Henry Ward Beecher:
AN AMERICAN PORTRAIT

THE SELECTION COMMITTEE
OF THE READERS CLUB

Clifton Fadiman

Sinclair Lewis

Carl Van Doren
Chairman

Alexander Woollcott

PAXTON HIBBEN

Henry Ward Beecher:

AN AMERICAN PORTRAIT

WITH A FOREWORD BY
SINCLAIR LEWIS

THE PRESS OF THE READERS CLUB
NEW YORK

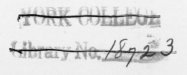

This book was first published, and copyright, by George H. Doran Company in 1927. The copyright is now in the possession of Sheila Hibben, from whom permission has been obtained for the publication of this special edition by THE READERS CLUB

The special contents of this edition are copyright, 1942, by THE READERS CLUB

PRINTED IN THE UNITED STATES OF AMERICA

FOREWORD

WHEN the Reverend Henry Ward Beecher was sued on a charge of adultery with the wife of his friend Theodore Tilton, the America of 1871 was ecstatically shocked.

For Mr. Beecher was, till his death in 1887, the archbishop of American liberal Protestantism. He came out for the right side of every question — always a little too late. John Brown's rifles were called "Beecher Bibles", and from the pulpit Beecher sold female slaves, to gain their freedom. He was referred to as "the greatest preacher since St. Paul", he was mentioned for the presidency, he was a powerful writer of trash, and all over the land, families got out the carry-all to drive into town and hear him lecture on everything from "The Strange Woman" to the cozy theory that a worker who didn't rejoice in bringing up five children on a wage of a dollar a day was a drunken gunny-sack.

Plymouth Church, in Brooklyn, paid him $20,000 a year, and in his pocket he liked to carry uncut gems. He would have been an intimate friend of Lincoln except for the detail that Lincoln despised him. He confided to many visitors that he was always glad to pray with Lincoln and to give him advice whenever the president sneaked over to Brooklyn in the dark, and the only flaw is that nobody except Beecher ever saw him sneak.

During the Civil War, Beecher went to England and helped out the American Minister by converting to the cause of the North some tens of thousands of Midlanders who were already converted.

He was a combination of St. Augustine, Barnum, and John Barrymore. He differed from the Reverend Elmer Gantry chiefly in having once, pretty well along in young manhood, read a book, and in being a Beecher, which was a special state of grace. His father, Lyman Beecher of Litchfield and Cincinnati, was a powerful hellfire preacher and progenitor, and his sister was Harriet Beecher Stowe, whose *Uncle Tom's Cabin* was the

vii

first evidence to America that no hurricane can be so disastrous to a country as a ruthlessly humanitarian woman.

At the sunlit height of Beecher's career came Tilton's suit for alienation of affection, and in Brooklyn and Litchfield they are still arguing about it. But its effect upon the protestant church, which might otherwise have taken over the whole government, is only beginning to be seen.

This book, the late Paxton Hibben's story of Beecher, was published in 1927. It had great praise, but it also met with a hush-hush campaign on the part of certain pious writers and editors and librarians that amounted to violent suppression. The Committee of The Readers Club believes that it is reviving a book which is more stimulating now than when it was first published, fourteen years ago.

Nothing could finally suppress and silence so courageous and intelligent a man as Paxton Hibben, not even his death, in 1928 when he was forty-eight years old. He had been a member of the American diplomatic corps in Europe and Latin America, well trained in the severe correctitudes of that caste, and he was a foreign correspondent of standing, yet he had taken the risk of vastly displeasing his superiors by his reports on Greece and the new Russia.

When he turned to biography, in this book, the exactness of his scholarship would suggest that he had all his life never strayed farther from a library than to the University Co-op, though actually it was his foreign training which enabled him to see the contrasts which make this portrait so human.

Beecher is here entire, from his boyhood, blundering, lonely, almost abnormal in the longing for friendly sympathy, through his frantic and fairly phony days as an ambitious young preacher on the Indiana frontier in 1837, up to his antimacassar splendor as a metropolitan pastor filled with pomposity and metaphors and the best oyster stew. He slapped the backs of all men, he tickled the ribs of almost all the current ideas, and he kissed a surprising proportion of the women.

The subtitle of the book is *An American Portrait*, and indeed here is the portrait of that blowsy hoyden of an America that existed when Grant was accounted a statesman and Longfellow an epic poet. Although Hibben never wanders from his scrupulous portraiture to give highfalutin panshots of the whole country, yet in understanding Beecher we understand everything that was boisterously immature in American religion, American literature, American manners, and the American relationship, ardent but sneaking, between men and women. We understand all the spirited spinsters who wanted to paint water lilies on the backs of the herded buffalos. We understand what we are still living down. Here is the story of our own grandfathers, which is one-quarter of our own stories. Though we speak with the brisk quack of the radio, our words are still too often the lordly lard of Henry Ward Beecher.

In discovering his emptiness, the country discovered its own emptiness and, as Captain Hibben says, "When the social history of the last quarter of the nineteenth century comes to be written, the Beecher case may be found to have had more to do with clearing the intellectual ground and freeing the minds of men from the clutter of the past than any other one episode."

Hibben does not spare his patient. The horsehair hypocrisies of Beecher are set down like fever symptoms on a chart. He does not flinch from the charming melodrama of Beecher's association with the wives of all the backers of his one-man show. Yet the book is never lip-licking and never a tirade. You see that, given the glacial hellfire of old Lyman Beecher, his son Henry would have to be a hypocrite, exactly in ratio to his own energy and imagination and desire for affection.

When it was published, this book was a little ahead of its time. The Committee believes that now it is just at its time.

SINCLAIR LEWIS

CONTENTS

AUTHOR'S PREFACE

died 1887

IN 1813, when Henry Ward Beecher was born, Hell was perhaps the most enduring reality in the lives of over half the eight
million people who made up this country.

The Bible was not merely inspired, it was the literal word of
Almighty God from cover to cover. God was Fear, and a Christian was one who crept into a church in terror like a child
hiding under the bedclothes during a thunderstorm. Human
slavery was more respectable, and respected, than education,
drunkenness a vast deal commoner than physical cleanliness,
gambling as recognized a diversion as golf to-day, and woman's
place was in the kitchen — or the brothel.

In the seventy-four years that Beecher lived all of this
changed.

The significance of the man is not that he lived as spectator or
even incidental participant through so many years during
which a tremendous transformation took place in the outlook
and the lives of men, but that the life and conduct of Henry
Ward Beecher were both barometer and record of these
changes. More than any other man, he was their voice. It is not
material whether Henry Ward Beecher was saint or sinner. It is
of less consequence still that he was neither crusader like
William Lloyd Garrison nor martyr like John Brown. An op-
portunist he was, certainly. He made no one uncomfortable,
least of all himself. But many a revolution dies stillborn because
when the bomb with which it might begin has blown up its
maker, there is no one to fan the spark it has left into flame.

Henry Ward Beecher threw no bombs. But for three quarters
of a century he blew diligently — blew hot and then blew
cold — upon the glowing sparks left by the bombs of others;
while the girders of a new order in the minds and the lives of
men were riveted in place — and the fires of a Calvinist Hell
burned to ashes.

It was not Beecher who struck the shackles from three million

xiii

human beings, though he played a not inconsiderable rôle in the drama of negro slavery. Nor was it Beecher who made the first breach in the Puritan wall that prisoned the souls of men a century ago. But when Abraham Lincoln and Charles G. Finney were dead and gone, Beecher was still husbanding the ground they cleared.

So much, outwardly—to the sight of man: a great orator, a great actor—a showman, if one like. But nothing else were there not in the inner life of the man an evolution more extraordinary far than the progress about him. And even this, as an individual development, were of curious interest only. But what came to Beecher in his threescore years and fourteen, came to America also. He was not in advance of his day, but precisely abreast of his day—the drum major's part in more than one sense. Now we watch the serried ranks pass without wonder. But back at the head of the line, forty years ago, when Henry Ward Beecher in shako and with shining baton marked the step, the crowds cheered.

Beecher stood forth a prodigious figure, not by blazing a path in any wilderness, but by the fact that his inner experience was identical with that of millions of his fellow countrymen. His gift was merely that he was articulate while they were not. But he was articulate of the very intellectual processes and material growth by which the portentous America of to-day was evolving from the provincial, self-opinioned, ignorant and intolerant America of 1813. And he was articulate because the evolution that with others was merely the sweep of a current, was, in him, a conscious progress. He began in the flint-like faith of the Puritans—that cruel circle narrowed to the bounds of self where God as ringmaster cracked the whip. Joy was of the devil and self-righteousness the accepted countenance of virtue. He ended his days an apostle of evolution, an advocate of women's suffrage and the higher education of women, a clergyman who attended the theater and who drank his wine or beer when he felt like it. He rose to the supreme height of standing public trial on a charge of adultery, of which he was never legally acquitted and may indeed have been guilty, fitted in the end not by dogma but by growth and experience to preach God as "loving a man in his sins for the sake of helping him out of them."

TO SHEILA HIBBEN

Henry Ward Beecher:
AN AMERICAN PORTRAIT

Part I: The Puritan Prison

"Henry Ward Beecher was born in a Puritan penitentiary, of which his father was one of the wardens—a
prison with very narrow and closely-grated windows. Under its walls were the rayless, hopeless and measureless
dungeons of the damned, and on its roof fell the shadow of
God's eternal frown. In this prison the creed and catechism
were primers for children, and from a pure sense of duty
their loving hearts were stained and scarred with the religion of John Calvin."

ROBERT G. INGERSOLL

CHAPTER I

1813

MIDSUMMER 1813.

For a brief moment in Europe there is peace. . . .

The Grande Armée has been shattered on the plains of the
Dnieper. By a miracle, Napoleon flings together a new host—
youngsters led by untrained officers. Prussians and Russians are
stopped short at Bautzen. . . . There is an uneasy pause—for
new intrigue, new combinations . . . The Corsican's arm is
about Metternich's shoulder (How he must have loathed the
touch!). "Ah! Metternich—how much has England paid you
to play this part against me!". . . Before Dresden, Jean Victor
Moreau, fresh from exile in Trenton, dies fighting against his
countrymen. . . . In Spain, Wellington smashes the army of
Jourdan and sends Joseph Bonaparte fleeing to the Jersey banks
of the Delaware. . . . Leipzig—Paris—Elbe. The end!

In Boston, God is publicly commended in solemn festival for
His part in the chastisement of the "ferocious military adventurer," and the Tsar of All the Russias hailed as Alexander the
Deliverer, "a name always dear to every lover of national freedom." In the District of Columbia "the news of *Buonaparte's
defeat* was received with a burst of joy and gratitude, such as a
virtuous and humane people would display upon the downfall
of tyranny, and the promised restoration of peace and prosper-

4   HENRY WARD BEECHER

ity to an *emancipated world.*" George Washington's adopted son was the orator of the occasion. . . .

Outside Boston harbor, the *Shannon* captures the *Chesapeake* with half Boston looking on. The dinners prepared for the victors grow cold — the Chesapeake's crew dines in Halifax . . . From New York, the *Argus* sails, bearing William H. Crawford as Minister to France. But she ends her trip in Plymouth, prize of the British brig *Pelican.* The boasts of Clay and Calhoun that Canada would be taken in a few weeks by a handful of men proved bombast. Michigan is in British hands. On Ontario, stalemate. On Champlain the British control the lake and threaten barracks and army stores at Plattsburg. On Erie, blockaded, Perry is building his fleet at Presque Isle. . . .

In another year, the smoke of Washington, burning, will drift down the Potomac . . . Half of Maine will be annexed to New Brunswick . . . Vice-Admiral Cochrane will order his fleet "to destroy and lay waste such towns and districts upon the coast as may be found assailable" — and none will stop him. The villages of Cape Cod will be laid under tribute by the British fleet — Brewster $4,000, Wellfleet $2,000, and so on. Stonington, Connecticut, will be bombarded, and Commodore Decatur, betrayed by his own countrymen, will fall at last a prisoner of the enemy. . . .

And two thousand miles from all of this, a little band of three hundred Americans — soldiers of fortune without plan, integrity or valor — defeat two Spanish armies and erect in San Antonio a government of the independent "State of Texas." For six months, in 1813, they realize the dream of Aaron Burr and anticipate the achievement of Sam Houston. Then a firing squad in the chilly Southern dawn puts a period to a drunken debauch. . . .

But in Litchfield, Connecticut, the young ladies of Miss Sally Pierce's Female Academy two by two trip mincing down North street under the lofty elms to the tune of flute and flageolet. The young gentlemen of Judge Tapping Reeve's Law School look out from their classroom upon the windows of the young ladies of the Female Academy. And once a month they meet, in Deacon Buel's ballroom or Old Grove Catlin's tavern, to dance . . . Occasionally two of the students from the South step over the State line into New York, in their pink gingham frock coats, to fight a bloodless duel over some miss in a round, short-waisted gown of jaconet muslin and white satin Quaker bonnet lined with pink. Occasionally, also, they serenade Flora Catlin, the inn-keeper's daughter, "the most beautiful woman in Litchfield." . . . The war with England was no more to Litchfield in 1813 than "one between the Turks and the Crim Tartars."

Yet Litchfield, then, was the fourth town of Connecticut in size, and by no means out of the world. There the statue of George III uprooted from the Bowling Green of New York by the Colonists in 1776 was cut up and run into 42,088 Continental bullets by the patriotic ladies of the town. Ethan Allen was born there, and thither came the Marquis de La Fayette and Count Rochambeau as distinguished guests. There dwelt Oliver Wolcott, Jr., the successor of Alexander Hamilton as Secretary of the Treasury, and Gen. Uriah Tracy, United States Senator under Washington and Adams. Judge Tapping Reeve founded the first law school in America at Litchfield, where Aaron Burr, living with his sister Sally, Judge Reeve's wife, studied his law, and John C. Calhoun received his grounding in the doctrine of secession. From this same school in Litchfield, in the course of a quarter century, sixteen United States Senators, fifty Members of Congress, two justices of the Supreme Court of the United States, ten Governors, five cabinet members and countless judges went forth with the stamp of New England upon them.

Through the main street of Litchfield, overhung by elms and lined with dignified white houses, their deep dooryards aflame with peonies, the gaudy four-horse post coaches to and from Boston, New York, Albany, Norwalk, New Haven, or Poughkeepsie (where one could catch a sloop up or down the Hudson) clattered with a great cracking of whips and blowing of horns, while the sailing packet *Trident* brought the far orient to Litchfield's doorsteps through the Litchfield-China Trading Company.

At this period, in this place, only twenty-two years after the death of John Wesley — a year later than Charles Dickens and Robert Browning, and a few weeks after Richard Wagner saw the light at Leipzig — Henry Ward Beecher was born on June 24, 1813, the eighth offspring of Lyman and Roxana Foote Beecher.

It was the end of the old order in America, but neither Henry Ward Beecher's parents nor their neighbors and familiars knew it. Still in their powdered wigs with queues, their white-topped boots, or small-clothes and silk stockings of another day, the solid citizens of Litchfield — indeed of Connecticut and for that matter all New England — had as yet discerned no radical significance in the American revolution. They regarded mechanics as vulgar, pinned their faith to what were termed leading men in the community, and looked upon the old families as the proper guide in political no less than social matters. The federal government had merely taken the somewhat remote place of fat, sporadically insane George and his Ministers, and Connecticut folk were as opposed to being ruled from Washington as ever they had shown themselves to being ruled from Westminster. The war of 1812, then in progress, was not in their eyes an engagement of the nation, but "Mr. Madison's war," and even so mild a person as Roxana Foote Beecher announced that "We don't intend to do anything to support this war, not even to write letters." Only a short time before, Judge Tapping Reeve wrote General Tracy that he had seen "many of our friends; and all that I have seen, and most that I have heard from" believed the moment ripe for the separation of New England from the Union. Lyman Beecher was one of the closest of the friends of Judge Reeve.

The truth of the matter was that in their isolation and self-dependence the colonists of New England had evolved a conception of popular government different to that then and still prevalent in Great Britain. Judge Gould of the Litchfield Law School baptized "this late and invaluable improvement" *Representative Legislation*, and declared that "exempt, on the one hand, from the oppressive rigor of monarchial and aristocratic sway, and from the licentious turbulence of democracy, on the other, it forms the most rational, and, as experience has shown, the most effectual plan, that human wisdom has ever yet devised for the purpose of uniting social liberty with social order." What was uppermost in the minds of the ruling class throughout New England at this period was the peril from the "licentious turbulence of democracy," and both social and political life were organized to scotch this particular serpent.

To this end, from time immemorial, no more effective instrument has been devised than the church. It was the church, therefore, in Connecticut that constituted the bulwark against the encroachments of democracy.

And into a church, with this mission, Henry Ward Beecher was born.

Early New England was as much a theocracy as early Babylon, and much the same kind of theocracy. Travelers from abroad marveled at the extent to which religion was the dominant interest and the ministers of religion the dominant factor in New England life. "Clerical gentlemen have here an astonishing hold upon the minds of men," Fearon wrote in 1817; "the degree of reverential awe for the sanctity of their office and the attention paid to the *external forms* of religion approach almost to idolatry." For over a century, the Congregational Church had been the established church in Connecticut, and had successfully resisted every attempt to weaken its grip upon the thought and conduct of the people.

In this struggle, Lyman Beecher was a leader. His house was the rallying place of those who opposed the loosening of the strait ties of Calvinism upon the spirit or the constricting bonds of puritanism upon the behavior. Armed with the twin weapons wielded by the clergy of his day — education and the terror of divine wrath — Lyman Beecher and his fellows were conservative because it is simpler to compel men to fit their spirits into the mold of rigid dogma than to write a theological prescription that will meet the needs of mankind; but they were conservative also because conservatism meant no lessening in the power and prerogatives of the church. To have cemented into Christian brotherhood the centrifugal personalities of those intrepid and disagreeable pioneers who had sought opportunity in a new world might well have called for genius; but merely to arouse in each an uneasy concern for the salvage of his own soul, according to a highly specialized formula of which the minister alone held the secret, demanded no more than astuteness. The immediate rewards of the latter course were obviously greater. For those who held in leash the fires of hell exercised a tremendous power, and, correspondingly, developed a tremendous ego.

Such an one was Lyman Beecher.

We have his word for it that he was a great preacher. More dispassionate witnesses cast doubt upon that estimate. Many thought him dull. Harriet Beecher Stowe found his sermons as unintelligible as Choctaw. Certainly, to read, they are remarkably uninspiring, and, curiously enough, considering the stirring times in which he lived, with little or no application to the larger problems of the day. It is significant of the period that though the clergy were the recognized leaders in politics no less than religion, little or no politics was preached from the pulpit. The political work was done in conference meetings, lectures and family visits, and as complete a political program as was ever conceived in Tammany Hall worked out at the annual State meetings of the general association of ministers. Sermons, on the other hand, were essentially doctrinal, frequently abstruse to the point of metaphysical subtlety, and dealt for the most part with the none too promising chances of the preacher's hearers to escape eternal damnation.

The early fame of Lyman Beecher rested on his sermons on dueling and intemperance. Neither was a subject of transcendent importance: dueling was hardly, after all, a menace to the stability of society even in that day, while a temperance movement had been launched in Litchfield twenty years before the Beechers ever came there. Drunkenness was an admitted evil of that age, but it is not of record that Lyman Beecher, sipping his cider for breakfast, materially lessened the evil by his fulminations. It was an hundred years before Connecticut submitted to prohibition.

The heart of Lyman Beecher and of his contemporaries as well was in an entirely different type of pulpit oratory. They were only incidentally interested in social improvement. But let some gentler minister of faith deviate never so slightly from the stern Calvinism of Jonathan Edwards, and Lyman Beecher was upon him, full cry, with the thunderbolts of God "so excited by his own discourses that he could not sleep at night until he had calmed himself by scraping the strings of his violin and worked off his surplus enthusiasm by a double shuffle on his kitchen floor." If Lyman Beecher was ever assailed by doubt that he was the confident of God, it nowhere appears.

"I believe fully that we are no longer to trust Providence, and expect that God will vindicate His cause while we neglect the use of appropriate means," he wrote in an agony of impatience. "God never in this manner vindicated His cause; He never will."

Lyman Beecher, at least, neglected no means, appropriate or otherwise. He rushed up and down Connecticut like a Field Marshal, his coat-tails flying, dropping the notes of sermons from his hat, leaving his belongings in stages and inns, a little ridiculous to others but the chosen champion in his own eyes, austere, somber, of passionate temper and indomitable energy — the great gun of Calvinism — rallying the forces against the baptism of infants, against toleration, against innovation and democracy, against the separation of church and state. To him the efforts of other sects than his own to secure a foothold on the outskirts of salvation was "a revolution, the object of which was, by withdrawing the support of law, to scatter and destroy us . . . to shake the confidence of the community in the clergy." Lyman Beecher fought it, and when the tide of progress swept over him, it left him sitting with head drooping on his breast, his arms hanging inert.

"Father," said his daughter, "what are you thinking of?"

And in sepulchral voice Lyman Beecher replied:

"The Church of God!"

"On the whole," he wrote Dr. Nathaniel W. Taylor, his ally in the struggle, "I have decided to give up the ship, not to enemies who have determined to take it, but to Christ."

A pious resolve. But Lyman Beecher had no thought of keeping it.

Lyman Beecher had been the son of a blacksmith. The power that came to him as a minister of God had gone to his head. He conceived himself influential when he was merely active, eloquent when he was only wordy, efficacious when he was only bustling.

Henry Ward Beecher's mother was a totally different type. She was a dreamer of dreams in a world of hard reality. She read novels, played the guitar and spoke French. She even painted pictures — one of East Hampton, which her sister complained did not take in all the public buildings, as both windmill and meeting house were left out. Possibly for the same reason. Brought up by a doting grandfather — old Andrew Ward whose command had kept the fires burning at Trenton while Washington crept around to take the British in the rear — Roxana Foote was a lady in the days when there was such a thing. She was shy, with a deep stillness of spirit that was her defense against the poverty and drudgery of a minister's household and the blatancy of Lyman Beecher's turbulent existence. When he first came to her, fresh from Yale and full of the self-confidence of his junior-partnership with God, she saw in him the romantic figure of Sir Charles Grandison. Long before she died, he was merely the least tractable of her children. . . .

In after years, Henry Ward Beecher spoke of his mother as if he had known her well. He had not, of course, known her at all — he was only three when she died. But she stood in his developing consciousness for all that his life lacked; and there was, in point of fact, a real basis for the highly idealized image of his mother that Henry Ward created, as he grew up, to help him over the hard places.

For Roxana Foote was a person. She left behind her a tradition of fineness and reticence to be found nowhere else among the Beechers. She had loathed the moral exhibitionism of the female prayer meetings, and could never lead them as a minister's wife should. She could never bring herself not to believe that God's children love Him because He first loved them — a revolutionary doctrine for any one in Dr. Beecher's household. There is something infinitely pathetic in the picture of this exquisite creature struggling with Lavoisier's Chemistry so that she might teach it in the school she kept to supplement the meager earnings of her husband, taking in half a dozen boarders, spinning a rug and painting it with flowers, and reading Maria Edgeworth aloud to the children that arrived with clock-like regularity.

But for all her undoubted qualities, Roxana Foote Beecher dead was a tremendously more potent influence upon Henry Ward than ever she was likely to have been living. She came to be to him the Perfect Mother, around whom he built him a fantasy world where he could and did find refuge, in her company, from the impacts of experience — an unreal world, where the consequences of his transgressions were softened or turned aside, and where things were as he wished them to be. It was the tragedy of Henry Ward Beecher's life that he spent it in trying to superimpose this dream world, whose door Roxana Foote opened to him, upon the world of reality about him — and that he never quite knew which was which.

When Roxana Beecher found peace at last, Henry Ward was no longer the baby of the family. There was Charles.

"I heard Dr. Beecher preach her funeral sermon, standing in the little tub pulpit, while her coffin stood below it," wrote one of the young ladies of Miss Sally Pierce's Female Academy.

It was quite a public function.

CHAPTER II

LITCHFIELD

LYMAN BEECHER was perfectly agreed that it is not good that the man should be alone. Not that he or any one else had much chance to be alone in the Beecher house, even after its capacity had been doubled by spending what was left of poor Roxana's tiny fortune. There was Grandma Beecher, a fine specimen of Puritan character of the strictest pattern; Aunt Esther, Lyman's half-sister, the very embodiment of New England — "a place for everything and everything in its place" — who had kept the Beecher house since the days when Lyman and Roxana began their married life at East Hampton, Long Island. These two, happily, did not live in the same house with young Henry Ward — there would scarcely have been room for them. But Aunt Esther might just as well have done so; she ran the household. There were the older children — stern Catherine Esther, older by thirteen years than Henry Ward, and William and Edward and Mary and George and little Harriet (the second of that name — the first had died) only a year older than Henry Ward — the Harriet Beecher Stowe of the years to come. There was Charles, the baby, and the two negro bound girls, Zillah and Rachel Crook, and Betsey Burr, the orphan cousin, and Mr. Cornelius, Lyman's assistant, and Candace, the black washerwoman (who only came in, however) and anywhere from three to five young ladies attending Miss Pierce's school, who boarded with the Beechers and occupied the best rooms. Then there were, of course, visiting ministers — always somebody or other. A week after Roxana died, Lyman was writing for Drs. Neetleton, Tyler, Harvey and Taylor to come and spend several days, reading sermons to each other. Less than a year after her death, he brought home a stepmother to Roxana's children.

It was not, however, for the sake of his children that Lyman Beecher went to Boston to "buy him a wife," as the young ladies of the Female Academy maliciously put it. He scarcely seems to have known very clearly how many children he had in

those replete days. Lyman Beecher was engaged in what to him
was of far more vital concern than his or any body's else children, and he required some one to tell him constantly how vital
it was and how well he was doing it.

The war was over and the political pot was boiling furiously
in the last stronghold of republicanism. Fisher Ames declared
that "the incessant proselytizing acts of the Jacobins [meaning
the Jeffersonians] will sooner or later subvert Connecticut,"
and indeed it seemed so. To Lyman Beecher, the Democratic
organization was in very fact "a conspiracy, active, daring and
wicked, in the midst of the State for the destruction of our
Government," and its leaders quite simply infidels. He did his
best to combat the resistless trend. But in 1817 the Congregational ministers of the state got together to march in procession,
smoke pipes, drink rum and decide who was to be governor of
the Commonwealth, for the last time. The clerical ring that had
dominated Connecticut for two centuries was slung out like a
stone from a sling.

Nor was this political turnover the only revolutionary blow
struck at Lyman Beecher and the solid citizens of New England. A menacing heresy under the name of Unitarianism was
spreading. For seven years the mind of Lyman Beecher had
been "heating, heating, heating," as he put it, over the awful
peril to men's souls of this blasphemous doctrine. Now he
elected himself the champion of orthodoxy and sallied forth to
Boston to attack the fearsome thing in its lair. It is not of record
that Unitarianism was greatly shaken by Lyman Beecher's onslaught; but to Dr. Beecher and his friends "it was a perfect
victory."

One victim at least he could boast. Harriet Porter, of Portland, Maine, niece of the great Rufus King, heard Lyman
Beecher preach at the Park Street church. He was forty-two.
He was by no means handsome. There was much of the village
parson about him. But he was a crusader. He stood for the
waning conservatisms of New England of which the family of
Harriet Porter was typical. In the pulpit his facility gave a
superficial impression of profundity; in conversation, he cowed
opposition by his positiveness. Lyman Beecher remained only a
few days in Boston, but when he returned to the eight children
he had left in charge of his sister, he had found them a stepmother in Harriet Porter.

Where Roxana Foote had been a lady, Harriet Porter was an aristocrat to the tips of her ringed fingers. She belonged to a circle of cousins famous for their beauty, their cleverness and their popularity from South Carolina to Maine. They were related to every one and they visited everywhere — the Cabots, the Lowells, the Van Rensselaers, the Tappans, the Wadsworths, the Richard Derbys, the Allstons, the Pinckneys. Rufus King had been Minister to England under Washington and Adams and was to serve John Quincy Adams in the same capacity. He was twice candidate for Vice-President of the United States and had only just been defeated as the Federalist candidate for the Presidency. He was United States Senator from New York at the time his niece married Lyman Beecher, and one of the most distinguished men of the country. His half-brother, William King, had been first Governor of the State of Maine; another half-brother, Cyrus, was in Congress. Taking it all in all, the son of the New Haven blacksmith had come far when he married into the King family, and set young Henry Ward in a way to have a new mother of rare parts and wide connections.

But throughout his life, Henry Ward Beecher had little luck with women. He had none in his stepmother. Harriet Porter had passed the first flush of youth, and was still a spinster. It was a day when girls married in their teens — or had to take what they could get in the marriage market. "I have now only patiently to wait till some clever fellow shall take a fancy to me and place me in a situation, I am determined to make the best of it, let it be what it will" wrote one of Harriet's popular cousins. But Harriet herself waited in vain. Her thoughts gradually turned from dances and parties at Broad's, near Portland, to the vice of the day — absorption in the welfare of the soul. "For a whole month I sought and agonized," she wrote. ". . . The night found me — oh, I hardly dare recur to what I did and suffered. Often I was persuaded that life or reason must inevitably leave me. . . . I dread the recurrence of temptation, for I have no strength, no power of resistance; yet I know where my strength lies; but I am an infant in Christ." To one in such a frame of mind, Lyman Beecher was a guide to heaven without peer. So Harriet Porter married him, and came to live in the rambling, rat-infested, overcrowded parsonage at Litchfield. "A lady of great personal elegance who, having been in early life the much admired belle in general society, came at last, from an impulse of moral heroism combined with personal attachment, to undertake the austere labors of a poor minister's family." Thus Harriet Beecher Stowe. Dr. Nathan Lord had known Harriet Porter all her life. "She never made a mistake," he says. "She never attempted what did not become her, and whatever she attempted was well done. She was justly regarded as a model."

Which, for a boy of four, was pretty hard lines in the way of a stepmother.

Neither she nor any one else ever gave Henry Ward a toy. In all his child-life he never celebrated a fête. He was thirty before he attached any joyous significance to Christmas. One snowy night, on his way home from an errand at Gov. Wolcott's, he passed the little box that was called the Episcopal Church. The door was open and the light shone out, and inside he could see evergreens and hear the choir practicing Christmas carols. He stood for a long time in the cold and darkness, wistfully peering in, wondering what it was all about, and what manner of folk these Episcopalians were who took their religion gladly.

"That is about all I knew of Christmas in my younger days," Henry Ward said years later. "I never heard anybody speak of it. It was not known in the house of my father, for a Puritan of the Puritans was he."

That same summer of 1817, Henry Ward started to school, his bare feet pattering down the dusty road, his yellow curls flying, holding his sister Harriet by the hand. That summer, too, President Monroe toured Connecticut, and mounted on a white charger reviewed the State troops. But all the huzzas could not stifle the grumbling of labor out of work, or capital caught in the squeeze of tight money. There was beginning for New England what Lyman Beecher called "a state of things more ruinous than war; and which at this moment is filling the land with bankruptcies and distress, beyond the calamities of any war in which we have been engaged." Allowing for the exuberance of expression characteristic of all the Beechers, New England was in fact feeling keenly the change from farming and shipping as cardinal activities, to manufacturing. Toward the end of the same sermon, Lyman Beecher suggested a remedy: "It is indispensable," he said, "that children be early accustomed to profitable industry."

His own were. As he attended district school, Henry Ward hemmed towels and aprons and knit suspenders and mittens. At eight, he was up while it was yet dark to build the kitchen fire before morning prayers, held at sunrise. In winter, when the water in the well froze, he took the oxen sledge and drove it two miles, broke the ice of a stream, filled barrels with enough water for washday, and fetched it home. He dug tunnels through the snow to the woodpile, split and carried the wood, cried with the cold as he stamped his feet and slapped his hands to keep warm. And when the winter was gone, he hoed corn and potatoes in newly cleared fields, and took care of a horse and cow. Outside of that, and school, his time was his own.

The liberty was relative. Harriet Porter was much too occupied with the cares of a household comprising nine children — one of her own within a reasonable time — three other relatives, four young lady boarders, three domestics and numberless visiting ministers, as well as with the state of her soul, to bother herself much about Henry Ward. As for Lyman Beecher, he held with Jonathan Edwards that "as innocent as young children seem to be to us, yet if they are out of Christ, they are not so in God's light, but are young vipers, and infinitely more hateful than vipers." His eldest daughter Catherine, no mean disciplinarian herself, describes Lyman Beecher's method of handling his vipers:

"With most of his children, when quite young he had one, two or three seasons in which he taught them that obedience must be exact, prompt, and cheerful, and by a discipline so severe that it was thoroughly remembered and feared. Ever after, a decided word of command was all sufficient."

Cheerfulness was the dominant note in this formula. Indeed, boisterous humor was the very fabric of the family life of the Beechers, and of thousands of repressed Calvinists like them. Behind a protecting curtain of jollity lurked meannesses and sinister cruelties, exorcised from time to time by horseplay and uproarious laughter. Comedy was at once a defense and an escape. No need for affection, however impelling, was appealing enough to strip the grinning mask of gayety from the countenance of self-absorption that every true Puritan wore. When Lyman Beecher swung his baby daughter out of the garret window by her hands, it was great fun; and in a tradition of such

outbursts of humor, interspersed by lickings with switches cut
from the quince trees on the north side of the house, Henry
Ward passed his childhood. The pain of the chastisements soon
faded. But he put away the armor of broad humor — if indeed
he ever did put it away altogether — only after many years
and deep suffering had taught him to stand unsmiling in the
presence of his fellow men.

"Boy traps" Henry Ward called schools. In the Beecher
house there was not a single child's book to make a boy feel less
bitterly about learning his letters. Traveling Englishmen visiting
the Connecticut schools of that day were shocked at their
sordidness, their cruelty, their ugliness. "I have not a single
pleasant recollection in connection with my school-boy days,"
Henry Ward declared years afterwards. He had many unpleasant ones. His first school was at Deacon Collins', on Litchfield Green, where he sat on a bench with his chubby feet dan-
gling, while Miss Collins, a tall, kindly-faced woman, paid no
attention whatever to her little pupil. Next he was sent to Miss
Kilborne's, right atop the hill where the wind would catch
Henry and Hattie and almost lift them into the air. He was "a
little, fat, clumsy boy, that hardly feared anything visible, but
dreaded all mysteries, and shook with vague and nameless terror
at the roaring of the wind up in the high tree-tops — the great
elm trees that swayed and groaned as if they too were in cruel
hands." At Miss Kilborne's he received more attention — "a
rousing slap on the head for some real or putative misde-
meanor," and a helpless rage inside, in consequence. But he
learned nothing.

Miss Sally Pierce's school came next — a girl's school. Henry
Ward was the only boy and, of course, was never called upon
to recite. Once, he was tied to the bench, because he had
laughed at something. It was all he could do to keep back the
tears at the indignity; and when one of the older girls came to
him to kiss the shame away, he could not keep back the tears. It
was finally at the District School, a rough, unpainted building
in a treeless waste, that Henry Ward achieved at last a certain
protective indifference. He was no student, then or ever. But
the "tall, sharp, nervous, energetic, conscientious spinster whose
conscience took to the rod as a very means of grace," pounded
into him a minimum acquaintance with the three Rs.

Henry Ward managed to shuffle through the district school,

his education "in an extremely backward state, a poor writer, a miserable speller, with a thick utterance and a bashful reticence which seemed like stolid stupidity." So far as such knowledge as can be obtained from books went, it was precisely that. The Reverend Mr. Langdon, of Bethlehem, had a turn with the boy. His "method of instruction for beginners was a system of extended, minute and reiterated drilling." But it was not a whit more effective than any other.

Henry Ward was a stocky, well-set-up lad by now, with a moon face, blond hair cut close on top, and curling "soap locks" plastered against each red cheek in front of the ear. His stepmother had lost her first baby and was ailing. His brother, Edward, was at Yale, where his father was writing him never to be concerned in any disorderly frolic, not to buy a watch, never to use tobacco or tipple, not to accept the volumes a clever book agent had sold him, that he had no money to send him — and above all "Oh! my dear son, *agonize* to enter in! You *must* go to heaven; you *must not* go to hell!" But of Henry Ward there is no mention. "A hermit could not have been more solitary," he says of himself at this period.

He roamed a great deal among the misty wooded hills. He hated school. He hated his father's noisy, crowded house, where even the young lady boarders complained that there was no place to wash but a basin in the kitchen sink. He hated the dull, metaphysical sermons in church and the endless doctrinal discussions at home. He watched his father's cordiality to visitors give way to denunciations of them when they had gone, and puzzled over it. His stepmother's unsmiling coldness repelled him; he was afraid of her. And all about him, like a terrific pressure that he could escape only by fleeing to the woods, there was the constant lament of his father that "every one of my dear children are without God in the world, and without Christ, and without hope. I have no child prepared to die . . . their whole eternal existence is every moment liable to become an existence of unchangeable sinfulness and woe."

Henry Ward was pretty well inured to this sort of thing. He had heard it daily ever since he could remember. By the time he was eight, he knew more about decrees, foreordination, election, reprobation, and the excellent prospects of eternal damnation of an unsaved child than most theological students even of that day. It was the staple of conversation in Lyman Beecher's

house. God was indeed an infinite detective watching children
from above. And while it was all very well to dismiss such
things as the commonplaces of daily life, their very reiteration,
the passionate earnestness with which Lyman Beecher spoke of
committing a child to the grave without one ray of hope con-
cerning its future state, made the matter of sin and salvation bob
up at every turn.

Out of doors, among the trees and the birds and the flowers
and the rabbits and grasshoppers, with sunset and the eternal
hills, it seemed quite silly that God should elect John Smith and
Mary Jones and a few others — all of course resident in New
England and members of the Congregational Church in good
standing — to be saved, and damn the rest. But in the silent
hours of the night, the thought recurred: What if it should be
true? When one of his boy friends died, — "dropped into
eternity" Henry Ward put it — the whole question came
sharply home to the lad. He was terrified.

"At intervals, for days and weeks, I cried and prayed. There was
scarcely a retired place in the garden, in the wood-house, in the carriage house, or in the barn, that was not a scene of my crying and
praying. It was piteous that I should be in such a state of mind, and
that there should be nobody to help me and lead me out into the
light."

And there was no one. No one, at least, but a hardly literate
negro, who shared the boy's room with him — Charles Smith.
To his simple mind, there was a glory and a wonder about God
that transcended his awfulness. Charles Smith had no desire to
stand forth triumphant in the divine presence as one entitled to
eternal bliss. He was content to belong to the humble company
of the millions of God's joyous children. Alone of all the
Beecher household, obsessed as each member was with his own
personal salvation, this negro was captivated by the idea of the
salvation of mankind. He read his Bible to Henry Ward, glory-
ing in its sonorous phrases, and talked with the frightened boy
of his soul as something to be saved not damned.

"I do not recollect that to that day one word had been said to me;
or one syllable had been uttered in the pulpit, that led me to think
there was any mercy in the heart of God for a sinner like me,"

Henry Ward declared, in later years. And it was when he was
torn inwardly with these doubts of himself, of his father, of

God, that the boy was sent to Hartford to attend the Female Seminary his sister Catherine had just opened.

Once more he was the only boy among some forty girls. He had exchanged the sporadic tyranny of Lyman Beecher for the unrelenting surveillance of four older brothers and sisters — Catherine, Edward, Mary and George. He could no longer run away to the gray hills and fancy-peopled woods in search of peace. He must seek a sort of secret life within himself, behind ramparts of comedy and practical jokes. He had read little. The common expedient of identifying himself with some legendary figure taken from story-books was denied the boy. He must create a world of the very fibers of his being — the terrible hunger for affection that haunted him all his life; the questionings, the uncertainties, the fears that encompassed him; the loneliness and the longing for a little tenderness, a little beauty. He came to act in a play which was not Robin Hood's life or Siegfried's life, but his own life. The springs of action were furnished by the impact of experience upon his own sensibilities; the theme was the development of his own emotions; the stage settings his own imaginings. And from this hidden drama he never escaped — the dramatization of Henry Ward Beecher, played by Henry Ward Beecher.

At first he tried to escape. Once he sought the help of the great Asahel Nettleton, saver of souls. He was told to "Go away, boy!" Once — perhaps often — he sought the lady who was his stepmother. But in the gathering darkness, he found her kneeling beside her bed, praying for her own soul.

"I think it would have been easier to lay my hand on a block, and have it struck off, than to open my thoughts to her, when I longed to open them to some one,"

he says.

And so, in the end, he crept into his own room, where Charles Smith by the light of a single candle was reading his Bible:

"And we have known and believed the love that God hath to us. God is love; and he that dwelleth in love dwelleth in God, and God in him.

"Herein is our love made perfect, that we may have boldness in the day of judgment: because as He is, so are we in this world.

"There is no fear in love; but perfect love casteth out fear, because fear hath torment. He that feareth, is not made perfect in love.

"We love Him, because he first loved us."

And to the deep voice of the negro, the boy fell asleep.

CHAPTER III

BOSTON

HENRY WARD stood it six months among the girls at his sister's school. Catherine Esther Beecher was made of the same stuff as her father, and it was not the sort of stuff best calculated to inspire love of learning in a lad of Henry Ward's type. Harriet — Hattie they called her — was much closer to both Henry Ward and Charles than any one else in the family, little as she resembled either. She slept in the same room with them off and on until she was thirteen and generally served as a bridge between them and the pure intellectuals of the household, Lyman, Catherine and Edward. An omnivorous reader herself, she had a refuge and a resource that Henry Ward lacked. Sorry for his backwardness, she managed to teach him drawing and the rudiments of Latin and to keep his scholastic shortcomings as inconspicuous as possible. She succeeded so well that Lyman Beecher, writing to Catherine of his "family of beloved and affectionate children," overlooked Henry Ward entirely.

Indeed, save for the soul struggles of Edward and William, the salvation of Mary and Harriet, and above all the agonizing of George, "whose voice of supplication could be heard night and day" keeping everybody awake, as an appropriate preliminary to being received into the bosom of the church, Lyman Beecher exhibited scant interest in his off-spring. He had other fish to fry at this period. For despite his perfect victory over Unitarianism in Boston in 1817, that stubborn heresy refused to die. Lyman Beecher returned to the charge; and once, when the roads were so blocked with snow that the stages could not run, rode to Boston on horseback through the blizzard to make a new onslaught on the dangerously spreading doctrine.

Great events were taking place under the very noses of the Beechers, without apparently producing the slightest effect upon them. On February 26, 1821, the Missouri Compromise had been adopted by the narrow margin of six votes, desertions from the North. Three of these were cast by Connecticut men. While two of the "renegades" (Storrs and Hackley) represented New York districts, the third, James Stevens, represented Stamford, and the whole of Western Connecticut was particularly incensed at his stand.

"Nothing could exceed the popular excitement upon that occasion," wrote a resident of Litchfield. "The three members were burnt in effigy in various places and popular indignation rose against them. . . . No one, not present at the time, can tell how bitter was the feeling of New England against Southern Slavery."

Henry Ward danced with the rest of the boys around the fire on the village green when Stevens was burnt in effigy. But it is unlikely that he had the faintest idea what it was all about. The abolition movement had not yet begun, and slavery was not a burning question in Litchfield. The growing economic and political dominance of the South, however, was. There were still something under an hundred slaves held in Connecticut at the time. But public opinion in the State was notwithstanding peculiarly virulent against the South, highly prosperous through the employment of slave labor.

There was a good deal to be said for New England. The embargo and the war had played havoc with shipping, her leading industry. Her land was not fertile, and industrial development required a capital that could be obtained only with difficulty and at high interest rates. From all over New England those who would normally have constituted the class of industrial workers were constantly trekking westward, leaving the New England manufacturers short of labor. The family of Lyman Beecher were familiar with these groups of emigrants passing through Litchfield, bag and baggage, bound for the great open spaces of Ohio, Indiana and Illinois. With the inauguration of the Erie Canal in 1825, an almost endless procession began in Maine and Massachusetts and moved through Connecticut — "discontented cobblers," Dr. Timothy Dwight called them, "too strongly impressed that their fancied talents could not find scope in their own country to stay there." And as these long trains of rough-looking men and women, with their wagons drawn by four or six horses, passed through Litchfield or camped near the

town, little Henry Ward Beecher would hide under the bed or
in the sheltering darkness of cupboards lest he be kidnaped by
them and carried away.

The remainder of the Beecher family exhibited little interest
in this tremendous Western movement — or in the far-reaching
events bound up with America's relations to the Old World,
either. It was in 1821 that the same Alexander, so enthusiastically hailed by the friends of Lyman Beecher eight years previously as "the Deliverer," issued his ukase warning all and
sundry to keep off "Russian America," including posts near the
Golden Gate and the entrance to San Francisco Bay. And it was
while Lyman Beecher was absorbed in what he called "the war-
fare in Boston" that President Monroe made reply to the Tsar
of all the Russias in two little paragraphs which have come to
be known as the Monroe Doctrine. In the years that Henry
Ward was going to school, La Fayette returned to Litchfield for
a triumphal visit, and a splendid ball was given for him at
Phelps' Tavern. It was, beyond doubt, a memorable occasion.

But in the great world outside Connecticut other things were
taking place, no less stirring. A half-breed Mexican was crowned
Augustin I, Emperor of Mexico and Central America. In Car-
acas, maidens in white presented wreaths of laurel and posies to
Simon Bolivar, the Liberator. Dom Pedro I proclaimed the
Constitutional Empire of Brazil. José de San Martin and the
Irish bastard, Bernardo O'Higgins, between them freed the re-
mainder of South America from Spanish rule. Serbia and Greece
threw off the yoke of the Turk. Revolutions blazed in Spain, in
Russia, in Naples and Piedmont. Napoleon died on St. Helena.
Byron perished at Missolonghi.

Of all these events only two left an impression on the Beecher
household: Lyman Beecher was confident that if Byron "could
only have talked with Taylor * and me, it might have got him
out of his troubles." He felt the loss of Napoleon deeply. "Why
rein his character up by the strict rules of Christian perfection,"
he said with rare tolerance, "when you never think of applying
it to any other ruler or general of the day?" There was, presumably, a certain elasticity to the faith once delivered to
the saints, when applied to the great of the earth.

It was plain enough that as Lyman Beecher turned fifty,

* Rev. Nathaniel W. Taylor, professor of Didactic Theology at Yale.

Litchfield was too small a place for him. His peculiar talents were in demand in wider fields and, besides, Litchfield could no longer afford to support one who spent as much on travel and other interests outside his congregation as did Lyman Beecher. His two trips to Boston in 1823 however greatly widened his circle of contacts, and two years later he was duly called to Hanover Church, Boston, and accepted. On March 19, 1826, he was formally installed. Henry Ward Beecher was then not quite thirteen.

It never entered Lyman Beecher's head that his sons should not, all of them, become ministers. For that, they must go to college, and the new pastorate, paying better than Litchfield, meant that George could remain at Yale, William could go to Andover, and Henry Ward and his brother Charles to the Boston Latin School. "I am happy to say we are beginning to be really comfortable," Harriet Porter Beecher wrote.

As for Lyman Beecher, he was in his element. True, his war on William Ellery Channing, once he was in the presence of the enemy, seemed momentarily less urgent than establishing himself securely in church and community. To effect this, he sought a safe subject for his initial preaching, and fell back upon the old one of temperance that had served so well at Litchfield. In due season his "Six Sermons on the nature, occasions, signs, evils, and remedy of intemperance" were published and brought him no little fame.

Hardly were the Beechers settled in Boston however before reports began to pour in from Oneida County, New York, of a preacher at whose call "the spirit of God was shed down with a power that nothing seemed able to resist." It appeared that a great, strange, soft-voiced giant of a man, who knew less of the technology of the ministry than the youngest of Lyman Beecher's children, who had never owned a Bible until he was thirty, and insisted upon preaching from the floor of a church instead of grandly thrust aloft in a box-pulpit, was taking the whole countryside by storm. He did not preach in the approved fashion of Jonathan Edwards and the Calvinist fathers — he just explained what other people preached, so that simple folk with hungry hearts and faltering spirit understood and were comforted. He had a way of putting his view of the business of a minister of the Lord that to a man like Lyman Beecher was almost blasphemous:

"Great sermons lead the people to praise the preacher. Good preaching leads the people to praise the Saviour,"

Charles Grandison Finney declared. He was not interested in praise of himself.

Henry Ward Beecher was still a mere child. But he had been steeped in metaphysico-theological dialectics. Here was something new. With understanding eyes he watched the losing struggle his father waged against the rising "whirlwind of insane piety" led by Finney.

Not that Lyman gave up easily:

"Finney," he warned the evangelist, "I know your plan and you know I do; you mean to come to Connecticut and carry a streak of fire to Boston; but if you attempt it, as the Lord liveth I'll meet you at the State line, and call out all the artillery men, and fight every inch of the way, and then I'll fight you there."

To Lyman Beecher, the emotionalism aroused by Finney was just another device of the Evil One — "the mask must be torn off from Satan coming among the sons of God," he thundered. What particularly aroused him was Finney's treatment of women as if they had souls:

"A greater evil, next to the loss of conscience and chastity, could not befall the female sex," he wrote the Rev. Nathan Beman. "No well educated female can put herself up, or be put up, to the point of public prayer, without the loss of some portion at least of that female delicacy, which is above all price."

Yet within four years Finney was holding revivals in Dr. Beecher's own church in Boston, at Lyman's invitation.

It was something for the boy, Henry Ward, to think about — this defeat of the rigid Calvinism of his father by the rich emotionalism of Charles Grandison Finney. He did think about it. For the first time in his young life, Henry Ward Beecher had a glimpse of something in religion besides cruelty and fear. He saw, too, that this method, that drew instead of driving men and women sobbing to the feet of the Lord, was successful far beyond all Lyman Beecher's theology backed by God's eternal wrath. And at the same time he had an insight into the mechanics of the ministry of Christ that was revealing. Finney relates the incident:

"One evening when there was a large attendance, I tried to point out exactly what the Lord required . . . and pointed out the sense in which they were expected to forsake all, and deliver everything to Christ. . . . I was about to call on them to kneel down, while we presented them to God in prayer; when Dr. Beecher said: 'You need not be afraid to give up all to Christ, your property and all, for He will give it right back to you.' "

Henry Ward Beecher never forgot that.

He was making little better progress in Boston schools than he had at Litchfield. Impressions still came to him wholly through emotional channels. Where at Litchfield he had suffered from the terrible solitude of one never alone, in Boston his was the only slightly less depressing solitude of one to whom no more attention is paid than to an article of furniture. His one confident, Hattie, was in Hartford. Charles Smith, the negro, was no longer at hand. His stepmother was the same unapproachable person whom her daughter "never saw appear in the morning, or at any other time, with unneat or disordered dress." His father was so wrought up by his theological conflicts that "his prayers became upheavings of passionate emotion" and he had to have a load of sand placed in the cellar of his house, that he might work off his excitement by shoveling it from one side of the cellar to the other. Nowhere was intellectual self-reliance encouraged or even rendered possible for the boy.

"The era of fermentation and development was upon him," his sister Harriet says of Henry Ward at this period, "and the melancholy that brooded over his childhood waxed more turbulent and formidable. He grew gloomy and moody, restless and irritable."

In "Norwood," his novel, Henry Ward himself wrote impersonally of this time:

"There is a period, beginning not far from fourteen, in young lives, when childhood is widened suddenly, and carries its banks so far out that manhood seems begun, though as yet it is far off. The stream is ocean deep. Upon this estuary of youth the currents are shifting—the eddies are many. . . . The important organic changes which in our zone take place at the second full seven of years, produce important results even in the coldest temperaments . . . there is frequently an uprising like a city in insurrection. The young nature, swelling to the new influences with a sense of immeasurable strength—sometimes turbulent with passions, but al-

ways throbbing with excited feelings, led on and fed by tantalizing
fancies, — seems transformed from its previous self. . . ."

Turbulent passions, excited feelings, tantalizing fancies — he
knew them, did Henry Ward. Knew and tried to escape them.
In the frightening bewilderment of adolescence, the sea seemed
to him a refuge, a way of safety. Boston * in those days with its
forty thousand inhabitants was a great port cluttered with sailing ships, their romantic figureheads thrust over the roadway of
the waterfront, their sailors from many lands crowding the
waterside taverns, the exotic smell of them heavy in the Summer
air. Here came Henry Ward, day after day, his memory full of
the tales of his Uncle Samuel Foote, the sea captain, like the
tales of all seamen — hardships excised and adventures accented.

"How many hours have we asked and wanted no better joy than
to sit at the edge of the wharf, or on the deck of some newly-come
ship, and rock and ride on the stream of our unconscious imagination? We went to school in Boston Harbor," he writes.

The sea was more to Henry Ward than a background for
daydreams. It was indeed the gate of liberty — a way out of all
the loneliness and ugliness of the repressed type of spiritual life
that hemmed him in. He could see the ministry looming before
him — a life of controversies, betrayals, meannesses, intrigues
and the sharp bargaining of the cloak-and-suit trade. He knew
that inside out, and was fed up on it. But the sea — as he conceived it — was freedom from the browbeating of so many
elders. One might be a Christian if one chose without working
at it night and day. There was a warmth of comradeship, of intimacy, among those who followed the sea that Henry Ward
had never known with any one, and that his whole exclusively
emotional being cried out for.

So he planned to run away to sea — as his Uncle Samuel had
done . . . And just there tragedy overtook him — the tragedy
that lay behind all the boisterousness and humor for which he
came to be famous in later years. For when he tried to run
away, he could not do it. He could not make the momentous decision. He had been too many years the seventh child, told always what to do and what not to do by an endless succession of
those in authority. He hated all that he had so far experienced

* About the size of Medford, Mass., or Hamilton, O., in 1920.

of the life that lay before him — its hypocrisies, its false enthusiasm, its spurious cheeriness and expansive contentment under the eagle eye of those entitled by the position of a minister in the community to pry into the minister's inner life. But these were, after all, little burdens that one might carry a vast weight of, if they came not too rapidly — miniature crosses of which one could bear an armload, when one great cross would crush. Henry Ward Beecher could make the small decisions, day by day, though he saw clearly enough where they led. He could not make the great, irrevocable one, from which there was no turning back.

And so, when his plan to run away to sea had matured, it was he himself who surreptitiously betrayed his purpose to his father. For once in his life, Lyman Beecher may perhaps have been gifted with a sort of revelation into the heart of another. Or possibly it may only have been adroitness. At all events, he met his son half way, and seeming to yield to the boy's desire to go to sea, declared himself ready to send Henry Ward to a school where he could obtain the technical instruction essential to a navigator.

So, one Fall morning before dawn, with all his meager belongings in a hair-trunk lashed behind, short, round, red-cheeked Henry Ward Beecher climbed into the waiting Albany stage, bound for the Mount Pleasant Classical Institution at Amherst. As the stage rolled away, Lyman Beecher heaved a sigh of relief.

"I shall have that boy in the ministry yet!" he said.

And every morning when the family gathered for prayer, Lyman Beecher prayed for Roxana's two youngest:

"Oh, God! May they become good ministers of our Lord Jesus Christ!"

CHAPTER IV

AMHERST

THE sons of Lyman Beecher were precisely the sort of "indigent young men of promising talents and hopeful piety" for whose education "with the sole view to the Christian Ministry"

Amherst College had been chartered in 1826. It was a day when all institutions of higher learning were feeders for the church, and Amherst was no exception. Edward and George had gone to New Haven, where Lyman Beecher's alter ego, Dr. Nathaniel Taylor, dispensed a brand of compromise orthodoxy that was somewhere between the Unitarianism of Harvard and the rigid Calvinism of Princeton, leaning towards the latter. To Lyman Beecher this was the only truth, and he would gladly have sent all his sons to imbibe it. But Henry Ward's studies at the Boston Latin School had not succeeded in fitting him even for the modest college entrance requirements of that day. So he was packed off to Amherst, to attend the Mount Pleasant Classical Institution, just opened on a very pretentious scale by two recent Amherst graduates "to combine the highest advantages of public and private education."

The tuition at Mount Pleasant was $250 per year, exclusive of uniforms and books, and the number of students limited to one hundred — a very select school indeed for a son of Lyman Beecher. But in return for a glowing tribute to the new school, to be used in its catalogue, Henry Ward was accepted for $100. The institution, Lyman Beecher wrote, for publication, "awakens my gratitude to God as a merciful provision for children and youth at the most critical period of their lives." Privately, however, he was not so enthusiastic, and in the end he was "exceedingly dissatisfied with the results of three years' study there and an expense of more than 800 dollars," as he wrote the President of Amherst. The canny doctor was not above pretending that he had paid the full price for Henry Ward's schooling.

Nevertheless, whether it answered the purposes of Lyman Beecher or not, the Mount Pleasant Classical Institution was a godsend to Henry Ward. In the New England of that day, the school was a remarkable one. To begin with, it made an especial effort to secure students from abroad, contact with whom could not fail to be an extraordinary experience for one brought up in the bosom of orthodoxy as young Beecher had been. In the three years that he spent at Mount Pleasant, he was schoolmate of almost two hundred youths from the ends of the earth, including six Greeks, four Colombians, two English lads, two Canadians, a Brazilian, a Cuban and a score of boys from the Southern States. One, indeed, in after years came to be Roman

Catholic Archbishop of Baltimore.* At the time Henry Ward Beecher made this lad's acquaintance, Lyman Beecher was holding forth in New York on the Catholic Church as "a ferocious beast" and "the mother of harlots." Indeed, it is to be doubted whether, had Henry Ward's Puritan father fully realized the awful perils to which his son was exposed among communicants of the Roman, Greek and Episcopal churches he would have permitted his offspring to attend Mount Pleasant, or Amherst, either.

Half a mile from the town of Amherst "on a commanding eminence surrounded by a noble grove of oaks and chestnuts," as the catalogue put it, the amazing building of the Mount Pleasant School overlooked the whole countryside. Here, as at Litchfield, Henry Ward could escape the realities of Latin, mathematics, grammar, and military drill — "dull as dullness itself" — in the somber, poignant beauty of the Berkshire foothills. There was excellent coasting and skating in winter and fishing, swimming and riding in summer. The boys roasted chestnuts and green corn in ovens they built of stones. Henry Ward even had a tiny garden of his own where, lonely and greatly over-awed by the magnificence of the place and the wealth of his fellow students, he found refuge in raising pansies and asters.

The program of the Classical Institution was as pretentious as its buildings with their white Doric columns. Theoretically, student offenders were tried by a jury of their peers chosen from a "Class of Honor" of the higher ranking boys to apply "the simple Principles of the science of Heaven." "The precautionary and controlling influence of the Law of Love" was the declared aim. But practically these benign pronouncements in no wise interfered with "the awful discipline and floggings of old and young" or generous use of a snake-haunted dungeon. Pupils, except in special cases, were not allowed to leave the grounds of the Institution "but in company with an instructor or guardian." Not, of course, that they did not.

Henry Ward was fourteen. He knew a little Latin and some English grammar, and that was about all. He still spoke "as if he had pudding in his mouth," and had no conception of how to study, and no desire to learn how. That, however, was the job of William P. N. Fitzgerald, a young man of no little ability

* James Roosevelt Bayley.

who was instructor in mathematics, natural philosophy and drawing at the Mount Pleasant Institution.

Just what the author of "Six Lectures on Temperance" would have said had he known that in addition to a large number of Catholics Mount Pleasant boasted, as its star instructor, a twenty-year-old ex-cadet who no longer ago than May of that year had been expelled from West Point for drunkenness, disorderly and riotous conduct and four other offenses growing out of an enthusiastic celebration of Christmas 1826, it is hardly safe to hazard. The affair was so scandalous that President John Quincy Adams refused to intervene. Fitzgerald had stood first at West Point in mathematics and natural philosophy, and was second on the list of most distinguished cadets, and for all his unfortunate escapade was a young man of parts who knew his business.

The school day began with military drill at half past four in the morning and ended with evening worship at eight o'clock at night. There were vacations of two weeks in April and three in August. It was scarcely a gay life for a growing lad. Young Beecher roomed at first with Fitzgerald, and was completely fascinated by the dashing West Pointer so little older than himself, whose life was already glamorous with rakish experience. Yet Fitzgerald was stern with his youthful charge. Once when Henry Ward was half way through the demonstration of a problem at the blackboard Fitzgerald snapped out: "No!" Taken aback, young Beecher began all over. But when he reached the same place, "No!" barked the instructor again. Henry Ward sat down, and the next boy took the problem. When Fitzgerald thundered "No!" to this youngster, however, the lad went right ahead, finished the problem, and was duly commended.

"Why," complained Henry Ward, "I recited it just as he did, and you said 'No!'"

"Why didn't you say 'Yes!' and stick to it?" replied Fitzgerald. "It's not enough to know your lesson. You must *know* that you know it. You have learned nothing till you are *sure*. If all the world says 'No!' your business is to say 'Yes' — and to prove it."

It is by no means certain that Henry Ward ever did learn this lesson.

For all his admiration of Fitzgerald, his real schoolboy hero was a more romantic person even than the expelled West Pointer, and the passion Henry Ward Beecher conceived for Constantine Fondolaik endured thirty years. Fondolaik was a Greek of Smyrna whose parents were killed by the Turks in the massacre of 1822. Somehow he had managed to escape, to be picked up by a sailing vessel and fetched to Boston. He had been adopted by a Mrs. Newell of Amherst. In the Institution he served as a monitor, commanding one of the divisions of the boys at military drill — a debonair, handsome, daring leader, exceedingly popular.

For this exotic youth, with his background of mystery and adventure, so different to anything indigenous to New England, Henry Ward Beecher developed a devotion that was close to passion. Byron was the almost fabulous figure of that day. When he died, Hattie, Henry Ward's imaginative sister, had flung herself on her face in the grass and cried bitterly. But for Henry Ward, the Greek was a Byron in the flesh. He worshiped Constantine.

"He was the most beautiful thing I had ever seen," he declared, years afterwards. "He was like a young Greek god. When we boys used to go swimming together, I would climb out on the bank to watch Constantine swim, he was so powerful, so beautiful."

Through Henry Ward's whole course at Mount Pleasant and the first two years of college at Amherst, the intimacy of this curiously assorted pair continued. Obviously, it was a relationship not without peril to young Beecher. But it developed no abnormal manifestations, and others among the Mount Pleasant boys besides Henry Ward Beecher bore witness to the enduring influence for good exercised by the Greek lad. Henry Ward's feelings for Fondolaik were not so exclusive that he did not pass through the usual adolescent stages of attraction to the opposite sex. Indeed the attachment which resulted in his marriage was formed under the eyes of Constantine Fondolaik.

Nevertheless, the imprint of the Greek upon Henry Ward Beecher was indelible. Here for the first time, Lyman Beecher's son obtained in unstinted measure the affection he had always craved. The extent to which this miracle affected him may be judged from the compact into which he and Fondolaik entered in 1832, when Henry Ward was nineteen, two years after he had graduated from Mount Pleasant:

"We consider ourselves as *brothers,* and we are bound together by ties and obligations as strong as can be placed upon us. But we rather rejoice in the relationship, as now it has converted our former friendship into brotherly love. As formerly we were connected by nothing save voluntary friendship, which could be broken off, so now we are connected by a love which *cannot* be broken; and we have pledged ourselves before God and his angels to be as written above. But we do not 'sorrow on this account — far from it, we greatly rejoice — for we have not done this thoughtlessly, but being convinced by *three years*' friendship that we mutually love one another; and from this time are now assumed new duties and obligations. And to all the foregoing we cheerfully and voluntarily subscribe our names. And now may God bless us in this our covenant and in all our future ways, and receive us both at last in heaven.' "

To this document, with its revealing interweaving of religion and a somewhat less ethereal sentiment, Henry Ward signed himself "H. C. Beecher," the C representing "Constantine," Fondolaik's name, which for several years during the height of this romantic relationship young Beecher adopted as his own middle name. Indeed, though Constantine Fondolaik died of cholera within a few hours of his return to Greece in 1842, he was still a very living memory to Henry Ward. Beecher named his third son for Constantine in 1848, and a year later, writing his wife from Amherst, he seemed to see the dead Greek boy "rise up to greet me, as he never will greet me," as he stood alone under the chestnuts of Mount Pleasant grove and looked out on the valley where he and his schoolboy hero had lived their intimate life together. Henry Ward returned to none of the reunions of the Mount Pleasant boys in after years — the one he would have sought was no longer there.

Sum and substance, young Beecher — "Hank," as he was called — gained of his romantic association with Constantine Fondolaik not only the affection for which he had hungered ever since Roxana Beecher died, but an emotional development that gradually became the formula of his relationship to his fellow men. In the arid intellectuality of his contacts with his father, with his brother Edward and his sister Catherine, he had withdrawn within himself, behind a protective wall of suppressions, until he appeared — and indeed was — stupid. His mental processes were defensive. He had formed a habit of avoidance of issues that he never altogether lost. He was unable to deal with emergencies in reasoned, logical fashion, and well in the way to become incapable of dealing with them at all — a mere creature of inhibitions. But in his intimate companionship with this Greek lad his sensitiveness expanded, came to take the place of reflective judgment. Never quite cut loose from the Lyman Beecher in his make-up, the mainspring of his action nevertheless became a sort of readily responsive emotionalism, a sentimental rebound that served as counterpoise to the ingrained shrewdness of his New England upbringing.

It was in this interplay of motives that, after Henry Ward had been at Mount Pleasant a year and a half, he delighted the heart of his father and created for himself a world of perplexities and soul-searchings by being "converted." Mount Pleasant was far from a religious school. The boys played cards, smoked, swore and enjoyed instead of mortifying themselves on Sunday. To Henry Ward, who in the old days in Litchfield had been sent to fetch tobacco and rum for the ministers' meetings in his father's parlor, such conduct should not have been too shocking. But the periodic revivals which swept over the country, and especially the one which at this period was following in the wake of Finney, changed the entire complexion of everyday events. In one of these emotional upheavals Henry Ward was entrapped and made a member of his father's church on a wave of feeling before he had half worked out what his religious convictions were, if any. Indeed, it was long after he left Amherst before he could, conscientiously, have called himself a Christian in the highly technical sense in which the term was used by such professional Christians as his father. Yet Henry Ward found nothing incongruous in remaining a member of a church, while assailed with doubts of his own sincerity, possessed by the accepted egoism of a thumping soul struggle. Nor did Lyman Beecher.

It was in his second year at Mount Pleasant that an influence was brought to bear upon Henry Ward which, while less fundamental than that of Constantine Fondolaik, was of enduring practical significance. John E. Lovell came to the Classical Institution as instructor in elocution. So far as Latin and Greek were concerned, young Beecher was making little headway; in mathematics he was plodding along, and in English losing ground. All of these studies demanded a type of intellectual equipment which the boy lacked then, and lacked always.

Oratory, however, was different. Here a pinch of emotionalism was worth a pound of cogitation, and facility of illustration outweighed argument. The emotionalism newly released through his relationship with Constantine Fondolaik became through this medium not a source of lurking shame, but a distinct asset. Instinctively Henry Ward felt that if he could only achieve the simple concurrence between the emotional equipment he possessed and his daily activities, he would have accomplished in his teens what many another spends half a lifetime to effect.

Young Beecher was, it is true, subject to extremes of feeling, extending from despair over the welfare of his soul to exaggerated gayety and practical jokes; but these were mere emotional states that could be turned with advantage into oratorical expression. All the boy lacked to complete the chain from his inner consciousness to his external life was self-confidence and technical training in the mechanics of elocution. This latter John E. Lovell supplied.

It was not that Henry Ward deliberately set about acquiring the tools of a preacher, or of a sea captain, either. He simply set about learning to do something that he could do successfully, like any other American. It was not easy, but it was easier than mathematics or theological disputation, and what is more, in that day when the sonorous phrases of Webster and Hayne and Clay and Calhoun were reverberating through the land, it was a highly desirable accomplishment. In Lovell's conception it was merely a question of the mastery of a certain fixed technique. Not Demosthenes was more exacting in his method than the author of "The United States Speaker." "It is while the organs of the voice and the limbs are yet flexible . . . that the seeds intended to produce the garland of the orator should be sown," he declared. Lovell remained only a little over a year at Mount Pleasant, but in that time he planted a world of seed in the fertile soil of Henry Ward Beecher. Gestures, including posture of feet, employment of hands and the facial expression, were left to no spontaneous impulse of the moment. They were rigidly classified and prescribed, with plates to illustrate their proper execution, and the aspirant for the orator's garland was drilled until he could perform them in his sleep. He was given words to pronounce, not a dozen, but a thousand, times, until the precise inflection and intonation had become ineradicable habit. In these days, Henry Ward wandered through the woods about

Amherst shouting "justice" and "circumstances" to the trees and the rabbits, no doubt to the vast astonishment of the latter. As he lost self-consciousness and embarrassment, growing more expert, he was given Webster's Bunker Hill oration or Clay's "Influence of National Glory" or his own father's "The Moral Effects of Intemperance" and "The Necessity of a Pure National Morality" to master — over and over again until his exacting instructor was satisfied. In the end, when Henry Ward Beecher left Mount Pleasant at seventeen, he was possessor of a specific accomplishment — which is vastly more than most youths of his age could say then or now.

Indeed, while Constantine Fondolaik was of course the hero of the graduation exercises, delivering the speech of Cataline before the Roman Senate and taking part in an Italian dialogue in the original tongue, Henry Ward was not without his honors, also. He was the old sea-dog, Captain Tackle, in a comedy scene with Jack Bowline; he was Warwick, in an heroic dialogue between Earl Warwick and King Edward. And all by himself, as the climax of a modest program of thirty-two numbers, he thundered the fearsome warnings of the prophet Joel:

"Let all the inhabitants of the land tremble, for the day of the Lord cometh, for it is nigh at hand: A day of darkness and gloominess, a day of clouds and thick darkness . . ."

with gestures.

CHAPTER V

ESCAPE

"After much deliberation & some hesitation I have concluded to send my son Henry to Amherst," Lyman Beecher wrote his Reverend Brother, President Heman Humphry. "One of the reasons of this decision is that in his preparation at Mount Pleasant he has been taught carelessly & has formed a habit of getting his lessons (I speak of the languages specially) superficially. So far as I can learn, until Mr. Newton came he was suffered to write almost entirely without parsing & scarcely retained the knowledge & use of his grammar which he carried thither. . . . To retrieve this loose setting out in any college may be difficult. But I understand that teaching by pro-

fessors and having smaller classes & more particular attention can be
& is paid to each student than might be practicable at Yale. . . ."

JUDGING from the sample, it is by no means clear what standards of grammar Lyman Beecher would have considered satisfactory. It was hardly to be expected in any event that Lyman
Beecher would appreciate what his son had got out of the
schooling at Mount Pleasant. He meant Henry Ward to be a
minister, and in his conception religion was a logical business.
Wandering sheep were herded, not led, into the fold by beating
down their intellectual resistance. Emotion had nothing to do
with conversion — or at least so he liked to believe. Wherefore
the equipment Henry Ward had acquired at Mount Pleasant
was in Lyman Beecher's estimate worse than useless.

In his own blundering way he understood his son and was
worried about him:

"Tho I have good hope of his piety yet his temperament & spirit
is of a kind which would make him susceptable to Southern influence assailing him on the side of honour & spirit," he wrote in the
same letter. "So far as I know his conduct has been circumspect, but
on the whole I shall regard his safety greater in Amherst than at
New Haven whither I was minded to send him in the indulgence of
a natural affection for my own Alma Mater."

It was the day of the Webster-Hayne debate in the Senate,
and feeling against the South ran high in New England. It was
scarcely as yet an open question of slavery; and even had it
been, Lyman Beecher would have been relatively unaffected.
He was opposed to slavery, as were the majority of New England clergymen; but it was not to his mind an evil comparable
to Unitarianism or the growth of the Roman Catholic church in
America. As his war upon the former had failed so far to blast
the heresy root and branch, Lyman Beecher now turned to the
more promising task of assailing Catholicism. An increase in
Catholic immigration to the United States had set Dr. Beecher's
mind again to "heating, heating, heating" over the danger of the
union of church and state in this country, as a quarter of a century before his mind had heated over the awful perils inherent
in Unitarian doctrine. The population, it is true, was only about
five percent Catholic, or a shade under what it now is; but in
Lyman Beecher's concept the Catholics were "as if they were

an army of soldiers, enlisted and officered and spreading over the land."

He was by no means alone in this feeling of panic. Early in 1830 Dr. Skinner wrote him that "Brother Peters, lately returned from a journey in the West, can tell you some things which would fill you with concern for the cause of Christ in that region." Evidently Brother Peters did so, for Lyman Beecher wrote his daughter Catherine shortly thereafter that "Catholics and infidels have got the start of us" in the West, and to his son William he boasted that "nearly $20,000 have been raised in money, and agencies . . . to preoccupy the Valley * before his Holiness." The Tappans were the principal contributors.

The means decided upon to combat the faith the immigrants who had settled the Ohio and Mississippi Valleys had brought with them from Ireland and South Germany was the erection of an orthodox, Calvinist theological seminary at some strategic point in the West, and as the district about Cincinnati had been largely settled by New Englanders, the Queen City appeared to be an appropriate spot.

There were a number of reasons why Lyman Beecher should be considered for the head of such an enterprise, and more still why he should have been glad to accept the task. He was now fifty-five. He had been four years head of the principal orthodox Calvinist church in Boston, an indefatigable pamphleteer in theological controversies, a prolific writer for the religious press, and a leading exponent of the ideas of Jonathan Edwards. Nevertheless, the stern doctrine he preached was so little appreciated in the community that when his church burned, the firemen refused to try to extinguish the flames, singing instead:

> "While Beecher's church holds out to burn
> The vilest sinner may return!"

Lyman Beecher had secured his son Edward the pastorate of the Park Street church, in Boston; but Edward's incumbency had not proved altogether satisfactory, either. On the whole, it began to be evident that the Beecher family had overstayed its welcome in Boston. It was time for them to be moving on, and Lyman Beecher was well aware of it. Only a few weeks before

* Ohio River Valley.

Henry Ward came home from Mount Pleasant for the last time Lyman Beecher wrote his daughter Catherine:

"I have thought seriously of going over to Cincinnati, the London of the West, to spend the remnant of my days in that great conflict, and in consecrating all my children to God in that region who are willing to go."

The "conflict" in question was that with the Roman Catholic church. He was even then preparing "a series of lectures on Catholicism in which he sounded an alarm in respect to the designs of Rome upon our country" for the following January. Henry Ward's days at home were spent in an atmosphere of a portentous decision. He had scarcely arrived when his brother Edward received a call to the presidency of Illinois College. The air was full of talk of the West, and when Henry Ward returned to Amherst, to enter college, it seemed more than likely he would be left to his own devices during four years, while those of his family not similarly situated * settled a thousand miles away.

It was therefore in depression of spirit that Henry Ward began his college course in the fall of 1830. At his father's suggestion, he roomed his first year in a private family, not in one of the college dormitories, with George Homer, a Boston Latin School boy, two years younger than himself. The two boys were left very much alone, as the other boarders at Mrs. Shepard's were seniors, one of them a Southerner of the type Lyman Beecher was anxious to have his son avoid.

The Rev. Joel Newton, whose arrival at Mount Pleasant in Henry Ward's last year was regarded with such satisfaction by Lyman Beecher, had been useful principally to instill additional piety in the lad, as if he had not had quite enough during his early years. Five weeks at home made it worse, so that when he came to Amherst it is small wonder his "Private Journal" began with entries on "Proof of a Hell," and his Saturday evenings were devoted to exhorting his classmates to a higher life and more constant activity in religious work.

Constantine Fondolaik, however, was still at Amherst, and the intimacy between the two was growing to the point where they were ready to pledge one another "that we will love and watch over one another, seeking by all means in our power to aid and

* Charles at Bowdoin and George at New Haven.

make each other happy." Not that Henry Ward had not, while in Boston, entertained a budding passion for the daughter of a neighbor. Even now, back among his old friends and associations, he still scrawled "Nancy" on the pages of his "Private Journal" — and little else.

In his studies Henry Ward just managed to scrape through. Every week there was an exercise in declamation, and Thursday afternoons were devoted to study of the historical books of the Bible, in addition to regular college classes. In athletics, however, he did better. Henry Ward was robust — "lusty," Oliver Wendell Holmes called him — and "chiefest among the football kickers."

Nevertheless, when the May vacation came in 1831, he was glad to get away. His classmate, Ebenezer Bullard, prepared for college in the more modest Amherst Academy while Henry Ward was at Mount Pleasant, invited young Beecher and Henry Ward's familiar, Constantine, to spend the holidays with him at West Sutton. Lyman Beecher was with difficulty able to raise the $93 that Henry Ward's tuition, board, lodging and washing were costing him. He had no money for coach fare. So the three boys tramped the fifty odd miles.

The Bullards were New Englanders of the earliest Puritan stock. Two of Ebenezer's brothers had graduated from Amherst. Artemas Bullard, the father, was a tall, florid, blue-eyed, straight-nosed, fine-looking country physician who "belonged to the school of domestic economists who regard industry and subordination as indispensable in a wise administration of family government." The mother, Artemas' second wife, was a descendant of Sampson Mason, the Baptist and Dragoon of Cromwell's army. She had been a bit battered by bearing ten children; but her spirit was unbroken. She was what one might call unflinching. Ebenezer was four years older than Henry Ward Beecher, and his next youngest sister, Eunice, was a year older.

Eunice had been to school at Hadley, only a few miles from Amherst, while Henry Ward was at Mount Pleasant. They had much to talk about. She had her father's strong features, and blue eyes, and her golden-brown hair fell about her face in a fringe of ringlets. She was intense, her lips quivered as she talked, and she was more than a little superior and patronizing towards this self-conscious young friend of her brother's. After all, his education was just beginning, while she was already teaching school.

It was precisely what Henry Ward needed more than anything else in the world at this particular juncture of his life — such a self-possessed, capable, older girl as was Eunice Bullard to whom to anchor his rapid emotional development. For in the distinguished family of Lyman Beecher Henry Ward was a negligible quantity. Catherine, the oldest, now past thirty, was the apple of Lyman Beecher's eye, and possessed an intellectual virility that none of the boys boasted. William and Edward were safely in the ministry, already colleagues rather than sons to their father. George, in whom Lyman Beecher discerned the greatest promise, had been sent to Dr. Taylor, to whom Dr. Beecher felt he owed his best. Mary was Mrs. Perkins. How far Henry Ward was from his brothers and sisters at this period is revealed in an entry in his diary. He had stopped at Hartford to see his sisters. He went first to Mary's "and sent word that I wished to see Mrs. Perkins. After waiting awhile she came down stairs, and did not know me, and I had to tell her who I was. About five o'clock I went to see Harriet and Catherine. Catherine knew me, but Harriet did not." And Harriet had been the beloved companion of his childhood days! Henry Ward's stepmother had a three-year-old baby and two other small children of her own to worry over, had she been given to worrying over children. And so far as Lyman Beecher was concerned, he committed Henry Ward to God and President Humphry of Amherst, in humble hope but scant confidence of the outcome.

And indeed the boy was neither brilliant nor studious. What attention he attracted in his family, at school or at college, was captured in the comic rôle. No memory of him at this time is complete without reference to some piece of clowning cited to illustrate the irrepressible levity of this adolescent, and in fact so transparently revealing his intensified craving for normal companionship. It was only here, among strangers, that for the first time in his life Henry Ward Beecher was regarded as himself, without apology. And it was to this girl of poise and evident intelligence that he felt he could look for understanding of all the heart-hunger that lay behind his pathetic buffoonery.

When Henry Ward left West Sutton, he knew that Eunice Bullard was to teach school at Clappville that summer, and had

determined to pass through Clappville on his way home to
Boston at the end of his freshman year. Meanwhile he returned
to college with the serious-minded intention of establishing a
daily prayer-meeting and praying for a revival, shocked at the
low state of morality into which Mount Pleasant had fallen. In
due season he was elected to the Athenian Society, one of the
three literary and debating societies of Amherst, common in
American colleges in that day, which gave diplomas to members
performing a certain number of debates, orations and disputations. But he took no active part in its program at first. The
legend that he was a distinguished debater and public speaker
at college is without foundation. He was more active in college
fights between "Sodom" — East Amherst — and "Mt. Zion,"
where the college stood.

What was far more to the point than Henry Ward's desul-
tory membership in the Athenian Society was the founding, in
his sophomore year, of two literary publications, the *Sprite* and
the *Shrine*, published anonymously by rival groups of Amherst
undergraduates. Of the *Shrine*, Beecher's Freshman year room-
mate, George Homer, was assistant editor, and Henry Ward's
literary career began right there. Contributions were signed
by fictitious initials, and it is difficult to trace their authorship.
None is remarkable. It is significant, however, that Garrison's
"Thoughts on African Colonization," in which the pretense
that the slavery problem could ever be solved by shipping the
negroes back to Africa is annihilated, was reviewed at length —
and not favorably — in the *Shrine*. It is even more significant
that an Anti-Slavery Society formed at Amherst in 1832, as a
consequence of Garrison's publication, "was disbanded by the
authority of the Faculty." Amherst was no place for Abolitionists. Henry Ward Beecher was not a member of this evanescent
organization. But he belonged to the College Band, and paraded, magnificent in a white suit and black cap.

Henry Ward saw Eunice Bullard again at the end of his first
year, as they had planned. Between them, they arranged that
he should teach school at Northbridge during his winter vacation, boarding at her aunt's, while she would be visiting her
aunt at the same time. He was homely, Eunice thought; but at
least he displayed a romantic persistence in seeking her out in
this marked way. After all, he was the son of the great (to orthodox folk like the Bullards) Dr. Beecher, and not such a bad

match. West Sutton was a small place, and she might do much worse. Once, when she was only twelve years old, Eunice had been sent to the market town twelve miles away to buy the supplies for the whole family — and had acquitted herself admirably. She was nineteen now, and had been teaching a year. She ought to know her own mind. And she did.

In Boston Henry Ward found the question of Lyman Beecher's Western venture virtually settled. There was a certain amount of coyness still to be displayed, but if anything were calculated to induce Dr. Beecher to accept the presidency of Lane Theological Seminary it was the news that his doctrinal views were being attacked in Cincinnati as contrary to the Presbyterian confession of faith. The deciding factor, however, was another consideration. Lyman Beecher had just conducted, to his own satisfaction, a controversy with Dr. O'Flaherty of the Roman Catholic church in Boston, and having tasted blood was eager for the fray in a vaster field.

"Dr. Beecher's great motive in going to Cincinnati was to oppose the influence of the Roman Catholic church in every way," writes his daughter Harriet, adding that "he frequently attacked it in the pulpit and in the press."

The custom, among the indigent young men of Amherst, to earn some of the cost of their education by school teaching and a little free-hand preaching during vacation stood Henry Ward in good stead in his romance with Eunice Bullard. Ostensibly, he was thus engaged at Northbridge. In reality, he was desperately seeking security in some one to love and to love him, in place of the already disintegrating family relationship now on the point of disappearing altogether in the West. Henry Ward must have some one to cling to him; he must have an audience favorably predisposed to his efforts; he must have some one to whom to confide the soul-searchings expected of all self-respecting Calvinists not actually ministers of God. With Constantine, however profound the affection that bound them, the Greek was the leader, the lord, the hero — Henry Ward was back in the old familiar rôle he had enacted since childhood, of worshiper. It did not help him a particle to get on his own feet.

Nor was it essential that the person whom he must find to take this rôle in his life, if he were not to sink under the weight of his Calvinist inhibitions and the small regard in which he was held by the Beecher family, should necessarily be Eunice Bullard. He had already experienced a fleeting passion for a plump little blue-eyed blonde at Hartford, who later became known to fame as Fanny Fern. Even during his courtship of Eunice Bullard, a girl in Northbridge almost captured him. "But Miss Bullard had preëmpted me," he says, "and would not let me up." She did more than that. She attended the evening prayer meetings he addressed in Whitingsville in the intervals of his school teaching, and admired him unblushingly. "Not once did he hesitate for a single word," she wrote. It was just what Henry Ward needed. He felt that he dared not let go this precious confidence in his abilities for the first time displayed by an attractive young lady older and intellectually better equipped than he.

So one evening he slipped her a note: "Will you go with me as a missionary to the West?" Would she? She had had no other intentions since she laid eyes on Lyman Beecher's son. Dr. Artemas Bullard felt otherwise about the match. But in the end, when Henry Ward returned to Amherst, he was engaged to Eunice Bullard.

His own family also failed to take the engagement seriously. Justifying himself to one of his brothers for the step, he wrote that "no term since I have been in college have I studied so much as last term; no year accomplished so much as the last." It was the obvious effect of his attachment for the girl. He had a moral support of his own now and the self-confidence that went with it. He went about the country delivering lectures on temperance — re-hashes of his father's famous discourses on that subject. Dr. Spürzheim had launched phrenology on Boston, and phrenology was precisely the sort of thing that would stand for science to Henry Ward Beecher. He read all he could find on the subject, and together with Orson Squire Fowler, a classmate, who later became the publisher of the *American Journal of Phrenology*, he toured near-by towns delivering lectures on phrenology while Fowler examined the heads of the curious.

All his life Henry Ward Beecher believed profoundly in phrenology. He held that

"it brings new aid to the statesman, the lawyer, the physician and the minister of Christ in their benevolent efforts to benefit society and gives them a new power over the intellect and the will."

He liked to feel that this "new power" was his. And believing that he could and did possess a magic power, he began indeed to exercise one.

At the beginning of his Junior year, Henry Ward registered from Cincinnati. The great removal of the Beecher family had at last taken place. Ebenezer Bullard had also gone West, and Constantine Fondolaik disappears from the picture. Henry Ward was left with only Eunice Bullard to tie to. He was rooming in the college dormitories now, first with David Gould and later with Chauncey Howard. As both had the law, not the ministry, in prospect, the terrible pressure of professional Christianity was somewhat removed from Henry Ward.

As the end of his college course approached, he rushed to make up all the debates and disputations he had been due to perform before the Athenian Society throughout three years. For a month he attended every meeting, discussing prohibition, the abolition of slavery in the District of Columbia, whether it was desirable for students in college to enjoy female society (Henry Ward in the affirmative), and whether the tendencies of society are towards perfection. He also delivered his required oration — "On the comparative importance of the three professions, medicine, law and theology." Towards the end of his Senior year, also, he· was elected president of the Society of Natural History. The Society sported a gold fraternity pin and discussed such scientific subjects as phrenology. On his election as president, Henry Ward delivered

"an able address upon the subject [phrenology] expressing the futility of the objections offered against the science, and exhibiting and defending its fundamental principles."

Otherwise, he was not conspicuous. He earned considerable sums (for his age and that day) from his teaching and his lectures — once as much as $10 for one lecture, of which he devoted eighty-five cents to the purchase of an engagement ring for Eunice. What was important in these activities was that Henry Ward learned that he could, at a pinch, make a kind of living — that he was economically free.

He roomed alone his last year. There had been no revival at Amherst since early in 1832. For two years and a half, therefore, he had not been tossed about on the tumultuous waves of religious emotionalism. Dr. Bullard exhibited sufficient hostility to his engagement to Eunice to keep the attachment alive, and Eunice herself, cool and clear-headed, devoted nevertheless to him, gave him self-assurance. Lyman Beecher was safely embarked upon new theological warfares in the West, and left his unpromising son, happily, alone. Out of these elements, Henry Ward Beecher began to fashion the tools of individual development, free of the shadow of his Puritan prison.

When he graduated, Hattie made the journey from Cincinnati to Toledo by stage, thence by boat to Buffalo, by canal boat to Albany, and by stage to Amherst. Of the thirty-nine men who received degrees, twenty-six had some part in the commencement exercises.

But Henry Ward Beecher had none.

Part II: Ambition

"In the controversy then arising through the land in relation to slavery, Mr. Beecher from the first took the
ground and was willing to bear the name of Abolitionist.
It was part of the heroic element of his nature always to
stand for the weak, and he naturally inclined to take that
stand in a battle where the few were at odds with the
many."

HARRIET BEECHER STOWE

"His common sense enabled him both to guess instanta-
neously and infallibly the present temper of an audience,
but also to read the signs of the times and know in season
what course on his part would put him into the true current of popular tendency. He never wasted much time or
strength in beating up against wind and tide. He felt for the
current and found it."

WILLIAM CLEAVER WILKINSON

CHAPTER VI

1835

In his sermon on the death of Wendell Phillips in 1884,
Henry Ward Beecher cast back to his college days. The Civil
War was then long over. Lincoln had freed the slaves. The
Abolitionists of half a century previous had won the day.

"I was chosen by the Athenian Society," said Beecher, "to debate
the question of African colonization which was then new, fresh and
enthusiastic. . . . Fortunately I was assigned to the negative side of
the question, and in preparing to speak I prepared my whole life.
I contended against colonization as a condition of emancipation . . .
and advocated immediate emancipation on the broad ground of
human rights."

It is an apt story — but there is not a word of truth in it. As
so often he did, to give added effectiveness to an illustration,
Beecher put the incident in the first person. And telling it so,
he came to believe it. His sermons and writings are full of such
examples, and no great harm done, either. In this case the rec-

46

ord of that debate at Amherst still exists. It took place on July 10, 1833, on the question: "Is the Colonization or Anti-Slavery Society more worthy of patronage?" The debaters were Mortimer Blake and Robert T. Conant. Henry Ward Beecher, lately elected president of the Athenian Society, was in the chair. He took no part in the discussion.

It is significant that the victory in this debate was carried off by those who spoke for the Colonization Society. That was the side of the controversy over slavery favored by Dr. Lyman Beecher and virtually every other New England clergyman of standing. No other opinion would have been tolerated in the Beecher family in 1833. None other was tolerated by the Faculty of Amherst.

In common with the vast majority of the population of the United States at this period, Henry Ward Beecher could see nothing in the slavery question to become exercised over. It had all been threshed out in the Beecher family five years before. Fresh from his Baltimore jail, William Lloyd Garrison had come to Lyman Beecher as "then the head of the evangelical clergy of New England, if not of America," to beg his aid in forming an organization that would really do something to end slavery, not palter with it.

"He was bitterly disappointed in finding him [Dr. Beecher] indifferent to the appeal," wrote Oliver Johnson. " 'I have too many irons in the fire already,' said the Doctor. 'Your zeal is commendable; but you are misguided. If you will give up your fanatical notions and be guided by us (the clergy) we will make you the Wilberforce of America.' "

The prospect of becoming the Wilberforce of America failed to allure Garrison. He could cipher as well as the next man. In fifteen years the American Colonization Society had managed to ship less than 1,500 blacks to Liberia, while the three million slaves held in the South were increasing their number by normal procreation at the rate of 150,000 a year. Faced with these figures, Garrison held that those who claimed to deplore slavery while at the same time advocating colonization as a means of doing away with the evil were just so many hypocrites. What is more, he said so in plain terms, and Lyman Beecher sat in Julien Hall, in Boston, his thick lips pursed and a frown on his face, listening to that rash young man in stern disapproval. When Garrison, persisting, wrote him, Dr. Beecher ignored the letter. And when Samuel J. May actually preached against slavery in the Rev. Ralph Waldo Emerson's church, it was Lyman Beecher who replied, from his own pulpit, "exhorting his hearers to support the Colonization Society, and sneering at 'the few foolish whites' who were opposing it, and advocating the immediate emancipation of slaves, 'reckless of consequences.' "

All of this was while Henry Ward was still a Freshman in Amherst. He was steeped in this handy if somewhat remote view of the slavery problem.

But in Cincinnati slavery was no longer an academic question; it was a very practical element in the daily life of those who dwelt there, as Lyman Beecher speedily found. It had its practical aspects even for young Henry Ward, still in Amherst. For Arthur Tappan was the financial mainstay of Lane Theological Seminary, the paymaster of Lyman Beecher as it were — and Arthur Tappan had suddenly gone over to Garrison and the Abolitionists. The Colonization Society, he wrote, was "a device of Satan, to rivet closer the fetters of the slaves, and to deepen the prejudice against the free colored people." He wanted to know where Dr. Beecher stood on the subject. Lyman was more tactful than candid:

"I am not apprized of the ground of controversy between the Colonizationists and the Abolitionists," he replied. "I am myself both, without perceiving in myself any inconsistency. Were it in my power to put an end to slavery immediately, I would do it; but it is not. . . . I trust God has begun, by the instrumentality of both, a great work which will not stop until not only the oppressed are free, but Africa herself shall have rest in the Lord along her extended coast and deep interior."

He felt that the colonization scheme possessed the advantage of enabling the negroes deported to Africa to "carry to that country the Christianity of their masters." He had no patience with the persistent agitation of the question.

It was when Henry Ward, approaching the end of his college course, was preparing to join his family in Cincinnati that Lyman Beecher was forced to face a problem whose outcome confronted Henry Ward with the first crisis of his existence. The discussion of slavery at Lane Seminary reached an acute stage. Harriet Martineau, who was visiting in Cincinnati at the time, summed up the situation:

"Ohio borders on two slave States; and Lane Seminary looked for a large measure of its resources to that portion of American Society with which slavery was incorporated. Freely, therefore, as the students were permitted to act on every other moral question, this, of slavery, must be interdicted as dangerous. The Faculty forbade discussion and association on the question, from the moment the students began to employ their *leisure hours* in establishing Sunday Schools, lyceums, and circulating libraries among the free colored population of Cincinnati and while the body of the Trustees and Professors were acting as partizans of the Colonization Society, and the President [Lyman Beecher] and his brother professors were making colonization speeches, which were circulated in the newspapers, they framed a set of laws repressive of speech and action on this subject among the students. . . . There was no step left for the conscientious but to withdraw. They withdrew. Out of forty theological students, only two returned the next year; and of classical students only five out of sixty."

So it came to pass that when Henry Ward Beecher tucked his Amherst sheepskin under his arm and started West, after two years of freedom from the mental and moral domination of his father and his sister Catherine and his brother Edward and all the rest of the Beecher tribe, he was bound for a school which had gone to pieces on the rock of intellectual liberty — with Lyman Beecher as usual holding the fort against free speech.

Henry Ward went first to West Sutton. Eunice Bullard never did think him handsome, but now, at twenty-one, he was perhaps more nearly so than at any other time in his life. Rather under medium height, he retained for a brief period a still adolescent slenderness of body and an as yet undefined leanness of face, with rounding chin, prominent nose and the large mouth of his sister, Hattie. But his lips were fuller than hers — heavy, sensuous lips even then, that lent an almost feminine softness to his countenance. A coaxing, wheedling face, save for the eyes. Whatever hardness was in the man was in them — blue or gray, as one liked. Frequently they seemed opaque. The blond curls of his babyhood had turned dark. He parted his hair far over on the left side and wore it just to his stock in the back; it was not until later that he affected the long mane sweeping his coat collar.

In Henry Ward's whole appearance there was a sort of wistfulness that was deceptive. "I always regarded him as a big boy, rather than a man at all," one of his intimates said in after years. Many did. They were beguiled.

Young Beecher spent only two days at West Sutton. He was full of trepidation at the prospect of submerging in the family melting pot the little individuality he had so laboriously won. It rested on so fragile a foundation! Once, at Amherst, he had asked Prof. Snell why he should be required to study mathematics, since he was preparing to be a preacher.

"To discipline your mind," said the professor.

"If that's all, I sha'n't go to class any more," Henry Ward retorted. "My mind gets enough discipline inventing excuses to you for not being there."

A vision of long vistas of inventing excuses to Lyman Beecher for cutting classes in a Seminary with only five students depressed Henry Ward. All his boyhood had been spent in that sort of thing — doing something he should not have done, and then living in an agony of fear lest it be discovered.

"I had not the courage to confess, and tell the truth," he said of those earlier years. "First, shame hindered me; second, fear . . . And when I got to going wrong, I went on going wrong. . . . I was afraid of being found out; and then I prevaricated a little; and that made the matter worse. . . . The terror would come that I might be found out; and for days, when my father came home, I would watch his face to see if he looked as though he knew it; and I showed conscious guilt, and the anxiety and pain grew on me . . . and out of that depression and low state it was easier to be tempted again; and I got into another wrong, and that made my case worse yet, and I became more and more uneasy. So one thing led to another and I was under a sense of condemnation. The very fear which I experienced bred suspicion and jealousy, and irritation, and unhappiness."

It was the recommencement of all of this that Henry Ward Beecher saw ahead of him, at Lane Seminary. And it was precisely against this that he sought the talisman of Eunice Bullard's love, her devotion, her confidence in his destiny. More than anything else his own individual emancipation seemed desirable to Henry Ward Beecher. He could never compass it alone. He was too easy-going. He would be too surely overweighted by the phalanx of his father and his stepmother, his brothers and sisters. But Eunice would be both excuse and support. Assured of her, he felt that he possessed a magic charm to fend from him whatever menace the future might hold.

Henry Ward Beecher went whistling out to the great open spaces of the Far West, at Cincinnati.

"Ohio," wrote Lyman Beecher, "is not a frontier State, or Cincinnati a new settlement, or the work demanded here that of a pioneer. On the contrary, Cincinnati is as really a literary emporium as Boston, and is rapidly rising to an honorable competition."

The Rev. Andrew Reed, of the British Congregational Delegation, was not quite so lyric. "I was struck by the number of barbers' shops and grocers, or grogshops," he wrote from Lane Seminary; "it should seem that no man here shaves himself, and that Temperance has not yet fulfilled its commission. I believe there are not less than 200 grogstores in Cincinnati," he added.

But it was a far weightier business than temperance that took Lyman Beecher back East the same year that his son, Henry, came West. Lane Seminary was sadly in need of money, which was a serious matter for the Beechers. Arthur and Lewis Tappan, just at that time, were financing the young students of Henry Ward's age who had abandoned Lane in the interest of free speech and the abolition of slavery, and finding them a new and less restricted sphere at Oberlin, where Dr. Beecher's old rival, Finney, was to have charge of their theological training. To Lyman Beecher, the whole slavery discussion was a tempest in a teapot. He had come West to fight the Catholic church, and for that purpose he now made his plea for funds. Harriet Martineau describes with what success:

"The removal to Cincinnati of Dr. Beecher, the ostentatious and virulent foe of the Catholics, has much quickened the spirit of alarm in that region," she wrote. "It is to be hoped that Dr. Beecher and the people of Cincinnati will remember what has been the invariable consequence in America of public denunciations of assumed offenses which the law does not reach; namely, mobbing. It is to be hoped that all parties will remember that Dr. Beecher preached in Boston three sermons vituperative of the Catholics the Sunday before the burning of the Charlestown convent by a Boston mob."

Lyman Beecher did his level best to stir up racial and religious prejudice against recent European immigrants, "through the medium of their religion and priesthood as entirely accessible to the control of the potentates of Europe as if they were an army," he declared. It did not seem to occur to the doughty doctor that the High Command of this potential army was right distant from the front.

But a Theological Seminary with no students and no money, buttressed by a little private war on the Roman Catholic church, was not what Lyman Beecher really would call trouble. He had that, too, in addition. It took the form of an assault upon his orthodoxy, as a fit and proper exponent of the Presbyterian creed. And this was indeed a momentous matter, not just for Dr. Beecher, but for his sons who were to come after him in the ministry — Henry Ward included. It was on the eve of Lyman Beecher's epic struggle to retain his place in the bosom of the Presbyterian church that young Beecher reached the metropolis of the West, and settled down to the relative luxury of Walnut Hills.

It never seemed to matter to Lyman Beecher how much money he received, he was perennially hard up. He was particularly so now, albeit he was not only president of Lane Seminary but also pastor of the Second Presbyterian church — "the aristocratic, rich church of Cincinnati," Henry B. Stanton called it — attended by such solid citizens as Judge Jacob Burnet and John H. Groesbeck, and, occasionally, by young Salmon P. Chase, only slightly older than Henry Ward Beecher, but already a marked man. Yet the great, rambling brick house at Walnut Hills, situated in a spacious yard of tufted grass, half concealed from view by acacias, locusts, rose-bushes and vines of honeysuckle and clematis, was more comfort than the Beechers had ever known before. Catherine and Hattie kept a school in town; William had a church near by, at Putnam, Ohio; George had one at Batavia. Henry and Charles were two of the five theological students at Lane; but as Lane was, by charter, a manual training institution where every student was "expected to labor three hours a day at some agricultural or mechanical business," neither should have been a drain on the family resources. Only the younger children — Harriet Porter's brood — were unproductive. Socially, Lyman Beecher's position established the family. General Edward Porter, a cousin of Harriet Porter Beecher, John P. and Samuel Foote — the same Uncle Samuel who had set Henry Ward to dreaming of ships and the sea — were leaders in the highly pretentious literary circles of the Queen City — chunky with culture, as a wit of the day put it.

As for that "noble class of young men, uncommonly strong, entirely radical, and terribly in earnest" who had left Lane Seminary high and dry over the question of their right to discuss slavery — to Henry Ward and the handful who remained at Lane, they were just "a little, muddy stream of vinegar that went trickling down to Oberlin." Henry Ward had only contempt for such fanatics, silly enough to wreck their careers over the 740 ignorant negroes who then inhabited Cincinnati. It was not slavery, but theology that caught Henry Ward Beecher in its grip at this particular juncture of his life.

If anything could have disillusioned Henry Ward Beecher as to the profession upon which he was about to enter, it would have been his father's heresy trial. The sheer trickery of the interminable proceeding that absorbed a year and a half of the life of the whole Beecher family; the politics; the personal jealousies obscuring what inconsequent doctrinal points were at issue; the ignoble triumphs and rankling defeats — there was in this fantastic comedy meat for the digestion of a young man about to embark upon a lifetime of a like career. It finished Henry Ward's younger brother Charles — he abandoned not only the ministry but Christianity itself, tucked a fiddle under his arm and set off down the river, an itinerant musician in search of a philosophy somewhat more harmonious than that of John Calvin. It finished Henry Ward's stepmother, too. She had spent her days in a whirlpool of just such meaningless, perfervid polemics as this. She had had enough. When the pother over Lyman's orthodoxy was at its height, she dropped quietly out of the cast. Already it was plain that her children were not of the same breed as those of Roxana Foote. They were growing up less complex and less inclined to compromise than Catherine and Hattie and Henry Ward and the rest. They were exhibiting symptoms of an intellectual integrity impervious to sentimentality. Roxana Foote had surrendered early; but Harriet Porter maintained herself impregnable to the last. Somber, austere, withdrawn, she had brought Henry Ward nothing, and she took nothing from him. Fifteen months later, Lyman Beecher at sixty-one married him another wife.

But Henry Ward Beecher was made of sterner stuff than his

brother Charles—or perhaps simply more pliable material. He shrank from none of the doctrinal gymnastics which the elder Beecher performed to escape the odium of heresy. Henry Ward squired his father during his trial before Synod at Dayton—they went up by canal boat, loaded down with theological treatises—and the young man was able to appraise in all calmness the narrow range of mind and spirit of these Scotch-Irish guardians of the faith once delivered to the saints:

"I never saw so many faces of clergymen and so few of them intellectual faces," he wrote. "The predominant expression is that of firmness (in many cases deepening into obstinacy), kind-heartedness, and honesty. As for deep thought seen in the eye or lineaments—for lofty expression—for the enthusiasm of genius—for the expression which comes of communion of great thoughts, with the higher feelings of poetry and religion, and even of speculation, there is an utter want of it."

For the first time, in a practical manner, it was demonstrated to young Henry Ward Beecher that even in face of deep-rooted mistrust and determined opposition, a clergyman could do about as he pleased if he were but glib enough, supple enough, when called to account.

"Is is possible to reconcile that man's whole career with a sound, honest, straight-forward purpose?" Dr. Miller of Princeton wrote Asahel Nettleton, of Lyman Beecher. "I fear there has been somewhere such a tampering with conscience as will be found to eat like a canker both into character and usefulness."

But to Henry Ward, his father was admirable. There was great rejoicing among the Beechers at the old man's triumph. But back East, many shook their heads.

"Born to be a leader, under some circumstances, this eminent man failed at this time in an essential attribute of leadership and moral and religious enterprises," wrote Lewis Tappan. "He had previously avowed in his lectures at the Seminary, as was understood, that true wisdom consists in advocating a cause only so far as the community will sustain the reformer."

That, too, Henry Ward Beecher believed profoundly. "To Lyman Beecher," wrote Henry Ward a few years later, "I owe my principles, my knowledge, and that I am a Minister of the Gospel."

CHAPTER VII

CINCINNATI

The Beecher policy of ignoring the slavery issue somehow or other failed to dispose of the problem. Many of the students who had left Lane Seminary "were slaveholders themselves, and many were heirs apparent to an inheritance of slaves." Under the spell of that enthusiasm which the Trustees of Lane had sought in vain to quench, these had freed their slaves; some even went back into the South, whence they had come, to carry the new gospel of Abolition. One of these young men, Amos Dresser, was taken by a vigilance committee in Nashville. He was given twenty lashes on his bare back, in the public square of the city. Seven Presbyterian elders were participants in the function. As the heavy rawhide whistled through the air, Dresser prayed.

"God damn him — stop his praying!" the mob screamed. But they did not stop it.

At the same moment Henry Ward Beecher, at Dayton, was ridiculing the Abolitionists in the Presbyterian Synod for their stand on the far more important matter of Dr. Beecher's theological ideas. It was at this time, also, that Lyman Beecher wrote his son, William, at Putnam, Ohio:

"As to abolition, I am still of opinion that you ought not, and need not, and will not commit yourself as a partisan on either side. The cause is moving along in Providence, and by the American Union, and by colonization, and by Lundy * in Texas, which is a grand thing, and will succeed, as I believe; and I hope and believe that the Abolitionists as a body will become more calm and less denunciatory, with the exception of the few he-goat men, who think they do God service by butting everything in the line of their march which does not fall in or get out of the way."

Henry Ward was willing, so far as he was concerned, to let the question of slavery rest there. He had other things on his mind. Catherine Beecher, at thirty-five, had already achieved a certain fame as an authoress (female writers were not yet

* Benjamin Lundy.

authors) with two books to her credit, and one in press. Now little Hattie bowled the rest of the Beechers over by winning a prize of fifty dollars offered for a short story by the *Western Literary Journal and Monthly Review*. She was definitely launched on a career of letters, and by no means averse to patronizing her younger brother on that account. Of Cincinnati at this time, Ebenezer Smith Thomas, editor of the *Daily Evening Post*, wrote, a little incoherently perhaps:

"It is in her Literature, her Authors, her Arts, her Artists, and her numerous Literary, Scientific and benevolent institutions, that has given her a name, not only among the cities of the great Valley, but of the civilized world, that will go down to the most remote posterity."

Mrs. Trollope thought somewhat less of the Queen City. She quotes one of the leading literary lights of the place, not without a certain malice:

"Shakespeare, Madam, is obscene," he said to her; "and thank God, *we* are sufficiently advanced to have found it out."

In such a literary forcing house as this, Henry Ward felt that those talents he had already displayed in college magazines would be worse than hidden in the earth unless he made something of them. He therefore tried his hand on a series of anonymous articles dealing with that ever burning (for the Beechers) subject of the Roman Catholic peril. The *Daily Evening Post* published them.

Young Beecher was enchanted. He found theology a dull business at best, and goodness knows he got little enough of it, what with Lyman Beecher running up and down the country fighting heresy charges and Henry Ward's new brother-in-law, Calvin Stowe, rushing off to Europe on a mission for the State of Ohio. Young Beecher had plenty of time to write, and to read, too, if he were so minded. Inspired by the general literary atmosphere of the Western metropolis, he did begin to read, omnivorously: Webster's and Hayne's speeches; Bulwer's and Scott's novels; and Shakespeare. "Phrenological works — the religion of bumps — with Shakespeare, were his textbooks then," wrote one of his classmates. Dr. Caldwell, "the Spürzheim of America," had organized a Phrenological Society in Cincinnati, and young Beecher belonged. He found Shakespeare a "wonderful writer" whose works might "with moderate caution be safely put into the hands of the young." But he recognized that "no one ever heard one speak as Macbeth, as Hamlet, or as Iago, for no one ever spoke so. Passion, or indeed nature, never marches in heroic measure," he adds sagely.

But Henry Ward found then, and indeed all his life, the greatest difficulty in remembering what he read. "I shall be obliged to collect my general scattered feelings into a definite, tangible form," he wrote in his journal, at Lane Seminary; "and if I always did that after reading I should have more numerous ideas of things and of their forms, and more correct ones." He was both too indolent and too little introspective for diary-keeping of any value:

"I am not enough contemplative to make a record of reflections and feelings very definite," he sets down; and adds: "I never could be *sincere.*"

After all, it was neither by contemplation nor reflection that impressions came to young Henry Ward Beecher in his Seminary days; but through emotional reactions, tempered by a saving common sense. He wallowed in sentimentality. But he kept clear of entanglements. It was by no means easy for one as demonstrative as young Beecher, and who craved affection as consumingly as he. Captain Marryatt wrote that he "saw more handsome women at Cincinnati than in any other city of the Union; their figures were more perfect, and they were finer grown." Charles Fenno Hoffman, the poet, was of like opinion:

"What would most strike you in the streets of Cincinnati would be the number of pretty faces and stylish figures one meets in the morning," he records. "I have had more than one opportunity of seeing these Western beauties by candle-light; and the evening display wrought no disappointment of the morning promise."

So Henry Ward also thought. In the three years he spent at Lane at least three young ladies held him enthralled. When one of them married, he wrote her in a perfect ecstasy of passionate incoherence, telling her that she knew how well he loved her — how *deeply* I love *all* when I love at all, as he put it. He would, he said, cherish her memory forever, with deep affection, single-hearted affection — Oh, Catherine, it will be long ere I find another for whom I shall feel all that I did and do for you — May *God* bless you, for *He alone* can give that fullness of blessing which my heart craves for you — *remember* that *one* here says

he will not *forget* — I will never forget you. He went on to
pray God to give her the light of His countenance, to keep her
near to Him and give her wisdom and patience and success in
the wifely duties to which she had been called. God grant you
may never feel the sickness of heart which those whom you
love have, he prayed, and may your love be undisturbed from
within and from without and ripen and mellow and be eternal
in Heaven. He could not, he said, express the earnestness and
intensity of his desire for her full happiness. He would pray for
her, he assured her, and if he could ever do more, you know
how sure I will do it. I do love you, he once more assured this
bride, and I *shall ever*. And now my prayer to God and my
heart's full desire is for your full happiness here — oh! Catherine, for your fuller joy hereafter!

It was probably as well for Henry Ward that the lady in
question was going to New York to live.

Not that these little affectional excursions afield in any way
dimmed young Beecher's devotion to Eunice Bullard — whose
being is mine, whose feelings are mine, as he wrote this same
Catherine Dickinson. Eunice, he felt, would swell the tide of
grateful memory and embalm in her heart and his all those joys
which Catherine had awakened, he wrote.

When he wrote Eunice, however, "theology predominated
in his letters," she says. Two of her brothers were in Cincinnati
with him. The tie that bound him to her — his need for affection, for emotional expansion — was only the stronger with distance. It was not merely a stimulated need, evoked when he and
Eunice could be together, dormant otherwise. It was a need as
essential to Henry Ward Beecher as his breath. No relationship
in his family had ever satisfied, or ever would. Lyman Beecher
and his son dwelt on different planes. Edward and Catherine,
with their cold logic, were as strange to him as Chinamen. Once
he and Hattie had been close; but now Hattie was on the thresh-
old of that world of romance of which she was to be, throughout her life, the rather bewildered heroine. Amid all these self-
absorbed, ruthless entities, Henry Ward, like a child in a
nursery, eager to talk, to play games, to make believe, to experience the vast release of laughter or tears, met only prohibi-
tions. He was forced to find his release where he could, in Constantine Fondolaik, or Catherine Dickinson, or whomsoever he

could fasten upon. His family called it his "genius for friendship." It was only heart-hunger.

It was in May, 1836, that opportunity knocked at Henry
Ward Beecher's door. Prof. Stowe had sailed for Prussia. Ly-
man Beecher's heresy trial was to reach its final stage in the
Presbyterian General Assembly at Pittsburgh, and he wanted
his assistant in the Second Presbyterian Church of Cincinnati,
the Rev. Thomas Brainerd, with him, to help him in his fight.
But Brainerd's main business was the editorship of the anti-
Catholic weekly which the Presbyterian pastoral association of
Cincinnati had established as artillery in the great war against
what it called the "ambitious ecclesiastical influence" of Rome.
The Cincinnati *Journal* boasted only 3,600 subscribers, and was
"always fraternal in its spirit towards the South." Hattie Stowe
called it "our family newspaper"—meaning the Beecher family. Henry Ward's articles in the *Daily Evening Post* had fully
qualified him to conduct an anti-Catholic publication. So when
Brainerd went East with Dr. Beecher, Henry Ward was left in
charge of the *Journal*, on a salary of $500 a year—at twenty-
three the man of the Beecher family.

Two months previous, James G. Birney, a gentleman of im-
peccable connections, a Princeton graduate, a man of substance,
a member of the Presbyterian church in good standing, and a
Southerner born and bred, who had conducted an Abolition
paper, *The Philanthropist*, at New Richmond, up the Ohio river
a way, moved his press to Cincinnati. Birney's abolitionist activities had never aroused any great enthusiasm in Cincinnati's
best circles. In January, 1836, Ebenezer Smith Thomas and a
number of other editors and politicians had even called a mass-
meeting to "exert every lawful effort to suppress the publication" of Birney's paper, as they quaintly put it. But Birney
ruined the meeting by appearing at it in person and making a
speech which "disarmed the madness of the multitude"—a
highly dramatic example of what could be done with a hostile
audience, young Beecher thought.

It was not until July of the same year that anything further
happened. What occurred then, Hattie Beecher Stowe describes, writing her husband:

"Yesterday evening I spent scribbling for Henry's newspaper
(the *Journal*) in this wise: 'Birney's printing press has been

mobbed, and many of the respectable citizens are disposed to wink at the outrage in consideration of its moving in the line of their prejudices.'

"I wrote a conversational sketch, in which I rather satirized this inconsistent spirit, and brought out the effects of patronizing *any* violation of private rights. It was in a light, sketchy style, designed to draw attention to a long editorial of Henry's in which he considered the subject fully and seriously. His piece is, I think, a powerful one; indeed he does write very strongly. I am quite proud of his editorials; they are well studied, earnest and dignified. I think he will make a first-rate writer."

But there was not a single word in Henry Ward's editorial on the rights and wrongs of slavery. Henry Clay himself could not more haughtily have ignored the whole burning question. Young Beecher confined himself to the safe ground of the evils of mob rule. Every year that he lived in the atmosphere of pressure of Lyman Beecher's family, the complete independence of the individual seemed more desirable to Henry Ward Beecher. It had come to be a fetish with him, scrupulously kept in the background while he achieved his own relative freedom of action under a smoke screen of buffoonery — of the pranks and antics by which a medieval court jester was permitted unlimited liberties of speech and behavior. But here was an opportunity to express himself on the one subject which seemed to Henry Ward vital, without involving himself in the discussion at all. He let himself go.

What Henry Ward wrote had no general influence. It deterred neither Judge Burnet, a pillar of Dr. Beecher's church, nor Henry Ward's own uncle, John P. Foote, from leading the movement to drive Birney out of town. Its sole indelible effect was produced upon Henry Ward Beecher. For the first time in his life Henry Ward crystallized in his own mind a conviction that had its genesis in the badgered days of his childhood in the crowded Litchfield parsonage, that had grown through all the years he had listened to Lyman Beecher lay down the law as if he were God's mouthpiece, and that now in the futility of heresy trials, growing strife among the Presbyterians, and the pathetic failure of Lyman Beecher's whole Western enterprise, rose supreme as the one tenable philosophy of life: the principle that every man is a law unto himself, responsible directly and only to his God; and that the pressure of society upon the individual — whether by mobs in the street, or the mob rule of the family in the home — is a thing of evil.

It was precisely this conviction that made it so difficult for Henry Ward Beecher to face the issue of slavery. He regarded slavery as a sin, as did all the Beechers, but he could conceive of no right by which the Abolitionists could impose their will upon the people of the South. After all, slavery stood written in the fundamental law of the land, and who attacked it, attacked the Constitution, the rights of private property, and the whole organization of society in America. Henry Ward was as yet unwilling to set himself up as an anarchist.

Nevertheless, the mobbing of James G. Birney gave him something to think about.

"As might have been expected, Birney refused to leave," Hattie Stowe wrote; "and that night* the mob tore down his press, scattered the types, dragged the whole to the river, threw it in, and then came back to demolish the office . . . Henry sits opposite me writing a most valiant editorial, and tells me to tell you he is waxing mighty in battle . . . A regular corps of volunteers was organized, who for three nights patrolled the streets with firearms and with legal warrant from the mayor . . . and we really saw Henry depart with his pistols with daily alarm, only we were all too full of patriotism not to have sent every brother we had than not have had the principles of freedom and order defended.

"But the tide turned. The mob, unsupported by a now frightened community, slunk into their dens and were still."

Henry Ward Beecher was captivated by editorial work, and relinquished his job with reluctance when Brainerd returned to Cincinnati in October. It had brought him into touch with a world of folk he would never have met otherwise. In a very real sense, Cincinnati was one end of the road of romance. Every distinguished foreigner who pretended to see America visited the Queen City — from Sir Charles Augustus Murray to Charles Dickens, "gorgeously attired, and covered with velvet and jewelry." Henry Ward loved to drop into the dingy, tobacco-stained room of the Court of Common Pleas, where General William Henry Harrison, fallen upon evil days under

* July 30, 1836.

a Democratic administration, had been found a sinecure by his friends, and listen to the doughty old Indian fighter orate with bombastic pedantry — all innocent of the exalted fate that awaited him. He knew brilliant, drunken Charles Hammond, of the *Gazette,* one of the ablest of the country's editors who still wore the queue of his Revolutionary sires, and Judge McLean, almost as perennial a candidate for the Presidency as Henry Clay, and "rich, eccentric, shrewd, but sometimes partially deranged" Nicholas Longworth. He went to parties in parlors palatially lit by dozens of candles, where "the gentlemen spit, talk of elections and the price of produce, and spit again. The ladies look at each other's dresses till they know every pin by heart; talk of Parson Somebody's last sermon on the day of Judgment, or Dr. T'otherbody's new pills for dyspepsia" — or so Mrs. Trollope described the social functions of Cincinnati.

But Henry Ward Beecher's Cincinnati years were even more remarkable for the men he might have known and did not. There was James G. Birney, who did more, perhaps, for the abolition of slavery in the United States than any other one man; there was the Rev. Elijah P. Lovejoy, who came and went between St. Louis and Cincinnati absorbed in the same high enterprise; there were Asa Mahan, who had resigned as a trustee, and John Morgan, who had resigned as a professor of Lane Seminary, over the question of slavery, and Theodore Weld and Henry B. Stanton (whom Elizabeth Cady subsequently married), who left Lane for the same reason. And there was that upstanding young man of whom Abraham Lincoln was to say later: "He was about one and a half times bigger than any other man I ever knew" — Salmon P. Chase.

CHAPTER VIII

LAWRENCEBURGH

IT WAS that gentle, vague old mystic, Calvin Stowe, who gave Henry Ward Beecher his first glimpse of a Christianity he felt he could preach. Henry Ward had not been at Lane Seminary a year before he knew that the Calvinism of Lyman Beecher and Jonathan Edwards was not his message. He had neither the

philosophical grounding nor the dialectic skill of the old divines
—nor a mental equipment that would ever acquire either.
Purely emotional in his religious reactions, Henry Ward could
not for the life of him see what "the transactions of Adam and
Eve, nobody knows how many thousand years ago in the Garden of Eden," with the conditions attached thereto "of guilt,
wrath and penalty running down through the thousands of
years and including every child born from that day to this," had
to do with what Jesus Christ preached up and down the dusty
roads of Palestine. It worried him tremendously. He was shar-
ing a room with Prof. Stowe at the time, as long ago, haunted
by similar doubts and fears in Litchfield parsonage, he had slept
in the same room with the negro, Charles Smith. And now, as
then, in intimate contact with one of humble faith, Henry
Ward Beecher gradually came to see in Christianity something
besides the iron face of God.

Long years later, he described the revelation:

"It then pleased God to lift upon me such a view of Christ as one
whose nature and office it is to have infinite and exquisite pity upon
the weakness and want of sinners as I had never had before. I saw
that He had compassion upon them because they were sinners, and
because He wanted to help them out of their sins. . . . There rose
up before me a vision of Jesus as the Saviour of sinners—not of
saints, but of sinners unconverted, before they were any better—
because they were so bad and needed so much; and that view has
never grown from me."

Of course no such vision came to Henry Ward Beecher at
Lane Seminary. If this was, in fact, his conception of Christianity in his early ministry, it was by no means what he
preached then, nor for many years thereafter—not, indeed,
until he himself came to know what it was to need so much
from a Saviour of sinners not of saints. But he did, even then,
get a glimmer of the inadequacy of a religion of fear—and
that, after all, was a great deal for a son of Lyman Beecher to
achieve.

One other incident marked Henry Ward Beecher's Seminary
years. In January 1837, as young Beecher's course was approaching its close, a debate was held between the Right Rev.
John B. Purcell, Catholic Bishop of Cincinnati, and the Rev.
Alexander Campbell, founder of the "Christian" church, then

making great headway throughout the West. The Rev. Thomas J. Biggs, formerly a professor at Lane, was one of the moderators of the debate, and for nine days the discussion absorbed the attention of every church member for miles up and down the Ohio river and far into the interior of Ohio, Kentucky and Indiana.

It was a revelation to Henry Ward Beecher. Never an original investigator, he had accepted what he had been told as to the evils of popery and the subtle designs of the Roman hierarchy to capture the United States, body, boots and breeches. And now suddenly he found that assertions he had heard repeated all his life as equivalent to gospel were without the remotest foundation in fact — that alleged documents that had been passed from hand to hand as far back as Henry Ward could remember, as definitive proof of the fearsome machinations of the Catholic church, had about the same evidential value as fairy stories. When Bishop Purcell, with suave good humor, said that "the abuse of the Catholics . . . is a regular trade, and the compilation of anti-Catholic books . . . has become a part of the regular industry of the country, as much as the making of nutmegs, or the construction of clocks," Henry Ward Beecher felt waves of doubt sweep over him as to the authentic bases of all the complicated fabric of organized belief upon which he had been brought up since childhood.

"I made up my mind distinctly that, with the help of God, I would never engage in any religious contention," he says. "I remember promising Christ that if He would strengthen me and teach me how to work I would all my life long preach for His kingdom and endeavor to love everybody who was doing that work. Not that I would accept others' belief, not that I would embrace their theology, not that I would endorse their ecclesiastical organizations; but whatever instruments might be, if they were sincerely working for the kingdom of Christ I would never put a straw in their way and never strike a blow to their harm."

In principle, at least, Henry Ward Beecher had riven the last fetter that chained him to the Calvinism of his father. Yet he knew his own weakness. He knew that if he remained in Cincinnati under Lyman Beecher's eagle eye, he would never in the world have the courage to follow his own bent. Harassed, he took his problem to the one person he felt was devoted to him — Eunice Bullard.

"I have always freely shown you how I am perplexed and troubled about some of the doctrines I shall be called upon to subscribe to if I secure a license and am ordained as an Evangelist," he wrote her. "There are some points which I must not, *will* not subscribe to. . . . But what will the result be when I go up before the council for examination? If they believe themselves what they expect me to assent to, they will not license me. How can they? I *can not* assent. What then? Preach I will, licensed or not. On that point I am determined. If I can do no better, I will go far out into the West, build a log cabin among the lumbermen and trappers, or whoever may seek employment in the forests, and devote myself to assisting in trying to interest them in religious services, far from the busy haunts of men. What will you do if this is the only course left me? Will you go with me into the wilderness?"

Henry Ward was not yet twenty-four, and his little essay at heroics really deserved a more sympathetic treatment than it received. Eunice replied that she considered the promises given in betrothal just as binding in God's sight as the marriage vow. She counseled him to be cautious.

In due season, Henry Ward was examined. He assented to everything he was asked to assent to, and was licensed to preach without difficulty.

Henry Ward had already preached quite a bit about the neighborhood of Cincinnati — and had not done any too well at it. He was therefore greatly excited when Martha Sawyer came up from Lawrenceburgh, and asked him to try his hand in the Indiana river town, which served as the Eastern gateway of the State. Miss Sawyer was a remarkable woman just started on her twenties — a singer of no mean talent, with the highest social connections in Indiana. James Whitcomb, later governor of the State, "would have married her if she had been rich," report had it.

The little Presbyterian church in Lawrenceburgh had staggered along for some eight years, more dead than alive. It was hardly a brilliant opening for a son of the Beecher brood — but it was an opening, and it had the advantage of being far enough from Cincinnati for Henry Ward to do about as he pleased. On June 14, 1837, he received his formal call. He accepted promptly.

The schism in the ranks of the Presbyterian church, between the strict Calvinists of the "Old School" and their scarcely less strict opponents of the "New School," of which Lyman Beecher's heresy trial had been one of the early symptoms, was approaching an open break. There was incredible bitterness of feeling. Every Presbyterian church in the country seemed to be — and, indeed, was — on the point of flying asunder. And Henry Ward Beecher, while licensed to preach, was still un-ordained. Lawrenceburgh lay in Miami Presbytery, a strong-hold of that very Scotch-Irish element of "Old School" Pres-byterians which regarded all the Beechers as no more Christian than so many Turks. Facing a certain conflict, Henry Ward suddenly felt the need of all the moral support he could com-mand. His mind turned to Eunice.

He wrote her, first. But the post was slow in those days of no railways across New York or Pennsylvania to the West. Before his letter had well started, he borrowed $300 of his first year's salary in advance, and hurried East on its heels. Four days after Henry Ward's arrival in West Sutton, he was married to Eunice Bullard. He wore his brother George's best suit. But Eunice got up at one o'clock in the morning of the day before the wed-ding and sewed till six that night on the India mull frock that was her bridal dress.

They had been engaged seven years. In almost four years, Henry Ward had seen his bride for only two days, till he came on to marry her. In the three years he had spent in Cincinnati, he had sentimentalized over half a dozen girls — "as full of Satan as he could button up," one of his classmates at Lane said. But to Henry Ward Beecher, Eunice had always represented something of his own — a partner, an ally, who had that faith in his destiny that, down under his fears and uncertainties and protective buffooneries, he also had in himself. As he conceived her, there was in her that quality of the mother he had longed for all his life and never had. She would see through him — would come to know by heart all his evasions, his indulgences, the essential child-like combination of sentimentality and shrewdness, of emotionalism and ruthlessness, that was the very essence of his power and his weakness. It would make no dif-ference to her. Where he was impetuous, she would be cautious — tenacious where he was volatile. "Her character is uniform, and projects, if anywhere, in line of *affection*," he wrote in his journal.

Yes; he wanted that. He wanted that, indeed.

"A town with two distilleries and twenty devils in it," Henry Ward called Lawrenceburgh. It was hardly so bad as that. Lawrenceburgh had been in existence some thirty-five years, boasted a population of about 2,600, a well-edited newspaper, two schools, three churches, and was a thriving river town in the days when the great rivers brought gold and gamblers, fortune and folly — drunkards, politicians, itinerant evangelists, prostitutes, temperance lecturers, cholera, and long lines of sullen-faced blacks in clanking manacles to their muddy, reeking shores. In after years, Mrs. Beecher always spoke of her husband's salary in Lawrenceburgh as $300 a year. It was $500, and with pork at five cents, beef at six cents a pound, and flour at $3.50 a barrel, not so bad, at that. It was Lyman Beecher who began on $300 a year in a town much smaller and a parish much larger.

Eunice sold a cloak her father had given her for $30 to furnish the capital to start housekeeping. Henry Ward sold his gold Phi Beta Theta pin — and bought, of all things, a workstand for his wife. Mrs. William Henry Harrison, whose husband had just been defeated for the presidency, presented the bride and groom with a bureau, a pair of brass andirons, shovel and tongs, with which, she said, "I began housekeeping more than forty years ago." But they had no fireplace in the two rooms they fixed up, above a warehouse, to live in. George Beecher contributed a stove and Mrs. Judge Burnet some calico curtains. They had Henry Ward's single bed, from his room at Lane Seminary, and a mattress of husks. But they were young.

When Henry Ward first knew Eunice, she had had golden brown ringlets in a bobbing fringe about her face. He did not like it. His passion for phrenology was uppermost, and he felt that the curls spoiled the lines of her head.

"A good-shaped head is a greater beauty than a wig any time," he told her. So she brushed the curls out, and wore her hair closely folded around her head. She had, in addition, a good complexion, and where Henry Ward was not tall, she was even shorter — a slight thing, while he was stocky. Soon, his face rounded out. Under his chin appeared a fleshy fullness that gave him a smug look. He wore his hair well down upon his collar behind, now — Eunice cut it for him, as she did all his life.

Just what this strait-laced, small town, New England girl of the strictest Puritan upbringing expected in marrying a youngster she scarcely knew, fresh from divinity school, or why she ever thought she would like going far out into the West with him, to live in a log cabin among lumbermen and trappers, must remain a mystery. Perhaps under her serene, forceful exterior she was romantic, just as under his tergiversations and painful lack of confidence in himself, there was an ambition, a will to succeed, as hard and as undeviating as a steel rail. It may be that in these early days of unrelieved intimacy at Lawrenceburgh each saw into the heart of the other. Or it may be that neither ever did.

What is certain is that Eunice Beecher hated the life in Indiana with a bitterness that grew fiercer every year. In the first place, the Presbyterians were not of the elect in that part of the world. They were a hard-headed, horny-handed, close-fisted lot who took life and religion seriously. Many of the Presbyterians of Indiana had come there when life was really hard. They had carved their homes out of the wilderness, amassed what they possessed with incredible toil and sacrifice, and forged their judgments of character on an anvil of harsh experience. They had little patience with the wails of a twenty-five-year-old bride who regretted that she could not afford a servant and felt put upon to have to do sewing or take in boarders to piece out her husband's income. The people of Indiana were not kind to Eunice Beecher. She never forgave them.

Henry Ward called Lawrenceburgh "the very metropolis of whiskey." It was the beginning of the bold, bad days of fast steamboats and fast living along the great waterways of the Ohio and the Mississippi. Even in Cincinnati there were many gentlemen of the bar, merchants and others who habitually gambled, and Judge Burnet was wont to say that of nine young lawyers who came to the bar with him, all had become "confirmed sots and gone to untimely graves." Living at Walnut Hills, Henry Ward had seen comparatively little of any but polite drinking. He tells of a party among the Lane students at which one could not move from his chair all the evening, and was, after the feast, carried to bed — oh! how *uncanonical!* he exclaims. He was keenly interested in the efforts of Nicholas Longworth to cultivate wine grapes. But for whiskey he had nothing but horror.

When Henry Ward Beecher began his career as a minister of

the gospel at Lawrenceburgh, there were thus two great evils to be fought—drunkenness and slavery. He chose the former.

Henry Ward's brother, Edward, was of different stuff. He had been President of Illinois College five years when Garrison was mobbed in Boston. When Edward Beecher had come West to Jacksonville, he found anti-slavery sentiment already well-formed and active in all the States of the Northwest territory, but it was not until 1835 that he himself "became satisfied, from a careful examination of the history of experiments on this subject, that the doctrine of gradual emancipation was fallacious, and that of immediate emancipation was philosophical and safe," he says. He was the first of the Beechers to face the issue squarely.

Illinois had split from Indiana because Illinois was somewhat more tolerant of slavery than the Hoosier State. In the former anti-slavery sentiment crystallized about the figure of Elijah Lovejoy, who, at Alton, was trying to print an Abolition newspaper under the handicap of having his press dumped into the river every so often. To this group, who took seriously the declaration of the Presbyterian General Assembly that it was "the duty of all Christians . . . to use their honest, earnest and unwearied endeavors . . . as speedily as possible to efface this blot on our holy religion, and to obtain the complete abolition of slavery throughout Christendom," Edward Beecher gravitated. And just when Henry Ward and Eunice Beecher were settling down so cozily in their two-room apartment, Elijah Lovejoy and Edward Beecher, in the latter's house in Jacksonville, kneeling on the floor, their arms stretched out over the dining-room table, their hands clasped, were beseeching the guidance of God as to what they could best do to defend "the sacred right of a free press . . . the vital and essential principle of our nation's life."

Undismayed, they went ahead with the fight on slavery. And on the night of November 7, 1837, a mob incited by the Colonizationists, who led the opposition to Lovejoy, set out to destroy the fourth of Lovejoy's presses. And Elijah Lovejoy, standing at the door of the building that housed his press, etched in the moonlight, was shot down by an unknown hand, firing from the shadows.

In Lawrenceburgh, the *Political Beacon* carried a slashing editorial under the head "Fruits of Fanaticism," pointing out how unerringly God moved in His mysterious way to strike down the would-be disturbers of the established order. Henry Ward Beecher felt that his brother Edward had been most unwise in getting mixed up in any such business. He himself maintained a discreet silence. But over in Springfield, Illinois, a young lawyer, only four years older than Henry Ward, addressed a men's club on the perils of mob rule, with unmistakable reference to the Lovejoy murder. Lincoln was his name.

The truth was that Henry Ward Beecher had troubles he considered a vast deal more important than slavery. His church was such an one as George Bellows pictures in "The Prayer Meeting," and not exigent. "There was but one man in the church, and that was one too many," he said. He went to Cincinnati to raise money for lamps by which he could hold night services, and to buy hymn books with. At the instance of Martha Sawyer, he began the organization of a choir. Eunice had no music in her. But Henry Ward could listen to Martha Sawyer sing "I Feel Like One Who Treads Alone" and "Oft in the Stilly Night" for hours on end. She had a book of her songs all neatly copied out by herself. Henry Ward loved to pore over it with her.

He was far from satisfied with his preaching. "I had time to sow all my ministerial wild oats without damage to my people, for they knew little whether I was orthodox or not," he confesses. "I said a great many extravagant things in my pulpit and preached with a great deal of crudeness." He swept out the church himself, filled the lamps and built the fires.

In the snug little home of their own making, where he and Eunice lived, the windows looked out on the shining Ohio to the misty hills of the Kentucky shore. At night they could see the gaudy lights of steamboats, passing up and down the river, with their flashing poniards of flame stabbing the darkness when the furnace doors were opened. In one of the two rooms of their tiny apartment, Henry Ward wrote his sermons; in the other, Eunice cooked their meals. When he had written something that pleased his fancy, he would whistle, and she would fly to him, her arms covered with soapsuds or dough, and kneel at his feet to hear him read it. In the long winter evenings, with the wind from the river lashing the house with rain, they would sit by the red stove and talk of what they would enjoy—of all that they would have when success had crowned their efforts.

But never again did they have each other as wholly as in those first days at Lawrenceburgh.

CHAPTER IX

INDIANAPOLIS

WHEN Henry Ward Beecher came to Lawrenceburgh, he wrote out a little plan of campaign for himself:

"1. In different districts get men quietly to feel *themselves* responsible for the progress of temperance or Sunday Schools.

"2. Quietly to visit from house to house and secure congregations.

"3. Secure a *large congregation*. Let this be the *first* thing."

As means to these ends, he noted several methods: "Visit widely and produce a personal attachment; also wife do same." And: "Get the young to love me."

The church history records that during Beecher's ministry "additions to the church averaged about the same as under other pastors; his ministry was more noted for pulpit than pastoral labors." Evidently he did not visit widely. Nor, local legend has it, did "wife do same."

As President of the Central Board of Agency, Western States, Lyman Beecher had no difficulty in getting his son put on the payroll of the Home Missionary Society from June 15, 1837, for four and a half months' financial aid each year. The first year Henry Ward reported eight additions to the church,[*] seventy-five Sabbath School scholars, no subscriptions to temperance societies, no Bible Class, no Sabbath School library, with the remark: "several hopeful conversions." The second year he reported no new admissions to the church, without remark. The third year, he made no report at all. It was hardly a brilliant showing. But then Henry Ward Beecher had other fish to fry.

First and foremost, he had to be ordained as a minister of the gospel. Fortunately, the long awaited schism in the Presbyterian church came in the Spring of 1838, at the General Assembly at

* One was Eunice Beecher.

Philadelphia. Lyman and Edward Beecher were both there. Right in the midst of this theological earthquake, they were reminded that other matters than ecclesiastical differences occupied the public mind. Lyman Beecher described the events with the pen of a true reporter:

"The heavens at this moment are lighted up by the flames of the Abolition or Liberty Hall in Sixth Street. The mob have set it on fire. It was dedicated two weeks ago; cost $40,000. The anti-slavery society are holding a convention in it. . . . The bell of the State House is tolling again — there are cries of fire! The mob was seen this afternoon *en masse* parading the streets, rioting over the ruins of last night's conflagration, and threatening another. The heavens are lighted up. The African Hall, in Thirteenth Street, is on fire. The mob is cutting the hose that no water may reach it. . . . The police are on the ground, but do nothing but talk; in fact, they are not able; in heart, they do not wish to restrain the rioters."

Dramatic as old Dr. Beecher's account was, it did not greatly interest Henry Ward. But he was shaken to his foundations over the split in the Presbyterian church.

"That the division of our church was uncalled for; it was wicked; there was no doctrinal difference for it," he wrote at the time, "or any necessity of any kind except that which mad ambition and madder jealousy begets. If the Pacific Ocean rolled between the two belligerent parties in this unnatural division it would not be more an everlasting barrier than now exists to reunion. . . . I believe that the day of reunion will not come till human nature is changed and human experience reversed. . . . Every indication of Providence seems tending to break up large ecclesiastical establishments. . . . A hundred denominations would be more peaceable than two overgrown ones. The more, the more it will become absolutely necessary to tolerate, and toleration is a step-brother to charity."

Henry Ward Beecher lived to see the Presbyterian church reunited, without human nature being greatly changed, or human experience reversed, either. But long before that, he himself had left the Presbyterian fold.

It was in September following the great schism that Henry Ward finally applied for ordination — out of sheer bravado, to the "Old School" Miami Presbytery, at Oxford, Ohio. He tells with gusto how cleverly he befooled those country parsons, playing a rôle and playing it so well that their cross examination failed to reveal a flaw in his orthodoxy, handling with consummate skill the catchwords of those doctrines of theology with which he had been familiar ever since he could lisp:

"I could state them very glibly. I was ready with explanation of every single point connected with them. I knew all their proofs, all their dodging cuts, all their ins and outs," he recounted, later. "They questioned, and questioned, and questioned. Some of them I answered directly, some intelligently, and others somewhat obscurely. . . . The Presbytery, without a dissenting voice, voted that I was orthodox — to their amazement."

But Henry Ward Beecher knew that he was not orthodox. So, evidently, did these hard-headed old Scotch-Irish preachers. For they did not ordain him. It was by a "New School" Synod, which Lyman Beecher and his friends formed in Cincinnati, that Henry Ward Beecher was finally made a minister of the gospel in full and regular standing, on November 9, 1838. Lyman Beecher installed him and Calvin Stowe charged his people. It was quite a family affair.

It was that same eventful Summer that Henry Ward Beecher pushed wide open another door of opportunity for himself — and, incidentally, took his first open stand on slavery.

Ever since the foundation of the American Colonization Society, it had been the custom to dedicate the Fourth of July to laudation of its high purpose and to taking up a collection for its pecuniary needs. The latter were obviously great, if some three million negroes were ever to be shipped to an Africa they had never laid eye upon — and, from all they could learn of the place, never wanted to. In 1838, the Hon. Milton Gregg, the editor of the *Political Beacon*, for whom Henry Ward had done odd editorial jobs from time to time, proposed that this time-honored custom be followed in Lawrenceburgh. The *Political Beacon* accordingly ran a four-column appeal for funds for colonization of the blacks, signed by the Hon. Henry Clay and other distinguished slave-holders, and Henry Ward Beecher's church was selected as just the place to hold such exercises.

All the country round turned out. Farmers came in wagons, with the whole family, or horseback, their wives on pillions. The bell on the Baptist church gave the signal for assembling. Arthur St. Clair, the most patrician of Indiana's aristocracy, presided. Henry Ward's choir, that he and Martha Sawyer had created, gave its first public performance, "enhancing the interests of the occasion," said the *Political Beacon*. It was a great triumph for Henry Ward Beecher. But greater were to come.

Dr. Brower, whose justly famous drug store also kept port, madeira and sherry wines and a "full supply of Methodist books," read the Declaration of Independence with sonorous effect. And then Henry Ward Beecher stepped to the front to second a resolution

"That while we recognize the legal and constitutional existence of domestic slavery in some of our sister States, and disclaim any right to interfere in the relations that there exist between master and slaves, we approve the colonization of the free blacks upon the coast of Africa or elsewhere."

He did not go into just how the blacks were to become free, so as to enjoy the inestimable privilege of being deported to Africa — "or elsewhere." But he made it very clear that it could never be accomplished by the methods followed by the Abolitionists.

Indeed, as Henry Ward Beecher warmed to his subject, he held his audience spellbound and astonished every one, even Eunice, by his oratory and the derision with which he riddled the incendiary theories and criminal conduct of the Abolitionists:

"He hit off, in a very happy manner, the ridiculous notion (to say the least of it) entertained and expressed by some, that Colonization was nothing more nor less than *Abolition in disguise*," said the *Political Beacon*. "And he went on to show, that so far from there being any identity of feeling and interest subsisting between them, they were in fact the antipodes of each other — and that, in principle and practice, their doctrines were, ever had been, and of necessity ever must continue to be, totally irreconcilable one with the other; and that the better and surer way to get rid of the evils of the one, was to promote and sustain the interests and objects of the other."

So successful was Henry Ward's appeal that $20 was raised to solve the problem of slavery by colonization.

Nevertheless, that Fourth of July was a turning point in the life of young Beecher. He had been the obscure pastor of a third-rate church, in a small, drab, God-forsaken Ohio river town. Suddenly, over night, he was a leading citizen of a place which was also the front door to a great and growing State. What he had said on the head of slavery was what the greater part of the solid, respectable folk of Indiana wanted desperately to believe. They were opposed to anything which would upset conditions and imperil their hard-won fortunes. They had fought Andrew Jackson and the "Loco-focos," as they called the Democrats, because they believed Jackson had upset the country's finances. Now they were as opposed to agitation of the slavery question, because they feared the abolition of slavery would play havoc with the country's economic stability. Here came young Beecher, who gave them sound, Biblical reasons for keeping things as they were. They nodded their heads, spat, caressed their beards with bony hands on which the veins stood out like whipcords, and pronounced Beecher a level-headed, promising young man.

Doors opened to Henry Ward that he had not dreamed of entering when he came to Lawrenceburgh a year before, with sixty-eight cents in his pocket, a few old sticks of secondhand furniture, and a bride. In Madison, there was the home of Jesse Whitehead, candidate for the legislature that year, whose pretty wife was half his age, and the cleverest, most charming and ablest lady of her years in Southern Indiana. He rode over frequently to see her. Of course Eunice could not go, what with the new baby and all. But Rebecca Whitehead became the most active advocate of young Beecher's talents in the foremost political and social circles of the new State. Martha Sawyer, too, contributed her mite to the making of Henry Ward Beecher. She was the intimate friend of the daughters of Samuel Merrill, who had been Treasurer of Indiana and was President of the State Bank, and to them she sang his praises. So that when Samuel Merrill came to Lawrenceburgh on his rounds of his branch banks, he heard Henry Ward preach, and was pleased by him.

It was the inconspicuous foundation of great things for Henry Ward Beecher. Nor was he unaware of it; but he was worried by the ineffectiveness of his preaching. "For the first three years of my ministry I did not make a single sinner wink," he says. And just then, there came to the Ohio valley an amazing figure, the like of whom that emotion-starved Western land had never seen. The Rev. John Newland Maffitt was a Methodist, but doctrine was not his strong point — "a sort of pulpit actor, as well as orator," James Silk Buckingham called him, "who sometimes preaches for fifteen or twenty nights in succession,

draws crowded houses every night, and often adds from fifty to
a hundred members to the Methodist body in a single evening. . . . His addresses are described as being more to the
imagination than the reason; his voice is spoken of as melting
and tender, his imagination fervid; and his language eloquent
and amatory."

Here was a model indeed for young Beecher. It was plain as
a pikestaff to Henry Ward that the day of theological argu-
mentation in the pulpit was gone. Those who attended church
in his generation would lack that background of exclusive absorption in religion that had been the heritage of the church-
goers of Lyman Beecher's day. Other interests had taken the
people captive — politics, business, pleasures of divers sorts. Men
and women could no longer be bullied into decent living. But if
somehow he, Henry Ward Beecher, could just preach "Christ
as being God because He knew how to love a sinner," and do it
in a way vivid enough to make people want to come to church,
not attend solely because they were afraid of hell fire, then
surely he had something that could go on when the followers of
Lyman Beecher's method were preaching to empty pews.

Henry Ward Beecher did not achieve this result at once, or
indeed very rapidly. Sunday after Sunday he would come home
from his service with a headache and the determination to quit
the ministry and buy a farm. He might have done so save for his
success in activities incidental to the ministry. Slavery he left
severely alone; but he lost no opportunity to strike at the evil
of drunkenness.

It was the day of oratory, when a ready flow of words was
passport to almost any honor. Henry Ward had not yet mas-
tered the art of leading men; but at invective he asked odds of
no one. And as he poured out the vials of his wrath on the distillers, grocers and coffee-house keepers of Dearborn County,
his fame as a public speaker spread. There was more than a little
truth in his boast that he could have made a fortune and become
a second Henry Clay had he turned his attention to the law instead of the gospel.

Yet his saving common sense restrained him from extremes.
It was early in 1839, at the local temperance convention, that a
proposal came up to extend the temperance pledge to include a
promise not to sell grain to distillers. Henry Ward was on his

feet at once. Suppose the farmer did know that his corn would be turned into whiskey, said he, how silly to hold the farmer morally responsible for what was plainly the distiller's sin! There were, of course, no distillers in his audience — but many farmers.

"A sensible young man," they said. And they elected him delegate to the State Temperance Convention to be held in Indianapolis in May.

Meanwhile, the wheels of fate were turning. The previous November thirteen members of the "Old School" Presbyterian church in the State capital had decided to form a "New School" church. Samuel Merrill was a leading spirit in the enterprise, and his two daughters, Catherine Merrill and Mrs. John L. Ketcham, with the latter's husband, were founders of the new church. The Rev. S. Holmes, of New Bedford, Massachusetts, was first called, and when he declined, President James C. Young, of Center College, Kentucky, author of "a powerful and faithful exposure of slavery." But he too refused. When Henry Ward Beecher turned up in Indianapolis in May, the new church had been five months in search of a pastor. Mrs. Ketcham had heard a great deal about Beecher from her friend, Martha Sawyer; her father, Samuel Merrill, had heard the young man preach, and liked him.

So on May 12, 1839, Henry Ward was invited to preach a trial sermon before the thirty members of the new church. And on the following day the congregation unanimously resolved to call the Rev. Henry Ward Beecher from his little church on the banks of the Ohio to the State capital. "Which call," say the church records, "was accepted."

That Fourth of July in Lawrenceburgh Henry Ward Beecher was the hero of the occasion. He was chosen orator of the day, and no bones about it, this time. His speech "was a rich treat," and the Hon. Milton Gregg flattered himself he would have the text of it for publication in the columns of the *Political Beacon*.

"I delivered the Oration from meager notes," Henry Ward replied to this request, "and it would require both time and labor, from them, to write out the address for the press. My approaching removal will prevent my employing the time necessary."

Henry Ward Beecher was through with Lawrenceburgh.

CHAPTER X

ASCENT

WHEN Henry Ward Beecher, now twenty-six, opened his eyes the first time in Litchfield parsonage, Col. Joseph Bartholomew and a handful of men were chasing Indians from the very spot where Indiana's capital stood in 1839. A month later, Maj. Zachary Taylor finished the job.

Indianapolis was only slightly larger than Lawrenceburgh when Henry Ward received his call. But it was the State capital, and as Mrs. Ketcham put it "we had cultivated and educated men as well as ladies who made our society delightful." Indeed, there was the framework of an imposing culture: two literary societies before which debates were held and lectures given on questions of the day; an historical society (albeit little history as yet); a Handelian society for music lovers; the usual quota of Bible, tract, missionary and benevolent societies; a library, a lyceum and atheneum, an academy, a female institute, a high school, a county seminary for higher education, two newspapers, a three-story brick hotel that had cost the fabulous sum of $30,000, a brewery, a millinery shop and a soda fountain. William Morris called the fine old wooden houses of Indianapolis "among the most comfortable and characteristic of truly American objects." But he had probably never been there.

Nevertheless, there were certain manifest disadvantages about the place. It was separated from the rest of civilization by sixty miles of mud or slush, with unbridged streams, floating corduroys that were worse than no roads at all and fathomless mudholes into which travelers were frequently dumped regardless of rank or fortune. President Van Buren was stood on his head in one, with no more ceremony than if he had been an itinerant preacher. The river bottom lands bred malaria, for which the sovereign remedy was Peruvian bark and whiskey. Or just whiskey.

To add to the normal difficulties of life, the financial panic of 1837 was just making itself felt in Indiana. Nobody had any money. Men with thousands of acres of rich farm land and dozens of eligible town lots were no better able to pay their debts than those who had not ground enough for a grave. Yet they were an hospitable folk — "the strangest mixture I have ever seen," said the Hon. Charles Butler of New York. The more substantial citizens were Yankees, of the type Henry Ward had watched trek through Litchfield in his boyhood days. But there were Kentuckians, also, of a class that had not been slave-holders in their native State, and a recent influx of "Pennsylvania Dutch" — a shrewd, hard-working, forthright people as a whole, blunt of speech and unpretentious in their way of life.

Little Harriet Eliza Beecher was a year old when her father was called to Indianapolis. She was teething, and Eunice, too, was ailing. So Samuel Merrill had them fetched to the capital in his private carriage, with his daughter, Julia, to do the honors of the journey. And when they arrived, they were his guests until they could find a house of their own. Eunice hated Indianapolis from the first moment. She could not feel drawn to the people as to those of Lawrenceburgh, she wrote her mother. "There is more *profession* of interest, but I doubt if I shall find as much *heart*." Mrs. Ketcham hardly knew what to make of the new minister's wife. "I had never seen such a woman: she could be as beautiful as a princess, and as plain and homely as possible. So she could be sparklingly bright and bitterly sarcastic, even against her own father," she wrote. "Mr. and Mrs. Beecher, like the rest of us, had very little to live on, though *we* were in houses of our own, and they in a very small one fronting off Market street on an alley back of it."

It was characteristic of Eunice's feeling towards Indianapolis that she insisted all her life that her husband's salary there was only $600 a year. As a matter of fact it was $800.

It was a handicap to Henry Ward, of course. Indianapolis was too small a place and the people too intimately thrown together for his wife's feeling not to become generally known. Even so casual a traveler as John Parsons, a Virginian, visiting Indiana in 1840, wrote of the Beechers:

"His greeting was hearty and sincere. I knew he meant his welcome and the invitation he extended to me to his church and his home. The latter, a neat, one-story cottage, in Market street, near New Jersey, I soon visited, meeting his wife, a rather discontented woman, complaining constantly of the chills and the unhealthy nature of the town."

She was, she said, "a harum-scarum girl" whose "only servant for three years controlled my house and relieved me of all responsibility, while I lived like a butterfly regardless of unswept stairs and dusty corners." This may be doubted. But Henry Ward did wash the dishes and diapers on occasions, and they took in three young gentlemen boarders, all of whom in due season became elders in Henry Ward's church.

There was no church building when Henry Ward came. "We met for worship in an upper room of the Seminary, small and low, and under the stairs the sheep lay," wrote Mrs. Ketcham. Young Beecher was standing on his own bottom, at last — and not quite as pleased as he thought he would be at his complete isolation from Lyman Beecher. His first shock came at the meeting of the Indiana Synod of the Presbyterian church, two months after his arrival at his new charge. As clerk of the Synod, he read a resolution passed the previous year on the subject of slavery: "This Synod feel called upon in the providence of God to make an explicit avowal of their views on this subject," it ran; and went on to memorialize the General Assembly in "strong language":

"This Synod . . . feel constrained to say that if ever the time should come when our church should . . . do anything that would imply that slavery is not a palpable violation of the law of God, it would be most distressing evidence of a departure from the principles of God's word and a flagrant dereliction of duty. If this be so, then it follows that the church ought to take speedy and decisive measures to purify itself from this long-continued and enormous evil."

Poor Henry Ward was stripped even of the convenient refuge in colonization which had served him so well at Lawrenceburgh. Said the Synod:

"Nor do we believe that the Colonization Society, however laudable its objects and however successful its efforts, will supersede the necessity of vigorous exertions on our part."

Nothing in the life of Henry Ward Beecher is more revealing than the account which he gave, thirty-five years later, of sentiment in Indiana at this time in respect of slavery. "I remember when no prayer meeting or church gathering allowed men to speak on the subject of liberty," he declared. "I remember when in Presbytery and Synod it was considered a heresy to advocate freedom."

Indeed, Henry Ward speedily found that not only did his Synod and his Presbytery make it mandatory upon him to denounce from his pulpit what one old Indiana preacher called "the God-dishonoring and hell-deserving nature of slave holding," but his own particular church also expected it of him. With one exception, every leading man in his congregation was against slavery: Samuel Merrill, trustee of the church, was a Vermonter, into whose home Frederick Douglass came as an honored guest; Dr. Luke Munsell, elder and clerk of the church, was a Kentuckian, but "a firm abolitionist" who had worked with James G. Birney while Henry Ward was still in Amherst; John L. Ketcham, who succeeded Munsell as elder and clerk, traveled at his own expense over half the South and all the way to Canada to establish the freedom of the husband of Beecher's colored maid. Had Henry Ward Beecher been so minded, he could have preached against slavery from the moment of his arrival in Indianapolis, and had the unqualified support of his church and his congregation.

But while there were plenty of Abolitionists in Indiana in 1839, the anti-slavery movement as yet lacked that wide, general appeal which young Beecher liked to feel characterized any cause he advocated. Even so, egged on by Synod and Presbytery, he might have taken a chance save for an incident that occurred a few months after his coming to the capital. Calvin Fletcher wrote it down in his diary:

"Jan. 2, 1840.

"This night a mob was assembled in consequence of the marriage of an intelligent white girl of 18 or 20 to a negro or mulatto. A family, it is said originally from Massachusetts, who emigrated to Missouri; there the father purchased a farm and the negro in question, died, and the family with the negro set out for Massachusetts, and while on the way the mother and three daughters and the negro stopped at this place, where they have stayed for 2 or 3 weeks past. They were visited by several of the most respectable and one of the young ladies was employed to play upon the organ at the Episcopal church, after the death of Mrs. Morrison. It is said the young ladies are intelligent. The licence was abstracted from the clerk on the application of the mother. Her story was that it was the injunction of her deceased husband to the negro to take care of his family, and she consented to the marriage etc., for such reasons etc. The par-

ties were married at Crouder's over the river, 2 miles distance, on
New Year's eve. Jim Johnson, J.P., refused to marry them but
Squire Weaver consented, and said the ceremony, and on this eve
(2nd Jan.) when I was leaving my office at ½ past 9, heard the mob
as they proceeded up the street in good order singing "A Long
Time Ago." They proceeded over the river to Crouder's. The
negro man fled. They took the woman and made her ride in on a
horse, and marched her up and down the street. Dr. Stipp undertook to interfere, and was knocked down and much injured. This
affair has created much excitement. There is not an individual in the
place to my knowledge who justified the white family who have
submitted to indignity."

On mature consideration, Henry Ward Beecher decided to
leave the subject of slavery alone.

The new church grew slowly. It was not until six weeks after
he was installed that Henry Ward admitted to membership one
Mary Harmon, first fruit of his evangelical labors. It was uphill
work. Overawed by his father and his elder brothers, Henry
Ward had come to look upon himself as a sort of infant
prodigy. He had cultivated a boyishness of manner that was
semi-protective — a means he had had to employ all his life to
penetrate the stern self-absorption of his elders in the family.
With it had gone a spontaneous and disarming vanity, which
helped him to retain what his boyishness won.

Henry Ward used this method now, among these strangers.
But it failed of effect, in great measure. He was no infant prodigy to them. Indeed, the Rev. Phineas D. Gurley, who came to
the "Old School" Presbyterian church from which Henry
Ward's congregation had separated, was three years younger
than he, and a young man of dignity and force who, in due
time, became pastor of President Lincoln's church, in Washington. A quarter of a century later, Samuel Bowles, of the Springfield *Republican*, passed a judgment on Henry Ward Beecher
which many people in Indiana already felt: "He has no reverence, and he inspires none, only wonder and admiration for his
mental gymnastics and his physical freshness and vigor." He had
a way, after his evening service, of walking across the road to
the Governor's Circle, where the young bloods of the town
congregated, leaning against the fence, and challenging them to
jump the fence or do other stunts with him. What is more,
Henry Ward could jump that fence easily. Once at a picnic in

Governor Noble's woods, he rolled down hill with the children, amid shrieks of gayety. At the Ketchams' he would play Post Office, and Hunt the Keyhole with the young folk; or Dumb Orator, with Mr. Ketcham doing the reciting while Henry Ward supplied the gestures. "Mrs. Beecher was almost as good as he," wrote Mrs. Ketcham. "What actors they would have made!"

What the good people of Indiana did not understand was that the horse-play, the swagger, the insolence, of young Beecher was the merest mask to cover a diffidence he seemed unable to master — deep-seated misgivings that held him captive. "It was singular to note how distrustful Mr. Beecher was of his ability to succeed," Eunice wrote. "In his earlier work this lack of confidence was sometimes painful."

"I would think the church was getting on its legs to march, and it would fall flat again," he wailed. "I sent for my father, but he wouldn't come; said I must fight it out alone."

Stern old Lyman! Henry Ward begged Calvin Stowe to come to his aid, too. And Stowe did come. It was a godsend to young Beecher. Eunice's second baby had died still-born, and she was complaining bitterly of the fever and ague, as the Hoosiers called malaria. The money to build the new church was to be raised. Henry Ward's congregation seemed at a standstill. He seized the opportunity of Stowe's coming to dump the whole business on the generous, burden-bent shoulders of his brother-in-law, and went East on a visit. Two young ladies of Indianapolis made the journey in his care — Julia Merrill, and Betty Bates, who lived just across the way from the Beechers' cottage.

It was a memorable journey. They went by stage through Columbus, Ohio, to Cleveland, starting at two o'clock in the mornings, and bouncing over the rough roads until eleven at night. But it was nothing to the hardships of the lake trip to Buffalo, what with seasickness and all. They were glad of the comfort of the luxurious passenger canal boats that bowled along so smoothly through the Erie Canal, at six miles an hour, to Albany. There for the first time in the lives of any of them, they not only saw but actually rode in a steam train, at the dizzying speed of sixteen miles an hour, as far as Schenectady. At Schenectady they returned to the less romantic travel of a stage coach, across the old, familiar, wooded hills of New England, past Litchfield on its lofty, wind-swept perch, to Worcester.

Betty Bates was only fourteen, but in that day many a girl was married and had started a family at fourteen. Her mother was one of the founders of Henry Ward's church, a cousin of Senator James Noble and Governor Noah Noble, of Indiana. Her father had been born in Cincinnati when that city was still Fort Washington, and was the first sheriff of Marion County. She herself was a romantic young person of rare and exquisite beauty to whom Henry Ward Beecher was as near God as anything she ever expected to see this side of the Day of Judgment. She adored him; hung upon his words, breathless; gazed at him with star-like eyes; and fluttered red and white every time he touched her. It was worship, open and unabashed, for all the world to see—and it was just what Henry Ward Beecher needed in that hour more than anything else on earth.

"He was excessively sensitive to praise and blame," his sister, Hattie Stowe, said of him; "extremely diffident, and with a power of yearning, undeveloped emotion which he neither understood nor could express."

Henry Ward was better at expressing his yearning emotion than Hattie gave him credit for. But Eunice was not. The work of being a preacher's wife in the West was incalculably harder than she had bargained for. She had been through childbirth twice in three years. At twenty-eight, a woman was looked upon as no longer young in that day. And Henry Ward in new surroundings, with new friends and an ever-widening sphere of interests, was growing constantly, while she was tied to kitchen and cradle. Nor could she help herself.

When Henry Ward Beecher returned to Indianapolis, he was like a new man. He had found what he required.

That Fall, Beecher's new church was dedicated, and the State Synod held its meeting in Indianapolis. It adopted a thumping indictment of slavery on eleven counts "as a heinous sin against God and our brethren" and left Henry Ward in a position of high embarrassment, with all his congregation aware that his silence on slavery was out of tune with the attitude taken by his church. And when the Rev. Philip S. Cleland, of Henry Ward's own Presbytery, followed this action by distributing broadcast a sermon ridiculing those timorous souls who were "thrown into convulsions by the word *Abolition*," it so upset Henry Ward that he did not attend Synod the following year.

Yet he would not be budged. "Secure a *large congregation*. Let this be the *first* thing," he had resolved in Lawrenceburgh. And that was what he was about. He even took in Elijah S. Alvord, the principal professional gambler and money lender of the capital — a very splendid gentleman, who wore whiskers, which was considered foppish, and owned the finest house and the fastest horses in town. Indeed, Henry Ward was fascinated by Alvord — drove his horses, used his house, and scandalized his church by retaining the gambler on its rolls when everybody in town knew how he made his money. Charles Beecher turned up from down the river, his violin under his arm — "in face and form an Apollo" wrote Mrs. Ketcham — and all the female hearts of Indianapolis went pit-a-pat over this handsome musician, with "the darkness of doubt overshadowing him." But Henry Ward put his brother to work training a choir, and ordered a new and magnificent organ for the church, to boot.

He was launched now, was Henry Ward Beecher. He organized a State Horticultural Society, was elected its president, and rented two lots from Calvin Fletcher for a garden where he grew prize-winning flowers and vegetables. He was invited to lecture at Indiana Asbury University, sat on the platform when Vice-President Johnson — "old Tecumseh-killer" — visited the Indiana capital, and saw his friend William Henry Harrison elected President of the United States. He was conquering his old diffidence as a horse is trained not to shy, by compelling himself to take part in everything that went on, to go everywhere, to be prominent on every occasion.

When President Harrison died, a ceremony was arranged of such pomp as the State had never witnessed. The Rev. Phineas Gurley offered the prayer and Governor Bigger was the orator of the day. But when the Governor sat down, Henry Ward Beecher sprang to his feet. He was not on the program, and he had not intended to speak, he said; but owing to the strong personal friendship and intimacy that existed between himself and General Harrison, when he saw the slow and measured tread of the procession and the evident and deep solemnity that marked the countenances of the people, he could not avoid giving vent to his feelings. It was a surprise to every one — as no doubt it would have been to the late President — to learn how intimate he and Beecher had been. But Henry Ward had worked out a homely picture of Harrison the man, rather than the hero, as he had known the old Indian fighter in the days of his obscurity in the dingy courtroom in Cincinnati, and he presented it with dignity and pathos. Those who heard him found his speech the very reflection of their own thoughts.

He was in demand as a lecturer — at Wabash College on Education; at Indiana University on Intolerance; at Laporte he denounced the modern tendency to educate young men for the overcrowded professions and praised the German system of teaching them practical farming. But he had not learned to preach yet, and he knew it. It was the Apostles, he says, who taught him the art:

"I got this idea: that the Apostles were accustomed first to feel for a ground on which the people and they stood together; a common ground where they could meet. Then they stored up a large number of the particulars of knowledge, which belonged to everybody; and when they had got that knowledge that everybody would admit, placed in proper form before their minds, then they brought it to bear upon them with all their excited heart and feeling."

By this formula, Henry Ward Beecher at last tried out what he called his "first real sermon." It broke no images, touched no sore spots, opened up no new trails. He was careful about that. He merely marshaled the thoughts that were in the minds of his hearers and gave them tongue — with force and conviction and dramatic power — all that he had learned at Mount Pleasant from John E. Lovell. And he swept his audience before him.

"I never felt so triumphant in my life," he says. "I cried all the way home. I said to myself: 'Now I know how to preach!'"

"I would give anything if I could say the things I think as Mr. Beecher can," said Samuel Merrill.

But there were dark spots in his ministry as well. On May 6, 1841, Mary Harman, the first sheep Henry Ward had welcomed into the fold, was expelled from the church for being "guilty of a breach of the Seventh Commandment." And on the following Sabbath, Henry Ward Beecher read from his pulpit the sentence of excommunication pronounced against her, and the reason therefor.

And at thirty Eunice Beecher's hair turned gray. She dyed it jet black.

Part III: Realization

"He has no difficulties at all. He is not a reformer, an innovator, a teacher of new or unwelcome truths, a champion of unwelcome principles. The popular drift befriends him. His equivocal position as minister of an Orthodox Congregational Society makes him attractive to both conservatives and liberals. Nothing radical enough to shock the former, nor conservative enough to displease the latter, he retains people of all descriptions."

THEODORE PARKER

CHAPTER XI

1847

HENRY WARD BEECHER was thirty when he felt, at last, that he knew his trade. He was at that period of his life when he was least good looking — "plain not only in feature but in form," Mrs. Ketcham said. He called himself "a lubberly fellow." He had tried whiskers, and abandoned them — whiskers were regarded with disfavor in Indiana in those days. His hair was rather stringy, very long and waved to one side in an opulent lock in front. As he preached, this lock would fall over his face, and he would brush it back with a sweeping gesture. His dress was sloppy. He went about with his trousers tucked in his boot-tops, and no dignity. He would be pitching manure in his garden one day and preaching the next. When the house of his Methodist colleague, the Rev. W. W. Hibben, burned down, he helped carry water like any fireman. Once he came in from a long trip on horseback, late for church. He strode up the aisle just as he was, in his oldest coat and green baize leggings, spattered with mud. He began the service without comment. Eunice writhed at his disorderly habits and unceremonious behavior. But Henry Ward Beecher did not care.

Physically powerful and full-blooded, he had no patience with what he called "slender health." And slender health was what Eunice Beecher enjoyed.

"One whose attention is, for years, directed to his own body, who watches his pains, and minutely studies every hour of his life, is apt to become extremely selfish," he preached on one occasion, and went on to speak at length of those who spent "their life thinking about themselves; fretful, peevish, dissatisfied, forever arguing some future evil — a burden to their friends, a curse to themselves."

His audience nudged one another and whispered behind their hands — "He ought to know — Mrs. Beecher — pss — pss —"

What Henry Ward Beecher craved was a sense of power. He would go out to Uncle William Bradshaw's farm and chop down one tree after another "just to hear 'em fall," he said. When a giant maple began to shudder under the swift, vigorous strokes, he would wipe his face on his sleeve and feel, for the moment, that he was master even of himself — that he had exorcised all the vacillations, the uncertainties, the fears, closeted within him. He acquired a certain incomparable arrogance that gradually took the place of the horse-play of his first pastoral years. Ex-president Van Buren visited the Indiana capital, and signified his intention to attend Beecher's church.

"Will it make any difference to you?" Elijah Alvord asked Henry Ward.

"No difference," he replied. "I should preach to him just as I would to any other sinner."

But Martin Van Buren was not to be outdone.

"How did you like Beecher's sermon?" Alvord asked the late President, hoping to cadge a compliment for his friend.

"His trousers don't set very well," said the Red Fox dryly.

Beecher rode hither and yon over the State helping in revivals.

"How hopeless and wretched did I feel when Jewett sent for me to come over and help him! I had no effective sermons. I did not know how to preach in a revival," he said, of the first of these experiences, at Terre Haute. "Hardly was my saddle empty before Jewett was at my elbow. 'You have done well to come. You must preach tonight.' . . . In a moment the cloud lifted. The reluctance was gone. It has been so all my life. At a distance I dread and brood and shrink from any weighty enterprise; but the moment the occasion arrives, joy shines clear, and an eager appetite to dash into the battle comes."

Just now, he was dreading and brooding and shrinking in respect of slavery. In the governorship campaign in 1843, there was an Abolition ticket in the field, headed by two men of the highest standing. That same Fall, the irrepressible Synod of Indiana, with Lyman Beecher present as his son's guest, adopted a resounding open letter on slavery, drafted by Elder Stephen C. Stevens, former Justice of the State Supreme Court, and addressed to the Christian brethren in the slave-holding States. Even Lyman Beecher had come out against slavery, at last.

As Henry Ward and his Elder, John L. Ketcham, rode home from Lafayette together, belly deep in mud, after the Synod meeting closed, young Beecher had about made up his mind to take the plunge on slavery. But at Pendleton, a short way from Indianapolis, they ran into an incident that set him back again into reticence.

A group of Abolitionists, including a white woman speaker and a former slave,* whose part it was to recite his escape, were holding meetings. The good folk of Pendleton were possessed of minds that could conceive of but one possible explanation of the presence of a white woman and a negro man in the same company. Accordingly, they mobbed the Abolitionists. The ringleader of the riot was duly arrested, pleaded guilty and was jailed. But three hundred mounted men armed with rifles galloped into Indianapolis and demanded his release — and Governor Whitcomb pardoned the man.

On the subject of this abject yielding by the Governor to intimidation, Henry Ward was outspoken:

"What can the community expect but growing dishonesty, when the Executive, consulting the spirit of the community, receives the demands of the mob, and humbly complies, throwing down the fences of the law, that base rioters may walk unimpeded to their work of vengeance or unjust mercy?"

But on slavery he had nothing to say. Indeed, Henry Ward Beecher was formulating a practical philosophy for a successful minister of the gospel, which he shortly imparted to his brother Charles:

"Preach little doctrine except what is of mouldy orthodoxy; keep shires etc. way off to pasture. They will get fatter, and nobody will all your improved breeds, your short-horned Durhams, your Berk- be scared. Take hold of the most practical subjects; popularize

* Frederick Douglass.

your sermons. I do not ask you to change yourself; but, for a time, while captious critics are lurking, adapt your mode so as to insure that you should be rightly understood."

And as he advised, so he did.

But somehow or other it just did not seem to work. For all the steady growth of his church and the devotion of the major part of his flock, Henry Ward seemed powerless to prevent losses, not simply by people leaving the church because they did not like him — few did that — but through the horrible, public process of sin, discovery, and a consequent excommunication pronounced by Henry Ward Beecher, himself, from the pulpit. He could not, in the end, save even his friend Elijah Alvord, the gambler. For Alvord indiscreetly boasted that if there was a brick in his magnificent house that had not been won at poker, he would take it out and insert another. Of course, after that, there was nothing Henry Ward could do about it. But the Beechers remained on terms of intimate friendship with the Alvords, notwithstanding; and when Mrs. Beecher's cousin, Julia Bullard, came to marry Stoughton A. Fletcher, the banker, it was in the Alvords' magnificent house that the ceremony took place — poker bricks and all.

Every Spring, Henry Ward held revivals and labored mightily to save brands from the burning. One year, he staged a colossal baptismal party on the shores of White river, in conjunction with his Baptist and Methodist colleagues. Thousands assembled along the banks to witness the wholesale immersions, preceded by a joint service by all three ministers, and Henry Ward added an hundred members to his fold. Nevertheless, John Montgomery had to be excommunicated for "highly vicious and grossly immoral conduct," and James M. Smith for habitual intemperance, and numerous others for the same; and Elisha Bilby and his wife Caroline had to be suspended from the privileges of the church for having, as the church record put it, "previously to their marriage been guilty of Fornication with each other" — it was discouraging. Particularly so when the Presbytery finally came down on Henry Ward with a sharp rebuke for the loose way his church was run, and ordered the rebuke spread upon the church's records.

Of course, too, the more prominent Henry Ward Beecher became in other lines — as a public speaker, as an horticulturist, as a Henry Clay Whig, as an indefatigable worker to close everything up tight on Sunday and a relentless enemy of gambling — why, the more embarrassing it became for him to have to try one of his Elders for drunkenness, or the leading member of his choir for "rumors unfavorable to his chastity." Henry Ward knew as well as the next man that something was wrong with his system. And so, to meet the emergency, he planned a series of "Seven Lectures to Young Men on Various Important Subjects," as he called them.

They were the fine flower of grandiloquence, and they embodied the philosophy of Henry Ward Beecher's life at this period. "Having watched the courses of those who seduce the young," he declared, from the lofty height of his thirty years, "I felt an earnest desire to . . . direct their reason to the arts by which they are, with such facility, destroyed." The moral pointed by two hundred pages of rhetoric was, quite simply: *Run away!* "A young man knows little of life; less of himself," said Henry Ward. "He feels in his bosom the various impulses, wild desires, restless cravings he can hardly tell for what . . . You are safe from vice when you avoid even its appearance; and only then."

He had his word to say about politics — "Let the hand of discipline smite the leprous lips which shall utter the profane heresy, *All is fair in politics*" — and strongly backed the protests of the Rothschilds, Baring Brothers and other foreign bondholders against "an infamous repudiation of just debts, by open or sinister methods." But it was on "The Strange Woman" — "a subject which is interwoven with almost every chapter of the Bible" — that Henry Ward really did himself proud. When he announced that he was actually going to speak on "that Vice upon which it has pleased God to be more explicit and full than any other" there were murmurs in his congregation. That was something men talked about in barrooms and brothels, not churches, people said.

They were unduly alarmed. The famous discourse proved to be devoted largely to literary criticism. He would, Henry Ward said, not willingly answer at the bar of God for the writings of Chaucer and Tom Moore, but he preferred the downright, and often abominable, vulgarity of Swift to the scoundrel-indirectness of Sterne. Shakespeare started out a sadly immoral fellow, but in the end "left the dramatical literature immeasurably purer than it came to him." Byron, Bulwer and Fielding, on the other hand, were no more than "the common sewers of society." French, said Henry Ward, is "the dialect of refined sensualism and licentious literature; the language of a land where taste and learning wait upon the altars of impurity." As for the Strange Woman herself: "From the lips of the harlot, words drop as honey, and flow smoother than oil; her speech is fair, her laugh is merry as music. The eternal glory or purity has no lustre, but the deep damnation of lust is made as bright as the gate of heaven!"

One has a curious, frightening glimpse of Henry Ward's own mind.

It was on Popular Amusements, however, that Henry Ward Beecher surpassed himself. The Theater, he felt, was an expiring evil, a clumsy machine of literature not to be compared with the popular lecture, the pulpit and the press.

"I am told that Christians *do* attend the Theatres," he said. "If you would pervert the taste — go to the Theatre. If you would imbibe false views — go to the Theatre. If you would efface as speedily as possible all qualms of conscience — go to the Theatre. If you would put yourself irreconcilably against the *spirit* of virtue and true religion — go to the Theatre. If you would be infected with each particular vice in the catalogue of Depravity — go to the Theatre. . . . It is within the knowledge of all, that men, who thus cater for public pleasure, are excluded from respectable society. . . . Christian and industrious people are guilty of supporting mere mischiefmakers — men whose very heart is diseased, and whose sores exhale contagion to all around them. We pay moral assassins to stab the purity of our children."

It was what nine people out of ten thought in that day — or said they thought. The *Indiana State Journal* ran three columns of review of the Lectures, quoting copiously. Thomas B. Cutler, a journeyman printer on the *Journal*, proposed to Henry Ward to print them in book form, and the Hon. John D. Defrees, the editor of the *Journal*, got half a dozen leading citizens of the State, including United States Senator Oliver H. Smith, Calvin Fletcher and Samuel Merrill, to write an endorsement of the book. Judge McLean of Cincinnati, who had narrowly missed being President, *earnestly* recommended it "to the study of every young man who desires to become eminently respectable." The Indiana State Synod momentarily withdrew its attention from slavery to resolve that "every father should place it in the hands of his sons; it should be in every Sabbath School Library, in every steamboat, hotel and place of public resort" — the Gideon Bible of its day.

From the odium of his silence on slavery, Henry Ward Beecher had, for the moment at least, redeemed himself.

The immediate practical result of this triumph was that the publishers of the *Indiana State Journal* launched a farm monthly with Henry Ward Beecher as editor. Henry Ward was enchanted. He abandoned the little cottage which, Eunice said, was so small that she had to go out of doors and make up the bed through the window. Her father had finally broken his neck, and with a little money from his estate, they bought some land and had a house built which Henry Ward painted. Thither flocked Beechers and Bullards in droves — Henry Ward's halfbrothers, Thomas and James, to live; Hattie Stowe — by now the distinguished authoress — to visit; Lyman Beecher to make flying trips; Eunice's brother, Dr. Talbot Bullard, and his wife, to settle permanently in Indianapolis; her youngest brother, Oliver, to join the household; and her sister, Maria and Maria's family, and her brother, the Rev. Artemas, and his family, passing through. It was like the old Litchfield parsonage.

But to Henry Ward Beecher it was immense relief. There were three children now, and Eunice's hands were more than full. Henry Ward got up before dawn and did his editorial work, largely with the scissors, by candle light. After that, he was a free man. He burrowed in the extensive libraries of Calvin Fletcher and Samuel Merrill. He read all the books he warned the Young Men against — George Sand, Eugene Sue, Bulwer, Dumas père, M. de Balsac, as he spelled it. He had read "Pickwick Papers" in the columns of the *Political Beacon* at Lawrenceburgh; but he felt that Dickens presented a shockingly low standard of virtue and dealt with "the most vulgar of mankind." He raced Elijah Alvord's horses against time along level stretches of road, and went on long rides with Betty Bates, now grown to lovely womanhood.

By the end of a year, the *Western Farmer and Gardener* had 1,200 subscribers and an exchange list that took it, with Henry Ward Beecher's name, into every newspaper office in the country. Even Horace Greeley's *Tribune* quoted from it. Between his "Seven Lectures" and his farm journal, Henry Ward was rapidly building him a reputation that reached beyond the boundaries of Indiana. His comments in the *Farmer and Gardener* were by no means confined to agriculture. Every issue had its exhortations to temperance (combined with recipes for making rhubarb wine — add a bottle of brandy for every five gallons). There were warnings to young girls; the solemn assurance that burned okra cannot be distinguished from the best Java coffee; a series of travel articles by Thomas K. Beecher, now twenty-one; a discussion of why 70 percent of the farm girls of England become prostitutes. Slavery, however, was never mentioned.

Yet with the elections and the impending annexation of Texas, slavery was the one topic uppermost in every one's mind. Even when Henry Clay was defeated by trying to be on both sides of the Texas question at once — bound to be right one way or the other, albeit never President — the agitation did not cease. Judge Stevens ran for governor on the Liberty Party ticket, and made a speech from the steps of the Indianapolis Court House:

"We must teach the abolition of slavery through the doors of 20,000 churches," he said. "We must bring them on the side of Jesus Christ instead of slavery. . . . We are told that our plan is seditious and factious; that we are agitators — yes, agitators. Well, Christ was an agitator. . . ."

Back at the edge of the crowd Henry Ward Beecher listened with his hands clenched and the muscles of his throat working, eager to leap up, as he had done at Harrison's obsequies, and twist that crowd around his finger with a new gospel of Freedom. But he did not dare — he did not dare.

The Fourth of July was a great day in Beecher's church, and he preached a great sermon. But before it ended there came through the open windows, from the street outside, screams and curses and the noise of many feet running and shouts of "Kill the damned nigger! *Kill him!*"

The service came to an abrupt close. The women hurried all the little girls, brave in their holiday white frocks and starched pantalettes, out a back door. The men, Beecher foremost among them, joined the crowd down the street, gathered about the horribly battered body of an old negro whom everybody knew — who had bought his own freedom in the sweat of his brow twenty years before. He lay in a pool of blood, his white hair strangely incongruous against the chocolate of his skin and the dull red of the blood.

"The niggers are gettin' too damn' thick — ought to be thinned out!" somebody growled. Somebody else suggested beginning with the Abolitionists. The mob moved down the street towards the house of DePuy, the editor of the local Abolition paper, *The Freeman*. They had gone only a little way when DePuy himself came running up — a slight, shy, near-sighted man, who wore glasses. With a yell, Jim Newland, a member of the City Council, leaped at DePuy and fell to beating him savagely. It was an unequal fight. Calvin Fletcher, followed by Henry Ward, shouldered his way through the press to where the figures struggled in the gathering darkness. Fletcher grabbed Newland, and Henry Ward turned to the Abolitionist.

"Get out!" he advised DePuy. "Run! You have no friends here!"

But DePuy only went as far as the office of *The Freeman*, where he started to set up an extra, with a report of the murder of the negro and the action of the mob. There Calvin Fletcher and Henry Ward Beecher found him, his clothing torn, blood- and mud-stained, his glasses gone, feverishly working by the light of a single candle at the type-cases, peering at what he set with near-sighted eyes. In the end, they persuaded the little man not to issue his extra.

"A newspaper account of the occurrence might prejudice the jury trying the murderer, and so prevent justice being done," was the quaint reason Henry Ward gave for his advice. As no effort was ever made to arrest the real murderer, the reason did not sound so well in the broad light of the following day.

The incident hurt Henry Ward Beecher far more than he liked to think. It went all over the country, and his part in it grew less and less heroic with repetition. People who had only recently read in his "Seven Lectures" Beecher's scornful denunciation of a state of affairs "when honest men and officers fly before a mob" raised their eyebrows. And then, there was his brother, Edward, who had stood beside Elijah Lovejoy, at Alton, while the mob raged outside the building.

One result of the affair was that that same Fall, the Indiana State Synod decided that it had stood for enough tergiversation on the subject of slavery. Aimed directly at Henry Ward Beecher, on motion of "Father" John M. Dickey, of Madison, a resolution was adopted calling upon every Presbyterian minister in the State "to preach on the sin of oppression, on the evils of slavery, and on the doctrine and laws of the Bible in reference to servitude." A memorial was addressed to the General Assembly of the Presbyterian Church "praying them to take firm and decided action against slaveholding." And the decision was taken that at every meeting of the Synod thereafter one of the ministers should preach, before the Synod, a sermon on slaveholding.

The action of his Synod left Henry Ward very little leeway. Yet he did not immediately comply. One John Hawkins, a reformed drunkard temperance lecturer of a type common in that day, furnished Henry Ward the excuse to be off full cry against his old enemy, drunkenness, instead of slavery. On hearing Hawkins, he gave himself up entirely to his feelings, he said, and was crying with great relish — "we could only by violent effort refrain from a downright oriental lamentation," he wrote, editorially. "Three or four boys in the seat before us squared around, and, regarding us as the more interesting spectacle of the two, leaned on their elbows and systematically watched our progress. We, nevertheless, cried enough in one night to answer for a dozen ordinary occasions."

Henry Ward did more than weep, however. In the columns of the *Farmer and Gardener* he made an onslaught on a Lawrenceburgh distiller, C. G. W. Comegys, who besides being a distiller happened also to be a church member — and could see no reason why he should not be. At least, so he wrote the *Indiana State Journal*, in somewhat astonished reply to Henry Ward's unprovoked attack. But Beecher would not have it so. He came back with a retort three thousand words long, in his best Lectures-to-Young-Men style, deriding the "evangelical distillery" of Comegys, excoriating the distiller, and holding him up to ridicule and contempt.

For once in his life Henry Ward Beecher had caught a tartar. Comegys was no rhetorician, but he knew how to touch his adversary on the quick. He told how Henry Ward had deserted a small, devoted church that had made great sacrifices to maintain him, to move on to a place with a better chance of fame and fortune, and recounted Beecher's boasts that he could have been as great as Henry Clay if he had gone into politics. Indianapolis grinned. Henry Ward's rejoinder rose to six thousand words. But the doughty distiller was ready for him:

"Let us see!" he wrote in reply. "Slavery — that is rather a delicate subject with the gentleman. . . . But slavery is an *evil*, and by its laws men without the exercise of their will or unalienable rights . . . are held by *iron law* fast in its chains. Does alcohol do that? Or does the distiller do that? Is any man chained so that he cannot *loose himself?* You cannot justify slavery, then, by talking about the making of whiskey. I make use of this in view of the gentleman's well known anti-slavery views, privately held. But his tongue cleaves etc. . . . It is not popular to denounce it! . . .

"Why is thy tongue still and thy pen idle when the sentiments of thy brother * and thy church on slavery are promulgated? Thou idle boaster — where is thy vaunted boldness? . . . When a moiety of true, philanthropic, Christian courage is needed — thou hast it not; thy tongue is still, thy hand forgetteth its cunning.

"You are greatly to be pitied — even by a distiller!"

It was cruel. For there was no getting away from it — the man was right. And everybody in Beecher's congregation knew it — everybody in Indianapolis — everybody in Indiana. There it was, spread all over the *Journal*, for all the world to read. Henry Ward had no answer to make. He could escape decision no longer. He must attack slavery openly or leave the country, a laughingstock.

And just as at Terre Haute — the cloud lifted. The reluctance was gone. The eager appetite to dash into battle came. Henry Ward Beecher preached against slavery at last.

But in his secret heart he made up his mind that he would leave the West at the first opportunity.

* Edward Beecher's "Narrative of Riots at Alton" had been published in 1838.

CHAPTER XII

PLYMOUTH CHURCH

"As a preacher he is a landscape painter of Christianity. Mr. Beecher has no model. He is the original of himself. He is always new. He imitates no man and no man can imitate him. The great power of Mr. Beecher over his congregation consists mainly in the clearness of his mental vision, the range of his thoughts, the deep interest he imparts to whatever he touches. He speaks as if conscious that he is telling the truth, and his audience believes he thinks so."

THUS Senator Oliver H. Smith, of Indiana, as shrewd a politician as that State of politicians ever boasted and one of the leading members of Beecher's Indianapolis church. His appraisal of Henry Ward Beecher at thirty-four is uncannily accurate. The personal magnetism that drew men and women to him, the power of giving himself that made others feel themselves his intimates, and the technical skill, become now a second nature, that enabled him to work his will of them — all of that was present in the man.

But there was also a certain something that inspired that last sentence in what Senator Smith wrote, with its curious little mental reservation.

Henry Ward himself felt it. He had been tremendously successful, not just as a minister of the gospel, but in a score of ways. He had taken a new congregation of thirty-three communicants, and raised the membership of his church to two hundred seventy-five. A church building had been erected, a splendid organ installed, a choir organized. He had gathered together a club of young men and a Bible class of what he called his bevy of girls — one his "handsomest girl," one his "dearest girl," one his "girl with the sweetest disposition." He was editor of a prosperous farm journal in a growing farming community, president of the State Horticultural Society, trustee of the Deaf and Dumb Institute, a lecturer in demand throughout the State, and a leader in the periodical crusades against drunkenness, gambling, theaters and the awful desecration of the Sabbath becoming all too prevalent with the growth of the city. Incontestably, Henry Ward Beecher was a person of consequence in the State of Indiana.

And yet, just as incontestably, there was something wrong. If Henry Ward had been compelled to tell what he thought it was, he would have said — with bewildered incredulity — that his people did not take him seriously. Just now, for example, towards the close of 1846, he was having difficulties with his church over the payment of his salary. They owed him $970, and $970 was a great deal of money in those days. To Eunice, such a sum represented servants and better clothing and some one to help her look after the three children (she had already lost two since they came to Indianapolis) and more ease generally. She was very bitter about it, and never ceased to remind Henry Ward that what the members of his church "wasted on parties and frivolous amusements every few weeks, would have comfortably supported their pastor's family a year, and given his wife an opportunity to rest and regain her strength," as she put it.

It was not difficult to persuade Henry Ward that the most effective way to bring his church to time would be to get some other church to call him elsewhere. There were plenty of business men from the East visiting Indianapolis who could manage it. He brought somebody or other home with him almost every Sunday, anyhow, and on these occasions Mrs. Beecher missed no opportunity to impress upon the visitors that she "longed for a broader and more brilliant sphere" for her husband. She did not have to sell Henry Ward Beecher to these strangers. He made his own good impression: his success as a preacher, his high standing in the community, and especially the genial common sense with which he waved aside the radical ideas which appeared to be gaining a deplorable currency, appealed to them. No one knew better than merchants and note collectors from New York the peril that resided in the half-baked theories, loose in Europe, that hordes of immigrants were fetching into the United States. In France, Louis Blanc was openly advocating socialism; Karl Marx was flourishing in Germany; in Italy, Mazzini was giving tongue to all sorts of hare-brained and dangerous ideas; Louis Kossuth, in Hungary, was demanding equal rights for everybody. Even in conservative England, the Chartists were bent on upsetting the established order and Parliament itself was considering a ten-hour day for industrial workers. Revolution was in the air in 1847.

Now there was no such nonsense about young Beecher:

"Let a man be a mechanic, a lawyer, a physician, a merchant, or what he will, he will find that he must conform to the wishes and opinions of those by whom he is surrounded. . . . Men are accountable for their *feelings* and their *opinions* as well as their conduct. It may seem strange to say that men are held accountable for their opinions; but they are, and will be forever — and that, too, in the freest land, and under the most liberal government. . . . Let any prominent man in either of the great political parties of this country stand up and affirm his repugnance to any one of the great principles of his party. . . . What will be the result? They cannot imprison him . . . but they can ostracize him."

So he preached. It was the kind of preaching substantial business men liked to hear, backed up by good, sound texts from the Bible. When bankers like Charles Butler returned to New York, they carried with them the report of Lyman Beecher's son as "an extraordinary young man, gifted as to talents, a remarkably fine speaker — eloquent, indeed — a wonderful knowledge of human nature, and a tact, if I may so speak, of exhibiting it, which carries you along irresistibly with him," said Butler. "Old Dr. Beecher more than lives in his son again," he added.

William T. Cutter, a collector from New York, had been a member of Lyman Beecher's Boston church, so it was no trick at all to enlist his aid to obtain young Beecher an Eastern call. A letter from him suggesting a church newly established on Brooklyn Heights by David Hale, proprietor of the *Journal of Commerce*, enabled Henry Ward to secure an entirely satisfactory and business-like settlement of the salary question with his Indianapolis church. He could have remained in Indianapolis if he had desired it.

But in his heart of hearts, Henry Ward Beecher did not desire it. He felt that, somehow or other, he had got off on the wrong foot in Indiana. There had been little things — the DePuy incident, the Comegys affair, the whole matter of his hesitation over the slavery question, of which, since he had taken the plunge, he was secretly ashamed. And now came another. There had not been a scandal in the church for two years when old Dr. Munsell, one of the founders of the church, and its first Elder, was seen drunk in public on several occasions, and Henry Ward was compelled to read from his pulpit the good doctor's confession and repentance, while the doctor sat there with red face sunk into the velvet collar of his Sunday coat. And on top of that, Elders Graydon and Ketcham reported that Owen Tuller "while he insisted that the rumors about him on the subject of chastity were very much exaggerated, he admitted that he had occasionally been guilty of adultery." Henry Ward was furious. On the following Sabbath, in the breathless hush of the crowded church, Henry Ward Beecher pronounced "that Owen Tuller, for the crime of Adultery, be, and he is, excommunicated from this Church as a member thereof."

Perhaps, thought Henry Ward, that prescription for a successful preacher he had given Charles was not just the proper formula, after all. He had been young, and had made mistakes. If only he could do it all over again! He knew so well, now, just how a great church could be built up — if he had the chance to try it.

And there was Betty Bates. She grew lovelier every day — so slim and tall, with her curling, Titian hair and her violet eyes. It was all very well for Henry Ward Beecher to tell himself it was not his fault that she felt toward him as she did. What was it he had said to those Young Men? "Your only resource is to avoid the uprising of your giant passions." Avoid. Run away . . . Henry Ward took pen in hand and wrote to Cutter discreetly — but clearly enough:

"It has occurred to me that my situation and my conversation with you were a little *queer*, and it was worth while to state exactly where I stood. . . . I have no plan for staying here, or for going to the West, or for going to the East. . . . I do desire above every other thing to have a heart prepared to receive that welcome *call*, joyous to everyone who has tasted of the powers of the world to come, *to go up and labor in a higher field*. . . . I believe that Christ will surely lead you wisely, if you will *be* led; and that he will point out to you what enterprises it will be wise for you to undertake, and to what one of his multitudinous servants you should apply for help."

Brother Cutter was promptly led to David Hale, indefatigable founder of churches, and Henry C. Bowen, whose wife, Lucy Maria Tappan, was a daughter of that very Lewis Tappan who had been associated with Lyman Beecher in missionary enterprises for a generation. She was twenty-two, recently married, and knew all about Henry Ward Beecher. David Hale had never heard of him. Hale had positive ideas on what was and what was not the function of churches. Slavery, he felt, for example, was "altogether a foreign and distant subject with which, as churches, they should have nothing to do."

Where Indianapolis, with a population of 4,000 boasted sixteen churches, Brooklyn with its sixty thousand had only thirty-nine. It was a field in which a church could not possibly fail. So that when Hale and Bowen and John T. Howard* got a chance to buy the property of the church of that intrepid old slavery-fighter, the Rev. Samuel H. Cox, in Cranberry street, Brooklyn, at a bargain, it was good business sense to do it. And having bought the property, the next thing to do was to get together a congregation to rent it from them. The whole process was a recognized and highly profitable industry in that day. Church property was tax free, and readily rentable for lectures during the week, as well as for Sunday services. It was a safer and more paying investment than public utilities later became — on much the same principle.

Naturally, the immediate success of any new church depended a good deal on the minister. The trinity, Bowen and Hale and Howard, would like to have had Lyman Beecher, whose name by then was one to conjure with. But Dr. Beecher was still conducting a sort of rear-guard action against the Catholics in the Ohio valley, combined with frontal attacks on the "Old School" Presbyterian church everywhere, and could not be spared from the fighting forces of the Lord. So the Brooklyn group had to be content with one of Lyman Beecher's sons. When Henry C. Bowen said he would defray the expenses of a young preacher of whom he had heard to come on from Indianapolis to speak at the twenty-first anniversary meeting of of the Home Missionary Society in May 1847, the secretary of the Society was only too delighted to put young Beecher on the program.

So it came about that Henry Ward and Eunice and the children all journeyed to New York at the expense of Henry C. Bowen, leaving Calvin Stowe holding the fort for Henry Ward

---

* Seth B. Hunt was a co-purchaser, but did not join in forming Plymouth Church.

in Indianapolis. But Beecher's congregation knew nothing of the real purpose of the trip, nor of Henry Ward's hopes in connection with it.

Henry Ward Beecher was not self-deceived when he went East. He knew that to the church world — which, after all, even in that day, was only a small part of New York — he was merely one of Lyman Beecher's preacher sons. At thirty-four, he was not even particularly young, compared to Richard Salter Storrs, recently established in the Church of the Pilgrims, in Brooklyn, or Theodore Parker, Wendell Phillips, Charles Sumner, Robert Bonner, Horace Greeley, Charles A. Dana, Henry J. Raymond or George William Curtis. Nevertheless, he felt, he had gone through an apprenticeship that they had not, out in that Middle West towards which, more and more, the balance of power in the country was gravitating. He knew the nation as a whole as no one of these other men, emerging as leaders, ever would know it. They might divine what the public should want — Henry Ward Beecher knew what it did want. And he stood ready to purvey it.

"I am strong in will and purpose, or I never could have done what I was set to do," he said afterwards, of this turning-point in his life. In that crucial hour of his test in New York, Henry Ward Beecher was strong indeed. Badly dressed, his hair a little too long and stringy, his face a little too round and moon-like, his carriage a little too self-conscious, his figure a little too short, he stepped before the audience that packed the great Broadway Tabernacle and looked out over the row of heads. All week he had sat there listening to nothing but dull speeches on dull subjects, and his heart leaped within him. His subject was of his own choosing: "That the circumstances of the West require its ministers to be men of apostolic stamp, and to labor on apostolic principles." There he stood — a living example of his thesis. He was bold:

"Nothing that relates to the acts of men, to liberty, to social forms and duties, but has been called up for discussion," he said, his voice filling every corner of the place. "There is alarm abroad at this universal inquiry and agitation, but I for one bless God for it! . . . The country is divided; all kinds of new thoughts, new theories, new-fangled notions of every kind are abundant as leaves in the spring. What will be the end of all this? I think there is no danger. . . . All is right if there are agitation and disturbances.

These things pass away; but with God, who works on a pattern which no man knows, they do not pass in vain."

He took the one worry that was preoccupying his hearers in that day of change and robbed it of its terrors. He caught his audience up by their coat-tails and flung them out among the stars. And they belonged to him. They were his men, his creatures, in the hollow of his hand.

"We would not be invidious in selecting in the mass of speeches made this week in the Tabernacle, one for particular perusal. But we cannot avoid directing attention to that of Rev. H. W. Beecher, of Indiana (worthy scion of the name)," said the *Express*. "The best speech, thus far, in 'Anniversary Week.'"

The only fly in Henry Ward's ointment was that parenthesis.

He had his own figure of the Brooklyn group: $1,500 for the first year, $1,750 the second, and the third year and thereafter, the same salary as the Mayor of Brooklyn — $2,000. Bowen was so afraid Henry Ward would get away that he wrote him thirty letters between Beecher's first coming in May and his return to stay, in October. Before Henry Ward Beecher had been gone from Indiana three years, he was receiving over four times his Indianapolis salary, and his Brooklyn church had grown from twenty-one to three hundred and forty-three communicants.

Out in Indiana, there were some shrewd guesses as to the real cause of Beecher's leaving.

"We presume he goes to Brooklyn, where he has a call backed by a salary of $2,500 or $3,000 per year," the Brookville *American* announced. "It takes a good deal of piety to continue in charge of a church at $500 or $800 per year, when he has so much louder calls."

This Henry Ward indignantly denied. He did his best to persuade the good folk of Indianapolis that Mrs. Beecher was dying and that he could save her life only by "removing temporarily to the sea-coast" of Brooklyn. But she had managed the long, difficult journey by stage, canal and primitive railroad from Indianapolis to the East and back again, with three children, in two months; and the people of Indianapolis rather felt that the little fiction about her health was intended for posterity — which it was. Indeed, Henry Ward Beecher's Indianapolis parishioners did not quarrel with his reasons for leaving them.

After all, he was not for them—after eight years, they knew it. Perhaps he was too supple for them; perhaps they were too austere for him. "Each saw in the other promising possibilities, but each had to submit to some things merely bearable in the other," Henry Ward's associates on the *Journal* summed it up.

The young men to whom he had delivered the famous lectures presented him with a gold watch that cost $125. Calvin Fletcher, whose brother Eunice Beecher had miraculously nursed back to life, gave her a set of silver spoons—"An Award for Merit for Restoring an Individual, after his Physicians and Others had given him up." And on the day when the railroad came at last to Indiana's capital, bringing with it prosperity and fortune to those who had held on through so many years of hardship and patient faith, Henry Ward Beecher left.

Thousands turned out to see the first train come puffing up the shining rails. Samuel Merrill, now president of the railroad, made a speech from the top of one of the cars, flower-bedecked, and the Governor made another. The young men and young ladies of the town piled into the train and took their first ride behind a locomotive. Noses got red and shiny from the Indian Summer sun and the refreshments. Lawrence Vance, one of Henry Ward's deacons and Betty Bates' brother-in-law, was conductor of this first train. And Betty Bates was there, too— proud and beautiful, her violet eyes swimming. But Eunice Beecher had gone on back East with the children several weeks before.

When night fell, and the crowd all trooped back to town, shouting and screaming along the dusty road, Henry Ward Beecher was left behind, the first passenger out of Indianapolis on the new railroad.

"The car was no car at all—a mere ex tempore wood box and even sometimes used for hogs when without seats," he wrote back; "but with seats, for men—of which class *I* (ah! me miserable!) happened to be one. At eleven o'clock I arrived in Madison not over proud of the glory of riding on the first train from Indianapolis."

Brooklyn, of course, was not New York; but in many ways the two were more closely in touch in 1847 than half a century later. New York life was still concentrated at the lower end of Manhattan Island. From the Astor House by Fulton Ferry one could be in Brooklyn in a jiffy, and for such old-fashioned folk

as still lived in Beaver street, it was nearer to go to church on
the Heights than at St. Mark's Place or St. John's Park. Fashion-
able life centered in Bond street, with its shade trees, and Great
Jones street, and Colonnade Row in Lafayette Place. The
younger married couples, who had to begin modestly, were
going way out towards Union Place, where Fifth avenue ended,
or even to Gramercy Park, where there were only scattered
houses.

Lady Emmeline Stuart Wortley found New York "certainly
handsome, and yet there is something about it that gives one
the idea of a half-finished city, and this even in Broadway itself," she wrote. "Crowds of carriages, private and public, are
to be seen in Broadway, passing and repassing every moment,
filled with ladies beautifully dressed in the most elaborate
Parisian toilets." What worried her most was the rapidity of
transportation. There were twenty-four omnibus lines, and
over four hundred busses that went whizzing along "like insane
vehicles" hardly stopping to take on passengers.

Taking on passengers was in itself quite a trick for a bus, considering the voluminous skirts women were wearing, that
seemed to grow bigger and bigger every year. When the
Beechers arrived, however, they were still within reason, and
the poke bonnets and the little velvet tippets or the lace shawls
worn in the streets were as modest as any one could wish,
despite the embroidered stockings that appeared whenever the
wearer climbed into a carriage. The men, of course, looked
like nothing so much as Lucien de Rubempré or Nicholas
Nickleby, with their frock coats fitting snugly at the waist and
flaring out like ballet skirts, their skin-tight trousers in huge
checks or stripes, held under the boots by straps. Enormously
tall chimney-pot hats surmounted faces completely surrounded
by whiskers.

But Henry Ward Beecher was smooth-shaven, would not
wear the conventional stove-pipe hat, and let his trousers flop
loose after the Western fashion. It was not just that he preferred
to be different to others, but that he felt it a distinct part of
his job to build up as rapidly as possible a character for himself and his church that would make Plymouth Church a land-
mark and its pastor a prominent figure. Only so could he justify
the confidence placed in him by the group that had financed

the new church. And only so could he ever hope to escape being one of Lyman Beecher's preacher sons, and become Henry Ward Beecher.

The investment character of his church was a matter that every metropolitan minister of that day was expected to bear in mind. Pews were auctioned off to the highest bidder and church scrip bore seven percent interest. A popular preacher was, also, a better real estate advertisement than whole pages of publicity. Indeed, such a preacher as Henry Ward Beecher proved, readily secured pages of publicity for the neighborhood in which he officiated. For it was the day when churchgoing was the only amusement permitted the godly, and divine services received the attention from the press later accorded theaters and social activities.

David Hale's passion for founding churches ran to Congregational communions for obvious practical reasons. A Congregational church was administratively independent. Its pastor was responsible to God, his congregation, and to no one else. This was precisely the form of ecclesiastical organization that most appealed to Henry Ward Beecher. Back in Indiana he had twice been censured by the Presbyterian Synod for the careless way his church was run, and he did not like it. He had been born into Congregationalism when it was still the State religion of Connecticut. It suited him.

Accordingly, on November 11, 1847, Henry Ward Beecher was duly installed as pastor of Plymouth Church, a Congregational body. Dr. Heman Humphry, to whom (and God) Lyman Beecher had committed his son seventeen years before in the humble hope that he might be useful in the world, pronounced the invocation. Edward Beecher, now back in Boston, delivered the sermon. The Rev. Joseph P. Thompson, of the Broadway Tabernacle, charged the people. And Dr. Richard Salter Storrs, who had entered Amherst the year after Henry Ward graduated, extended the fellowship of the churches.

"At my first coming, I had no plans," said Henry Ward. "I had marked out no future. I had no theories to establish, no system to found; no theories to demolish, no oppugnation of any kind."

But six months before, when he had preached his first sermon to those who now formed his church, he stated his faith:

"There is a day of terror coming when God will call you to account for all the Divine efforts made in your behalf," he had said. "As for myself, I know what I will do when God calls my soul to Him. I know when I shall look back upon my life, it will be folly to attempt to justify anything I have ever done. I will turn to Christ and say: 'Thou hast promised to save me if I would trust in Thee, and I have trusted in Thee, and now I claim the fulfillment of Thy promise, O Lord. Here I am, and my only hope is in Thee.'

"And then Christ will throw about me the shield of His righteousness — not because I am not a sinner, but because I am a sinner, loved and shielded of Christ."

There was no account in the newspapers of Henry Ward Beecher's first sermon in Plymouth Church. But the *Courier and Enquirer* did report that, the night before his installation, Mrs. Beecher was violently assaulted by a colored man, who wrested a package from her and made his escape.

CHAPTER XIII

BROOKLYN

THERE were a number of reasons why the advent of Henry Ward Beecher on the metropolitan scene created no particular comment. For one thing, troops were beginning to straggle home from the Mexican war, and the political pot was boiling furiously. As a loyal Whig, Henry Ward had denounced the war at its inception. But as success followed success south of the Rio Grande, he flung himself into the emotional current and hurrahed with the best of them for *victory!*

Then, too, he had to get settled in his new surroundings. He had driven a canny bargain in the matter of his new salary, but for the time being was not only without funds but had left a world of debts behind him in Indianapolis. These latter Henry C. Bowen paid, and bought Henry Ward a new outfit more suited to Eastern fashion standards, to boot. Mrs. Bowen took Eunice and the children to the shops and fitted them out handsomely. Poor Eunice lost another baby shortly after her arrival and was due to have her sixth child in January. Life was literally just one baby after another for Eunice Beecher.

Yet she was not lonely in Brooklyn as she had been in those early days in Indianapolis. Here were her own people — New Englanders, for the most part. Besides, her sister, Lucy, was settled in New York; and her youngest brother, Oliver, and his wife, had come on from Indianapolis evidently determined to share the fortunes of Eunice and Henry Ward for life; and Grandma Bullard; and Henry's stern old Aunt Esther still bringing up the Beecher progeny; and a whole new tribe of Henry's own mother's relatives, the Footes — the very same Justin Foote with whom Lyman Beecher had stopped on his way to his first church at East Hampton, Long Island, near half a century earlier. How Brooklyn had changed in that time! Where now stood Plymouth Church was a turnip patch then, with Uncle Justin's the only house for miles. Now Brooklyn had grown from a village to a regular city with four banks, a public library, twenty-four policemen and a brand new City Hall!

For his part, Henry Ward had his church to organize and build up and get on its financial feet — the same problem he had had in Indianapolis, with Henry C. Bowen playing the rôle of Samuel Merrill. Henry Ward had been through it before, and he knew the whole routine of it, down to just the right psychological moment to go away and leave his congregation without him for a few months, as he had done out West. He was not in the least worried by the task; but it did take time and tact. The first five years of a church's life are the hardest, he always said:

"If a church were consecrated, active and energetic during the first five years of its life, it would probably go on through generations developing the same features. . . . Consequently I went into this work with all my soul, preaching night and day, visiting incessantly, and developing as fast and as far as might be that social, contagious spirit which we call a revival of religion."

But the main reason why Henry Ward Beecher stuck so closely to his job as a Congregational minister in those early years, and left such side-issues as politics and slavery alone, was David Hale. David Hale and Henry C. Bowen were his two financial backers, the owners of the property of Plymouth Church, and the guarantors of its existence. Hale was a strange mixture of prejudice and principle. He had bought the Broadway Tabernacle and turned it into a Congregational church because its elders had refused Lewis Tappan the right of free speech on slavery — and this though he disagreed violently with Tappan's views. In four years, Hale had been instrumental in founding eight churches in Brooklyn, as well as others in Detroit and Western New York. He was a great admirer of Lyman Beecher, but regarded Lyman's anti-Catholic activities as mischievous. On the head of slavery he minced no words:

"The anti-slavery agitation, conducted as it has been, has been the worst thing for the interests of religion. . . . The great mass of Christian people have become utterly sick of it. We wish the ministers were as sick. Some are."

Henry Bowen, on the other hand, had married into the Tappan family and the Tappan point of view. The rules for the employees of the Tappans, in the days of their affluence, included:

"Total abstinence; not to visit proscribed places nor remain out after ten o'clock at night; to visit a theatre, and to make the acquaintance of an actor precluded forgiveness; to attend Divine service twice on Sundays, and every Monday morning to report church attendance, name of clergyman and texts; prayer meeting twice a week, and must belong to an anti-slavery society and essay to make converts to the cause."

It is not of record that clerks in Bowen and McNamee's "princely establishment" at 112 Broadway had to live up to quite these stringent regulations, but Henry C. Bowen was as pronounced an anti-slavery man as David Hale was the contrary. Tact, not to say plain common sense, demanded that Henry Ward under these circumstances set about building up a church to stand back of him before he launched into anything else.

Consequently, when the American and Foreign Anti-Slavery Society, of which Arthur Tappan was president, held its annual meeting some eight months after Henry Ward's arrival in Brooklyn, Beecher found that the fatigues of auctioning off the pews of Plymouth Church the evening before for some $8,500 made it impossible for him to attend the anti-slavery meeting. It was pure chance that did, finally, involve Henry Ward Beecher in the slavery controversy. The association of Methodist ministers of New York had arranged a meeting at the Broadway Tabernacle to raise funds to buy the freedom of two mulatto girls, daughters of a free father and a slave mother, who, when they were to be sold following the legal status of the mother, attempted to escape and were recaptured. To give the affair a non-sectarian character, various ministers of other denominations were invited to take part. Dr. Dowling, for the Baptists, and Henry Ward Beecher for the Congregationalists, were scheduled for a few remarks. The veteran Abolitionist, Alvan Stewart, was to be the speaker of the evening.

But they reckoned without their Henry Ward. A great many points in the slavery question confused him still; but here before him was precisely the one thing in the whole slavery problem that was clear to Henry Ward Beecher. On the constitutional question of how slavery was to be abolished, he was by no means decided. Indeed, he held that slavery could not constitutionally be abolished against the will of the Southern States. He had no use for the methods of the left-wing Abolitionists, Garrison, Phillips, and Theodore Parker. The law, the logic of the situation, as he saw it, was insurmountable, and screaming about it both undignified and futile.

But a case like this was different. It was no longer a matter of abstract reasoning, but of concrete emotion. The issue was not, to his mind: "Do you believe in the abolition of slavery at the price, perhaps, of war or disunion?" but "Shall this girl — almost as white as you are — be sold for money to the first comer to do as he likes with?"

"A sale by a human flesh dealer of Christian girls!" he cried, and went on to dwell upon the horrors awaiting female slaves. "Suppose them so comely that no price less than $3,000 would purchase them. Suppose this, and act as you would act then!"

These are Christian girls — Methodists. It is not just a question of women who will drift into one immoral relationship after another, like so many animals. These are girls who have seen the Light, who know good from evil, whose souls have been saved by the immortal Redeemer. What may come to them as slaves will not be merely a pollution of the body, but a profounder, more agonizing wound — they will resist, they will pray, they will struggle — but they will be tempted beyond their strength or violated by brute force.

He sees all of this — as if he were an actor in it, himself. It is more real to him than the crowded church filled with sobbing, hysterical women, with shining-eyed, trembling-handed men, vicarious participants in a tremendous drama of heroism, cruelty, sex, blood — yes, and virtue triumphant! For they tear the money from their pocketbooks — they pay the price of the virginity of these girls.

Just so in years to come, like appeals to save Christian Armenian girls from the horrors of Turkish harems would move similar audiences to frenzied generosity. The institution of slavery had nothing to do with it.

"Of all the meetings I have attended in my life, for a panic of sympathy I never saw one that surpassed that," Henry Ward said afterwards.

But to Henry Ward Beecher the sale of the Edmonson sisters was more even than columns of publicity in the New York newspapers and sudden fame in his new field of labor. It was a revelation. Here was the means and the method of power over vast multitudes of people — here was a subject beside which his lectures to young men on drunkenness and harlotry were mere exercises in elocution. More than that. Here also was the key to his own dilemma respecting slavery: he would treat it no longer as an academic discussion of constitutional powers and State rights, but as a human question, in which God, the sanctity of the home, chastity, salvation, bodily purity, the patriotism due a nation unrent, Christ's love and the blood of atonement, could all be brought together in one stupendous emotional appeal that would achieve what Garrison and the rest of the Abolitionists had come no nearer to accomplishing in twenty years of what Beecher termed their "ruinous absurdities."

On his way home across the ferry that night, Henry Ward Beecher stood in the chill darkness that so suddenly and so completely had succeeded to the light and the excitement of the Tabernacle, and turned these things over in his mind. The intoxication of the meeting was still upon him. He felt his power, as a runner feels his second wind and settles into his stride. Not, perhaps, in so many words did he say to himself: "This is the path I must follow and this the pace I must maintain." But at the bottom of his consciousness there formed an unquestioning confidence in the efficacy of a swift emotional rush to attain whatever ends might be desired — even the rebirth of mankind and the redemption of the world.

In the morning the old New England shrewdness returned,

and the old uncertainties and doubts of himself. There was also David Hale to consider, and others like him in Plymouth Church.

And then, providentially, the church burned down, and a fortnight later David Hale died.

Henry Ward Beecher knew exactly what he had to do now: he must erect a church that would be neither David Hale's church nor Henry Bowen's church, but Henry Ward Beecher's church. It must be big enough to grow into. That amazing evangelist, the Rev. John Newland Maffitt, had recently been holding revival meetings of over three thousand persons in Brooklyn. Well, Plymouth Church must be able to handle even that many. The old church burned on January 30, 1849. By mid-February Beecher writes of the prospect of raising $100,-000: "I do not regard the enterprise as *quite* sure, though looking favorably." But it was not Henry Ward Beecher who raised the money to build Plymouth Church. "I carried the subscription paper, day after day and evening after evening, and saw with my own eyes nearly every subscription that was made," said Henry C. Bowen. Plymouth Church might be Beecher's church — but it was his church, too.

Meanwhile, many things happened in the great world.

In the course of 1849, some 150,000 people rushed to California, mad over gold. It was clear that the old difficulties over the admission of Missouri and Texas as slave States must shortly come up again over California. When the Missouri Compromise was reached, neither Texas nor California was in the Union at all. The South took the position therefore that the best way to settle the status of this new territory was simply to extend the Missouri Compromise line westward to the Pacific. New Mexico and Arizona were unsuited to slave development anyhow, and such a solution might have saved both pride and politics in the South, without materially enlarging slave territory.

But the anti-slavery forces had, by now, grown into a great political party that in 1848 polled 300,000 votes and held the balance of power. The leadership of the movement was passing from those interested in the welfare of the slave into the hands of those interested in securing political and economic dominance, in the name of the slave. They were bent on so hedging in the slave-holding States that they could neither expand nor live on their own resources, thus using economic pressure to wrest from the South its political control of the country. As this ancient process involved neither violation of the Constitution nor civil conflict, those who cried out against being reduced to a state of ruin in the name of higher morality were made to appear truculent, rebellious and a menace to the peaceful continuance of the Union.

The Southern States were, in point of fact, none of these things. They were that most pathetic of modern anachronisms, a people forced to depend on a purely agricultural economy in a rapidly industrializing world. Under the circumstances, the Southern planter was hardly concerned with the morals of his slaves or whether they could read the Bible or not. What bothered him was that the economic value of slave labor appeared to be growing less and less. He was caught in the cogs of an economic law which, conceivably, might be just as much God's law as the seventh commandment.

But Henry Ward Beecher and thousands of clergymen like him in that day (and this) knew no more about economic law than they did about the paleolithic age. What interested them was the seventh commandment. They regarded slavery as a sort of gigantic debauch on the part of the slave-holders, in which female slaves were seen not as the economic liability they really were, but as the unwilling victims of their masters' lusts. They attacked slavery not so much as a cruel exploitation of man by man, as upon the ground of its wickedness as an incentive to grossly immoral behavior.

Which was not in the least the matter at issue.

Ever since he had left his editorial scissors sticking in the desk of the *Western Farmer and Gardener*, Henry Ward Beecher had itched to write again. Some 20,000 copies of his "Lectures to Young Men" had been sold—a promising beginning, certainly. Henry Ward had, moreover, a lively belief in the possibilities of religious journalism, fortified by unbounded confidence in his own resources as a religious writer. So when Henry C. Bowen and his partner in the dry-goods business began to turn over in their minds the idea of a religious weekly, Henry Ward was hot in support of the project. Three Congregational clergymen—Drs. Leonard Bacon (a lifelong friend of Lyman Beecher), Joseph P. Thompson and Richard Salter Storrs—were accordingly secured to act as an editorial board, and *The Independent* launched in December 1848. The choice of Joshua Leavitt as managing editor of the new paper was based on his twenty years' experience in just such work.

But Joshua Leavitt happened also to be one of the founders of the New York Anti-Slavery Society back in the days when a mob sacked Lewis Tappan's house and burned his furniture in the street. He had been for James G. Birney for President, on the Liberty Party ticket, when Henry Ward Beecher was voting for that staunch old pro-slavery Virginian, William Henry Harrison. It was plain that if Henry Ward Beecher was to write for a paper under Joshua Leavitt's management, he would have to come out against slavery more openly than he had yet ventured to do since coming East.

Beecher was at first reluctant to burn his bridges. Slavery had been at the bottom of a good deal of his trouble in Indiana, and that was precisely what he wanted to avoid any repetition of. Aside from the one incident of the Edmonson sisters (which he had been at some pains to explain was merely an act of Christian philanthropy divorced from the general question of slavery), he had trodden with meticulous care in respect of slavery since his arrival in Brooklyn. He did so now, in writing for *The Independent*, sticking closely to the proved and familiar subjects of the "Lectures to Young Men" — temperance, the hideous moral perils of dancing, a defense of sudden conversion tempered by a warning against employing reformed characters to reform others (so often they did not stay reformed!), and a description of Henry Ward Beecher revisiting his childhood New England home. His début in the metropolitan press was dedicated to "Vicious Reform Literature," with special reference to certain periodicals purveying salacious matter in the guise of a crusade against vice. The *National Police Gazette* was just then hounding that incomparable evangelist, the Rev. John Newland Maffitt, on a charge of seducing a member of his flock, the step-daughter of the judge of the Brooklyn court. Maffitt's "heart had literally burst" over the affair, his physician attested, at the autopsy. It was quite the scandal of the day.

The more anti-slavery *The Independent* became under Joshua Leavitt's guidance, the more marked grew its "unparalleled accession of subscribers." With this practical demonstration of the popular trend before him and Joshua Leavitt and Mrs. Bowen, Lewis Tappan's daughter, to egg him on, Henry Ward Beecher finally took his courage in both hands and opened up on slavery in the columns of *The Independent*, two years and a half after he had first come East.

His specific target was not slavery, however, but Louis A. Godey, the editor of *Godey's Lady's Book*. Godey had denied that he had ever attacked "Southern Institutions" in his magazine, and Henry Ward fell upon him. Godey, he said, was little better than a slave himself, "as anxious for the shame of supple servility as the slave for the manliness of liberty." Godey, he went on, might have a white skin, but his liver was whiter still:

"If he has had in his magazine one word in favor of love, of the family, of the sacred relation of parent and child, husband and wife, mother and sister . . . then he has aspersed Southern Institutions, whose very foundations are laid in the negation of all these. Is this the magazine for our sons and daughters to read? . . . Are these the men who are to direct the reading of our children? Are their magazines to lie upon our tables?"

This hurricane of rhetoric left the readers of *Godey's Lady's Book* gasping. It had never occurred to them or to Louis Godey, either, that its chaste pages were a suitable vehicle for anti-slavery propaganda. Had Godey been a large, choleric gentleman with a thick neck, Henry Ward Beecher's crusade against slavery might have ended as suddenly as it began. But as nothing happened to Henry Ward, he began to get up steam in earnest.

The week after Beecher demolished Brother Godey, Henry Clay spoke in support of his Compromise Measures to a Senate so crowded that the *Tribune* correspondent could not get near enough to hear his voice. Considering how much his own tergiversations during the seventy odd years of his life had contributed to the need for a calmness of spirit that now no longer existed, Henry Clay did the best he could. He appealed for concessions by both North and South, "not of principle, but of feeling, of opinion in relation to matters in controversy between them." He was afraid of what might happen to the country if emotion unseated judgment over the slavery issue.

He appealed in vain to Henry Ward Beecher. The whole slavery question was a matter of emotion with him. What opinion he had was rooted in feeling.

"The struggle now going on is a struggle whose depths lie in the organization of society in the North and South respectively; whose causes are planted in the Constitution," he wrote in *The Independent*. "There never was a plainer question for the North. . . . It is her duty to refuse her hand or countenance to slavery where it now exists. . . . If the compromises of the Constitution include requisitions which violate humanity, I will not be bound by them. . . . If my patriotic sires confederated in my behalf that I should maintain that instrument, so I will to the utmost bound of right. But who, with power which even God denies Himself, shall with compact foreordain me to the commission of inhumanity and injustice? I disown the act. I repudiate the obligation. Never while I breathe will I help any official miscreant in his base errand of recapturing a fellow-man for bondage."

It was gallantly, bravely said. Henry Ward Beecher was right. The Fugitive Slave Law was nothing more than the rendering effective, through Federal instead of State operation, of a specific provision of the Constitution of the United States. If slavery was wrong, the Constitution was wrong and ought to be torn up. True, during the five years he had spent on the banks of the Ohio, he had seen many a hunted negro returned to bondage under the Fugitive Slave Law adopted by the Founding Fathers in 1793. While Henry Ward was at Lane, James G. Birney and Salmon P. Chase, single-handed, had fought in vain to save the mulatto girl, Matilda Lawrence, from "a fate worse than death"—and it had been Beecher's friend, William Henry Harrison, who as clerk of the court had signed the papers delivering the girl up to be sold to the highest bidder in the slave mart of New Orleans. Henry Ward Beecher had managed to worry along under the Constitution of the United States for thirty-seven years without outcry.

But in the last fifteen years times had changed—thanks to Birney and Garrison and Wendell Phillips. Public opinion had veered around. Just before Henry Ward Beecher launched his bold pronouncement, Horace Greeley had trumpeted the same sentiment in the columns of the *Tribune*. Henry Ward found himself shouting with the multitude. It was beginning to be a popular pastime in the North to attack slavery, and as the slaves who escaped were only three one-hundredths of one percent of those remaining in bondage, the Fugitive Slave Law was by all odds the safest feature of slavery to assail.

Henry Ward Beecher did not limit himself, however, to the Fugitive Slave Law, passed "without much opposition and with

slight notice" on September 18, 1850. It was the Constitution
of the United States he was bent on overturning, by force and
violence if necessary. It was an immoral instrument, and he, as
a Christian, would not be bound by it:

"As a Christian nation we have a right to interfere in this matter,"
he told the American and Foreign Anti-Slavery Society. "In this
nation the law of Christianity is the only authorized law for all men.
. . . We are not to cease our exertions until the victory is accomplished. I know not how long I may live, but as long as I do live, I
will not, as one man, cease my endeavors or hold my peace unless
the vile monster is driven from the land. Peace! — there shall be
none to the system or its upholders while a fragment of it remains!
Peace! — there shall be none until God in His infinite mercy takes
us from the face of the earth — or the vile stain is removed from
America!"

The voice was Henry Ward Beecher's voice, but the hands
were the hands of Horace Greeley. Nevertheless, for Henry
Ward it was a stroke of genius. Elijah Lovejoy had died for the
faith. Samuel J. May, Samuel H. Cox, William Lloyd Garrison,
James G. Birney, Lewis Tappan, the Grimké sisters and a host
of others had suffered at the hands of mobs. In this distinguished
company Henry Ward Beecher now took his stand, without
pain, without labor.

"He sat down amid the most vociferous applause and waving
of handkerchiefs by the ladies present," recorded *The Independent*.

CHAPTER XIV

NEW YORK

THE wave of popular sentiment against slavery on whose
crest Henry Ward Beecher, under the tutelage of Joshua
Leavitt, now sought to balance himself was the result of no
sudden conversion of the average citizen to a gospel of color-
blind love. As Henry Ward himself said, "for thirty years
everything that has opposed the current of anti-slavery feeling
has been swept down by it." In the relatively few years since
mobs had wrecked the printing presses of Birney and Lovejoy,

it had come to pass that "almost every press in the North is as anti-slavery as those were which mobs demolished." It was none too early for Henry Ward Beecher to fall into step with the marching millions.

Neither were Henry Ward's scathing remarks on the Constitution news to any one. Eight years before, Wendell Phillips had cursed the Constitution in Faneuil Hall, and only the year previous in the Broadway Tabernacle under Henry Ward's very nose, the American Anti-Slavery Society headed by Phillips, Garrison and Theodore Parker, had adopted Edmund Quincy's resolution declaring for "no union with slave-holders, either religiously or politically." Henry Ward had come a long way in the seven years since he ridiculed the Abolitionists that Fourth of July in Lawrenceburgh. But for the life of him he could not go as far as Garrison and Phillips and Parker. Nor, indeed, did his mentor, Joshua Leavitt, ask that he should. For Leavitt was twenty years older than Henry Ward and belonged to the right-wing anti-slavery group, in whose meetings no one tore up the Constitution. Quite to the contrary, they believed slavery could be abolished through the Constitution — they had a child-like faith that there was somehow a magic in political action that could conjure economic realities.

Yet in his heart of hearts, Henry Ward Beecher envied the younger men their intrepidity, their intransigeance, their intemperance of phrase and act. And when that doughty sporting-house proprietor, Captain Isaiah Rynders, with his gang of Bowery b'hoys, drove Wendell Phillips from the stage of the Broadway Tabernacle, Henry Ward bestirred himself to get Phillips the use of Plymouth Church, and in person introduced the speaker. But as he had done in the case of the Birney riots in Cincinnati he was very careful now, also, to make clear to the audience that his action was solely in the interest of free speech, not agreement with Phillips' views. Writing to Oliver Johnson, later, however, there creeps into his letter a pathetic longing to be as sure of himself, as serenely conscious of righteousness, as this man, hardly older than he, who had been so long in the thick of things:

"I was amazed at the unagitated Agitator — so calm, so fearless, so incisive — every word a bullet. I never heard a more effective speech than Mr. Phillips' that night. He seemed inspired, and played with his audience (turbulent, of course) as Gulliver might with the Lilliputians. He had the dignity of Pitt, the vigor of Fox, the wit of Sheridan, the satire of Junius — and a grace and music all his own."

It was just before Henry Ward told the more conservative American and Foreign Anti-Slavery Society that "every minister that does do his duty must boldly declare and teach that the system of slavery is accursed of God and man," amid the unbridled enthusiasm of the Chautauqua salute, that Hattie Beecher Stowe turned up in Brooklyn. She brought her three babies (and another coming), on her way from Cincinnati to Bowdoin, where Calvin Stowe had just been made a professor. Harassed as usual for money, Hattie was not a little envious of Henry Ward's good fortune:

"Henry's people are more than ever in love with him, and have raised his salary to $3,300, and given him a beautiful horse and carriage worth $600,"

she writes — which is about as near accuracy as Hattie ever comes. Poor dear, desperately hoping by her writing to raise the combined resources of the Stowes to $1,700, she lopped off a little from Henry's income!

Henry was more than prosperous. Plymouth Church paid him $3,500, and besides there were his contributions to *The Independent*, his royalties from the "Lectures to Young Men" (of which new and enlarged editions were in preparation), as well as a more than occasional fifty dollars and expenses for a lecture. Eunice was, at last, able to hire all the servants she wanted to. She had her own bank account and paid all the household bills out of it herself. But *The Independent*, the increasing calls for Henry Ward to speak on divers occasions, the rapidity with which his church was growing, the expanding circle of his prominence — these were taking him away from his wife and that home on which she now staked everything to hold her husband to her. She began to look back upon the trials of Indiana with something akin to regret. "With all these discomforts, I had a far more thorough knowledge of Mr. Beecher's inner life, his thoughts and feelings, than I ever had after we came East," she says, pathetically. "When I got here to Brooklyn the public began to take my husband away from me. His study was no longer in the house but in the church. And when he went out, I used to gasp for breath, and my eyes would fill with tears, for it seemed to me as if we had quarreled."

It was true. The days when she had knelt at her husband's feet while he read her what he had written were gone. She was forty now — and forty in that day was not youth. There was more than a chuckle in the incident that had occurred on the trip East from Indianapolis in the Spring of 1847.

Then Eunice was making the most of her ill-health to fortify Henry Ward in his wavering purpose to seek a new field in the East. At every stop, he had to tumble out and fetch her something, while she complained to all and sundry of her sufferings. An old woman fellow passenger essayed to comfort her:

"Cheer up, my dear madam," she said, patting Eunice's hand. "Surely whatever may be your trials, you have cause for great thankfulness to God, who has given you such a kind and attentive son."

Eunice had hated her hard, unyielding father; but daily she grew more like him. Already her features were taking on that granite sternness they were to wear for forty-five years. There was no nonsense about her, but a good deal of nonsense about Henry Ward, she felt — his sentimentalism and its obverse, his boisterous gayety; the facile tears; the horse-play and the crude, sometimes almost vulgar, humor — and above all, the amazing, incomprehensible effect of all this upon vast audiences of otherwise sensible people, strait-laced in their suppressions, whose sole emotional outlet seemed to be the sobs and the laughter Henry Ward knew so well how to evoke. Eunice found all of this very childish in his audiences, and none too good for Henry Ward, either. To her, he was already too sensitive, too easily moved — vain, pleasure-loving, tender, sensuous — essentially a child still. She must mother and protect him. But how was she to fend for him, if he were constantly being taken away from her by a thousand enterprises that flattered his vanity and stimulated his ambition?

It was into this domestic struggle, just beginning to be acute, that Hattie dropped, with all her own incurable romanticism, her sentimentality unashamed, her extravagant rebellions against the inhibitions of their common childhood. It was an emotional debauch for both Hattie and her brother in which Eunice saw all she had been seeking to shore up during the three years since they had come to Brooklyn — of balance and sturdy, ground-gripping sensibleness — swept away. Hattie left, all attuned to receive from Edward Beecher, in Boston, the impetus to "write something that would make this whole nation feel what an accursed thing slavery is." Henry Ward remained, to attack slavery with new flights of sentimentality:

"There is no sensual vice which we are taught to abhor, which Slavery does not monstrously engender," he wrote in *The Independent*, May 23, 1850. "Among freemen, the road of honor lies *away* from animal passion, from sensation, towards Conscience, Hope, Love and Spiritual Faith. But Slavery sharply turns the wretch downward and teaches and compels him to evolve the task of life from such motives as are common to him with the ox, the ass, and the dog. The slave's pleasures are his appetites. His motives are, almost of necessity, those which religion most earnestly dehorts us. . . . This vast abomination which seethes and smokes in our midst; which is enervating and demoralizing the white by the oppression of the black; in which adultery, fornication and concubinage exist, that in comparison with it, a Turkish harem is a cradle of virgin purity . . . in this huge, infernal system is the destruction of men, soul and body."

With which parting shot, Henry Ward went abroad for the summer.

In Europe he saw Art for the first time. Music he had already discovered, even before the day of Martha Sawyer, in Lawrenceburgh. In Indianapolis, congregational singing had been as essentially a part of the effect he achieved by his preaching as costume and stage setting to a play. It had been more than that, even. For music furnished the channel for his own emotional release. It was with heart swollen by the sensuality of melody that he stepped forward to preach his most affecting sermons; and at their end, when in direct hortation he could twist the screws no tighter without risk of bathos, he swept on into prayer and let himself go, swung his hearers into an emotional ecstasy — and then floated them safely back to earth again on the wings of music.

Art naturally was more personal — it could hardly become a tool of his trade and, so, commonplace. As even so far back as Mount Pleasant he had raised flowers to satisfy his sense-hunger, so now, in the galleries of London and Paris he clutched at a gratification to be had of painting, and readjusted in his own mind the Puritan barriers to its enjoyment. It had been simple enough with music: congregational singing after all was worship, and so, desirable. With sacred painting, a similar adjustment was possible. But what was he to say in the face of Rubens' voluptuous nudes whose very themes were pagan? He could not approve, of course — found the "women not alone plump, but fat," and made his comment that Rubens

"was twice married, and his *second* wife he seems to have loved entirely, as she is forced into almost every picture which contains a female face. . . . In the abduction of the Sabine women, a fine Roman has had the luck to get *his* wife, the finest woman of the crowd. . . . This fondness for his wife is amiable enough, but it redounds to the credit of his heart more than to the fertility of his fancy. I soon am tired of his women,"

he adds, and protests that his favorite artist was the sentimental Sir David Wilkie — a story in every picture. But it is to Rubens that he devotes most space.

On his return voyage from England, Henry Ward launched into another of those impassioned and futile controversies which seemed to intoxicate him as theological battles delighted Lyman Beecher. The ship on which he sailed, being a British vessel, held Sunday services according to the rite of the Church of England. Henry Ward wanted a service of his own. It was not permitted. No sooner was he on dry land, therefore, than he fell afoul of Mr. Cunard (who had been a passenger) in the columns of *The Independent*. In sheer self-defense, Mr. Cunard intimated that the reverend gentleman was not altogether truthful. Instantly, Henry Ward was off to a counter-attack:

"While my principles forbid me to employ falsehood, yet if I should attempt it, I should conscientiously endeavor to lie well," he says. "What I have said will be very much to the personal prejudice and to the damage of the reputation of your steamers. Why, then, if the door is open, do you not, if I am a false witness, convict me of it? I stand ready to prove whatever I have said before the courts of my country."

Twenty years later there were those who recalled how sharply Henry Ward Beecher had indicated recourse to the courts as the only sufficient defense against slander.

Henry Ward had not been back in the United States a week when the Fugitive Slave Law became effective, and James Hamlet, a negro, was promptly arrested under its provisions in New

York and taken to Baltimore. Immediately, Beecher was to the fore with an account of "The Fugitive Slave Bill at Its Work." It was a bit premature, of course. But that did not deter Henry Ward Beecher. As one reads his articles, as they follow one another in *The Independent*, visions rise of the roads from the South congested with escaping blacks, jostled by long lines of United States marshals dragging their shrieking victims back to bondage.

As a matter of fact, the new Fugitive Slave Law was not conspicuously successful. Public opinion, on the whole, experienced not so much indignation as a tremendous relief over the adoption of the Compromise Measures. In Boston a salute of an hundred guns celebrated the conjuring of any further danger of a split in the Union. In New York ten thousand people called a mass meeting at Castle Garden to approve the action of Congress. Life proceeded without discernible dislocation. Zachary Taylor died and was buried, with a funeral procession five miles long attended by a quarter of a million people. Mrs. Amelia J. Bloomer, "a quiet, domestic, religious woman" of Homer, New York, designed a costume for women that set the whole world (outside of Mohammedan countries) rocking with laughter. It consisted of a skirt reaching slightly below the knees under which pantaloons came down to and were gathered in at the ankles. Henry Ward Beecher approved the idea — but only for country wear. Jenny Lind arrived, and Barnum sold the seats for her first concert for $30,000 — at auction, just like the pews of Plymouth Church. The Rev. John Hughes was made Roman Catholic Archbishop of New York, and the seeds of the Know-Nothing movement — native, white, nordic, Protestant, one hundred percent American — began to sprout.

To Henry Ward Beecher all of these activities were as nothing. After twenty years of mental anguish, he had found at last a formula that took care of the slavery problem, and neither Congress nor any one else was going to send him back to his doubts. It was probably at this period that, according to Hattie Stowe, he rode till midnight through a blinding snow storm to meet his sister at Brunswick, Maine, and talked till morning of "what we could do to make headway against the horrid cruelties that were being practised against the defenceless blacks." Hattie's unsubstantiated account of the conference is hardly evidence that it took place — she could never resist the dramatic. In any event, nothing appears to have come of it — the horrid cruelties had being going on quite a while. They continued quite a while longer.

"Henry told me that he meant to fight that battle in New York; that he would have a church that would stand by him to resist the tyrannic dictation of Southern slaveholders," Hattie continues. "I said: 'I, too, have begun to do something; I have begun a story, trying to set forth the sufferings and wrongs of the slaves.' 'That's right, Hattie,' he said; 'finish it, and I will scatter it thick as the leaves of Vallombrosa.' "

Thus encouraged, Hattie did finish "Uncle Tom's Cabin," and it was duly published serially in the *National Era* of Washington, under the editorship of that same Dr. Gamaliel Bailey who, fifteen years previously, had edited *The Philanthropist* for James G. Birney, in Cincinnati. But neither Hattie nor Henry Ward Beecher knew him then — he was looked upon as an Abolitionist.

Henry Ward displayed very little interest in his sister's project to "write something that would make this whole nation feel what an accursed thing slavery is." Indeed, he did not even read "Uncle Tom's Cabin" until over a year after it appeared, and then only because everybody else had read it. He was intent upon his own personal adjustment of the slavery evil.

Plymouth Church did not worry him. Its members were largely of New England stock, opposed to slavery both by education and conviction. Besides, he rather avoided slavery as a topic in the pulpit at this period — out of eighty sermons only one touched the subject, and that was confined to "the duty of Christians to fugitive slaves." It was in *The Independent* that Henry Ward Beecher developed his peculiar solution of the slave problem; and his articles in *The Independent* were signed only by an asterisk.

The extreme Abolitionists he rejected outright. He regarded Garrison as "one of the most unfortunate of all leaders for the best development of anti-slavery feeling." Garrison, Beecher thought, lacked that "conciliation, good-natured benevolence, or even a certain popular mirthfulness" which he himself possessed and proposed to put to use. The occasion, he felt, required "a noble soul, deeply and truly benevolent." Benevolence is the word he uses over and over again. He refuses to denounce slave-holding as a sin *per se*, and longs to see a spirit of forbearance among anti-slavery men. Love is his remedy for slavery—love and Christian piety. "Let those who desire to emancipate the slave remember that there lives an Emancipator who for more than four thousand years was engaged in this very work and with unfailing success," he reminds the more ardent. Just how freedom of that kind would help the four million negroes then in bondage is far from clear; but Henry Ward cannot lose "confidence in the power of God's truth to overthrow an evil even so gigantic as that of slavery."

"We will not dispute about subtle questions of the right or wrong of slavery *per se*," he writes in *The Independent* in 1852. "If ever there was a solemn call laid upon a church, we feel that it is a call of God to arise, and (we will not say now to abolish Slavery, since that might seem too much,) bring the truth of the gospel to bear upon the community, until a change is effected in the legislation, which is now a shame to Christianity, and a disgrace to the very name of just laws."

In an address to the American Anti-Slavery Society on May 12, 1853, with William Lloyd Garrison presiding and all the left-wing Abolitionists sitting on the platform, he rebukes them for meddling in God's business:

"My earnest desire is that slavery may be destroyed by the manifest power of Christianity. If it were given me to choose whether it should be destroyed in fifty years by selfish commercial influences, or, standing for seventy-five years, be then the spirit and trophy of Christ, I had rather let it linger twenty-five years more, that God may be honored, and not mammon, in the destruction of it."

And when Horace Greeley, not a little nonplussed by this attitude, suggested in *The Tribune* that for his part he would

"wish to take the sense of *those in bondage* before agreeing to the twenty-five years' postponement for the glory of Christianity. If *they* are willing to endure . . . till 1885 in order that Christianity might reap the glory of its [slavery's] overthrow, why then we should think about it. . . ."

Henry Ward Beecher was not to be shaken. He replied to Greeley at once:

"Our highest and strongest reason for seeking justice among men is *not* the benefit to men themselves. . . . I believe my own aspirations having a base in my natural faculties, to be influenced and directed by Christ's spirit. The mingled affection and adoration which I feel for him is the strongest feeling that I know. Whether I will or not, whether it be a phantasy or a sober sentiment, the fact is the same nevertheless, that that which will give pleasure to Christ's heart and bring to my consciousness a smile of gladness on His face in behalf of my endeavor, is incalculably more to me than any other motive. I would work for the slave for his own sake, but I am sure that I would work ten times as earnestly for the slave for Christ's sake. . . . This sentiment does not spring from any indifference to the slave, but from a yet greater sympathy with Christ Jesus — the slave's only hope, my only hope, the Saviour of the world!"

As for just how slavery was to be ended to the greater glory of God, Henry Ward knew that, too:

"Our policy for the future is plain. All the natural laws of God are warring upon slavery. We have only to let the process go on. Let slavery alone. . . . We do not ask to interfere with the internal policy of a single State by Congressional enactments; we will not ask to take one guarantee from the institution. We only ask that a line be drawn about it; that an insuperable bank be cast up; that it be fixed and forever settled that slavery must find no new sources, new fields, new prerogatives, but that it must abide in its place, subject to all the legitimate changes which will be brought upon it by the spirit of a nation essentially democratic. . . . Time is her enemy. Liberty will, if let alone, always be a match for oppression."

But Frederick Douglass, who had been a slave himself, was unimpressed by this high-sounding rhetoric.

"With a good cow-hide, I could take all that out of Mr. Beecher in five minutes," he said.

CHAPTER XV

POISED

THE Kansas-Nebraska Bill was not the product of one of the South's best minds. Stephen Arnold Douglas, its author, was what was known in that day as a Northern man with Southern principles — that is to say, a practical politician. Franklin Pierce, another of the same kind, had been elected President by an overwhelming majority in as dull a campaign as the country had seen for many a day. The real power in Washington was the handsome Senator from Mississippi, now Secretary of War — Jefferson Davis, son-in-law of the late President Taylor. The one substantial benefit accruing from Pierce's election had been to the cause of American letters: the President's old college mate, Nathaniel Hawthorne, was made Consul at Liverpool, where he could write "The Marble Faun" in peace.

"The nation," said Abraham Lincoln, "has passed its peril."

There were, of course, all manner of interesting things going on, even before the Kansas struggle reached a crisis. Crinoline appeared to have come to stay, to the immense discomfort of passengers on the New York busses. Wire hoops were not as generally worn as is supposed; they were cumbersome and if inadroitly handled apt to surprise both wearer and bystander. But by wearing a dozen or more starched and flounced petticoats the same general effect was achieved with more certain modesty. *The Independent* said crinoline was "tasteful, elegant, and healthy. Besides, the industrial interests involved in skirt manufacture are immense." Large straw hats with ostrich plumes went with the crinoline, and high laced boots long enough to reach well up the calf of the leg, whose shape they were supposed to set off to advantage. Gentlemen varied the monotony of previous styles mostly by the form and luxuriance of their whiskers. Thackeray visited the United States as the first of a still unbroken line of British literary lecturers, and Rachel, the French tragédienne, blazed a trail Sarah Bernhardt was to tread into a boulevard.

Louis Kossuth arrived on an American warship, to raise funds for a revolution in Hungary; but most of the money raised went for public dinners and meetings. He spoke in Plymouth Church — at $5 a ticket. Fanny Wright, the suffragist, sued her husband for divorce, and immediately the godly saw in the fact evidence of the depths to which women who bobbed their hair would sink. Adelina Patti made her début at Niblo's Garden, at the advanced age of eight, and Lola Montez, Countess of Lansfeldt, an Irish girl with a Spanish name and a Tyrolean costume, set New York by the ears with the suggestiveness of her dancing and the candor of her conduct. Phineas T. Barnum opened a theater of "moral domestic drama" played by E. A. Sothern; he had the astuteness to call his theater a "Lecture Room," so church members who regarded theaters as immoral could attend. James H. Hackett became impresario of Italian Opera at the Academy of Music; the public, however, found Fourteenth Street rather too far up town. But the real sensation of the day was "Uncle Tom's Cabin," at the National Theater, embarked on a run of two hundred successive nights.

Hattie's triumph as a dramatist — *The Independent* pronounced St. Clair the greatest tragic figure in English literature since Hamlet — failed to budge her brother from his stand on the stage:

"It is notorious that the Theatre is the *door* to all the sinks of iniquity. . . . Half the victims of the gallows and the Penitentiary will tell you, that these schools for morals were to them the gate of debauchery, the porch of pollution, the vestibule of the very house of Death,"

he declared. Dion Boucicault wrote protesting against this "passionate exclamation of your intolerance of opinions not your own" and ridiculing Beecher's "rampant virtue" on the subject of the drama. But Henry Ward simply reiterated his belief that the theater was and ever would be "an institution by its nature confirmed as the Arch-minister of vice and the stronghold of Evil." He had never been in one, and he would not step foot in such a place, he said.

Indeed, Henry Ward Beecher scarcely seemed content unless engaged in acrimonious controversy with some one, from William Cullen Bryant, of the New York *Evening Post*, to John Mitchell, the Irish patriot. In defense of an error of Hattie's in "Uncle Tom's Cabin," he ran twelve solid columns in a single issue of *The Independent*. He flayed unsparingly every one who ventured to differ with him on any subject. His brother Charles finally felt constrained to point out that "railing and vituperation are not mentioned by the Apostle as forming any part of the panoply of God."

But Henry Ward had to externalize his inward struggles somehow, and vilification was, after all, merely the journalistic mode of the day, of which he could quite properly take advantage to let himself go — to get it out of his system, so to speak. And he did. Words intoxicated him, and for all he went on at a great rate about the "bottomless licentiousness" of slavery, under which "every year thousands of women are lashed for obstinate virtue, and tens of thousands robbed of what they have never been taught to prize," he also wrote with simplicity and sweetness of birds and trees and flowers. He loved such things, as a child might, and liked to write about them. But most of all he liked to write (and to talk and to preach, also) about himself. His own reactions to everything from art to the Know-Nothing movement were a constant source of wonderment to him. Something would come up, and immediately he would ask himself: "Now what does Henry Ward Beecher think of that?" Straightway, he would find his own opinion tremendously interesting, and would write it, or say it in public. Then, perhaps, the same matter would bob up again in a week or a month, and again he would go through the same fascinating process, and write or say something further on the subject—as frequently as not quite different to what he had said before.

Once in a while, however, Henry Ward's cock-sureness got him into difficulties. In one instance, he recommended a novel by Solon Richardson of the *Tribune*, rejoicing in the title of "Hot Corn." Immediately, the office of *The Independent* was swamped with protests. It appeared that, in the work in question, "houses of dissipation are opened, their inmates made dramatis personæ, their language and disgusting orgies more or less set forth"—in a word, by no means the sort of book for the parlor table of a religious home. Henry Ward was forced to admit reviewing the novel without reading it. But the incident furnished him opportunity to make a significant confession:

"There are things no man should see, no man should hear, no man should think. There are things a mere contact with defiles like pitch, burns like coals. The monstrous ingenuities of passions, the hideous charms of occult iniquity, strike through the imagination a taint that years cannot clean," he says. "No man can read the reform literature of France, at least not such as Sue, and Sand, issue, and not regret to the day of his death that he ever touched it."

This time, he spoke from knowledge.

From the hour of Hattie's success with "Uncle Tom's Cabin" all the Beechers suddenly became possessed with the itch to publish. Hattie herself emitted books like a barrage—anything bearing the name of Harriet Beecher Stowe sold phenomenally. Catherine Beecher brought out four books in two years, covering hygiene, religion, domestic economy and education, bringing up her literary output to seven books. Edward, in the same time, published two colossal tomes: "The Conflict of the Ages; or The Great Debate on the Moral Relations of God and Man," in 550 pages, and the other, almost as voluminous, a sort of bible for the Know-Nothings entitled "The Papal Conspiracy Exposed" — copiously illustrated. Charles issued, separately, two sermons besides a treatise on spiritualism. Neither was old Lyman Beecher to be outdone by his progeny. He published his "Works," in three volumes. Even Eunice, finally relieved of further child-bearing, penned an anonymous romance of her life in the West in which she vented her spleen on those who had, she felt, been unappreciative in Indianapolis. Henry Ward, in the face of all this Beecher output, was hardly gallant about his wife's modest effort.

"Tell Derby," he said, "if he wants to be fool enough to publish a book written by my wife, to go ahead."

The bookstalls were cluttered with Beecher products, and Henry Ward was not one to be behindhand. He prepared a selection of his *Independent* articles for book publication. But that was not at all the sort of thing he meant to get out. He wanted something that would run into the tens of thousands of copies, like "Uncle Tom's Cabin," and be a lasting monument. Even Henry Ward realized that people were not going to read sermons forever — indeed, they had already stopped reading those of the great Jonathan Edwards. But so long as Christian worship endured, they were not going to stop singing hymns — the older the better. It was an inspiration. He would compile a collection of hymns wide enough in range to be used by any evangelical church. They would be his selection, with an elaborate introduction by Henry Ward Beecher — the "Plymouth Collection." It was a stroke of genius.

No sooner said than done. It cost more than he had anticipated to have music printed, and Brother Bowen had to help out. Charles, too, with his knowledge of music, performed the greater part of the work, and John Zundel, the organist of Plymouth Church, assisted. But it was Henry Ward Beecher's book, just as he wanted it, with the tunes printed right with the words for the first time in history. Henry Ward was enchanted. He sat back and waited for the encomiums.

They did not come. Despite extensive advertising and a warm recommendation of the book from Beecher's own pen, in *The*

Independent, it was received with no enthusiasm. One journal had the temerity to ridicule the use as a religious tune of the air to which "Tippecanoe and Tyler Too," had been sung. The New York *Evangelist* said the collection was better suited for Christy's Minstrels than a church. A great many poked fun at it.

In common with most inveterate jokers, Henry Ward Beecher had no sense of humor where he and his were concerned. He was furious with the criticisms. He clamored that he was the victim of a conspiracy, and beginning with five and a half columns of *The Independent* he ended by devoting the whole front page to his indignation with his critics. He fell upon professional choir singers "whose unwashed lips that all the week sang the disgustful words of glorious music in opera with all the inspiration of vanity and brandy"; and when the son of Dr. Leonard Bacon, one of the editorial board of *The Independent*, had the effrontery to edit a rival hymnal, Beecher rose to almost hysterical heights of resentment and invective.

Henry Ward emerged from this controversy in no very lovely light, when all was said and done. He had sought with peculiar ferocity to ruin the career of young Bacon, who was just entering the ministry and was the son of one of Lyman Beecher's dearest friends. Dr. Bacon, the father, had assisted at Henry Ward's installation at Plymouth Church and was even then a colleague of Beecher's on the very paper in which Henry Ward's attack on his son was printed. As in the Comegys case, Beecher had not hesitated to misrepresent facts to such an extent that he was compelled publicly to retract. He had displayed an almost childish vanity and ill humor. On the whole, the incident was one a young man who had just come to work on the staff of *The Independent*, after a brilliant initiation in journalism under Horace Greeley's eye, might have done well to ponder. The young man's name was Tilton — Theodore Tilton. Beecher had recently married him to Elizabeth Richards, a Sunday School teacher in Plymouth Church and the step-daughter of a judge of the Brooklyn court.

But it was upon the Kansas-Nebraska Bill and the repeal of the Missouri Compromise that Henry Ward Beecher lavished his choicest rhetoric and displayed his greatest enthusiasm. In the logic of Senator Douglas' proposal that if the inhabitants of States had the right to decide whether they wished slavery or not, the inhabitants of public lands about to be erected into Territories should consistently enjoy the same privilege, Henry Ward Beecher had no interest whatever.

"The simple question is: Will you allow the people to legislate for themselves on the question of slavery? Why should you not?" said Douglas. "The legal effect of this bill is neither to legislate slavery into these territories nor out of them, but to leave the people to do as they please."

Now Henry Ward Beecher believed in democracy in theory; but he regarded slavery as a religious matter. People left to themselves, he felt, were inherently vile and could be counted upon to embrace vice every time unless restrained by legal or moral considerations — preferably both. The Missouri Compromise line was just such a legal and moral restraint drawn to save the North from contamination by a system of "animalization of three millions of men in the bosom of a Christian land, under the cover of Democratic institutions." He would as lief consider abolishing the seventh commandment as the Missouri Compromise — to his mind, they served a like end.

"It is notorious," he insisted, "that slavery is maintained for reasons of profit, of politics, of indolence in the whites, and of motives of passion even worse than these."

Beecher was far too late a comer in the anti-slavery campaign to contribute any striking ideas to the discussion, beyond his most recent contention that God would take care of the matter. But even his plea of a higher law than the Constitution, Seward had voiced in the Senate two months before Beecher advanced the same view. Seward heard Beecher preach in 1854. "It was a noble speech — sermon it was not," he said. "He is a man who seems, in going through a discourse of an hour, to act a dozen parts, from the deepest tragic to the broad comic." But Henry Ward Beecher left no intellectual impression whatever on Seward.

With the opening of the Kansas struggle, Beecher came forward with the idea that this renewal of the slavery controversy was certain to end in conflict. But the conceit was Sumner's. Indeed, until Chase, Sumner and Seward had all spoken out in the Senate on the Kansas question, Beecher was still asking himself: "Ought not every minister to speak? . . . If not in the pulpit, then in private?" It was not until he made a trip into New England, and found there every minister already speaking — a monster petition in circulation among the clergy signed, among three thousand others, by Lyman Beecher — that Henry Ward began to feel that in the particular case of Kansas it would not do to leave matters wholly in God's hands:

"At length God seems to have caught the wicked in their own craft," he cries. "It is not in the power of all the men of the North to develop so earnest a feeling against slavery and for liberty as is now finding tongue and giving itself forth all over the North. . . . *For the last time* God has called upon the North. . . . Let the *conscience* of the North settle this question, not her *fears*. God calls us to a religious duty!"

It was the particular form this divine behest took, as Henry Ward interpreted it, that got him into a world of trouble two years later. The Kansas-Nebraska Bill had become law, and the struggle for Kansas was on. A group of colonists were going from New Haven to Kansas, and Henry Ward spoke. "The Northern settlers have gone there with rifles in their hand, which they are determined to use if necessary," he said. He hoped that this group would "want for nothing while you have it in your hands to give it," and quoted: " 'Inasmuch as ye do it unto the least of these, ye do it unto me.' " Promptly, Prof. Silliman of Yale pledged a Sharp's rifle, and the pastor of North Church another — and Henry Ward Beecher pledged Plymouth Church to contribute twenty-five rifles, to promote the just and peaceful settlement of the Kansas issue.

All of Henry Ward Beecher's careful, painstaking effort to maintain a moderate attitude towards slavery went overboard with a bang. Whether he liked it or not, he found himself suddenly classed in the public mind with the extreme Abolitionists. Frivolous people called Sharp's rifles "Beecher's Bibles" and the irreligious dubbed Plymouth Church "the Church of the Holy Rifles." Church folk from one end of the country to the other quoted the sixth chapter of the Gospel according to St. Luke to him, and asked with some asperity how he applied it to his recent course.

It all seemed very unfair to Henry Ward Beecher. The Rev. George B. Cheever and an hundred other ministers he could name had been far more pronounced in their anti-slavery position than he. Occasionally he had been a little exuberant in the way he expressed himself — "We will war it to the knife, and the knife to the hilt!" he had said, once; "America *shall be free!*" But he had never preferred disunion to a continuance of slavery, as did Garrison, Phillips and Parker:

"I cannot reckon myself among those who have advocated disunion, either by policy or from principle," he declared, in Boston. "I never have gone, I cannot go with them."

Beecher's was, in fact, a different approach to the problem. Departing from his conception that the liquidation of slavery was safer in God's hands than in those of the politicians, he arrived, all unconscious of its significance, at a profound truth that the Abolitionists wholly overlooked:

"The policy of the South is not one of vexatious haughtiness. It is a policy the necessity of which springs from the very organization of their society, from the irresistible nature of their industrial system. They cannot help themselves," he maintained. "These events in the South come from a law stronger than volition, from a law which underlies society, and compels its movements."

And elsewhere:

"Many men are prating about the reconstruction of society; but when society improves it is to be the result of that change which comes from growth, not reconstruction," he said. "The change to be wrought in society will never be wrought by man's prescience, but by the elements of society itself. It is to change, but only as the plant changes, when one joint shoots out a higher one."

Unfortunately, this was a view not very clear to Henry Ward Beecher himself at this time, nor indeed for many years. Sentimentality was what the public cried for in the fifties — Alice and Phœbe Cary, Fanny Fern, John B. Gough, Mary J. Holmes — tears, oceans of tears. When Beecher's adventure with the Sharp's rifles raised a storm about his ears, there was one way out for him, and Henry Ward Beecher knew that way better than any one.

Just at that moment, Dr. Storrs of the neighboring Church of the Pilgrims was appealing for funds to purchase the freedom of a slave girl. It was a common practice. In churches all over the country, subscriptions were constantly being solicited for that purpose. One took the minister's word for the existence of the slave in question.

But Henry Ward Beecher had an inspiration. He sent to Staunton, Virginia, for a beautiful mulatto girl around twenty, who was, he said, "to be sold by her own father [white] to go South — for what purpose you can imagine when you see her." Afterwards, there was some question of the authenticity of this story; but it served its purpose. Beecher led her up to stand beside him on the broad platform of Plymouth pulpit, almost surrounded by the gaping throng, dressed from head to foot in virginal white. He bade the girl loose her hair, and it fell in shining waves to the floor. And then Henry Ward Beecher read to his congregation from that very chapter of St. Luke that had been cited against him in the matter of the rifles — "Give, and it shall be given unto you; good measure, pressed down, and shaken together, and running over . . ."

"How much for her?" he cried, imitating the rasping voice of a slave auctioneer. "Will you allow this praying woman to go back to meet the fate for which her father sold her? If not, who bids? Who bids?"

Eunice Beecher tells what followed:

"Tears of pity and indignation streamed from eyes unused to weeping. Women became hysterical; men were almost beside themselves. For half an hour money was heaped into the contribution boxes, while those to whom the baskets seemed too slow in coming, threw coin and banknotes upon the pulpit. Women took off their jewelry and put it into the baskets. Rings, bracelets, brooches, piled one upon the other. Men unfastened their watches and handed them to the ushers. . . ."

And all the while, Beecher tore at the hearts of his audience with his appeal. He brought forth heavy iron slave-shackles, cast them on the floor before him and trampled them under foot in a frenzy of righteous wrath, while Sarah cowered beside him, her glorious hair half-concealing her. She was freed, of course. In time, she went to live near her benefactor at Beecher's country place, at Peekskill, for the remainder of her days. She never married.

Henry Ward Beecher heard no more of Sharp's rifles.

For all the importance his family and friends — and even Henry Ward himself — came to give to these activities of his, in later years when the anti-slavery rôle had proved the heroic one, they were distinctly secondary to Henry Ward Beecher at the time. Primarily, he was a preacher. As such he was known among his contemporaries, and it was not until many years later that he began to regard himself as anything else. At the close of his first decade in Brooklyn, Plymouth Church had 1,241 members who paid $16,254 a year to hear Henry Ward Beecher. Some 2,000 applicants could secure no pews.

It was a stupendous achievement, not by any means solely accounted for on the ground that Brooklyn at that time was scantily supplied with churches. Neither was it hard pastoral labor — he was incurably indolent; nor a genius for organization — he was incredibly disorderly. But Henry Ward Beecher was possessed of limitless energy that threw him into countless personal contacts every day of his life. And to each of these he brought a fountain of inexhaustible emotionalism from which he poured out sympathy, sentiment, self-revelation, benevolence, tenderness, and what he called love, without stint.

His day began at six, with visitors even before breakfast: people to marry, people to bury — "a young man from the country wishes your name on a circular for a school. A young woman is failing in health by confinement to sewing; does not know what to do; cannot go away to the country; does not wish charity . . . While you are attending to these, the bell is active, and other persons arrive to take the places of those that go . . ." So he describes it. He speaks of "his ten thousand services to individuals, to the unfriended, the tempted, the poor, the afflicted, the perplexed; the giving of counsel to the weak, encouragement to the desponding; the taking care of men, one by one . . ." Henry Ward Beecher could afford to smile at Horace Greeley's suggestion that he be elected to Congress. He reached far more people in a more effective way, and with a more personal fame to himself, than ever he could have done in Washington.

Not that Henry Ward was indifferent to politics, even in this early day. He was always dabbling in politics. He even commended Mayor Fernando Wood for his administration of New York — the same Fernando Wood who, said Philip Hone (once Mayor himself), "ought to be on the rolls of the State Prison" — as amazing a political adventurer as ever rose from keeping a three-cent grog shop. Henry Ward used to drop into Windust's restaurant, near the office of *The Independent*, where he would dine with Wood and Forrest, the actor. He liked Fernando Wood, as he had liked Elijah Alvord, the Indianapolis gambler —and so far as Henry Ward Beecher was concerned, that ended the matter. He formed his likes and dislikes in that passionate way.

So, also, did Eunice. But while Henry Ward had many likes and few dislikes, with Eunice it was the other way around. Just now she was really ill. She had ended her period of child-bearing in a blaze of glory with two pairs of twins, but had lost three of them. They were moving into a great, stone house, requiring more domestic management than she felt capable of, and not only had old Lyman Beecher come to live with them, with his third wife, but the rest of Henry Ward's family and her own relatives as well were constantly camping on them. William Beecher wanted his daughter given the advantage of a season in the East—at Henry's, of course. The house on Columbia Heights was a sort of caravanserai, and Eunice Beecher hated it. She hated the lecture trips that took her husband out of her sight for days and weeks. She hated and feared the adulation he was receiving more and more. And most of all she was afraid of the new friends he was making, among people of radical views —she who embodied all the conservatism of a small New England village. *The Independent* had actually endorsed woman suffrage, and while Henry Ward had not yet done anything his wife considered so abandoned, he had called the horrid Bloomer costume "the only dress that is *really* decent."

Eunice Beecher knew very well that Henry Ward never got any such ideas as that at home. She suspected that he got some of them from that brilliant young assistant managing editor of *The Independent*, with whom Henry Ward was beginning to spend so much time. Eunice did not trust that fellow, Tilton— he was too good-looking and too self-sufficient to be a really moral character. Besides, he wrote poetry.

Indeed, poor Eunice sensed very strongly that her husband was getting out beyond his depth. She knew how wholly his equipment was emotional—and in that part of his life she no longer played any rôle. She knew, moreover, how impulsively he was apt to espouse any cause that appealed to his sentimentality, and how passionately to prosecute it. She had little confidence in that saving quality of shrewdness that he had of his

Connecticut forebears. She had never yet seen it save him from any of his follies — but that, perhaps, was because she saw from inside.

As Eunice Beecher's hold upon her husband slipped, he was left groping hungrily for the emotional stimulus he must have, or collapse. His emotionalism was all he had, and it was not indefinitely self-renewing. There was something poignantly personal in his plea in *The Independent* for those whose

"great and peculiar need is a Christ who knows all their weaknesses of disposition without feeling disgust, who knows all their sins without bitterness; who knows their faults and foibles without contempt; who knows their practical, daily difficulties, their cares, their family troubles, their business perplexities, and who knows just how all these things, acting on the peculiar temperament which each possesses, hinders their piety, mars their joy, fills them with doubts, and afflicts them with burdens."

If ever a body needed just that, it was Henry Ward Beecher at this moment. He needed it far more than ever he had in those days almost twenty years back when, suddenly called upon to face the future, he had fled to West Sutton to marry Eunice Bullard. For now he had climbed higher. Now he was launched upon enterprises whose infinite ramifications he did not see, and could not have grasped had he seen them. All about him were the jealousies any success engenders. All about him, too, were those to whom Henry Ward Beecher and Plymouth Church were a profitable investment, solicitous for their capital — those who had been wounded by the passionate intemperance of his slashing attacks — those who, it may be quite honestly, believed that any such exalted emotionalism, any such transcendental sentimentality as Henry Ward Beecher purveyed, was a force for danger, not development.

Against all of these he had only two weapons: what he called "benevolence" — the geniality that for all its disarming, boyish quality somehow generally managed to win through to what he wanted; and, in reserve always but always there, the shrewd, hard, common sense of his New England fathers.

With these as armor, Henry Ward Beecher climbed at last to the pinnacle and surveyed the world.

It was lonely up there, he thought.

Part IV: Spring Tide

"This church [Plymouth Church] is simply the most characteristic thing of America. If I had a foreigner in charge to whom I wished to reveal this country, I would like to push him in, hand him over to one of the brethren who perform the arduous duty of providing seats for visitors, and say to him: 'There, stranger, you have arrived; *this* is the United States. The New Testament, Plymouth Rock, and the Fourth of July — this is what they have brought us to!'"

JAMES PARTON

CHAPTER XVI

1860

THEODORE TILTON was not quite twenty-one when the Rev. George B. Cheever persuaded him to come to the staff of *The Independent*. While still in his teens he had been a reporter for the *Tribune*, where Horace Greeley thought highly of him. On leaving the College of the City of New York, he went to work on *The Churchman*, then the New York *Observer*; but he left the *Observer* because he did not like its equivocal attitude towards slavery. "No youngster on the New York press gave finer promise of a brilliant and useful career than Theodore Tilton," says a contemporary.

"He had been early trained to sympathy with the Abolitionists, who, in his childhood, were persecuted and abused by the pro-slavery leaders in both political parties; and the fiery eloquence of Dr. Cheever, the leader, for many years, of the religious anti-slavery party in New York, had made a deep impression on the pale, thoughtful, freedom-loving lad. He longed to share in their trials and triumphs, and while yet a child, ranged himself with them, to take his share of the contempt, insult, and obloquy which greeted them on all occasions, and his share also of the coming glory and honor, which ever his boyish vision foresaw for them in the speedy future.

"What was at first, perhaps, only the sympathy of a sensitive boy, abhorring oppression, injustice, and wrong, soon came to be

one of the deepest convictions of his nature; and it is not surprising
that though his friends were desirous that he should qualify himself to enter the ministry in the Congregational church, he should
have preferred the career of a journalist."

Tilton's advent on *The Independent* made a very marked difference indeed in the paper. Joshua Leavitt, to whom the bulk
of the actual editorial work fell, was what Henry Ward Beecher
called "venerable" by now, and a journal that, in five years, had
become "the largest religious paper in the world" (or so it
boasted) was badly in need of young blood.

It was the day of the Weekly Family Newspaper of a distinct
religious cast. De Tocqueville marveled at the tremendous rôle
played by church affiliation in the United States — not just socially, but even commercially. In Indianapolis, Henry Ward
Beecher had led a regular crusade against turning the Sabbath
into a "day of *mere* bodily rest." Church going, he contended,
was obligatory on decent folk; certainly neither railway trains
nor street cars should be allowed to run on Sunday. He urged
prohibition with a plenary right of search and seizure in the en-
forcing authorities:

"We ask that liquor dealers and their dwellings be treated as we
treat counterfeiters," he said. "We propose to treat men who keep,
for illegal and criminal traffic, the implements of death to the citizen [meaning bootleg liquor] just as, in time of war, we would
treat those suspected of treasonable intercourse with the enemy."

He considered stock brokers dangerous and bankers possessed
of too much power:

"The General's sword, the Marshal's truncheon, the King's
crown, are not the strongest things. The world's strength lies in
the million hands of producers and exchangers. Power has shifted.
No matter who reigns — the *Merchant* reigns. No matter what the
form of government is, the power of the world is in the hands of
the people. The Kings are weaker than the Bankers. War cannot
convulse the world — but Capital can."

As for card playing and betting on the races he argued that
"professional gambling can be regarded as nothing less than a
crime . . . to rank with thefts, assassinations and murders."

These ambitious efforts to expand the decalogue represented
no rare point of view. Solid, respectable citizens shared this
view, or kept their dissent to themselves. It was therefore small

wonder that a religious journal reflecting this somewhat restrained outlook on life should gather a tremendous circulation
in a relatively short time; and not surprising, either, that a young
man of the promising talents of Theodore Tilton should prefer
religious journalism to the coarse vulgarity of the daily press.
The latter, according to Henry Ward, was devoted to

"reporting the prurient details of divorce cases at disgusting length,
repetitious columns of news from the prize fighter's ring, the police court reports, the details of salacious scandal, and the hateful
histories of dissipated life, in which men that are rich, no one
knows how, fester in loathsome vices and break forth in disgrace-
ful crimes."

It is difficult for readers, nowadays, to visualize newspapers of
this character.

There were also practical reasons why Henry Ward found
young Tilton so valuable a friend. Tilton was well known in
newspaper offices, and no one better than Henry Ward Beecher
knew the importance of publicity. What with his auctions of
slave girls, his "Beecher's Bibles," his acrimonious controversies
with a score of public men (including the New York City
Council for serving champagne at a dinner), and his relationship
to the author of "Uncle Tom's Cabin," Henry Ward had not
done so badly in keeping in the public eye. But he had reached
the point where he really needed a first-class publicity man who
could put his heart into the job. Theodore Tilton was precisely
that.

Indeed, he was more than that. For Theodore Tilton believed
in Henry Ward Beecher as he did in God. Never had Henry
Ward been more completely successful in carrying out his early
resolve "to get the young to love me" than with this glorious
young giant with his shock of golden hair, his great, appealing
blue eyes, his poetic intensity, his religious fervor—and his
hero-worship of Henry Ward Beecher.

"From my boyhood up, you have been to me what no other man
has been—what no other man can be. While I was a student, the
influence of your mind on mine was greater than all books and all
teachers," Tilton wrote Beecher, several years after their intimacy
began. "You are my minister, teacher, father, brother, friend, companion. The debt I owe you I can never pay. My religious life;
my intellectual development; my open door of opportunity for

labor; my public reputation; all these, my dear friend, I owe in so great a degree to your own kindness that my gratitude cannot be written in words, but must be expressed only in love."

It was the spontaneous and generous expression of a very young man towards one twenty-two years his senior who had overwhelmed him by the gift of an unreserved intimacy.

The obligation was by no means all on the side of Theodore Tilton. Hitherto, the columns of *The Independent* had been filled with matter by Beecher; now, in addition, there began to appear items about Beecher and about Plymouth Church, from the pen of a worshipful admirer. It was Tilton who arranged for the publication of Beecher's sermons in *The Independent*, thus not only adding greatly to Henry Ward's income but at a single stroke increasing his audience from the three thousand who could attend Plymouth Church to the more than 100,000 readers of *The Independent*. Before Tilton came to *The Independent*, the paper was not only religious but sectarian, its contributors clergymen not widely known outside church circles. And it lost money.

Theodore Tilton revolutionized all that. With astounding rapidity he developed into one of the really great editors of the country. Elizabeth Barrett Browning, Kossuth, Whittier, Greeley, Bayard Taylor, Seward, James Russell Lowell, Garrison, Wendell Phillips, Francis Lieber and William M. Evarts became contributors. *The Independent* coined money. Almost over night, Henry Ward Beecher's articles were appearing cheek by jowl with the work of the foremost writers of the day. The effect on his fame and his personal fortunes was incalculable. The door of Robert Bonner's *Ledger*, with its million readers and the colossal advertising Bonner gave his writers and the fabulous sums he paid them, was suddenly opened to Beecher.

It was more than opportunity for Henry Ward Beecher — it was financial salvation. He had gone deeply into debt to purchase his new house. The panic of 1857 pushed him to the wall. Everything he owned was mortgaged, and he was at his wit's end to save himself from ruin. When Bonner learned of his embarrassment, he presented Beecher with $10,000 in cash, on the sole condition that Henry Ward would never reveal the gift. It was Eunice who told.

It was not just in the field of journalism that Theodore Tilton

squired his hero. In Plymouth Church he acted as superintendent of the Sunday School and a leading figure in the younger
generation upon whom the future of the church must, of
course, rest. Tilton, Bowen and Beecher came to be known as
"the Trinity of Plymouth Church" — there were even those in
the communion who saw in Tilton's handsome, ascetic features
and golden locks a resemblance to the Savior.

Indeed, in some such guise this brilliant, adoring young man
must have come to the hungering emotionalism of Henry Ward
Beecher. For, save for such brief excursions into the field of
politics as his support of Frémont in the campaign of 1856,
Henry Ward was wholly absorbed in the throes of a terrible
inner struggle. For Frémont, he could do little. Lyman and Edward Beecher (and even Henry Ward in his younger days) had
worked a mischief with their attacks on the Roman Catholic
church which now came home to roost. Frémont was not a
Catholic, but he was said — and widely believed — to be one.
All that Henry Ward could do could not now mend the damage
the Beechers and their like had done in rousing unreasoning
terror of Catholic dominance.

It was neither by politics nor the rapidly approaching crisis
in respect of slavery that Henry Ward Beecher was profoundly
stirred towards the close of the fifties. It was the imminent peril
of his own soul. With that amazing lack of reticence with which
he made pulpit capital of every emotion he had ever experienced since the death of his mother, Henry Ward Beecher
stated his own domestic problem:

"Domestic unhappiness comes from the fact that people do not
know or do not enough recognize the peculiarities of each other's
natures. They expect impossible things of each other. If a flaming
demonstrative nature and a cool, undemonstrative nature come together, neither of whom understands or makes allowance for the
peculiarities of the other, there can hardly fail of being unhappiness."

Certainly no more flaming, demonstrative nature than that of
Henry Ward Beecher ever came into contact with a cooler, less
demonstrative one than that of Eunice! Even in his children,
poor Henry Ward had not that for which his heart cried out:

"We carry our children as heavy burdens," he wrote; "their
faults, their excesses, their temper or indolence, or quarrelsome-

ness, seem to us intolerable. We never look so homely as when we see our own deformities in our children."

Tottering on the verge of fall, Henry Ward became incoherent in his self-revelation:

"How many noble natures gave over to celibacy and virginity the wondrous treasures of multitudinous affections. And when the periods of heart-swellings, in hours when the secret tide set in upon men from the eternal ocean, and carried out upon mighty longings and yearnings, toward God, before whom they poured forth in mingled sobs and words those affections which were meant to be eased in the relations of life, but which hindered and choked, found tumultuous vent in mighty prayer to God!"

It was to God that now he took those perilous longings and yearnings meant to be eased in the normal relations of life. The panic of 1857 had left the whole country sobered — a "strange, sad time" a Brooklyn newspaperman, Walt Whitman, called it. People were terrified by the future, and in their fear sought God. The last of the great religious revivals swept the land from end to end — "a general outpouring of the spirit," according to *The Independent*. The *Liberator* called it an "emotional contagion without principle."

Into this seething cauldron of emotionalism Henry Ward Beecher flung himself in quest of his own salvation quite as much as that of those who thronged the daily services at Plymouth Church. "It seemed as if, after a time, we had got over the old shame connected with tears." It was a sort of gigantic hysteria, in which people sobbed and laughed and told their dreams (it was before the day of Freud) and sang Henry Ward's favorite hymn, "The Shining Shore."

"We lost all power to *listen*, and could only *feel*," said one of the participants.

And as indefatigable as the Pastor, helping him, cheering him, constantly at his side, swept into the same vortex of emotional intoxication with him, was Lucy Maria Bowen, Henry C. Bowen's wife.

What this protracted emotional ordeal brought to Henry Ward Beecher, he reveals as candidly as he did his need:

"The consciousness of being loved . . . always produces a reaction in every generous nature. It produces a sense of unworthiness, it produces sadness, and a sense of sinfulness and inefficiency, and that too in proportion as the affection received seems pure, and rich and noble," he writes. "There is always the apprehension that our being loved is a phantasy which, like a dream, will not bear the light, and that it will leave us sadder all the rest of our lives."

Indeed, this experience that came to him in this crisis and so swiftly stilled the longings and yearnings that had tortured Henry Ward, was not without its moments of self-probing:

"Every man is living two lives — an exterior one and an internal one. They are not always, or often, either parallel, or morally alike. And not once in a thousand times can one infer from the outward life what is in the interior," he says. And he adds: "He is a brave man that dares ask to know himself."

In all this maelstrom of internal struggle, where the resources of which he disposed were of a nature to betray rather than shield him, Henry Ward Beecher had one firm rock to cling to — Theodore Tilton. "Thou, younger, God-given," Henry Ward called him. And as, long ago, at Mount Pleasant, beset by the temptations, the hot longings, the "wild desires, restless cravings" of adolescence, Beecher had found strength in a passionate friendship with Constantine Fondolaik, so now in this terrific upheaval of his full manhood, he found surcease and new courage in Tilton.

Of their intimacy, as it came to flower in 1858, Tilton wrote seven years later:

"Then, what hours we had together! . . . What mutual revelations and communings! What interchanges of mirth, of tears, of prayers! The more I think back upon this friendship, the more am I convinced that, not your public position, not your fame, not your genius, but just your affection has been the secret of the bond between us; for whether you had been high or low, great or common, I believe that my heart, knowing its mate, would have loved you exactly the same."

They had little in common — so little, indeed, that only Beecher's almost pathetic need of the younger man could have kept their intimacy intact so long. For Theodore Tilton was that combination of seer and enthusiast doomed to travel a rough road, and rough roads were not in Henry Ward Beecher's calculations. "I love you for the utter recklessness of consequences with which you adhere to what you believe to be just, and the valor with which you defend the irresistible conclusions of right reasoning," Matt Carpenter once wrote Tilton. Henry Ward Beecher was anything but reckless, and intellectual valor was no part of his endowment. But he was Theodore Tilton's hero in those early days of their association, and a hero's rôle he must play, will he, nill he, if Tilton had anything to say on the subject.

Every Wednesday Beecher devoted to *The Independent*. He was up at six, ate a Spanish mackerel, drank a cup of coffee, and was off across the ferry to the editorial offices in Beekman street. He would saunter into the sanctum, hunt for a quill, whittle it a while in meditation, and then with blots, spatters, scratches, and dashes for punctuation, write his article. By eleven he had finished, and the product went to the compositor. It was then that he gathered in Tilton, and off the two started up Broadway, to rummage book shops, artists' studios, museums of curiosities, furniture stores, picture galleries, together, arm in arm. Tilton, who loved books for what was in them, would finger volumes over affectionately; but Beecher would buy them for the sheer luxury of buying — books that he never looked inside of, whose pages he never cut.

After a while, they would work back to the office, to read proof. Henry Ward would lie down on a lounge and close his eyes, and Theodore would read Beecher's article aloud. And then began the struggle between these two. For the old world in which Henry Ward Beecher had been born and raised was crumbling. He stood in the presence of a convulsion of social and moral forces. Greater minds than his were confused and hesitant, and Henry Ward Beecher was cannily bent on having a foot safely in both camps.

But Theodore Tilton would not have it so. His hero must lead. With fanatic energy he would push and shove his idol back onto its pedestal, thrust the banner of captaincy in his hand — and then stand off and cheer. Henry Ward loved the cheering, but he found Tilton's insistence on a knight-errantry for which he had no stomach a bit irritating.

In one respect, Tilton accepted Beecher's leadership implicitly. With the older man's break with the Calvinism of the past, in which Theodore also had been reared, he had no quarrel. When Henry Ward defined his new-found spiritual message: "I will worship love that sacrifices itself for the good of those who err, and that is patient with them as a mother is with a sick child," that was what Tilton, too, believed. Henry Ward went farther. He could not worship God. God was too far, too vague, too awful. But Christ he could visualize:

"A dim and shadowy effulgence rises from Christ, and that I am taught to call the Father. A yet more tenuous and invisible film of that arises and that is the Holy Spirit. But neither are to me aught tangible, restful, accessible," he says. "But Christ stands my *manifest* God. . . . I bear Him in my thoughts hourly, as I humbly believe that He also bears me. For I do truly believe that we love each other!"

Beecher had been silent on slavery for some time when John Brown was caught at Harper's Ferry. The Dred Scott decision passed with scant notice. But the tragedy of John Brown appalled him. He felt himself directly involved in the bloody business. It was of no use to tell himself that long before he had urged the sending of rifles to Kansas others had done so, or that if, in fact, John Brown had carried one of "Beecher's Bibles" at Harper's Ferry, his was a cracked brain crazed by events for which the South, not Henry Ward Beecher, was responsible. Beecher thought he had been preaching Love as the remedy of all the evils of the world. And now the work of his preaching was not love, but death.

"We have no right to carry into the midst of slavery exterior discontent," he cried. "Does any man believe that this vast horde of undisciplined Africans, if set free, would have cohesive power enough to organize themselves into a government, and maintain their independence? If there be men who believe this, I am not among them. . . . It is true that slavery is cruel. But it is not at all certain that there is not more love to the race in the South than in the North. . . . By all the ways consistent with the fearless assertion of the truth, we must maintain sympathy and kindness toward the South. We are brethren, and I pray that no fratricidal influences be permitted to sunder this Union. There was a time when I thought the body of death would be too much for life, and that the North was in danger of taking disease from the South, rather than they our health. That time has gone past. I do not believe that we shall be separated by their act or ours."

It was the best amends he could make. But the thing would not down. Hardly had he got the vision of the body of John Brown swinging from a sour apple tree out of his mind when the question arose in Plymouth Church of contributing funds to the American Board of Foreign Missions, whose communicants in the Cherokee Nation were slave-holders. Fifteen years before, in the Indiana State Synod, he had joined in condemning the very action now proposed. But fifteen years is a long time, and Henry Ward Beecher felt, somehow, that there was blood on his hands. He supported the slave-holding missions.

In the eyes of Theodore Tilton, fanatic Abolitionist, this was not just weakness — it was treason. Treason to his hero. He stood there in the crowded lecture room of Plymouth Church, his finger leveled at Henry Ward Beecher like some implacable fate. He brought out John Brown's rifle, and told anew the story of "Beecher's Bibles."

"Wherever I go, whether in the stage, in the railroad car, in the ferryboat, or on foot up and down the streets, I am perpetually accosted with the question: 'Is the Pastor of Plymouth Church changing his views? Is Mr. Beecher becoming more conservative?'" cried Tilton.

To Beecher, this blond young giant seemed to be marshaling every word Henry Ward had ever uttered into a vast mob that hustled him forward, crying: "We are your words and your masters! You cannot turn back! You cannot turn back!"

Tilton spared his hero nothing. Female suffrage had always been a delicate subject for Henry Ward to touch, owing to Eunice Beecher's "disgust" with "talk of woman's wrongs and the cramped and downtrodden condition in which she lived."

"I have no sympathy for the new woman . . ." Eunice asserted. "What is the ability to speak on a public platform or the wisdom that may command a seat on a judge's bench compared to that which can insure and preside over a true home?"

But Tilton would have it that Henry Ward must take a stand on suffrage. So, between Lucy Stone and Robert Dale Owen, the Communist, on the stage of the Cooper Institute, Henry Ward Beecher burned his domestic bridges behind him:

"The most natural and proper method of introducing reformation into public affairs, is to give woman a co-ordinate influence there," he declared. "What man that is gross, what man that is corrupt, would not be blighted before woman's vote?"

It was Mrs. Tilton's brother, Joseph Richards, who invited Abraham Lincoln — "a lawyer with some local reputation in Illinois," as the *Times* put it — to lecture in Plymouth Church.

Henry Ward knew of Lincoln only as one of the unsuccessful candidates for the Vice-presidential nomination on the Frémont ticket. He did not even hear the lecture, which was not held in Plymouth Church, after all, but in Cooper Union. It would scarcely have interested him if he had, for the Western lawyer took precisely the opposite position to that held by Henry Ward Beecher. In Beecher's view, so long as the South was guaranteed its constitutional right to slavery in the slave States, the whole North was free to call Southern slave-holders criminals, immoral persons, thugs, murderers, liars and heathen; and the South was bound to stand it without precipitating any break in the friendly relations between the two sections. But Lincoln saw the matter in quite another light:

"What will satisfy them [the South]? Simply this: we must let them alone, but we must convince them that we do let them alone," he said. "Cease to call slavery *wrong*, and join them in calling it *right.* . . . If our sense of duty forbids this, then let us stand by our duty, fearlessly and effectively."

An oasis of hard sense in a desert of sentimentality. Accept without squirming the consequences of opposition to slavery. If you are going to stand in one camp, get your foot out of the other.

Perhaps this speech did elect Lincoln. It did not clarify things much for Henry Ward Beecher, however. When Lincoln spoke in New York, and the following day attended Plymouth Church, Beecher had other things on his mind. A horse had run away with Eunice Beecher, and thrown her out of the chaise in which she was driving with two of her children so that she fell on the right side of her head. She was never quite the same afterwards.

And just the Sunday before, Henry Ward had ransomed another slave girl in Plymouth Church:

"The rain never fell faster than the tears fell from many of you that were here," he said afterwards, recounting the exploit. "The scene was one of intense enthusiasm. The child was bought and overbought."

In such activities as this no other consequences were involved than emotional release, felt Henry Ward. No war would be brought on, no blood shed, by contributing money to purchase pretty slave girls out of bondage.

During the Lincoln campaign, when thousands of "Wide-Awakes" paraded Broadway in capes and képis in an unprecedented torchlight procession, Henry Ward Beecher was only mildly active. Frémont he had regarded as "a clear, fresh, able, honest, heroic man." Lincoln, in Beecher's estimate, was merely "a considerate, prudent, honest politician." He never did see much in Lincoln.

Nevertheless, rather to Beecher's astonishment, Lincoln was elected. The returns were hardly in before Henry Ward was climbing on the bandwagon:

"The time has come when the public mind must take some position and make some expression," he said, in Boston. "I, for one, do not believe in union for the sake of it. . . . There is almost but one question: . . . 'Do you think that the South will secede?' My answer is: 'I don't think they will; and I don't care if they do.'"

It was merely an echo of Horace Greeley's editorial in the *Tribune*, three weeks previous, and all very well for Henry Ward. But Plymouth Church, also, had to be heaved over onto the right side of the fence. Wendell Phillips and others among the dyed-in-the-wool anti-slavery leaders had been mobbed. Plymouth Church, however, had been invidiously overlooked. It was time something was done about it.

Accordingly, on December 16, 1860, a mob-scare was duly staged for Plymouth Church. There were two hundred policemen in the audience and a whole company of police concealed in the lecture room next door. At the close of the service Henry Ward was escorted to his home by a determined bodyguard of the brethren of Plymouth Church.

But the provisions for the mob were faulty. None appeared.

CHAPTER XVII

ENGLAND

Henry Ward Beecher was Hyperion, now. His long locks, in which just a few threads of gray were beginning to appear, were curled a little. He affected low, square-toed shoes like one of the Puritan Fathers. His wide-brimmed felt hats were made to order and there was a costly elegance to his clothes, worn with such studied carelessness. His over-red cheeks were full and under his chin were soft folds of fat. Fowler called it a sensuous face. "He seems to me a stump speaker who has mistaken his way and stumbled into a church," wrote Adam Badeau. "He would be more at home . . . in the House of Representatives, with his feet on the desk, interrupting the speaker, or talking against time." Dr. Thomas Nichols, the Scotch divine, referred to Plymouth Church as "the temple which seemed to have been created chiefly to the honor and glory of Mr. Beecher," and Theodore Parker dismissed Henry Ward as "of not great intellect or great knowledge."

Nevertheless, Henry Ward Beecher was a man of consequence in the land. Charles Dudley Warner embodied three of his most fervent passages in a "Book of Eloquence" — just such another book as Lovell's "United States Speaker" of Henry Ward's Mount Pleasant days. Only now, here he was, cheek by jowl with his distinguished father — and with Webster and Hayne and Patrick Henry as well! David Bartlett included Henry Ward Beecher among his living American reformers and Maturin Ballou ran a piece about the Pastor of Plymouth Church in his *Pictorial Drawing-Room Companion*, accompanied by a picture of our hero resplendent in Galloways. He spoke with respect of Henry Ward's "foreign journeys." George W. Bungay devoted one of his "Crayon sketches of noticeable men of our age" to Beecher, Buttre made engravings of him, Thomas Hicks, of the National Academy, painted his portrait * — as did Frank B. Carpenter, who, later, was to immortalize Lincoln and his cabinet.

On the whole, Henry Ward felt, not without reason, that he needed a larger frame. So at the height of the hysterical enthusiasm of the revival of 1858, he launched a project for a bigger church edifice, to stand forever a monument to the immensity of the audiences Henry Ward Beecher had been able to attract and to hold spellbound — a perfect leviathan of a church, to seat six thousand people and cost a quarter of a million dollars.

Ever since the funds for the existing church building had been raised single-handed by Henry C. Bowen, Beecher had resented Bowen's quiet dominance in the affairs of Plymouth Church. Whatever else might be said of Henry C. Bowen, no one ever hinted that he lacked appreciation of the value of a dollar, or

* Frontispiece.

that there was much of anything he would not do to get and keep one. "No man ever left his employ with a good opinion of him," was the verdict on Brother Bowen of Plymouth Church. He was Henry Ward's age, thin, sallow, sunken-eyed, with a face like parchment and a flowing beard. Eunice Beecher particularly disliked him. There were special reasons just then why Henry Ward feared him and would have been happy to wrest Plymouth Church from the grip of Brother Bowen. He tried it now, choosing H. B. Claflin to head the Committee to raise funds to build a Greater Plymouth Church.

The project failed disastrously. It cost Plymouth Church $25,000 and no little prestige.

It was a lesson to Henry Ward Beecher that came at a critical moment. Whether civil war was to follow the election of Abraham Lincoln or not depended a vast deal on just such men as Henry Ward Beecher. Everybody knew where Garrison and Wendell Phillips and Theodore Tilton and others of the left-wing Abolitionists stood. But it was men like Greeley and Beecher, first on one side and then on the other, and great numbers of bewildered folk who read the *Tribune* and attended Plymouth Church, who held the balance of decision. In Plymouth Church, "up to the time of the war, slavery was not made the subject of discussion more than once or twice a year," says Beecher. His people were not really prepared for war. And now that Henry Ward had to make up his mind which way to swing them, the lesson he had just received of the importance of such merchants and business men as Henry C. Bowen, who stood to lose everything they possessed by war, dictated the attitude he adopted towards the South, in Plymouth pulpit:

"Our Northern apathy to freedom and greed of commerce are a thousand times more dangerous than Southern rage and threat," he said, on Thanksgiving Day, 1860. "Let us have firm courage, kindness of temper, willingness to make concessions in things of mere policy, but no concession of principles. . . . We honestly wish no harm to the South or its people; we honestly wish them all benefit. . . . All that belongs to the South; all that with liberalist construction was put in the original bond, shall be hers. Her own institutions were made inviolate in all her States. . . . We will not aggress on you," he pledged. "Keep your institutions within your own bounds; we will not hinder you. We will not take advantage to destroy, or one whit to abate, your fair political prerogatives.

. . . You shall have the Constitution intact, and its full benefit. The full might and power of public sentiment in the North shall guarantee you everything that history and the Constitution give you."

This sort of talk made Theodore Tilton sick at his stomach. Just ten years before, as a college youth, he had cheered himself hoarse when Henry Ward Beecher thundered, "As long as I do live, I will not cease my endeavors or hold my peace unless the vile monster [slavery] is driven from the land." And now it was a matter of common talk that he welcomed with complacency the adulation of a lot of silly women in his church. In fact, the thing grew so notorious that some of the leading men of the church got together and deputed one of their number to speak to Henry Ward about it. The forces of progress were on the eve of a titanic struggle, thought Tilton, and the man who should have been their commander was sating his ego with cheap flattery and associations fraught with danger.

Perhaps Beecher was not so forthright in respect of slavery, now that the conflict impended, as some of his earlier pronouncements would seem to have foreshadowed. But he did not lack his courage, on occasions:

"The supreme fear of Northern cities is pecuniary. But even for money's sake, there should be a settlement that will stay settled," he preached, borrowing generously from Charles Sumner. "The corrupt passions which lead in the Southern States to all the gigantic evils of slavery, in Northern cities break out in other forms. . . . The same thing that leads to oppression of laborers among us leads to oppression on the plantation. The grinding of the poor, the advantages which capital takes of labor, the oppression of the road, the oppression of the shop, the oppression of the ship, are all of the same central nature, and as guilty before God as the more systematic and overt oppression of the plantation. . . . If we have said: 'To agitate the question imperils manufacturing, imperils shipping, imperils real estate, imperils quiet and peace,' and if then we have sacrificed purity and honesty — if we have bought the right to make money here by letting slavery spread and grow there — we have been doing just the same thing that they have."

Which was bold enough to satisfy even Theodore Tilton.

It was precisely because he felt that he had made far-reaching concessions to the Southern point of view at the last moment that Henry Ward Beecher was the more incensed when Roger A. Pryor and two staff officers of Gen. Beauregard's command demanded the surrender of Ft. Sumter, and failing to get it, war began. Beecher suddenly had not abuse enough to heap upon the South—they were a lot of poltroons down there, anyhow:

"There has been a spirit of patriotism in the North; but never within my memory, in the South," he declared, after war had begun. "If you have peace, you are to stigmatize the whole history of the past; you are to yield your religious convictions; you are to give over the government into the hands of factious revolutionists; you are to suppress every manly sentiment, and every sympathy for the oppressed. . . . I utterly abhor peace on any such grounds. Give me war redder than blood and fiercer than fire. . . ."

But, alas! no one would give Henry Ward Beecher war redder than blood, or any other kind. The war languished. The less impetuous Lincoln sought, first, some compromise whereby a general conflagration might yet be averted. And when that was prevented by the dyed-in-the-wool Abolitionists, the President bent every energy to retain in the crumbling Union those whom Beecher dubbed "the border-State eunuchs."

To Henry Ward Beecher, this was a futile business. "Since war is upon us, let us have the courage to make war," he said. He did his part. His eldest son, Henry, enlisted for three years before he was twenty-one, and Plymouth Church subscribed $3,000 to the regiment in which young Beecher was an officer. Henry Ward addressed recruiting meetings, blessed flags, preached warlike sermons and wrote warlike articles for *The Independent*. He was as busy as a Major General—and a good deal busier than some of the Major Generals at that juncture. He ran down to Washington to see why his son's regiment was not sent to the front at once, helped to get boys into the army —or out of it—organized welfare work for the soldiers, and a hundred other things. But mostly he exercised the inalienable right of non-combatants in time of war to criticize the government. Thanks largely to Henry Ward Beecher a people enduring a good many other evils with commendable fortitude were not also compelled by law to hold their tongues.

There were several reasons why Henry Ward Beecher fought Abraham Lincoln so implacably. First and foremost were his very close personal ties with Frémont, through the Howards and Raymonds. John Tasker Howard was the third of the triumvirate with Bowen and David Hale to found Plymouth Church. The closest intimates the Beechers had in Brooklyn from their arrival were the Howards, and Mrs. Howard's family, the Raymonds. They were the backbone of Plymouth Church. Eunice Beecher nursed little Henry Ward Beecher Howard at her own breast, and now that Eunice was suffering so severely from her accident, Mrs. Howard was indefatigable in attendance on her.

Howard was a promoter, associated with Frémont in the latter's ill-starred Mariposa gold-mining venture, and when war broke out became one of the group surrounding Major General Frémont at his headquarters in St. Louis. Jack Howard and Ros Raymond were Frémont's aides. The only first-hand news Henry Ward had of the conduct of the war was their letters home, complaining of Lincoln's jealousy of Frémont, of the War Department's efforts to ruin him, of Frémont's greatness and the pettiness of Lincoln's administration. When Frémont was summarily removed on charges of graft and incompetence, Henry Ward Beecher was one of the earliest and most sympathetic visitors of the fallen general at the Astor House. The romantic element in Frémont's career appealed sharply to Henry Ward's sentimentality — as the disgraced West Point cadet, Fitzgerald, had captivated him at Mount Pleasant, as the dashing gambler, Alvord, had won his loyalty in Indianapolis, and as Theodore Tilton, the poetic knight-errant of reform, now held him in thrall. Frémont, he said, was "maligned and mistreated . . . unquestionably the most personally popular man in the country." Frémont was undoubtedly a dashing figure, with a certain courtly foreign grace. In Lincoln, Beecher saw only a man born among the very commonest of the common people:

"It would be difficult for a man to be born lower than he was," Beecher writes. "He is an unshapely man. He is a man that bears evidence of not having been educated in schools or in circles of refinement."

Not in the least that Henry Ward Beecher reproached Lincoln his humble origin. But he could see no glamour in the man because of it.

The second quarrel that Beecher had with Lincoln was that the President did not free the slaves at once. Henry Ward blew hot and cold on this subject, himself. But when Frémont did the trick in his military bailiwick on August 30, 1861, Beecher was confirmed in his opinion that Frémont was, thereby, a greater man than Lincoln—he was not of those who saw Frémont "a painted woman quoting the Scripture."

It would have been of relatively little moment whether Henry Ward Beecher invested Lincoln with his approval or not, had Beecher not, at this crucial juncture, become editor-in-chief of *The Independent*. For the war ruined Henry C. Bowen, as it did many another Northern merchant. All he had left as assets were *The Independent* and the obligations Henry Ward Beecher was under to him. Bowen therefore conceived the happy idea of rebuilding his lost fortunes by pooling both these assets in a single investment, by making Henry Ward Beecher the editor of his paper.

Beecher was enchanted. He had long felt the need of a wider audience than his pulpit commanded and a more homogeneous public than his lectures brought him. As the star contributor to *The Independent* he had wielded a very considerable influence. Tilton had made the paper the leading family newspaper of a religious cast in the country. He would continue to run it as Beecher's managing editor—"of whom we may not speak more, such are the ties of personal affection between us, lest it seem an imputed egoism," Henry Ward wrote. And Henry Ward Beecher, as editor-in-chief, would harvest the full fruits of a successful enterprise successfully conducted. Bowen would pocket the profits. Tilton would do the work.

Beecher had, at this moment, every reason to feel himself under the heaviest of obligations to Theodore Tilton. Charles Francis Adams called the headquarters of the Army of the Potomac "a combination of bar-room and brothel." In one or the other of those aspects Beecher's son, who was not yet even of age, was caught in a breach of discipline and forced to resign his commission in the army.

To Henry Ward Beecher it was a staggering blow. He felt humiliated and disgraced beyond any power to save him. In his grief and shame, he went to his friend, Theodore. And Theodore Tilton did not lose an instant. He went straight to Washington, and to the house of Secretary of War Cameron. Cameron had guests to lunch; but Tilton would not be put off. So the Secretary asked Tilton to stop to luncheon, also.

Theodore Tilton was a man of unquestionable charm. He turned a dull political function into a red-letter day for Cameron's guests. His wit, his personal magnetism, his physical beauty and rare culture captivated the company. When the guests departed, Tilton begged a commission in the regular army for young Beecher, got it with the Secretary's signature, and took it himself to the President. He secured Lincoln's name to the document, and fetched it back to Henry Ward Beecher. From that hour Eunice Beecher conceived a hatred of Theodore Tilton that was scarcely sane. He never entered Beecher's house again.

From his editorial post in *The Independent*, Beecher addressed a large audience of those who would, normally, have been staunch supporters of the administration. Lincoln was a minority President, and well aware of the fact. Even without the South, he required all his political strength intact to carry on his task. What Henry Ward Beecher now proceeded to do was to cut that strength, with all the force of his popular prestige as an anti-slavery orator, the editor of a great journal, and a mouthpiece of God.

"This is the common people's war. They furnish the men, the money, and its enthusiasm and patriotism. They *can* understand war. . . . What has Mr. Lincoln's education done for him — more than ours for us — to fit him to judge of military affairs? We are sick and weary of this conduct. We have a sacred cause, a noble army, good officers, and heroic common people. But we are like to be ruined by an administration that will not tell the truth, that spends precious time at President-making; that is cutting and shuffling the cards for the next great political campaign . . ."

he wrote. "The people are beginning to distrust their rulers," he says. "The President seems to be a man without any sense of the value of time. . . . This is not punishing rebellion. It is helping it." And again:

"Our armies have been managed as if they were a body of nurses in a foundling hospital, watching at every step lest they tread on a baby. . . . It is war that we are making — war first, war second, war wholly! It is not Politics. It is not Constitution-making. . . . It is War, absolute, terrible, and immeasurable War!"

All Henry Ward Beecher's doubts of the authority of the central government constitutionally to abolish slavery by naked decree, which had kept him silent on the subject of slavery so many years, suddenly evaporated under the influence of immeasurable war. On this he hammered away, week after week, in pulpit and out: the end of slavery must be decreed. Almost over night he became as radical as Garrison, and carried UNIVERSAL EMANCIPATION in capital letters in *The Independent*, as his program. "All men are born equal, and have certain inalienable rights—LIFE, *Liberty*, and PROPERTY," he declares. But the three billion dollars' worth of slave property which constituted the principal wealth of the South could and should, he felt, be wiped out with a gesture.

Even when Lincoln's Emancipation Proclamation, already drafted, was only being withheld at the suggestion of Seward, and after the President's messages of December 1861 and March 1862 had made pretty clear the course of Lincoln's mind, Henry Ward Beecher was implacable towards the Administration:

"Certainly neither Mr. Lincoln nor his Cabinet have proved leaders. Fear was stronger than Faith!" he says. "And never was a time when men's prayers so fervently asked God for a Leader! He has refused our petition! . . . Not a spark of genius has he [Lincoln]; not an element for leadership. Not one particle of heroic enthusiasm. . . . We must cease looking any more to Government. We must turn to ourselves. And the time may be here when the people will be called to act with a courage beyond all precedent. After . . . reverses have come, and our rulers are fugitives from the proud Capitol, should they deem the task of maintaining the sanctity and integrity of the National Soil hopeless, then this Great People . . . may yet be called to take up the despairing work and carry it forth to victory."

In the event of such a popular uprising against the Government as this, Henry Ward was confident God would take the leadership of the Union armies, presumably through the abler of His ministers. When Pope suffered the disaster of the second battle of Bull Run, Beecher held Lincoln responsible:

"At present, the North is beaten. . . . It is a supreme and extraordinary want of executive administrative talent at the head of the Government that is bringing us to humiliation," he wrote. "Let it be known that the Nation wasted away by an incurable consumption of Central Imbecility."

But this Great People as a whole sided with Lincoln rather than Henry Ward Beecher.

"We are coming, Father Abraham, three hundred thousand more!" they sang.

On September 14, 1862, at the suggestion of Henry C. Bowen, Henry Ward Beecher and Dr. Theodore L. Cuyler decided to go to Washington to urge upon the President the necessity of decreeing emancipation without further delay. They were to be very plain-spoken with Lincoln. Henry Ward could not leave at once, however. A week passed — and Lincoln acted without their advice. But even the preliminary emancipation proclamation, and the President's message of December 1862, did not satisfy Beecher:

"The President's message is very well in its way," he wrote. "It is pleasing to know the opinions of any intelligent man on public topics. But President Lincoln was not placed in the Presidential chair to read lectures to Congress on political economy, nor to manage a war with reference to New York politics, nor to undertake to draw out on paper how anyone may settle the questions of the next century. . . . There is the enemy. Defeat him."

To Henry Ward Beecher at this time, Lincoln could do no right.

Henry Ward's public performances were not confined to holding Lincoln rigidly to his job. He also played a billiard match with Phineas T. Barnum, at Irving Hall.

And then, suddenly, Henry C. Bowen's wife died at the age of thirty-eight, at the height of her attractiveness, the mother of ten children — a tragic figure, who had done a world of good in her life and perhaps no harm at all. But on her death-bed she made her husband a terrible confession. And it became impossible for Henry Ward Beecher to remain the editor of Henry C. Bowen's paper. Within two months, Beecher left the country. When he returned, Theodore Tilton had succeeded him as editor-in-chief of *The Independent*.

During the single year Henry Ward Beecher edited *The Independent*, he had never once let up on Lincoln. All over the country, clergymen read his editorials and took their cue from them. The effect was far-reaching and depressive. But somehow or other Old Abe only grew bigger in the popular estimate, and his critics more petty. Moreover, when the emancipation of the slaves for which Beecher had been clamoring at last became a legal fact, and still the South did not collapse, Henry Ward hardly knew what to suggest next. Little by little, he began to sense that he had put his eggs in the wrong basket, and to cast about him for a way to get them out again. A trip abroad might well present an opportunity to shift his ground without too obvious a retreat. He seized upon it.

So colossal a legend has grown up of Henry Ward Beecher's unprecedented service in the cause of the Union in England the following October, that it is just as well here to take stock of the actual state of Anglo-American relations in the Summer of 1863, not as presented by Hattie Stowe's admirer, Oliver Wendell Holmes, in a bit of war-time propaganda in lyric praise of Hattie's brother, but as they are revealed in the cold light of history.

"In 1863," says James Bryce, "the masses of the English people were with Mr. Lincoln." There had, it is true, been a time when relations had been strained. But the efforts of Archbishop Hughes, Bishop McIlvaine and Thurlow Weed, aided not a little by Queen Victoria and her indefatigable Consort, had ended all that long since:

"Lord Palmerston cannot but look on this peaceful issue of the American quarrel as greatly owing to her beloved Prince, who wrote the observation upon the draft to Lord Lyons, in which Lord Palmerston so entirely concurred." Victoria wrote, adding pathetically: "It was the last thing he ever wrote!"

That was early in 1862.

"Before our Parliament met," John Bright wrote Charles Sumner, February 27, 1862, "there was much talk of interference with the blockade, and much still said in favor of the South. All that has passed away. In London all has changed, and it is difficult to find a noisy advocate of the secession theory. The press has become much more moderate, and the great party that was to have driven the government into hostilities with you is nowhere to be found."

Grant's capture of Fort Donelson had done the trick.

No one knew this better than Henry Ward Beecher, and none better than he that addressing mass meetings in industrial centers like Manchester, Liverpool and Glasgow was a meaningless gesture, since the laboring class of England was without vote. Indeed, five months before he went abroad, he had published in *The Independent* a letter from the Rev. John Waddington, of England, adjuring Beecher to "look at our public meetings, where any fair statements of facts can be given, and you will find the public verdict unanimously on your side." Henry Ward knew before ever he went to England that if he were so minded he could talk there in public to his heart's content without altering the relations between the two countries so much as a finger's breadth.

However, if there was one thing that Charles Francis Adams, the American Minister to England, could get along very well without it was any one stirring up the question of Anglo-American relations. So when a group of clergymen urged Beecher, on his arrival in Liverpool, to make some public addresses on the war, and Henry Ward refused, "the loyal Americans" were "all tickled out of their boots at this decision." What they wanted of Beecher and other traveling Americans was "dignified silence."

There is something singularly child-like and engaging about the account which Henry Ward Beecher himself wrote in 1880 of his exploits in England. He is like Synge's Playboy — the relation of what he described to fact is so remote that, evidently, the affair had become a sort of saga in his mind — like his early anti-slavery debate at Amherst and his stand against slavery in Indiana. But now he treats of matters of international concern, and unsentimental chroniclers swiftly put events in their proper relationship. In Professor Adams' two comprehensive volumes on "Great Britain and the American Civil War" Henry Ward Beecher rates a footnote:

"I have not dwelt upon Beecher's tour of England and Scotland in 1863, because its influence in 'winning England' seems to me absurdly over-estimated. He was a gifted public orator and knew how to 'handle' his audiences, but the majority in each audience was friendly to him, and there was no such 'crisis of opinion' in 1863 as has frequently been stated in order to exalt Beecher's services."

Rhodes, Channing, McMaster and Charles and Mary Beard make no mention of Beecher's feat, in England.

"Popular opinion in England ran clear and strong in favor of the North," say the Beards. "The English masses believed in the triumph of freedom and prayed for the success of northern armies."

Even at the time intelligent folk were not befooled. Henry H. Bright wrote Nathaniel Hawthorne from England:

"Mr. Ward Beecher has been lecturing here. I regret to say that someone was unmannerly enough to placard the walls with 'secession' placards in black and red, quoting from a speech of his (Ward Beecher's) on the *Trent* affair, in which he was pleased to remark that 'the best blood of England must flow' in consequence. I'm afraid that Mr. Beecher found a portion of his audience inattentive, and given to groans and stamps; however, there was no *regular* row; and Mr. Beecher's audacity in lecturing at all had a trace of sublimity in it. Mr. Channing has also been lecturing in Leeds and elsewhere."

While the London *Era* recorded of Henry Ward's speeches that

"the Rev. Mr. Beecher (brother of the author of 'Uncle Tom's Cabin') is delivering very showy addresses, which immense crowds flock to hear. . . . As Falstaff says, 'He spoke very wisely, but we regarded him not!'"

In the face of the evidence, one is constrained to admit that Henry Ward Beecher's triumph in England, so celebrated by Oliver Wendell Holmes, was, after all, of no great political value to his country.

It was, however, of enormous significance to Henry Ward Beecher.

CHAPTER XVIII

FORT SUMTER

WE HAVE got to settle this question *by our armies*, and the opinions of mankind will follow," Henry Ward wrote Hattie Stowe, on his arrival in England. Unfortunately, Henry Ward felt, the Northern armies were badly led. When he reached London, he celebrated the Fourth of July by informing a large audience of representative temperance leaders from all over England that he could point out several great misfortunes which had befallen the armies of the North "owing entirely to the drunkenness of officers." He cited the defeat of Chancellorsville and charged General Hooker with being "under the influence of liquor" during the last part of that engagement. His remarks had a deplorable effect. Some of Henry Ward's staunchest friends felt that criticisms of that nature were hardly the kind of thing one talked about in foreign countries — England least of all.

Henry Ward himself was scarcely prepared for the unfavorable impression his remarks created — it opened his eyes, and he saw clearly that British sentiment had altered. The preponderance on the part of the North of what Lord Russell called "large masses, superior in numbers" had already made itself felt. In the United States it was generally believed that England was with the South, but Beecher's genius for sensing popular feeling now told him that this was no longer true. He divined that the time had come when any clear statement of the Northern position would be received in England with almost universal acclaim, and he who made it reap a great reward. Henry Ward Beecher itched to be that man.

But he wanted a good, smashing victory or two back home to add impetus to what he might say. It was not until he reached Paris, late in July, that the news of Gettysburg and the fall of Vicksburg brought him just what he needed. From that moment, Henry Ward literally ran through the remainder of his continental trip in his haste to get back to England to carry out his plan. Early in September he was in London again. There he found even such limited, if noisy, Southern sympathies as he had encountered two months previous rapidly dissipating. The moment had arrived for Henry Ward Beecher to trim his sails and come out as conspicuously and as dramatically in support of Lincoln as he had hitherto opposed him.

"The fall of the great fortresses, the repulse and escape of Lee, the defeat of Bragg, the capture of Morgan, and the fact that the Mississippi is now free from end to end, have wrought convictions here which are bearing fruit," said the *Era*, "and unless some extraordinary and unhoped for success on the part of the South should justify delay in an avowal that the North is victor, we may shortly look for the strongest recommendations to the Confederates to accept the fortunes of war, and succumb."

On September 25, James M. Mason, the Confederate Commissioner, played his last card, and Lord Russell declined the Southern overtures. A week later, at Blairgowrie, the British

Foreign Secretary, representing, according to the *Saturday Review*, "the nearly unanimous wish of his countrymen," expressed himself so unequivocally on solid ground of friendship for the North that even the New York *Tribune* was satisfied. Henry Ward had not a moment to lose — unless he spoke speedily, he was in danger of missing his opportunity altogether. Accordingly, he announced an address in Manchester for October 9.

The population of Manchester was particularly friendly to the North. There were, of course, a few cotton mill owners who were not, but they were scarcely of a type to hunt in mobs. Nine months before, Beecher himself had printed in *The Independent* a sympathetic address from the workers of Manchester to President Lincoln. It was the workers of Manchester who would make up his audience.

On the other hand, the very sympathy of Manchester folk with Lincoln made them suspicious of Henry Ward Beecher. No one in the United States had been more relentlessly hostile to the American President than he, and in addition, when the *Trent* affair brought the North and Great Britain to the brink of war in 1861, no one had been more violently anti-British than Beecher, either. He had written of an inevitable "deluge of blood" and prophesied that "the best blood of England must flow for the outrage England has perpetrated on America."

Henry Ward found his unfortunate phrases assailing England plastered all over the hoardings of both Manchester and Liverpool. They were a poor introduction of the Great American to any British audience. He had only himself to thank for the warm reception he received. Certainly, it is hardly fair to lay the blame at the door of the British public.

As the years passed, Henry Ward's memory of his English experience grew more and more heroic. Hamilton Wright Mabie furnishes a particularly dramatic account,* as he had it of Beecher:

> "On the day on which he was to make his first speech, he was in an agony of depression all the morning, feeling quite unable to bear up under the awful burden of the concentrated animosity of a nation; he felt something as he imagined Christ must have felt on the road to Calvary; he had never been so depressed before, and was never again under such a burden. He spent most of the morn-

* Lyman Abbott: "Henry Ward Beecher"; p. 253.

ing on his knees, without any help; but finally arrived at a point where his prayer took the form of an offer to surrender everything and even to fail if that was God's will."

No such strain was placed upon Henry Ward's magnanimity, however. The nation the burden of whose concentrated animosity he felt so keenly only became aware of his existence after the first three of his speeches had gone off successfully; and while he was jeered in Manchester and Liverpool, he was, on the contrary, cheered enthusiastically in Scotland and London. The New York *Tribune's* special correspondent found his Glasgow speech "rather egotistic, and certainly calculated to displease the sober common sense of England." The London *Herald* described his as "a bad copy of Daniel Webster's face, but coarse and heavy, with eyes which seem to fear to look straightforward; no one could, with an approach to truth, call the countenance intellectual." Nevertheless, said the New York *Times:*

"He could not have hoped for a greater personal triumph; but even he must have seen that in all the meetings he attended there was scarcely one person of influence. . . . But all of this is of little importance. The Government of England . . . takes substantially a Northern side. The North commands all the available resources of English munitions of war."

This was, of course, quite literally true. But Henry Ward Beecher could not admit it to himself. Personal triumphs were nothing to him — he had them every Sunday, with Plymouth Church applauding to the echo. But in England, for the first time in his life he had done a thing entirely on his own responsibility, without help from any one, and he was a hero only if what he had done was heroic.

"I was quite alone in England," he said. "I had no one to consult with. I felt the burden of having to stand for my country in a half-hostile land; and yet I never flinched for a moment, nor lost heart."

Indeed, if opposition to his speaking had not existed in fact, he must have created it in his fancy. For only so could Henry Ward Beecher at last free himself, at last stretch his wings and fly. In the face of his bawling audience in Liverpool, he stood there saying to himself: "Miserable creatures! Wait till I get you and I will twist you around my finger!" He did get them.

He did twist them around his finger. And then he went back to his hotel to sit long hours watching the colors come and go in a pocketful of opals he carried with him, as they lay on the table under the gaslight.

He had conquered. Not just his audience—he conquered audiences every day of his life. He had conquered Henry Ward Beecher. His hesitations were gone. He was a free man. Free of the menace of Bowen rubbing his hands like Uriah Heep. Free of Eunice and her jealousies and her inward contempt of his monkey-shines. Free of Theodore Tilton, driving him always to lead the charge, when what he wanted to be was a general, safe in the rear somewhere. He *was* a general now— and he conceived no limits to his power, no bounds to his ambition.

Yet curiously enough it was to Theodore Tilton that he wrote of his English experience as that stupendous triumph he wanted so eagerly to believe it. After all, Henry Ward Beecher was a practical man—and Tilton was a journalist. Henry Ward's confidence was not misplaced. Theodore spread the story over the columns not only of *The Independent* but of every metropolitan newspaper as well. It had all the elements of first-rate news, and long before Henry Ward's return the whole country rang with the account of Beecher's taming of the British. It tickled the vanity of the American to feel that at last England had been subjugated, whether it were so or not. Oliver Wendell Holmes, in *The Atlantic Monthly*, dubbed Beecher "Our Minister Plenipotentiary" quite as if Charles Francis Adams had never existed. The Mayor of New York presided at an immense meeting in Henry Ward's honor. In Brooklyn two mammoth meetings were held.

If Henry Ward Beecher had ever entertained serious doubts of his greatness, these were now dispelled. The political situation on the eve of the presidential campaign of 1864 conspired to send his thoughts skyrocketing. The one point of agreement among the dozen or more potential candidates for the presidency seemed to be that, whoever else might be chosen, Lincoln would not do at all. The war was a failure—Henry Ward himself had so declared with such ardor and frequency that *Vanity Fair* suggested Fort Lafayette's military prison as the proper place for him. As President, some one must be found who would call out what Henry Ward termed a "great unifying inspiration by which the Government may draw the people after it." Such a man, for example, as Henry Ward Beecher. In Plymouth Church he begged his congregation to pray for him

"not so much that I shall have strength for outward work as that I may not be seduced from the work of this ministry."

Indeed, there might have been a fair chance of Henry Ward's being seduced, save for an untoward incident which occurred on May 18, 1864. Joseph Howard, Jr., the son of Henry Ward's intimate friend of the trinity that ruled Plymouth Church, forged an Executive Proclamation calling for the draft of 400,000 additional soldiers and appointing a day of fasting and prayer. Grant's Wilderness campaign was at its bloody and terrible worst. The moment was well seized to produce the panic on the stock exchange upon which Howard counted.

It was Howard who was imprisoned in Fort Lafayette. Henry Ward Beecher had to beg his release from Lincoln in person. As the tall, "unshapely" man — as Beecher had called him — looked down at his rubicund visitor, he might well have quoted: "How unsearchable are his judgments, and his ways past finding out!" But all the President did was to write Secretary Stanton a little note: "I very much wish to oblige Henry Ward Beecher." Howard was released.

But the press that so shortly before had said of Beecher's speeches in England that "there has not been a more heroic achievement on any of our fields of battle" now took pains to point out that Howard had been an intimate of Beecher's since childhood, brought up on "the droppings of the Plymouth sanctuary." As a political possibility, Henry Ward Beecher faded out.

Nevertheless, the incident was not without its value to Henry Ward. He had made and sealed his peace with Lincoln, and got into friendly touch once more with Washington. Theodore Tilton was on familiar terms with the President — Old Abe had kissed Tilton's little daughter and unbosomed himself on the state of the country in an hour's private conference with Theodore. Now Henry Ward felt that he too had the entrée to the White House, and when Congress was on the point of adopting the Thirteenth Amendment to the Constitution, there he was, sure enough, congratulating the President just at the right moment to appear with Lincoln at a window of the

White House to share with the President the cheers of the crowd.

Henry Ward had heard talk of a peace conference with Confederate emissaries, and he beseeched Lincoln to have no truck with the treacherous rebels. Old Abe was amused. He told Henry Ward three stories — "two of which I forget, and the third won't bear telling," Beecher said. Curious, the one he remembered! And then, having sent his visitor away reassured, Lincoln did meet his old friend Alexander Stephens, Vice-President of the Confederacy, and the other Confederate Commissioners, and had a friendly chat with them. He felt there were things that Henry Ward Beecher would not understand.

To Beecher these casual contacts with the President were epoch-making. He wrote every one he could think of about them — including Lincoln. And when the President acknowledged two of these voluminous communications with a brief, courteous note, Henry Ward spoke in Plymouth Church of "the last letter I received from him" as if it were part of an intimate and highly confidential relationship. Yet at that hour, Henry Ward Beecher in his special world of folk religiously inclined exercised a tremendous influence of his own that required no reflected luster from a fictitious intimacy. But he could no more resist the romance of the rôle of confidential adviser to the President of the United States than he had been capable of presenting his English speeches in less than heroic light.

Of Lincoln's dour Secretary of War Henry Ward saw more than of the President. "All the elements of old John Adams: able, staunch, patriotic, full of *principle*, and always *unpopular*," he wrote Bonner. "He lacks that sense of other people's *opinions*, which keeps a man from running against them, & so, he is not unfrequently found with a plan pitched right into somebody who by *tact* might have been avoided." With his genius for publicity, Henry Ward suggested to Stanton the idea of sending a shipload of Sunday School teachers to Fort Sumter to raise the flag of the Union over the reconquered ruins, on the anniversary of the fall of the fort. Stanton could not, himself, go, but he issued a formal order that Beecher should go in his place, and deliver an appropriate oration on the occasion.

It was the first official connection Henry Ward Beecher had

had with the war. He was as delighted as a child with it. Brother Bowen, of Plymouth Church, organized a party of his own to go along in another ship, but Henry Ward Beecher and his family, William Lloyd Garrison, Theodore Tilton, Dr. Storrs of the Church of the Pilgrims, and some seventy-five others, were guests of the Government. The ceremony took place April 14, and the party learned of Lee's surrender on arrival at Charleston. Henry Ward broke down and cried like a child at the news, he said. Some of the women fainted. "Men clasped each other in convulsions of emotion. Many prayed. Some wept."

Beecher had prepared his address with great care, and it stands to-day an example of American oratory. But the strained effort he made to picture the people of the South as blindly misled by "ambitious, educated, plotting political leaders" hardly held water. On the whole, it was Theodore Tilton who sounded the popular note of the trip, and came away loaded down with flowers.

Yet for the hour of his oration, Henry Ward Beecher was incomparable. Not even the Secretary of War, whose representative he was — no, not the President himself — was his peer. He stood on a heap of stones, his slightly graying hair flying in the wind, his full face flushed by the Southern sun, his sonorous words echoing back from the battered walls. Officers of Army and Navy stood at attention. About him, a select group, were the flower of Plymouth Church — people of substance and standing in the world. The torn battle flag of Fort Sumter bellied above him. The war was over. He had won his long fight. Generously he gave credit:

"We offer to the President of these United States our solemn congratulations that God has sustained his life and health under the unparalleled burdens and sufferings of four bloody years, and permitted him to behold this auspicious consummation of that national unity for which he has waited with so much patience and fortitude, and for which he has labored with such disinterested wisdom. . . ."

But this belated tribute never came to Lincoln's ears. He lay dead.

Before the war ended, Beecher had been very positive as to the rights of the negro. The negro was a man, he said, and as a man, a son of God and brother of every other man, entitled to all the prerogatives of his manhood, including the vote. But when the war was over and what to do with the freedmen became a practical question, not just an appropriate subject of discourse, Henry Ward Beecher was quick to sense a popular reluctance to confer immediate enfranchisement on the negro.

This reluctance Andrew Johnson embodied, and Henry Ward Beecher was instantly drawn to the new President. They had much in common: the same itch for speech-making and a like facility at it; the same tendency to extravagant overstatement in ex tempore address; the same superficial egoism masking an internal timidity. Moreover, in the early days of his presidency, Johnson's ideas and Beecher's ran parallel:

"I would not shed blood, but no man that with his eyes open went into this rebellion should go unpunished, and if I were President of these United States, no such man should ever again have the power to shape a law, or elect a magistrate, or should stand otherwise than as a branded and disgraced traitor. Pardoned he might be, and suffered to live; but he should live as Cain lived,"

declared the minister of the gospel. The politician agreed.

But as peace became familiar again, both men altered their first hot ferocity towards the conquered South. To Henry Ward Beecher, slavery had been a sin — the resistance of a self-opinioned, scheming few to the ordinances of his God. Slavery kept the Bible from the slave; made a mockery of the holy institution of matrimony; and confronted both white and black with temptation to break the seventh commandment, which the existence of millions of mulattoes testified was, in fact, violated with deplorable frequency. But with the abolition of slavery, all of this, Henry Ward felt, would come to an end. The blacks could be taught to read their Bibles; marriages could no longer be broken up by the sale of one of the parties thereto; any further infractions of the seventh commandment would have to be with the consent of both sinners, who could be held morally responsible for their degraded conduct. The South once compelled to recognize this state of affairs, Henry Ward Beecher's concern with the war ended. He believed it should be forgotten.

Proceeding from quite different premises, Andrew Johnson came to the same belief, and Henry Ward felt a proud glow that he and the new President were at one. When Johnson issued his amnesty proclamation, Beecher wrote him his enthusiastic approval. Indeed, it seemed to Henry Ward that this was the position the public at large was certain to adopt. He put it forth himself at first tentatively, then boldly. On October 22, 1866, he delivered what the New York *Times* termed, in huge headlines, an "Unqualified Endorsement of President Johnson." The *Daily News*, the leading "Copperhead" newspaper, promptly congratulated Mr. Beecher that he had "emerged from the atmosphere of *The Independent* office . . . Escaped from associations that have hitherto eclipsed his truly admirable genius, we predict for Mr. Beecher, henceforth, a much less equivocal reputation than he has hitherto enjoyed."

All of this was incense to Henry Ward Beecher. He had long felt himself too straitly in intellectual leading strings to Theodore Tilton. Now at last he who had been in the wrong pew so long in regard to Lincoln was in the right pew with Andrew Johnson. He had never in his heart believed that the radical Republicans of the type of Sumner, Chase and Wendell Phillips represented any enduring political strength, anyhow. And as for Tilton, now in Henry Ward's old editorial chair on *The Independent* — Beecher found the slogan Tilton ran in caps: "The slave a man; the man a citizen; the citizen a voter," cheap claptrap. The negro, he held, could become a citizen only in due time, by undergoing "the hardships which every uncivilized people has undergone in its upward progress," which might take centuries. "I believe that that man's life is valuable who produces results," he declared six months after he had advocated immediate negro suffrage; "and that that man's life is worthless who produces no results."

It was therefore no surprise to Henry Ward Beecher to be invited to invoke the divine blessing on a convention of Johnson supporters in Cleveland in September 1866. He had the hay fever and could not go, but he wrote at length elaborating the views which, a month before, had been moved by the editor of the New York *Times* and adopted by a similar gathering endorsing Johnson at Philadelphia. Indeed, as he usually did when he felt he was on the right track, Beecher even went a little farther than any one else. The storm of disapproval which his light dismissal of the status of the negro to some indefinite future and his general commendation of Johnson's "restoration policy" evoked was like an unexpected blow in the face to Henry Ward. He could not understand it. Wrote Horace Greeley:

"It was ungenerous . . . to render his apostasy so base, so black, so hateful, so hideous. In pity, if not in decency, they [the committee inviting Beecher to Cleveland] should have put something into their letter implying or insinuating an assurance that he might serve his new masters without betraying God's poor, and shaming the honorable record of his past years."

The leading members of Plymouth Church formally repudiated in the press their pastor's stand.

"Mr. Beecher's public attitude at the present moment is the attitude of a man who is putting a great reputation to the ignoble use of debasing his country," wrote Theodore Tilton. "May God forbid that Mr. Beecher's great name shall be a feather's weight for the support of such a policy of dishonor and shame."

Poor Henry Ward was bewildered. His whole attitude towards the war and its aftermath had been rooted in sentimentality. Slavery and war hatreds alike, he felt, could be obliterated by one Christ-like gesture. There was something pathetic in his confidence that a handful of words would, somehow, transform the minds and hearts of men over night, like the phrase of a conjuror, and all the bitter things he himself had said and written about the South during twenty years evaporate, leaving no sting. He tried to deny that Plymouth Church's repudiation of his stand was genuine. But he was speedily undeceived. And then, before he had time to draft a dignified retreat, his hero, Johnson, spoke from the balcony of an hotel in Cleveland, drunk, the papers said.

It was the final blow. The world crumbled about Henry Ward Beecher's ears. In the eighteen months he had been backing the President, Johnson had succeeded in alienating Congress and placing himself in a position where he needed influential friends badly. To a supporter as widely known as Beecher, Johnson could hardly have denied anything in reason, and cabinet changes were imminent. Henry Ward had nursed fond hopes. But in the face of the onslaught of Greeley, Tilton, his brother, Edward Beecher, and his own church, the Great Preacher had to make the best of a bad business. He did it none too convincingly in a second letter, explaining that if things went so far that no choice would be left "but between a Copperhead Johnson party and a radical Republican" he could not hesitate. "Neither am I a 'Johnson man' in any received meaning of the term," he explained. "I accept that part of the policy which he favors, but with modification."

This, also, was unsatisfactory to the public — and particularly to Plymouth Church. For the first time, Henry Ward Beecher was frightened by the possible consequences of an act of his. He organized a public meeting in Brooklyn, at which he, who had been so used to march up and down a platform before admiring audiences tickling their sense of humor, working on their emotions, saying whatever he pleased, off-hand and without other consideration than his feeling of what the crowd wanted, read his manuscript — a straight-out party stump speech, of the kind to become so familiar in the generation following:

"You yourselves are witnesses that during the first three weary, dark and disastrous years there was an utter want of outspoken sympathy with our Government on the part of the Democratic party," he said. "I cannot belong to that party."

And, strangely enough, nobody laughed. Henry Ward's diatribes against the Government during the first three years of the war were, presumably, forgotten.

But Theodore Tilton did not forget. For Tilton had been a tower of strength to the radical Republicans during the days of Johnson's impeachment. He had gone to Washington himself and done the work of ten men to secure the President's conviction. A flaming sword, a crusader, was Theodore Tilton — right or wrong, an unflinching idealist. In his conception, his hero, Beecher, had betrayed the Cause. Of Beecher's meeting he accordingly wrote, in *The Independent*:

"The spectacle at the Academy of Music had in it a touch of humiliation which even the noblest passages of the address did not redeem. . . . Something of true moral grandeur is wanting to the position of a veteran who, after twenty-five years of service as a pioneer of political opinion, has nothing nobler to say in the present juncture than simply: 'I am not a Democrat.' "

And to his wife Theodore wrote:

"I believe he is not as morally great as he once was. I do not now refer to his political views. His political views have made no change in my feeling toward him as a friend. But there was an older virtue which has since gone out of him — an influence which used

to brighten my life when I came under its ray; an influence which
became gradually quenched like a vanishing dream."

So, many began to think.

CHAPTER XIX

LIVINGSTON STREET

WHEN Henry Ward Beecher returned from England in
1863, he felt he was out of a job.

Of course, he had Plymouth Church, which, with its fifteen
hundred members and its annual income of between $30,000
and $40,000, would have satisfied most preachers. The trouble
was that his English experience, especially in the legendary
form in which he swiftly came to view it, had entirely altered
Henry Ward Beecher's outlook. He took Oliver Wendell
Holmes' characterization of him as a Minister Plenipotentiary
seriously. Looking about him at the type of political timber
available for the gigantic task of reconstruction, Henry Ward
conceived himself the peer of any one of them. And no doubt
he was.

Unquestionably he had a colossal following. Henry Bowen's
office safe was full of old sermons of Beecher's, for which he
had already paid, so he continued to run them in *The Independent* — Bowen let nothing interfere with business. Henry
Ward also had a lyceum schedule calling for some fifty lectures
a year. Between those who read his sermons and those who
heard him lecture, he reached tens of thousands entirely aside
from the attendants upon Plymouth Church.

Yet Beecher was far from satisfied. For almost twenty years
he had wielded a gradually increasing power with tongue and
pen that he had come to crave. When he became editor of *The
Independent*, that power had a definite focus and he a definite
lever to exercise it. Now it had become dispersed again. He had
learned that most unwelcomely in the Johnson incident where,
deprived of the backing of his church and with Tilton's opposition, he had been helpless. Henry Ward felt that he must
have an organization of some sort, no matter how small to begin
with.

Beecher had no more than got back from England therefore than he made overtures to the Abolitionist Republicans, whose star seemed in ascendant, begging "the privilege to call myself a brother, only . . . and, where I differ from you, of having still your confidence that I mean right." The gesture was coldly received. He was not wont to speak at our meetings, remarked Garrison, dryly. It was finally in the modest camp of woman's suffrage that Henry Ward Beecher at last got political foothold. One day in the Spring of 1864, he overtook the gaunt figure of Susan B. Anthony, umbrella in hand, climbing the steep path to Columbia Heights, and slapped her on the back.

"Well, Old Girl, what do you want now?" he asked.

She was going to Theodore Tilton's to devise ways and means of raising money. The suffrage movement was always in need of funds, it seemed. So Henry Ward volunteered to take up a collection for her in Plymouth Church — and got $200. From that moment, he was launched.

Of course it made trouble at home for Henry Ward. But then, so many things now made trouble at home for Henry Ward that he did not care. Eunice despised the whole suffrage movement and all its supporters, while Henry Ward's sister, Catherine, was as unyielding an opponent of female suffrage as she had been of Abolition. The antipathy of both women to woman's suffrage was grounded not only in what they conceived to be good taste, but in fundamental considerations of morality. Suffrage agitation was not respectable, and that was a great deal worse than being immoral. For certain immoralities did indubitably exist in the world, and had for ages; but respectable people did not have to do anything about them or talk about them — or even know about them. "All pure love, all right thoughts, all religion, if you would have them live, must have their roots beneath the altar of the home," wrote Eunice Beecher. The husband she called the Household King whose part was to "battle with the great world outside, in whatever sphere his talents and duties call him." Suffrage advocates, she said, had deliberately "ignored the sweeter, more delicate and feminine home duties for the rougher, coarser duties that were ordained to be man's special work." She herself had organized a model household, she felt. Her children had never been permitted to treat their parents with such unbecoming familiarity as to say "Hello, mamma!" or "Hello, papa!" or anything uncouth like that. Indeed, Eunice Beecher believed that if children could not be brought up with becoming firmness by parents "too cruelly indolent to control children in their early youth as God commanded" they should be packed off to an institution where proper discipline could be provided.

To Henry Ward Beecher, all of this was very terrible. He had suffered so bitterly from loneliness and hunger for affection in his childhood; now he saw it all repeated in his own home, powerless to prevent it. As his children grew up, he wrote out from time to time the fears and uneasiness he felt over their up-bringing and published his observations in little articles in *The Independent.* Yet he hardly knew what to do about it, himself. There had been the trouble his own boy had got into in the army — and that Theodore Tilton had smoothed over in 1861. The Howard children had been like his own to him — yet there had been the hideous business of Joseph Howard's conviction of what might easily have been regarded as high treason. For the life of him, Henry Ward could not see where Eunice's model home had proved very successful in its working out. Certainly it was anything but comfortable.

For Henry Ward was a gregarious person, and loved to fetch friends, and even mere acquaintances who might become friends, home from church with him, or to meals. But when he did so, more frequently than not the atmosphere was hostile and embarrassing. Young Samuel Merrill of Indianapolis met Beecher in the street, on arriving in New York after his discharge from Sherman's army; and Beecher fetched him home to dinner. Catherine Beecher sat in the dining-room throughout the meal reading a book; but she did not even turn around. Mrs. Beecher could talk of nothing but the outrageous conduct of the returned soldiers — until Henry Ward gently reminded her that Merrill was himself a returned soldier and might prefer another topic.

Old Lyman Beecher had lived with Henry Ward for a little while, his mind more clouded than ever. But Eunice could not bear Lyman's third wife — or Lyman, either, for that matter. So the great Dr. Beecher of another day had to find him a little house around the corner in Willow street, where his wife's relatives took care of him till he died. And when Harriet Eliza Beecher, Henry Ward's only living daughter whom he had carried in his arms from Lawrenceburgh to Indianapolis, was mar-

ried, Eunice's behavior was such that Henry Ward wept when
he spoke of it.

Indeed, the difficulties in the Beecher household came to be a
matter of general knowledge. As far West as Chicago they were
"a common topic of discussion." Oliver Johnson, associated
with Beecher for years and who stuck by him through thick
and thin, called Mrs. Beecher "one of the most jealous women
that ever lived" and termed Henry Ward's life with her a "hell
upon earth." Even Henry Ward's elder brother William said
that she "separated Henry Ward from his kindred, from his
brothers and sisters, who were prevented from coming to the
house on her account." Brooklyn folk called her "the griffin"
and chuckled at the thought that she kept the Great Preacher's
door against visitors, like a dragon, opened and answered his
mail (though he had a secretary besides) and was so closely
the guardian of his purse that he had to sneak his extravagant
purchases of expensive books and rare engravings into the
house with all the subterfuges of a naughty boy.

Yet for all that, there was a good deal to be said for Eunice
Beecher. Henry Ward became more luxury-loving as he grew
older. He loved beautiful things, costly things, and purchased
them recklessly. At one time he had three exquisite Persian rugs,
one atop the other, on the floor of his drawing room, because
he could not resist buying them — though there was no place to
put them. He carried pocketfuls of gems about with him —
unfading flowers, he called them — because he loved to watch
the colors come and go in their cryptic depths, as a child might.
He was passionately fond of driving fast horses. And on the
platform of Plymouth Church, winter and summer, cost what
might, he kept always huge bouquets of fresh flowers.

It was not just that Henry Ward Beecher craved luxury with
a definite sensuousness — though that, too, was a corollary of
the very emotional influence he exercised over his audiences.
But power was essential to him. It was his sole means of escape
from his own inner uncertainties. Year by year, the great lesson that man cannot live by feeling alone was brought home to
him. Yet he could not accept it — dared not. For when feeling
ended with Henry Ward Beecher, nothing was left. He collected books, but he did not read them. He collected pictures,
but their only appeal to him was through his emotions. He
stood in the midst of a world of mysterious things of whose

significance he had not the vaguest comprehension. He could only tell their reaction upon him, as an individual — graphically, dramatically, until every one who heard him cried in his heart: "Yes! I feel that, too!" But neither for them nor for himself could Henry Ward Beecher interpret the experiences of life in terms of abstract ideas or eternal principles.

To Eunice Beecher all of this was quite simply incomprehensible. Hers was a world of fixed values. The ancient Puritan standards in which she had been brought up were not only unquestioned but unquestionable. There were tens of thousands of clergymen who preached the gospel of John Calvin Sunday after Sunday with neither histrionics in their pulpits nor applause in their churches. Right was right and wrong was wrong, and it required no great discernment to draw the line between them, and no great fuss about it, either. After all, Henry Ward was gray. His jowls were heavy. There were well-defined wrinkles in his neck. He could no longer write without a blanket about his legs, to keep them warm. Others might think he moved with a certain majesty of presence; but Eunice Beecher knew that it was extra weight about the waist. It was high time silly women left him alone, at last, she thought. And she told him so.

The very idea of advancing age was ghastly to Henry Ward Beecher. The carefully ordered household, where the routine had been unbroken for so many years that they seemed centuries, filled him with terror. The conversation at the breakfast table — "the vainest, the most vapid, the most juiceless, the most unsaccharine of all things" — day after day, appalled him. "I dread to go back to my own house," he said to Theodore Tilton once. And so he did. For his own house was himself — stripped of the lights and the faces beyond the footlights. Elsewhere, there were men and women, too, eager to have him call upon their sentimentality — make them laugh and cry and pray and cheer. Elsewhere, he felt the blood run hot in his veins at the quick emotional response he evoked, as one playing an organ. Elsewhere, he was a living, dynamic force — the Great Preacher. At home, he was only a grandfather.

The break with Bowen and Beecher's sudden retirement from *The Independent* brought all this sharply home to Henry Ward. For a little while after his return from Europe he haunted the office where he had been so many years the star contributor and so brief a space the Chief. He even wrote a few inconsequent contributions for his young successor, went on book hunts with him as of old, arm in arm along the busy streets — and came away from these associations in profound gloom. He saw the circulation of *The Independent* increase under Tilton's management by leaps and bounds — so rapidly, indeed, that Bowen offered his new editor a partnership at thirty. In 1865, Bowen had married again. By tacit consent the bitter past was buried between him and Beecher — or appeared to be, though Bowen would not step foot in Beecher's house. But for all that, *The Independent* seemed to want no more of Henry Ward Beecher than testimonials for Grover & Baker's sewing machines, Chickering pianos, Sapolio and Waltham watches, to boost the advertising end. Henry Ward wrote them. He even wrote one for a truss advertised to cure rupture. It appeared with his picture.

Not that there was any diminution in the friendship between Beecher and Tilton. Theodore knew all about the reasons for Bowen's break with Henry Ward — Bowen told his story one night, as the two men crossed on Fulton ferry, standing together in the early winter darkness watching the ice floes grinding in the river. They were like those ice floes, Theodore thought — these two men: swept in a current stronger than they, grinding each other to pieces. And God help anything caught between them! Bowen's tale gave Theodore a swift insight into the loneliness that beset Henry Ward, and the perilous expedients to which, perhaps, he had been driven in search of relationships in which his part might be that of a human being, with faults and frailties — not always a mouthpiece of God, living in a glare of publicity. He suddenly understood Beecher's passion for songbirds in cages, and why Henry Ward had them always about him.

Theodore Tilton was sorry for Henry Ward Beecher. He invited him to come oftener to his house, where Greeley and Wendell Phillips and Charles Sumner and Henry Wilson and John G. Whittier and many of the foremost figures of the radical Republican party were intimates. He thought it would aid Beecher to readjust himself to the abrupt cessation of editorial activities, after so many years — that perhaps, in such associations, Henry Ward might be led into new fields of creative work of value both to Beecher and to the country.

At first, Henry Ward, all agog over his excursion into national politics, was inclined to smile a bit at Theodore's proffers of hospitality. But with the fiasco of his support of Andrew Johnson and the isolation in which that adventure left him, Beecher suddenly bethought himself of his young friend's urgings, and dropped around to the little house in Livingston street.

But the stimulating circle of Theodore Tilton's friends was by no means Henry Ward Beecher's only resource in the peculiar crisis affecting both his inner and his outward life that followed his return from England. During the year of his editorship of *The Independent*, Henry Ward had written nothing for Bonner's *Ledger*—and it was through the *Ledger* that Beecher kept his touch with the masses. But now, with his triumphant return from Europe and the stoppage of his *Independent* articles, he was not only free to write for Bonner again, but with the tremendous publicity he had received for his English speeches, Beecher's name might really prove a card worth Bonner's holding. It was no surprise therefore when Bonner proposed to pay Henry Ward the record price of $24,000 to write a novel for the *Ledger's* columns.

They were curiously unlike in almost every respect—Bonner and Beecher. Sometimes disillusioned by what *Vanity Fair* called his "Sabbath harlequinades—motley in the pulpit," Henry Ward sought out Bonner's uncompromising uprightness as something stable and sure to cling to. There was a quality in Bonner that made Henry Ward's unending stream of jokes and comicalities singularly inappropriate in his presence. He held Bonner in awe. "I always made it a point of honor never to fail in any engagement I made with him," Henry Ward said. "This is what I would not have done for any other man living." It was what he did not do for Bonner, either.

When Henry Ward came to Brooklyn, Robert Bonner had been an obscure printer eleven years younger than Beecher. Now he was the proprietor of the weekly of the largest circulation in America, a millionaire who owned the fleetest trotters in the world. Every afternoon, in stove-pipe hat and Prince Albert, he raced his trotters himself in Central Park, against Cornelius Vanderbilt—and regularly showed the doughty Commodore the heels of Dexter or Rarus. Yet Bonner never bet on his horses. He did not belong to Henry Ward's church and did not agree with the doctrine that Beecher preached. But he knew Beecher — knew his strength and his weaknesses. And he was willing to back him.

Henry Ward himself had much less confidence than Bonner in his ability to rival Harriet Beecher Stowe as a novelist. "Oh, if I could make a story as easily as I can a sermon!" he wrote Bonner. "I have *dreamed* two *plots;* but forgot them as soon as I *waked.* . . . I hoped soon to have the use of my *head* — Then for a dash for immortality with R. B. driving! That would beat more than all the Vanderbilts on earth! . . . Give me your best wishes for a good intellectual impregnation, gestation & delivery."

But Henry Ward made no hand of it. "I am stuck. My team won't pull. They balk. One whole half day have I given, with all coaxing appliances. I have rubbed my head: looked in turn out of each window: up at clouds, down at grass; at a barn, the road, the hills, the river, in hope some kind spirit would come to my relief — None came!" he once wrote Bonner, about his weekly article for the *Ledger.* "I began an article on a Jackass this morning, & came near writing my own biography."

He found it even worse with "Norwood," his novel. The agreement with Bonner was made in January 1865. Henry Ward canceled all his lectures to devote his entire time to the story. But he was indolent with that irremediable laziness of active folk. Twenty months later his novel was still "all done but writing the verses," as he put it. That is, he had written little or nothing. He offered to substitute articles about Johnson, or Henry Wirz — that commandant of a Confederate prison who was executed after the war — or Stanton, whom Henry Ward regarded "*more* than any other THE man whom the war developed" — in short, he wanted to do anything else rather than write the novel he had agreed to write. But it was not all laziness. The truth was that he was horribly unsure of himself.

"In the earlier chapters I was almost in despair," he confessed. "I needed somebody that would not be critical, and that would praise it, to give me courage to go on with it." In the old days, he would have read his manuscript to Theodore Tilton; but now Theodore was away lecturing four months every winter, and when he was in town, terribly busy. So, instead, Henry Ward tried his opening chapters on Theodore's wife. "She was good enough to speak very enthusiastically of them," he said.

Indeed, Elizabeth Tilton was more than enthusiastic; she was flattered beyond all measuring that the great man should seek her out to consult as to the merits of his literary production. "Lib" Tilton was thirty-two, had been married ten years, borne five children of whom only three were then living — "an exquisite housekeeper, an ideal mother; a woman of wide reading and fine literary taste, of sunny temperament and affectionate disposition," Susan Anthony said. She was very tiny, with black hair that she wore in ringlets beside her cheeks, black eyes and dark skin. She was not pretty, but she had a little bird-like helpless way about her that made men feel big and strong in her presence. A Sunday School teacher, who would not permit her children to play with their toys on Sunday, to Lib Tilton religion was that exalted combination of sentimentality and emotionalism preached from Plymouth pulpit. She was the full flower of Henry Ward Beecher's teaching, in which she had been steeped for fifteen years. And when Henry Ward defined sympathy as "the act of throwing one's self in another's place, with a realization either of their joy or their sorrow, and then acting with them, or for them. In consequence of this interjected life, you participate in others' life. You know it. You make it your own," Lib Tilton felt that it was in this spirit that she was asked to help Beecher, when he came to her. And when he thundered from Plymouth pulpit:

"As men grow toward love, finer and finer are those interpreting sympathies by which they select out of the masses of men . . . those that by elective affinity are theirs by purity, by capacity, by self-denial; theirs by the power of humiliation; theirs because they can bear as Christ bore, and be Godlike, as he was, through suffering,"

she would close her eyes and feel herself lifted out of reality into some mystic sphere where she could somehow, by a complete abnegation, serve God through serving her Pastor. Her whole world was a world of transcendent sentimentality, from the days when she had been a model pupil in the Packer Institute and fed her mind upon the poems of Elizabeth Barrett Browning and the novels of Charles Reade and Mrs. E. D. E. N. Southworth, until the crowning moment when handsome, poetic, ambitious Theodore Tilton picked her out to marry.

The door of the house in Livingston street was spanned by an archway on which stood written: "And whatsoever house ye enter, ye shall first say: 'Peace be to this house.'" To Henry

Ward Beecher, peace did dwell in that house, with its walls almost covered with the best pictures, its tables littered with the best of books. He found there a sort of adoration "as a very Christ," — so Susan Anthony put it — that pushed back the years and banished his middle-aged dyspepsia and biliousness, and gave him new energy to achieve new triumphs in still untried fields — politics, fiction, or the production of some enduring work of literature, that would carry his name on when the sound of his voice had died away forever. All the affection that he had hungered for all his life was here, as a matter of course and without his asking. He felt there was no place in the world where he could get such inspiration as at Theodore's desk, while Lib Tilton, so tiny and so still, sat beside him in a low chair, darning her children's stockings.

"What a pretty house this is!" he said to her, once. And added wistfully: "I wish I lived here!"

And once he came with an armload of flowers. Lib wrote Theodore about it:

"After visiting with me twenty minutes he said: 'I am hungry to see your children.' 'Are you, really,' said I; 'Then come up directly and see them.' I had set apart this day for doll-dressing, as I had not time before Christmas. So he followed me up stairs where, for one full hour, he chatted and played with them delightfully . . . After this he invited me to accompany him to Mr. Ovington's, which call he had intended to make for some time. He said he had planned going there with his wife, and then to say to her, 'Come, mother, Mrs. Tilton lives right up here, let's call on her; she is all alone this winter.' "

But Henry Ward never did bring Eunice to call on Lib Tilton.

Nor was it just affection alone that Henry Ward Beecher found in the house in Livingston street. For there also came Elizabeth Cady Stanton and Susan Anthony and Laura Curtis Bullard and others among the leaders of that movement for woman's suffrage that in the late sixties so many women felt was on the very edge of success. With them, at Tilton's suggestion, Beecher joined in forming an Equal Rights Association that was to work for suffrage for women and for the freedmen. "All forward-looking minds know that, sooner or later, the chief public question in this country will be woman's claim to the ballot," Tilton wrote, in *The Independent*. Carried away by the enthusiasm of those he met at Theodore's house, Henry Ward agreed with this, and proudly claimed to have been a suffragist long before Tilton. He even offered to lecture for suffrage so soon as his novel for Bonner should be out of the way — and did so.

One other element bound Henry Ward Beecher into the household on Livingston street. Theodore Tilton had come a long way since he had refused a job on the New York *Herald* because he would not work on Sunday. Freed by Beecher's teaching from the Old School Presbyterian orthodoxy in which he had been brought up, he was now, just past thirty, testing not alone his religious beliefs, but the very social theories and ethical standards of a day peculiarly artificial in its outlook. He, too, had drunk deep of the sentimentality that flowed from Plymouth pulpit; but his mind was too active to accept emotionalism as a philosophy. Tilton felt himself in consequence subject to great oscillations of belief. These he took to Henry Ward Beecher, as an older man — his pastor and his friend — for assistance in finding a more secure intellectual footing. And loyally Henry Ward sought to help his friend:

"I look back upon periods when, if I had expressed the then results of thought and reading, I should have committed myself to views which I have outlived or left behind," Henry Ward wrote him. "I regard the labors of naturalists as indispensable to the final adjustment of truth, and I would encourage such men as Spencer to say whatever is given them, not because they bare the full truth, but because they bring out the truth, and because the human mind must pass through that stage before it will come to the rest and glory of the final Christianity, the second coming of Christ — morally, not historically — in which He shall reign in heaven and on earth over faith and science, and unite and harmonize both."

But to Elizabeth Tilton, these questionings in her husband were blasphemous. As his eager mind strove "to tear off little by little — since I cannot do it at a stroke — some of the bandages that have hitherto bound me blind," she swung farther towards a sort of intoxicated mysticism, in which love and faith and God and her Pastor were all confused — in which her senses and her sentimentality were inextricably interwoven with love of Theodore, a desire to save Beecher from "the evil influences which surround him," a belief that "there is no spot so sacred in all this earth as Plymouth Church," and a sort of

pathetic and terrible bewilderment in which she could write
her husband of Beecher:

"With all the earnestness of my being, I commit you both to
God's love. He has signally blessed you both, and He will help
His own beloved. Why I so mysteriously was brought in as actor
in this friendship, I know not yet. No experience of all my life has
made my soul ache so keenly as the apparent lack of Christian
manliness in this beloved man . . . I do love him very dearly, and
I do love you *supremely, utterly* — believe it. Perhaps, if I, by God's
grace, keep myself white, I may bless you both. I am striving. God
bless this trinity!"

It was more than could reasonably be expected that Henry
Ward Beecher should put aside an idolatry so rare. Besides, he
had need of it. The streams of emotionalism he was called upon
to supply from Plymouth pulpit flowed from no inexhaustible
spring. He was no internal combustion engine of sentimentality.
Here in the little house in Livingston street was more than he
required, literally poured out for him. And so he came almost
daily — so often, indeed, that people began to talk; he sent
books and pictures and giant baskets of flowers; he played with
Lib Tilton's children, and put her littlest baby to sleep — "laid
him down, and covered him up"; called her "a dreamer," and
read to her from the manuscript pages of "Norwood":

"All women marry gods, but sadly consent afterwards to live
with men. The quenching of their resplendent imaginations, the
discovery and full conviction that the husband cannot, by his
strength and goodness, dominate the heart and be sovereign in love,
at length produce a crisis. Some easily yield up the delusion . . .
Others there are, of diviner mould, who cannot lose faith in Love
. . . They know that there is a life which they never live; that
there might arise out of their hearts a love so great, so pure, so
commanding and satisfying, that all other experiences of fortune
would, in comparison, be of little moment."

When her Pastor read things like that to her, little Lib Tilton
was suddenly seized by panic. "While I long to be with you, I
am haunted continually with fears that your cheery face will
soon be shadowed and the dear head droop!" she wrote Theodore. "This thought is agony to me, and I have spent many
hours since your absence weeping because of it . . . *I am
afraid!*"

CHAPTER XX

FALTER

THOUGH Henry Ward had had grave doubts of his ability to write a novel, when he finally got into "Norwood," he was delighted. "There is not a single unpleasant memory connected with it," he said. There were so many pleasant ones! As he read Lib Tilton from his manuscript:

"It would seem as if, while her whole life centered upon his love, she could hide the precious secret by flinging over it vines and flowers, by mirth and raillery, as a bird hides its nest under tufts of grass, and behind leaves and vines, as a fence against prying eyes,"

her heart stopped beating in a sort of panic that he had divined her secret and seen through all her little subterfuges to hide it. He read her, too, of the trailing arbutus — "like the breath of love" — and a few days later brought her a water color of a trailing arbutus. That afternoon, when Susan Anthony came to call, Lib Tilton slipped her hand under gaunt Susan's arm and drew her to the mantelpiece where the new picture hung.

"My Pastor brought that to me this morning," she confided, her eyes all shining. Little Alice Tilton, Lib's youngest daughter, named her doll "Rose Wentworth" after the heroine of "Norwood."

In these days, Lib wrote Theodore, traveling through the West on his one-night stands:

"About 11 o'clock Mr. B. called. Now, beloved, let not even the shadow of a *shadow* fall on your dear heart because of this — now, henceforth, or forever. He cannot by *any possibility* be much to me since I have known *you*. I implore you to believe it, and look at me as in the Day of Judgment I shall be revealed to you."

And Theodore believed it. Perhaps she did, too.

Tilton was a little shocked to learn, in Chicago, that Henry Ward, his brother Edward, and a number of Congregational clergymen friendly to both, had inaugurated a determined campaign to oust him from the editorship of *The Independent*. Under Tilton's direction, *The Independent* had become a journal of "practical Christianity in which good men of all churches

— yes, and good men of no churches — can Christianly unite," instead of a narrow sectarian organ. It was precisely this "eminently unecclesiastical and catholic tone" that Tilton had absorbed in Plymouth Church. He could not understand why Beecher should assure him so warmly that he had not wandered from received opinions while he was at the same time secretly writing his brother Edward in vehement protest against what Henry Ward termed Tilton's heresies. After all, Beecher's brother Charles had recently been convicted of heresy, and his own doctrine was regarded by many as highly irregular. There were a number of things about his friend Henry Ward Beecher that Theodore Tilton never did understand.

First and foremost, he could not comprehend why Beecher set such store by the forms of orthodoxy. But Beecher was older and wiser, and he knew that in that day the organization of the church was still a tremendous factor in the social and economic life of the country. A man might be without the church and yet be moral; but he stood alone. Within the church, censorship of the conduct of fellow members was strictly enjoined — "no member of the church has a right to pass over without notice the dereliction of a fellow member from Christian duty, on the plea that the offense is not personal against himself" read the manual of Plymouth Church. And organized society supported the church member because he bore the guinea stamp of a morality assumed from his church membership, while upon a man not of the Lord's elect rested the burden of proving that he was not every conceivable brand of sinner.

No one knew all of this better than Henry Ward Beecher. He had been brought up on it. And, as in the days of his examination for the ministry out in Ohio, he kept himself scrupulously within the letter of orthodoxy. Plymouth Church he had created in his own image — big, prosperous, a little flamboyant, apparently self-sufficient — truculent, even — but for all that strictly a Congregational church. And when Henry Ward Beecher made his dramatic entry, flung his soft hat under a settee, wrapped his cape about him and sat looking from left to right and right to left over the sea of faces, he knew that there, in the midst of his own, he could do whatever he pleased. For these men and women who crowded pews and aisles came for certain things they could find nowhere else in an odor of sanctity: excitement, entertainment, secureness, hope, self-confidence, emotional release. These things Henry Ward Beecher gave them with all the weight of divine sanction. When he cracked his pulpit jokes, there were polite titters from the more costly pews and loud guffaws from the galleries; when he raised his voice in prayer, the tears streaming down his full cheeks, he could hear the little staccato sobs of women and the harsher sobs of men from every corner of the vast house; and when he rose to exalted flights of sonorous phrases, the applause began gently and swelled to a thunderous drum-roll of triumph. Plymouth Church was a great name in the land as Henry Ward Beecher's name was great. The members of Plymouth Church were share-holders in him. He could do no wrong.

Henry Ward had come nearest to it in his support of Johnson. It had been a warning to Plymouth Church — and a lesson to Beecher. With his mind full of the political rôle that he came to believe he had played in England, Henry Ward had dreamed for a moment of a career above and beyond Plymouth Church. The brutal logic of practical politics swiftly taught him that unless his words were the expression of what millions of sub-stantial, well-to-do, respectable citizens of the type that made up Plymouth Church were thinking — they might be never so eloquent, but they had no significance. In doctrinal matters, on the other hand, he was expected to be bold, to satisfy the urge of his congregation to feel themselves the forward looking members of the community. Tampering with the existing politi-cal and social order was, of course, perilous, and frowned upon. But for those who felt the cry of progress, there was much that might be done to soften the inflexible Calvinism of the early days of the church in America — and that Henry Ward Beecher did.

There was hell, for example. The day of profound belief in lakes of brimstone was waning — indeed, there were many peo-ple who had not the faintest idea what brimstone was. Yet there was, too, a certain reluctance to give up eternal punishment al-together — surely one was not going to meet murderers and adulterers and one's own pet enemies in heaven! It was just the opportunity for Henry Ward Beecher, and he met it to the complete satisfaction of Plymouth Church:

"Our Saviour is the foundation of this doctrine," he said. "The simple circumstance that it is a doctrine of which Christ is the author and teacher is to me the most convincing of all things."

Thus hell as an institution was preserved. But as all a good Christian (of any denomination) had to do was to be possessor of what Henry Ward called "the all-inspiring love-power" to be saved, hell became rather an historic relic than a living influence in the lives of men.

The writing of "Norwood" served other useful ends besides the pocketing of the $30,000 Robert Bonner finally paid for the novel. Thirty thousand dollars was a good deal of money, even for Beecher, and there was considerable criticism of his accepting so much. But Theodore Tilton came to Beecher's rescue in *The Independent*, and it all proved good advertising. So did the fact that "Norwood" was dramatized by Augustin Daly. It failed as a play, but Beecher was savagely attacked for permitting his work to be shown "among the quarreling, drunken, ogling, mincing, brutal women of the brothel and their like," who, he had said, were the frequenters of the theater.

"We have, it is true, often heard Plymouth Church called a 'playhouse' and the sermons preached there as good as plays," wrote Tilton in defense. "But we had supposed that Mr. Beecher had sufficiently atoned for the dramatic character of his sermons by the sermonic quality of his novel."

Henry Ward himself joined in the general levity with which "Norwood" was received by the critics.

"People used to accuse me of being the author of 'Uncle Tom's Cabin' — until I wrote 'Norwood,' " he laughed.

While Beecher's novel was appearing in the *Ledger*, he published, as a sort of set-off to it, a volume of "Prayers from Plymouth Pulpit," and was amazed to find that this, too, raised a tremendous uproar. So many good church folk were shocked at the very idea of a stenographer taking down a prayer to God in shorthand, for subsequent publication and sale. It took all of Tilton's eloquence in *The Independent's* columns to allay the storm.

The principal utility of "Norwood" had been to permit Henry Ward to drop quietly from public attention during the period of its writing, and while the incident of his support of Johnson was being forgotten. When Grant was nominated in Chicago, and it was certain that Chief Justice Chase would not be the choice of the Democratic Convention in New York,

Henry Ward Beecher took his stand. He never had been one of the self-styled "Liberal" Republicans, he said.

"I have liked Grant from the first," Henry Ward declared. "Solid, unpretentious, straight-forward, apt to succeed and not spoiled by success, wise in discerning men, skilful in using them, with the rare gift (which Washington had in an eminent degree) of wisdom in getting wisdom from other men's councils. I confidently anticipate that, great as his military success has been, he will hereafter be known even more favorably for the wisdom of his civil administration."

He was for Grant for a second and even for a third term. Grant, to Henry Ward Beecher, was the ideal American.

In August, little Paul Tilton died — the baby Henry Ward used to put to sleep while Theodore Tilton was writing from Illinois of the hunger of his heart to see "Paul with his toes held out to be named at the fire." Henry Ward came down from Peekskill for the funeral. There was no mourning. The little house in Livingston street was flooded with sunshine. Lib Tilton, bravely keeping back the tears, was dressed all in white.

On October 9, there was a great Grant meeting at the Brooklyn Academy of Music. Henry Ward Beecher was the orator. The hall was packed. Before the speeches began, an enormous canvas was unrolled from the ceiling, on which Thomas Nast's smashing cartoon "Matched!" was painted. Henry Ward outdid himself. He called the Southerners "Rebels." The only thing that could prevent civil war in the South again was to elect Grant and Colfax. "It is said that Gen. Grant is a drunkard," he thundered. "I do not believe a word of it. But if it were so, I had rather have Gen. Grant a drunkard than Horatio Seymour sober!" The applause was "tremendous and long continued." The crowd cheered and cheered. And tiny little Lib Tilton in the audience, hustled from side to side, could hardly get to Beecher to tell him how wonderful he was. But the next day was Saturday. Henry Ward's family was still at Peekskill. He was alone at home, writing his sermon. And she came to see him. She was still trembling with excitement over his great triumph the night before. Her heart was full of tears, still, over the death of her baby — Theodore could not bring himself to talk about Paul to her — she must talk to some one. So she came to her Pastor.

That was the tenth of October, 1868.

"Norwood" was still appearing in the *Ledger* and Henry Ward still writing furiously on it, to keep ahead of publication, when new literary adventures opened before him. So far Beecher had made relatively little from his books. Two volumes of selections from his sermons were published in England without authorization — "I had two children born and wasn't aware of it," Henry Ward laughed. Also, after the attacks of Edward Beecher and his friends on *The Independent* as "an infidel sheet" because Thomas Wentworth Higginson, Wendell Phillips and Charles Sumner wrote for it, Bowen ceased to print Beecher's sermons in its columns. Unless Henry Ward were willing to confine his influence to those who attended Plymouth Church in person, he would have to find a new method of having his sermons published.

Of course Henry Ward Beecher had no intention whatever of giving up his vast audience of hundreds of thousands who read his printed sermons. So when his friend Howard suggested a sort of Plymouth Church publishing firm, whose principal capital should be the literary productions of the Beecher family, Henry Ward was delighted. His initial contribution would be his sermons in weekly pamphlet form. And on top of that, he was to write an elaborate "Life of Jesus, the Christ," as Henry Ward worded it, from which stupendous profits might be expected. Beecher received, cash down, a bonus of $10,000 to start the work so soon as "Norwood" was out of the way. Meanwhile, Sam Wilkeson, of the *Tribune*, was taken into the firm partly to secure for the new publishing house his "Record of a Busy Life" which Horace Greeley had written for Bonner's *Ledger*, and partly because Wilkeson was just then handling the publicity funds of the Northern Pacific "pool" for Jay Cooke & Co. — a financial connection not to be sneezed at.

Henry Ward did not begin work at once. Robert Bonner could have told Beecher's new publishers a thing or two about the job they would have on their hands to get copy out of him. Bonner paid Henry Ward $200 a week for an article for the *Ledger*, and then hired a man to wait at Beecher's house with orders not to budge until the manuscript was placed in his hands. Instead of writing his "Life of Christ," Henry Ward presided at suffrage meetings, and sat for a portrait by William Page, of the National Academy, which Theodore Tilton was having painted. At Page's studio he met a classmate of Theodore's, Francis De P. Moulton, a young business man of excellent family and high promise, whom he found agreeable and cultivated. Moulton's wife was a member of Plymouth Church, but Moulton himself was not a church member. He and Henry Ward would walk down to the ferry together, and talk, in a casual way.

Frank Moulton represented a type in the life of America new to Henry Ward Beecher. Here was a young man whom the church had never touched — not even Henry Ward's own particular church, with all its tremendous concessions over the churches of Lyman Beecher's day, made for the very purpose of reaching out and taking possession of just such young men as Moulton and millions like him. This younger generation seemed to be moved neither by fear of future punishment nor hope of future reward, but to prefer integrity for its own sake. Once Tilton had written:

"It seems to me that the truest method, and the surest, of developing a Christian character, is never to swerve from one's own inward idea of right, whether or not this ideal be in conformity with the prevailing conventional notions of good men."

So Frank Moulton believed. And to Henry Ward Beecher as a Christian minister it was both a puzzle and a challenge that a man could so live. For when Beecher talked to Frank Moulton, he saw with lightning-lit clearness that the struggle against which old Lyman Beecher had fought was now really only just beginning in America. In it, he might be taken as representing one camp, and Moulton the other. Midway of these opposing forces lay many like the Tiltons, striving desperately to reconcile conduct with creed and threshing themselves to pieces in the effort — doomed in any event. But between the new generation of the Moultons and the older tradition of the Beechers the issue was clear: if the former won, Henry Ward saw plainly enough that the day of the vast nation-wide power of organized religion was over.

To Henry Ward Beecher any such outcome was unthinkable. Yet he had no specific program to controvert it. "The Christian principle was love, with a codicil: 'abhor that which is evil,'" he preached. But what was evil, in this new alignment of social and economic forces growing out of the war?

The group of women who gathered at the little house in

Livingston street — Susan Anthony, Elizabeth Cady Stanton, Henry Ward's own half-sister, Isabella Beecher Hooker, and the radicals among the suffragists — believed that women's participation in politics would prove a regenerating element. Lib Tilton was one of the editors of *Revolution*, the suffrage paper, and chairman of the executive committee of the Equal Rights Association. Under her influence Henry Ward became a vice-president of the more radical wing of suffrage workers, and made speeches for woman's rights:

"Now, when the red-hot plowshare of war has opened a furrow in this nation, is the time to put in the seed," he declared. "If you have radical principles to urge, don't wait until a quiet time comes, until the public mind shuts up altogether. We are in the favored hour, and if you have great principles to make known, this is the time to advocate them."

While the country was still rocking from the pandemonium of Black Friday and men were whispering behind their hands that Grant had made his millions out of an obscene compact with Jay Gould, Henry Ward was the lion of his sister's suffrage convention at Hartford.

"If you want to make your audience cry, take a cup of tea before you speak," he advised Susan Anthony. "If you want to make them laugh, take a cup of coffee."

"But you make them do both!" Susan exclaimed.

"I take a cup of each," rejoined Beecher, solemnly.

In New York, in Washington — from one end of the country to the other — people were too shocked by the stupendous corruption of the day to laugh or to cry, either. Compared with what had been revealed in six months of Grant's administration "the worst scandals of the eighteenth century were relatively harmless," wrote Henry Adams. The knavery that came to light "smirched executive, judiciary, banks, corporate systems, professions, and people, all the great active forces of society in one dirty cesspool of vulgar corruption." But Henry Ward Beecher was working on his "Life of Christ."

He took the manuscript sheets of his first chapter to the little house in Livingston street, and read them to Lib Tilton. He had read them to no one else, she said, and wanted to know how his opening chapter would sound. She was going to have a baby herself in a few months, and what her Pastor had written of the preparations for the birth of the Christ child thrilled her. She ran up stairs and fetched one of the scripture lessons she taught her class of poor mothers, on Mary the Mother of Jesus, as an example of woman's faith, and read it to him. She read him other things she wrote — even, sometimes, her letters to Theodore — and he "spoke to her in great admiration of them." He talked over with her what he was writing, too, and got her criticism and advice. "It was entering into her life, and, in a sense, giving her an interest in mine," said Henry Ward.

More and more he frequented the little house in Livingston street — "a place of peace" he told Lib it was. He loved to tell her, too, of the great pleasure he had in the way of her household, as he put it, "and how I was glad to resort to it, and that it was where people could not find me." Once he fetched his daughter-in-law, "Hattie Ben," along, and played with Lib Tilton's children — "held Flora on his lap and chatted with Alice to her great delight, and left two cakes of soap that would keep their hands from chapping." Once Lib and Henry Ward went shopping together, to buy a doll for his grand-daughter — as large as Lib Tilton's boy Carroll. But "such grown-up dollies do not live in Brooklyn," Lib wrote, disappointed.

"The house of the Tiltons' was the second home of Mr. Beecher, and scarcely a day passed that he did not visit it. He found here the brightness, congeniality, sympathy and loving trust which every human being longs for." Thus Susan Anthony, who loved both the Tiltons as her own family.

In the Spring of 1870, besides his lecture tour, Theodore had to be in Washington a good deal, too. Henry Ward took Lib for drives behind his new team of fast grays, and brought her his new volumes of "Sermons," of "Lecture Room Talks," and his "Overture of the Angels" — the second chapter of that "Life of Christ" which she had helped him write — each with its inscription from the giver. She put them all away in a little secret closet where she kept her precious things — the plaster cast of her dead baby's face and the picture of Mary holding the body of Christ in her arms, which came from her Pastor.

The period of uncertainty that followed his break with Bowen and the severance of his connection with *The Independent* appeared at last to be at an end for Henry Ward Beecher. The *Church Union*, a minor religious weekly distinguished

principally for the virulence of its attacks upon Theodore Tilton, was to be had for its debts, and Beecher's friends, the
Howards, proposed to take it on, in association with him, and
make him editor of a journal of his own. Henry Ward was en-
raptured with the idea. "If wisely managed I think there is
money in it: and if it does succeed there will be a good deal of
money," he wrote. He was right. Given a controlling interest
in the enterprise at its start, Beecher sold his holdings six years
later for $10,000. In the paper's management, however, Henry
Ward insisted on "a bishop's, not a curate's, place" — he had
produced only one chapter of his "Life of Christ" in a year and
a half, and felt a bit guilty about taking on additional responsibilities. "A dull paper that represents no new thought in morals,
religion or politics," it turned out to be, according to Elizabeth
Cady Stanton, "that floats on the name of Beecher, in spite of
Mrs. Stowe's heavy Scripture lessons and Edward Beecher's
theological antiquities." Eunice conducted a column of
"Motherly Talks"; the Rev. S. B. Halliday, Henry Ward's assistant at Plymouth Church, a religious department; Hattie and
Calvin Stowe and Thomas K. Beecher and Horatio King of
Plymouth Church all appeared in its staid pages. Marshall's
Household Engraving of Washington (it was the Stuart Washington, though the artist was not mentioned) was given as a
premium with each new subscriber. But to the enterprising who
sent in two new subscribers came "a new and superb steel-en-
graving PORTRAIT OF HENRY WARD BEECHER."

Once, shortly after Henry Ward took charge and the paper's
name was changed to *Christian Union* to please him, he failed to
send in his leading article. One by Calvin Stowe on eternal punishment was substituted at the last minute. When it appeared
many readers were shocked at this reversion to Calvinism. But
Henry Ward only laughed:

"The paper has only said the old things in the old way, and
nobody will notice at all," he said. "Merriam [the assistant editor]
is anxious that we should say what we think. Sometimes that
is very important. But no investigator ought to say all he thinks, for
his opinions grow and change from year to year . . . To run the
paper into such a discussion at this time would be to ruin its influence without accomplishing anything of good."

Yet Beecher was canny rather than cautious. Where money
was involved, he considered twice before acting; in other re-

spects he took tremendous chances without even a second thought.

It was just at the close of 1869 that a well-known journalist, Albert D. Richardson, was shot in the office of the *Tribune* by Daniel McFarland, with whose divorced wife Richardson was alleged to be living. There was an incredible to-do over the affair. Richardson attended the Rev. O. B. Frothingham's church, when he attended any, and Beecher was in no wise involved in a business which gave every promise of being highly scandalous. Two days before Richardson died and four days after he had been shot, Henry Ward married him to the lady in the case. Frothingham was present and could have done the job quite as well as Beecher — why Henry Ward did it is by no means clear, except that he could not resist the lure of the limelight.

The hurricane of popular disapproval of Beecher's act quite took his breath away. He tried to justify himself by charging McFarland with adultery; but the public would have none of it. The papers were full of the sordid details of the wretched affair: Beecher had married a divorced woman, about the legality of whose divorce there was serious question, to the lover who had broken up the Home; he had, they said, desecrated the sacrament and stood "for the sacredness of 'free love' principles." Henry Ward scuttled to cover. Horace Greeley had asked him to do it, he pleaded. But Greeley promptly said he did no such thing — with some of his most picturesque profanity. Robert Bonner finally came to the rescue: if, in his haste and excitement, Henry Ward had made the charge of adultery "without time to investigate it, on mere hearsay evidence, and without legal proof to sustain it, is it not a plain matter of duty on your part towards the accused to come out and say so publicly?" he wrote Beecher. Henry Ward thought it was. "The man was dying," he explained. "Was that a time for sifting evidence?"

But there were literal-minded folk who pointed out that Beecher admitted having held himself in readiness to perform the ceremony for two days, during which time he might, they said, have looked into the case a bit. And anyhow, they asked, what affair was it of Beecher's? Some even went so far as to imply that a man who bandied public charges of adultery around in that irresponsible way had no business in the ministry. Ultimately McFarland was acquitted and given the custody of the children — which only made Henry Ward's position worse. It was all a tempest in a teapot. But coming when it did and as it did, the incident stuck in the public mind.

One other matter at this time gave Henry Ward Beecher's friends cause for concern.

It was the day of easy money. From the President himself, accepting gifts right and left, to the Hon. William Marcy Tweed of Tammany Hall, every one who could seemed to be bent upon getting something for nothing — preferably out of the public. Men high in Plymouth Church were closely allied with enterprises that, a few years previous, would have drawn out the unsparing condemnation of their pastor. But now there appeared to be no clear conception of where speculation ended and peculation began. Joseph Howard ran a newspaper subsidized by Tweed, in the interests of the Tweed ring. "Tearful Tommy" Shearman, clerk of Plymouth Church and Henry Ward Beecher's personal attorney and intimate friend, was, as the New York *Times* put it, "one of Jim Fisk's most active lawyers, and the man who was personally mixed up with the grossest of the scandals which were perpetrated in the time of the corrupt Tammany Judges. He either suggested them or carried them out." "Elegant Oakey" Hall, a full partner in the Tweed Ring, presided at meetings at which Henry Ward spoke, and nobody thought anything of it. Sam Wilkeson, Jay Cooke's Man Friday in what the Brooklyn *Eagle* called the "Northern Pacific swindling games," was Henry Ward's business partner in the firm of J. B. Ford & Co., publishers of the "Life of Christ" and the *Christian Union,* and Col. John H. Puleston, another partner in the same firm, was Jay Cooke's New York representative in floating the Northern Pacific "pool." It was perhaps natural enough, therefore, that in January 1870 Henry Ward Beecher should receive from Jay Cooke & Co. $15,000 worth of stock in the Northern Pacific Railway, for the express purpose of "influencing the public mind to favor the new railroad. Beecher's aid," it was provided, "included the use of the *Christian Union* newspaper."

There was, of course, nothing dishonest in Beecher's share in this transaction. Gen. Horace Porter, President Grant's private secretary, accepted a similar offer "with alacrity," as did John W. Forney, of the Philadelphia *Press,* and Horace Greeley, of the *Tribune.* Jay Cooke even held a note bearing the President's signature. Nevertheless, there were friends of Henry Ward Beecher who felt that this was not exactly the rôle for the Great Preacher. At that moment, George William Curtis was calling the Northern Pacific "pool" a "huge robbery of the public domain," and before long the Brooklyn *Eagle* was to refer to it as a "fraud through which thousands of clergymen, widows and children have been impoverished or beggared." On the ethics of lending such a name as Henry Ward Beecher's to stock promotion, E. L. Godkin, of *The Nation,* was outspoken: "A newspaper, and especially a religious newspaper, stands in a very different relation to its readers from that of a broker to his customers. . . . Nor has an editor ever ventured to defend his selling his columns by the plea that he only sold them to good men for good purposes. The public would no more listen to such an excuse than it would listen to a judge's saying that he only took bribes from the right side."

It was to this growing worldliness in her Pastor that Lib Tilton referred when she had written Theodore so pitifully: "Oh, let us pray for him! You are not willing to leave him to the evil influences which surround him. He is in a delusion with regard to himself . . ." But Henry Ward himself felt none of this. He was in fine spirits, making his pastoral calls, and kissing his parishioners all around. Now that he had his own paper, he was determined to reconquer Bowen's support. One night at the house of Deacon Freeland, he met Bowen and pleaded with him, kneeling on a chair, his hand on Bowen's knee, tears streaming down his face, in an agony of contrition.

"Bowen, we must be friends," he cried. "There must be no break between us; it would kill me!"

And the next Friday, at prayer meeting, he announced to every one that he and Bowen and Theodore Tilton had cleared up all their differences, and resumed "the old relations of love, respect and reliance."

That Fourth of July, President Grant and Ben Butler came to Bowen's place at Woodstock, Connecticut, and Henry Ward rode on the engine of the President's special train and afterwards made a Fourth of July speech. And Beecher and Bowen and John Tasker Howard, the trinity who had conceived Plymouth Church, and seen it grow all the twenty-three years since its founding, ran a foot-race on Woodstock Common. Howard won, and Beecher and Bowen, their arms around one another, came puffing up to congratulate him.

Never had Henry Ward Beecher's life seemed to open before him so clearly and surely as on that day.

But Theodore Tilton was not there. For back in the little house in Livingston street, he had been sitting the night through on the side of the bed, while Lib Tilton lay stretched at his feet, her arms rigid across his knees, telling her story. It was not a new story, and in the cold language of the sworn statement presented to Plymouth Church, a sordid one:

"That on the evening of October 10, 1868, or thereabouts, Mrs. Elizabeth R. Tilton held an interview with the Rev. Henry Ward Beecher, at his residence, she being then in tender state of mind, owing to the recent death and burial of a young child; and during this interview an act of criminal commerce took place between this pastor and this parishioner, followed also by other similar acts on various occasions . . ."

In the next issue of *The Independent* there appeared a strange editorial from the pen of Theodore Tilton.

The Wreck of a Life

"When a man of unusually fine organization, with high-strung nerves, with a supersensitive conscience, with a tremendous sensibility to reputation, and with a boundless ambition, suddenly, by one act, sacrifices the slow honors of a lifetime, there is something in his self-destruction to excite the pity of mankind . . .

"To such a man the agony is that there is no restoration. The crime leaves an ineffaceable stain. He looks back upon a violated ideal. He can never again be his former self . . . He may become in many respects a wiser, nobler, cleaner man — taught by experience and chastened by suffering; but nothing can prevent the remainder of his life from being, to his own thought, a vanity. Whoever else may pardon him, he cannot pardon himself. Every day's sunshine will mock him, and make him see the shadow of his soul. No bird will ever sing in his ear without reviving his innocence as a memory and his guilt as a fact. He is like one who has lived his appointed span. The grave waits him. Death is his next friend.

"A man with a sword in his soul, giving him a wound that never heals, exciting in him an agony that never sleeps, filling him with a despair that never takes a ray of hope — if any human creature deserves sympathy, this is the man."

In this spirit, Theodore Tilton said no word to Henry Ward Beecher of what his wife had told him.

Part V: Climax

‣‣‣

"Excuses for moral delinquency are, therefore, usually processes of self-deception. At first they may not be; but at length a man who tries to deceive himself comes into that state in which he can do nothing else but deceive himself. A man can put out his eyes, inwardly, so that at last he will not see that a lie is a lie, and a truth a truth. Deceit may be known to be so at first. It then becomes less and less noticeable and finally the mind is falsified and lives without frankness, openness, truth or purity. And nothing is more common than that men may be in that state, and with a certain kind of exterior morality, making them noticeably good in external matters while they have actually lost power of moral discrimination in respect to their own inward habits."

HENRY WARD BEECHER, 1858

‣‣‣

CHAPTER XXI

1870

By MARCH 30, 1870, the political horizon of the country was cluttered with generals — and women. The generals, after the manner of their kind, were more or less taciturn. But the women were not.

The fifteenth amendment to the Constitution had been ratified and proclaimed. "After the negro, the women," Wendell Phillips had said, and with the backing of men of the influence of Benjamin F. Butler, Chief Justice Chase, George William Curtis and Thomas Wentworth Higginson, the women of the country were bent on getting the right of the suffrage for themselves, and getting it at once. It was the golden age when Lucretia Mott was still active and Elizabeth Cady Stanton, Susan B. Anthony and Anna E. Dickinson stumped the country from coast to coast for what were then known as "woman's rights." It was the golden age, too, of the birth of spontaneous disgust with corruption and cynicism in politics and business — of the day when thousands of men would march and cheer for Greeley and his plea that North and South clasp hands across the bloody chasm. And then vote for Grant, and more corruption.

The position of women left much to be desired. Mrs. Chickering came down from her country place to meet her husband in New York and attend the theater. In some way, she missed Mr. Chickering. It was too late to return to the country, so she went to an hotel. She was a lady of middle-age of the highest social standing and respectability. But no decent hotel would let a room to an unaccompanied woman. Mrs. Chickering finally agreed that one of the hotel's porters should sleep outside her door all night, and was permitted to stay. Women were buttoned up tight in frocks that extended from their chins and trailed on the ground behind, crowned with bonnets resplendent with ostrich plumes, and wore *chignons*, "outrageously large and improbable," fastened with jet pins. "The law of marriage demanding that in *no* case a man shall seek another wife while his first one lives is always imperative," Catherine Beecher wrote Susan Anthony. Divorce for any cause was social ostracism. Whoever transgressed the rigid rules of convention was promptly charged with being a "free love" advocate. In the seventies, love had to be paid for.

Henry Ward Beecher had given the suffrage leaders every right to count upon his active support. He had announced his conversion to suffrage as early as 1854, had gone on record in an address in 1860 on Woman's Influence in Politics which had been used as a suffrage tract ever since. He had been one of the organizers of the Equal Rights Association in 1865. "It needs only that women should have a conscience educated to their duty of suffrage, and it will be yielded," he wrote, then.

But suddenly the flame of political radicalism seemed to burn out in Henry Ward Beecher. The popular trend was plainly towards reaction. He found Grant "a man without vices." Measures to check the shocking scandals of the administration had, he felt, been "resisted only until it was seen that the people really demanded them." For the highbinders of the Tweed Ring, still at large and unpunished, he expressed his "sympathy with men who are suffering on account of their wrong doing."

He deserted that wing of the suffrage movement to which Susan Anthony and his sister Bella belonged for the more conservative group of Julia Ward Howe. "I am not so sanguine of the day when a woman's vote must be calculated by political assemblies as you may be," he wrote Lucy Stone in November 1870, and declined to be president even of the American Women Suffrage Association again.

Of his editorials in the *Christian Union* at this time only one, rejoicing at the Prussian victory over the French, was of significance: "The Lord has intrusted the leadership of Europe to a people whose race-mission it has always been to develop freedom, intelligence and pure spiritual religion," he wrote. He meant the Prussians.

And he saw no more of Lib Tilton. Once she wrote him while he was at Peekskill, in August, and begged him to come to her. He came and found her much depressed. "I cheered her the best I could and prayed with her just before leaving." The next day he called again. She would not see him. He learned nothing, he says, of what troubled her.

But others were learning.

For almost twenty years Theodore Tilton had listened to Henry Ward Beecher preach the following of Christ, from Plymouth pulpit. To Tilton it was not just an emotional stimulus — he took it seriously. He had no sense of humor and was incapable of achieving that practical separation of Christianity from daily life that enabled the brethren of Plymouth Church to sob over their souls on Sunday and go about gouging their fellow men the rest of the week with a clear conscience.

"Sometimes I get such an overpowering view of what it is to live the true Christian life that I feel like forsaking all else and following Christ — following him, I mean, not merely in a sentimental, reflective and emotional way, but in denying myself the things which I am mostly engaged in seeking and in enduring hardness as a good follower of Jesus Christ,"

Tilton wrote. Hard-boiled newspaper colleagues spoke of him as of Sir Philip Sidney — "the high-erected thoughts seated in a heart of courtesy." They thought religious journalism bad for him, as no doubt it was. Indeed, religion was Theodore Tilton's vice. He brought it into his daily life, not as a talisman or a fetish, but as a guide of conduct. And it played the very mischief.

So when little Lib Tilton told her tragic story that breathless July night, Theodore sought his Testament and read the Gospel according to St. John, down to where it stood written: "I am the light of the world: he that followeth me shall not walk in darkness, but shall have the light of life." And he took a great resolve, and went about his business as editor of both *The Independent* and the Brooklyn daily *Union*, as a lecturer traveling four months in the year from one end of the land to the other, as one of the leaders with Wendell Phillips, Horace Greeley and Charles Sumner of the liberal Republicans, as president of the radical wing of the suffrage movement, and an implacable opponent of the Tweed Ring in New York and the corruption of the Grant administration throughout the country — as though nothing had happened.

It did not work. Despite the enormous burden of multiple activities Theodore Tilton heaped upon himself, his mind could not let go of the story his wife had told him. He had to talk to some one about it. So he sought out the man he knew whose life was nearest what a Christian's life ought to be — Oliver Johnson. Johnson was one of the early Garrisonians, a wheel horse in every humanitarian movement for almost half a century, a man whose philosophy of life was quite simply to love his neighbor as himself. "You cannot paint too blackly the wrongs you have suffered," Oliver Johnson told his young friend. "On that point I make no plea in abatement, but I beg you to remember that nothing can change the law which makes forgiveness noble and godlike."

That was all very well, but what tortured Theodore Tilton was the fact itself, not what to do about it. All the months that this hideous business had been going on, Lib Tilton had written him letters of passionate devotion. Theodore did not understand. Perhaps a woman could help him. So he went to the oldest and most intimate friend he and Lib had, Martha Bradshaw. For twenty years the two families had been inseparable, and for eighteen years Martha Bradshaw had taught Sunday School in Plymouth Church. She was a deaconess of Plymouth Church — a Christian woman of the highest type. She revered Beecher as no man on earth, and what Theodore told her made her sick with misery and wretchedness. She could not help Theodore Tilton.

And poor little Lib Tilton, suddenly so buffeted about and tortured in mind and heart, was sadly in need of some one to talk to on her own account. It had all been so simple, with her Pastor by to assure her that she had committed no sin. But now she felt with Theodore that there was "a sort of mountain of clouds overcoming us." She longed to throw herself into the arms of some one who would understand. And just then along came Susan Anthony — wise, honest, homely, loyal, true-hearted Susan. Lib and Theodore had just had one of the bitter quarrels that were all too frequent now.

Elizabeth Cady Stanton tells the story:

"Mrs. Tilton remained with Susan throughout the night. In the excitement of the hour, amid sobs and tears, she told all to Miss Anthony. The whole story of her own faithlessness, of Mr. Beecher's course, of her deception, and of her anguish, fell upon the ears of Susan B. Anthony and were spoken by the lips of Mrs. Tilton.

"The next morning Mr. Tilton told Susan never to enter his house again. And she told him she should enter whenever she chose."

Which was Susan all over.

Susan had to be off on her lecture trip, and Lib Tilton was left alone again, with no one to go to for help in those difficult days. She feared and mistrusted her mother, Mrs. Morse — in fact, both she and Theodore thought Mrs. Morse should have been in an asylum long ago. But to whom else could she turn? It proved a mistake, however, for Lib to trust her mother with the tragic tale. Mrs. Morse's rage — curiously enough against Theodore — knew no bounds, and in despair, Lib fled at last to friends in Marietta, Ohio. But even there she was pursued by her mother's wild threats and her plea that she leave her husband. Frantic, Lib wrote Theodore in November 1870:

"For the agony which the revelation has caused *you*, my cries ascend to Heaven night and day that upon mine own head all the anguish may fall . . . Even so, every word, look or intimation against Mr. B.,* though I be in no wise brought in, is an agony beyond the piercing of myself a hundred times. His position and his good name are dear to me. Once again I implore you for your children's sake, to whom you have a duty in this matter, that *my past* be buried — left with me and my God."

But alas! she had told her mother — and her mother "told all the world." Mad as Mrs. Morse undoubtedly was, she was not one to waste tears on spilled milk. Also, she knew her Theodore.

* Verbatim testimony: Tilton vs. Beecher, Vol. I, p. 672: "Q.—Who was the Mr. B. of whom she spoke? A.—The Rev. Henry Ward Beecher."

He could forgive but he could not forget. He would be going back over the whole business for the rest of all their lives, as he had been doing ever since Lib's confession — and that, to Mrs. Morse's way of thinking, was just no life at all. Theodore had thrown away his best opportunities again and again to follow some ridiculous new-fangled notions like Abolition and woman's rights and God knows what all, filling the house in Livingston street with strange women like Susan B. Anthony and Elizabeth Cady Stanton — "free lovers," Mrs. Morse called them. Theodore made good money, but he spent every cent of it on silly things like pictures and books. Five hundred dollars for a portrait of Henry Ward Beecher! The very thought enraged Mrs. Morse so that she tried to cut the painting to pieces with a knife.

On the other hand, there was Beecher. A man of standing and influence who could get government jobs for his friends. He made a mint of money, too. Plymouth Church had just raised his salary to $20,000 a year, and he received as much again, or more, from his lectures and his books and the *Christian Union*. And he was generous with it.

Now if only Theodore would just leave Elizabeth for good — go to Europe, maybe — she and her daughter could live so happily together in a little house where Mr. Beecher could come again as of old, and she could call him her "dear son" and he call her "mother." So reasoned Lib Tilton's mother; and being a person of action, she set to work with the wish fathering the thought to spread stories of an impending separation of the Tiltons, of Theodore's cruelties and brutalities and infidelities and immoralities — not one of which had the faintest foundation in fact.

Theodore had other troubles as well. Thomas Murphy, President Grant's particular crony, had been appointed collector of the port of New York, a post for which he was conspicuously unfit, and Henry C. Bowen of Plymouth Church was hand in glove with him in one of the most fruitful grafts of the Grant administration, the "general order business" of the custom house. Naturally, Bowen wanted *The Independent* and the Brooklyn *Union* to support the Administration and back up his little private graft. He had just made a highly flattering contract with Tilton to be his editor for five years and he hardly thought Theodore would object. But whatever other faults Theodore may have had, his pen was not for sale. He refused to permit the papers under his editorship to do anything of the sort. And right then and there Bowen made up his mind to be rid of Theodore Tilton.

But even Henry Bowen could scarcely break a contract because his employee was conscientious. So when he heard the gossip about Tilton that Mrs. Morse was so assiduously spreading, it was music in his ears. And when, on top of it, Tilton printed in *The Independent* an editorial on "Love, Marriage and Divorce," Bowen felt that he had just the excuse he was looking for to compel Tilton to back up the political corruption he found so profitable — or get out. "Marriage without love is a sin against God," wrote Theodore. "Christ set forth an ideal of so faithful a fidelity that most marriages estimated by this standard would prove adulterous." In Plymouth Church circles any such ideas as these were considered revolutionary. Even Henry Ward Beecher, hardly clear of his scrape over marrying Mrs. McFarland to Richardson, felt that a man so tainted with heresy could not properly be retained on a religious paper like *The Independent*.

Of all this seething undercurrent of tale-bearing, intrigue and gossip in his church, Henry Ward Beecher swore he had no inkling whatever until early in December 1870, when, he said, Mrs. Morse sent one of the Tilton servants to ask him to come to her house and give his pastoral advice in a domestic matter. It was from this half-witted servant girl, Beecher declared, that he learned most of the gossip about Tilton; the remainder came from Mrs. Morse. The following day, Henry Ward returned with Mrs. Beecher, and while he and Lib Tilton remained alone together — in prayer, he says — Mrs. Beecher and Mrs. Morse went off into another room to plan a campaign of action.

To Eunice Beecher, who had always hoped the worst of Theodore Tilton, Mrs. Morse's lurid tales were thrice welcome. She promptly adopted Lib Tilton, and set forth with real enthusiasm to plant the stories of Theodore's rascalities right where they would do the most harm — in the ear of Henry C. Bowen, Tilton's employer. And Henry Ward, on his part, gave his advice, as pastor, "that a separation and a settlement of *support* will be wisest," as a solution of the state of affairs that had presumably arisen in the little house in Livingston street.

Five years later, on the witness stand, Beecher was asked:

"*Judge Fullerton:* 'Before giving the advice you did not see Mr. Tilton?'

"*Mr. Beecher:* 'I did not.'

"*Judge Fullerton:* 'Nor communicate with him?'

"*Mr. Beecher:* 'I did not.'

"*Judge Fullerton:* 'In any way?'

"*Mr. Beecher:* 'Not in any way.' "

In justice to Beecher it must be recorded that his advice (if he ever gave it) was not followed — that, instead, poor badgered little Lib Tilton returned to the house in Livingston street, and to Theodore. Indeed, when the great trial came, Mrs. Beecher, Mrs. Morse and Lib Tilton were never even called to the witness stand by Beecher's attorneys to substantiate his extraordinary story of that interview. There was no evidence, beyond Beecher's own unsupported word, that he had ever so far betrayed a friendship of fifteen years' standing or belied his profession as a minister of the gospel — or that the whole meeting at Mrs. Morse's (if it took place at all) was not perhaps just a little white comedy played to still the jealousy of Eunice Beecher over her husband's relations to the Tilton family.

And now events swept to swift disaster.

It was Christmas eve that Oliver Johnson came to Theodore Tilton with the news that "an avalanche" of malicious gossip about him had been poured into Bowen's ears, and on Christmas day Tilton accompanied by Johnson went to Bowen's house to have it out. The gossip against Tilton was speedily disposed of:

"I *know* that some of the stories told against him are false and that malicious persons are on his track, with the intention of hounding him down," Johnson assured Bowen. And there the whole matter might have ended.

But seven years before, just after the deathbed confession of his first wife, Bowen had written Theodore Tilton from Woodstock a letter full of a terrible anger against Henry Ward Beecher. "One word from me would make a *revolution* throughout Christendom," he had said, and had gone on to set down in writing specific charges against Beecher in terms which cannot be reproduced here of acts for which, if Bowen were to make them known, Beecher would be "driven from his pulpit and from Brooklyn in twelve hours." When Henry Bowen married again, Tilton dismissed the matter from his mind, as Bowen seemed to do. Now, however, Bowen brought it up anew, and

"as if to leave no doubt on the mind of either Mr. Johnson or myself, you informed us that Mr. Beecher had made to you a confession of his guilt, and had with tears implored your forgiveness," Tilton wrote Bowen, afterwards.

And Oliver Johnson, not to be outdone in Christmas spirit, added a contribution of his own:

"I also know something that you do not of the evidence against Mr. Beecher," he, too, wrote Bowen; "and if he denies his guilt in the matter whereof he was accused in that Christmas day interview at your house, he lies in the face of evidence that would convict him in a court of justice. *That evidence I have seen.*"

All of this naturally brought Theodore's own grief sharply to the fore — his wife had just had a miscarriage, and he was beside himself with worry. He had already confided in Johnson, so now he told Bowen, too, something of the story. And Bowen cried, "with terrible emphasis that he [Beecher] ought not to remain a week longer in his pulpit," and suggested that Tilton write, and he himself would carry, a demand upon Beecher that he "immediately cease from the ministry of Plymouth Church and quit the city of Brooklyn as a residence."

And Theodore Tilton then and there wrote such a note, and gave it into the hands of Henry C. Bowen.

From that moment Theodore Tilton, as his friend Frank Moulton put it, was a ruined man. He and all his affairs became a mere tragic episode in the war between Beecher and Bowen that had gone on for years, and that was to endure until both were dead. It was not just the matters set forth in Bowen's Woodstock letter to Tilton that lay at the bottom of the enmity of the two men — seven years had passed since then, and whatever he may have suffered at Beecher's hands, the first flame of Bowen's wrath may reasonably be considered to have abated somewhat. But to Henry C. Bowen Plymouth Church was his church. He had called together the little group that had founded it, in his own house. He had fetched Beecher, then a mere backwoods preacher, to Brooklyn — paid his expenses,

guaranteed his salary, housed him till he got settled and bought
Beecher the very suit of clothes he preached in. It was Henry
C. Bowen, not Henry Ward Beecher, who had raised all but
$150 of the church's $14,000 floating debt. For twenty years,
there had not been an activity connected with Plymouth
Church that Bowen had not fathered. Most of them he had
also financed. As for Beecher — "I have done more for him
personally than for any other man living or dead," said Henry
Bowen; "and I never stopped doing for him until I found out
he was an impure man."

And now Bowen suddenly saw the vast edifice of Plymouth
Church — *his* church — the church into which he had put
twenty years of his life and a fortune in money — threatened
by Beecher's "remissness and unreliability." It must be saved,
somehow. Tilton was nothing to him. Beecher was nothing to
him. If he could use Tilton to force Beecher out before the
whole structure of Plymouth Church came crashing about his
ears in scandalous catastrophe, so much the better . . .

So Bowen sent his boy around and summoned Beecher to
meet him in a couple of hours at Deacon Freeland's — he would
not step foot in Beecher's house. And when Beecher arrived,
Bowen handed him Tilton's letter without comment. Henry
Ward read it, and put it in his pocket.

"The man's crazy," he muttered, and sat for a long time in
the gathering darkness, in silence, drumming on the arm of his
chair.

"Do you know about Tilton's family troubles?" he asked
Bowen, at last. And he told Bowen what he had heard from the
Tiltons' servant, and the gossip he had had about Tilton from
Theodore's mother-in-law, and, warming to his subject, Henry
Ward told Tilton's employer that Mrs. Tilton had written him
from Marietta, Ohio, complaining of her husband's treatment
of her, and that he would like to show Bowen the letter. He
said he felt that Tilton was not a fit man to edit *The Independent*, and as for the *Union*, "I thought that as the editor of
the Republican organ in Brooklyn he would be found to be a
man that would get his paper into trouble." And finally, Henry
Ward said that Mrs. Beecher knew more about Tilton's moral
delinquencies than he did, and he begged Bowen to get further
details from her. And that he did and said all of these things
about a man who had been his intimate friend for fifteen years,

the Great Preacher five years later took his solemn oath in open court.

But all the back-stairs gossip Henry Ward detailed to Bowen affected Bowen not a whit. He told Beecher plainly that he had already made up his mind about Tilton — as indeed he had. And he came on away.

As Bowen walked home through the dark streets, he could see into houses where stood tinsel-decked, candle-lit trees in honor of the Christ child. Christmas spirit was in the air — but Bowen felt none of it. He was turning over in his mind what Beecher had told him. If there was a single shred of truth in any of it, he reflected, Henry Ward Beecher was required by the laws of Plymouth Church to do one thing, and only one: "In all cases of scandalous offenses, or any breach of morality . . . affecting Christian character, when efforts to bring the offender to repentance prove unavailing, the church should proceed to the act of excommunication . . . giving the reasons for the same, which should be publicly announced before the congregation, on the Lord's day."

Back in Indianapolis, Henry Ward Beecher had not hesitated in the case of Owen Tuller, Bowen thought. Why did he hesitate now?

CHAPTER XXII

THE UPPER ROOM

WHAT passed in the mind of Henry Ward Beecher that Christmas week of 1870, no one will ever know. Indeed, during the five terrible years that followed the man's inner life became so entrenched behind *cheval de frise* of words and moat of tears that he himself lost his way in contradictions and involvements — "days in which midnight came at midday and a horror of darkness," as he put it. And in those black days there was just one place Henry Ward could go for peace and comfort: the house of Frank Moulton — "as good a friend as God ever raised up for a man," Beecher called him — and Emma Robinson Moulton, his wife — "one woman in this world to whom I can go and talk of my troubles without reserve."

It was a strange fatality that drew Frank Moulton and his wife into the tangled web of circumstance that seemed to engulf every one in any way connected with Henry Ward Beecher in a terrific battle that for years filled whole pages of newspapers daily, obsessed the thoughts of millions of men and women, disrupted churches, shook the very foundations of the established order, and destroyed individuals as ruthlessly as if they had been thrown into the machinery of a stamping mill. Perhaps indeed when the social history of the last quarter of the nineteenth century comes to be written, the Beecher case may be found to have had more to do with clearing the intellectual ground and freeing the minds of men from the clutter of the past than any other one episode.

Frank Moulton was only one of the most casual of Beecher's acquaintances. Tilton he knew better, but not with any great intimacy, either. He and Theodore had been classmates at the College of the City of New York. When Frank graduated, he had an appointment to West Point, but did not feel physically strong enough for army life. Instead, Peter Cooper got him a job with the mercantile house of Woodruff & Robinson. In due season Moulton married the niece of Jeremiah P. Robinson, one of the partners, and at last became a partner, himself. He was an excellent business man, quite good looking, tall and stalwart, with a tousled mass of flaming red hair, large blue eyes and a Lord Kitchener mustache. Mrs. Moulton was shyly pretty, with a color that came and went—a direct, frank-spoken woman, with no nonsense about her. They were candid young people of culture and fineness, to whom life was a simple affair of straightforward loyalty and truth.

When Theodore Tilton returned to Livingston street from Bowen's he found Frank Moulton waiting to wish him a Merry Christmas. Theodore was seething with the whole story of his talk with Bowen and Oliver Johnson. He walked up and down the room with his giant's strides and told it to Moulton. Not Lib's part in it, of course—but what Bowen had said about Beecher and about the note he had written to Beecher. Tilton felt, somehow, that a great and dramatic act had been accomplished. Moulton felt otherwise.

And so did Lib Tilton. She had listened to Theodore's story in a fever of terror and weakness. She knew her Henry Ward Beecher better than Theodore did, for all their long association

—she had reason to. She knew that, under the surface geniality and benevolent, easy-going manner that the world saw as Beecher, there was something as hard as the precious stones he carried about in his pocket—something of the rocky hills of New England fortified by years of holding the passions and emotions of great masses of men and women in the hollow of his hand. Lib Tilton was afraid of Henry Ward Beecher. She had been afraid to tell him that she had confessed their relations to Theodore, though Theodore thought she had done it long ago. She was afraid, now, that in any fight between Bowen and Beecher she and Theodore and her little brood of children would be swept to destruction. And most of all, she was afraid of that hard-faced woman, Beecher's wife, with her beetling brows and her curt manner. Lib Tilton knew she could expect no mercy from Eunice Beecher.

Part of all of this Lib said to her husband, and begged him by the love he held for his children, if not for her, to get out of range of the firing while there was yet time. She gave him a note to Beecher saying that she had told Theodore everything, and that she "loved her husband with her maiden flame." Theodore was to take that to Beecher, say his say, and be done with the whole business. And then she and Theodore were to begin life all over again, with the New Year. For, a week before in *The Independent*, Bowen had printed a signed article about Tilton:

"Bold, uncompromising, a master among men; crisp, direct, earnest; brilliant, imaginative, poetic; keen as a Damascus blade and true as the needle to its pole in his sympathies with the needs of man, he was surely designed by Providence for the profession he had chosen."

Tilton was, he announced, to become the star contributor to *The Independent* and editor-in-chief of the *Union*. Bowen did not announce it, but Theodore Tilton under his new contract was to have the highest editorial salary paid anybody in that day. In every material way, the new year beckoned enticingly to Tilton and his wife. If only they could just wipe out this whole business about Henry Ward Beecher!

Well, Theodore was going to do his best to get rid of that, too. The day after Christmas, at the office, he informed Bowen that he was going to see Beecher shortly and have things out with him. It was like a thunderclap to Henry C. Bowen. God knows, he hated Henry Ward Beecher, and would like nothing so much as to see him destroyed. He had hoped that Tilton might do it. But here was Tilton going to talk things out with Beecher — instead of shooting him down, or publishing his infamy to the world, or something equally effective — and final. That was just like Theodore Tilton, Bowen thought. You could never depend on him to behave like anybody else. He was fed up with Tilton, anyhow, was Bowen — Tilton and his quixotic ideas about honesty in politics.

"If you ever dare reveal to Beecher the things I told you and Johnson about him, I'll fire you on the spot!" he roared at Theodore. And Theodore, white with rage, shouted back:

"I'll do just as I think best about that!"

Bowen slammed the door behind him. Strange, thought Theodore Tilton. What had happened to Bowen? He had been hot enough against Beecher the day before. And why did Beecher give no sign in response to the note Theodore had sent him? Had Bowen ever delivered it? Tilton waited until Friday for some move from Beecher. Then he went to Frank Moulton. This time he told Moulton the whole tragic story.

"Go tell Beecher I want to see him," he said. "Then let me talk to him here, in your house — I can't take him to mine."

It was prayer meeting night in Plymouth Church, when it was Henry Ward Beecher's habit to sit in a great arm chair in the lecture room and discourse on all sorts of subjects, less formally than in a sermon. It was what Henry Ward liked best about his ministry — it was all well enough to move the vast crowds that came to Plymouth Church to tears or exaltation by a sermon. But that was what the crowd came for. De Witt Talmage was doing that every Sunday right there in Brooklyn with crowds as big as Henry Ward's — or bigger. But the prayer meetings were the backbone of Plymouth Church as an organization. They were where Henry Ward kept his personal touch with his enormous flock. He submitted himself to a kind of cross-examination on anything and everything, with questions and answers flying back and forth and a great deal of jollity — "that royal, lion-like, defiant presence, fresh, hearty and jovial — a sort of evangelical Bacchus," as his admirers described him.

It was a wretched night, snowing and cold, and Henry Ward

was just starting out for his prayer meeting when Frank Moulton was announced. He had never been to see Beecher before, and Henry Ward was a bit surprised to see him now.

"Mr. Beecher, Mr. Theodore Tilton is at my house, and wishes to see you," Moulton said.

"This is Friday night! This is prayer meeting night! I can not go to see him," objected Henry Ward.

"He wants to see you with regard to your relations with his family, and with regard to a letter he has sent to you through Mr. Bowen," Moulton replied. "I think you had better go and see him."

Henry Ward Beecher stood there for a while in silence. Then he went to the door and called to George Bell, in the next room.

"Take the prayer meeting for me, please, George," he said.

He followed Moulton into the street. The wind blew great gusts of snow into the faces of the two men, blinding them. They could hardly walk.

"This is a terrible night," said Beecher. "There is an appropriateness in this storm . . . What can I do? . . . What can I do?"

"I don't know," said Moulton. "I am not a Christian. I am a heathen. But I will try to show you how well a heathen can serve you. I will try to do you some good. I will try to help you."

When they got to the house, Moulton sent Beecher up stairs to the front room where Theodore Tilton was waiting for him. And Beecher went up alone.

And now there come to be two sides to the story of Henry Ward Beecher. There is his own, for the most part unsupported by any confirmative evidence whatever. And there is the sworn testimony of Theodore Tilton, Mr. and Mrs. Moulton, confirmed in part by that of Martha Bradshaw, Franklin Woodruff and Lib Tilton's brother; and supported by the unsworn evidence of Elizabeth Tilton, herself. There were thousands of men and women, from one end of the country to the other, who believed implicitly that "the simple word of Henry Ward Beecher is worth more than the sworn testimony of an acre of other witnesses." Yet even in his own day, Henry Ward Beecher's unsupported word was not sufficient to convince a jury drawn from neighbors, who lived in the very shadow of Plymouth Church. It convinced the country at large even less.

Other thousands believed with Charles A. Dana, of the New York *Sun*, that "Henry Ward Beecher is an adulterer, a perjurer, and a fraud; and his great genius and his Christian pretenses only make his sins the more horrible and revolting."

As the healing years pass, there is less interest in Henry Ward Beecher's guilt and more in his genius — which is as it should be. For had he not possessed the genius, his guilt would have been a matter of no more consequence than that of countless other clergymen before and since, whom far less evidence has been sufficient to condemn. Clerical adultery was not invented by Henry Ward Beecher; nor clerical hypocrisy either. But if he was guilty of the adultery, it may be contended, he was also guilty of the hypocrisy. And if he was guilty of the hypocrisy, it may be argued that the scope of his genius should be widened to include the carrying of hypocrisy to greater heights than any other character in history.

These are judgments. They have no place in this study. Henry Ward Beecher did as Henry Ward Beecher was. No miracle was worked for him, or by him. Step by step, each subsequent act in his life is the consequence of its predecessors. In what follows, therefore, the acts of Henry Ward Beecher during this disputed period are presented as they are consistent with the life of Henry Ward Beecher revealed in these pages. It is thus his own attorneys plead that he should be judged.

To the interview between Henry Ward Beecher and Theodore Tilton, in the upper room at Frank Moulton's house, on December 30, 1870, there were no witnesses. According to Beecher it was a terrific indictment of his faithlessness, double-dealing, disloyalty to a friendship of many years, mischievous meddling and slander, entirely apart from any question of intimacy with Tilton's wife. But Theodore Tilton went on with his accusation. In Beecher's own words:

"that I had suffered my wife and his mother-in-law to conspire for the separation of the family; that I had corrupted Elizabeth, teaching her to lie, to deceive him, and hide under fair appearances her friendship to me; and that I had made her to be — that I had — that he had married her one of the simplest and purest women that he ever knew, and that under my influence she had become deceitful and untrustworthy; he said that I had tied the knot in the sanctuary of God, by which they were to be bound together in an inseparable love, had also reached out my hand to untie that knot, and to loose them one from the other — he drew from his pocket a strip of paper — and read to me what purported to be the statement of his wife to him that Mr. Beecher had solicited her to become his wife, to all the intents and purposes which were signified by that term."

To this terrible indictment all Henry Ward Beecher had to say was: "Mr. Tilton, this is a dream. She could never have made in writing a statement so untrue." Not until three years and a half later, and eight months after the specific charge of adultery had been made public — when the clamor of the whole country rendered some statement from Beecher inescapable — did Henry Ward Beecher ever deny to Tilton or any one else, in any document produced then or since, the truth of Theodore Tilton's arraignment. Indeed, on oath he stated:

> "*Judge Fullerton:* 'Didn't you consider it in the light of a false charge known to be so by Theodore Tilton?'
> "*Mr. Beecher:* 'I did not.'"

One does not have to be much of a psychologist to find this testimony of Beecher's exceedingly interesting, especially in view of its points of difference with the testimony of both Tilton and Moulton regarding that interview in the upper room at Moulton's house. For Theodore Tilton swore that what he then charged Henry Ward Beecher with was "sexual intimacy" with his wife, not what Beecher so quaintly termed "improper advances" to the lady. And to that Frank Moulton also swore.

This tenuous distinction indeed grew to be the very crux of a case prodigiously revealing, by that fact alone, of the incredible sham of the period. For, at this distance, the herculean efforts made by Henry Ward Beecher and his friends to convince the world that he stood accused not of adultery but merely of doing his best to commit adultery seem curiously futile. There appeared, in that day, to be a virtue in this defeatist viewpoint which has evaporated with time. The world does not stand still.

Henry Ward staggered from his interview with Theodore Tilton, his hand to his head, moaning, "This will kill me!" He had received Theodore's permission to see Lib Tilton once more, to satisfy himself of the authenticity of her confession. He went straight to the little house on Livingston street, with Frank Moulton beside him, plowing through the snow-drifts, in silence. At the door Moulton left him, and Henry Ward went in.

Poor little Lib was lying on a couch, with folded hands, still weak from her miscarriage — "as one dead," Beecher described her. There he was — her Pastor! After all these six hideous months, he had come back to her! He was saying things — asking her things . . . What difference did it make — all these quarrels and perils and warring interests? She took the pen he handed her. He held the inkstand. She wrote. . . .

When he told of it on the witness stand, Henry Ward wept. But that night it was Lib Tilton who wept. Henry Ward Beecher put the paper she had written for him in his pocket, and came on away. But after he had gone, Lib Tilton lay thinking a long time. It was so difficult to know what to do! . . . She did not want to hurt any one. . . . So, before she went to sleep, she wrote a little note to Theodore:

"Midnight.
"My dear Husband:
"I desire to leave with you here before going to sleep a statement that Mr. Henry Ward Beecher called upon me this evening, asked me if I would defend him against any accusation in a *council of ministers*, and I replied solemnly that I would in case the accuser was any other but my husband. He (H. W. B.) dictated a letter, which I copied as my own, to be used by him as against any other accuser except my husband. This letter was designed to vindicate Mr. Beecher against all persons save only yourself. I was ready to give him this letter because he said with pain that my letter in your hands addressed to him, dated December 29, 'had struck him dead and ended his usefulness.'

"You and I are both pledged to avoid publicity. God grant a speedy end to all further anxieties. Affectionately,
"Elizabeth."

And the following morning she wrote Frank Moulton and asked him to get back from Beecher the paper she had given him, so that both it and her written confession could be destroyed. Frank Moulton did so. Henry Ward was a bit reluctant at first to let go of the document; but as it had probably already served its main purpose in setting Henry Ward right with Eunice Beecher, he did give it to Moulton.

For Henry Ward Beecher was twenty-five years older than Frank Moulton. He had lived in a great number of widely different places and known all sorts and conditions of men. Man was the instrument upon which he loved to play as upon an organ — women the treble and men the bass — with a strong predilection to use of the tremolo stop. And he was shrewd, with the New England shrewdness of his fathers. Thirty-three years before he had begun as a preacher, at $500 a year. Now he made an hundred times that. He knew what people wanted, did Henry Ward Beecher — knew the joints in men's armor, and how to pierce them. It was his business to know these things. And he knew his business.

Henry Ward had done a good bit of thinking himself, since he left Elizabeth Tilton lying so white and still on her sick-bed. So long as she lived and Theodore Tilton lived, whatever secret it was these three shared between them was not safe. The retraction she had given him was worthless — he might make a collection of such written exculpations. They would avail him nothing if Lib Tilton were to tell her story. As Henry Ward saw it, he had just one course: he must bind Lib Tilton and her husband to silence by bonds of common interest. And as it was difficult, under the circumstances, for him to do this himself, he must enlist an ally to do it for him. And right there God raised up for him, as he put it, Frank Moulton.

First, Henry Ward knew that with a man like Moulton he must be candid.

"Of course, if this charge is made against me, if Theodore should make any charge against me, my defense would be the technical one of general denial," he told Frank. "But with you, since you know the truth, I would throw myself upon your friendship, and what I believe to be your desire to save me." And according to Moulton he went on to say "with great sorrow, weeping, that he loved Elizabeth Tilton very much; that the expression, the sexual expression of that love was just as natural in his opinion — he had thought so — as the language that he had used to her; that if he had fallen at all, he had fallen that way, through love and not through lust." And then, with infinite pathos, Henry Ward said: "My life is ended. When to me there should now come honor and rest, I find myself upon the brink of a moral Niagara, with no power to save myself — and I call upon you to save me." And he wept.

Moulton was impressed. Beecher was a great man — the greatest preacher in America, certainly — possibly the greatest preacher the world had ever known. And here he was holding out his two hands to Frank Moulton, tears streaming down his face, begging Moulton to save him. Frank Moulton was no prude. Beecher's weaknesses were none of his affair. Besides, there was more than Beecher involved. If this thing ever got out, it would strike a deadly blow at respectability, everywhere. Goodness knows, the country was in a sufficiently deplorable state, anyhow, what with post-war looseness of morals, and business and political corruption rampant. Moulton had no desire to see the world stood on its head by the revelation of any such scandal as this. While he was hesitating, Henry Ward went on to tell him that the preceding summer "Elizabeth Tilton had sent for him to come to her house, and told him she believed their relations were wrong. And he told me," Moulton swore, "he said to her: 'If you believe these relations wrong, then they should be terminated.' And he told me that he had prayed with her — prayed to God with her — for help to discontinue their sexual relations."

As he thought it over, it seemed to Moulton that however regrettable the whole business had been, it now was really ended. No one could change the past, but at least he could help prevent what had taken place from working any further mischief. So he promised Beecher to do what he could to manage Theodore Tilton, and keep the whole thing quiet.

From that time on, for the next three and a half years, Frank Moulton was engaged in little else. At all hours of day and night — sometimes even twice a day — before Frank was up in the morning and after eleven at night — Beecher was in and out of the Moulton house in Remsen street. Of course in time Mrs. Moulton was bound to know all about it; and in time, too, Moulton's business partners were going to have to know all about it, as well. And when Henry Ward was not flying around the corner to confer with Frank Moulton, the tall, thin form of Theodore Tilton might be seen striding to or from the house in Remsen street. In fact, just now when Moulton came home from his talk with Beecher on the last day of 1870, there sure enough was Theodore Tilton, waiting for him.

This time, for once in a way, Theodore had something on his mind besides Beecher. Bowen had fired him that very morning, giving no reason at all — just fired him. Of course, Tilton had a perfectly good claim against Bowen for some $7,000 for-

feit provided in his contracts; but collecting money from
Henry C. Bowen was no easy task. Later, Bowen made it plain
that it was Tilton's threat to reveal what he, Bowen, had said
about Beecher "that led me to discharge him summarily."
Tilton suspected that, anyhow.

Theodore was furious with Bowen, and in a mood of great
despondency. Here was Beecher, who had played havoc with
Elizabeth's life and his — and for all he knew to the contrary,
played havoc with Bowen's life as well — going scot-free; and
he, Theodore Tilton, with a wife and four children on his
hands, out of a job. . . . Frank walked the silent streets with
him for hours, telling him how sincerely Beecher had repented,
counseling him to put the whole horrible business behind him
and begin his life anew with the morrow.

And as they walked, the chimes rang in the New Year.

For the first time in seven years, Henry C. Bowen came to
the New Year's reception at the Beechers', and improved the
occasion to tell Henry Ward that he had discharged Tilton the
day before. It gave Beecher a sinking feeling in the pit of his
stomach that he was to grow fairly familiar with in the course
of the next few years. But he was not familiar with it yet, and
during the remainder of the thousand calls he received that day,
and until he could get Frank Moulton up stairs in his study,
where he could talk with him about this fresh danger, Henry
Ward was in a cold sweat of terror.

For Henry Ward knew his Theodore — none better. "Theodore Tilton attacks the objects of his hatred with the *élan* of a
man who never distrusts himself; whose cruelty is the double-
distilled cruelty of outraged vanity and outraged principles, of
which he is the avenger and the advocate," Eugene Benson had
said of him. Henry Ward felt in his bones that Theodore
would fight Bowen to a finish — and here he had been walking on a volcano, as he put it, urging Bowen to get rid of
Tilton! . . .

Everything depended on Frank Moulton now, Henry Ward
thought. And so to Frank he addressed his best efforts. "He
felt that he had done a great wrong, because he was Theodore's
friend, he was his pastor, he was his wife's friend and pastor,
and he wept bitterly," Moulton testified. Frank was deeply
moved by the tears and the protestations. He told Henry Ward

that if he would just write that to Theodore, he was absolutely certain it would fix everything. "For I know he loves his wife," said Moulton.

But Beecher was too agitated to write. Instead, he walked up and down the room pouring out his contrition while Frank did his best to get it all down, to show to Theodore. When the ground had been pretty well covered, Moulton read the production over to Henry Ward,* and Beecher signed it. But nowhere in it was there any denial of the truth of Theodore Tilton's terrible accusation:

> "*Judge Fullerton:* 'I now ask you again to give this jury any message you sent by Mr. Moulton, any word that you spoke upon that subject coupled with a request that it should be communicated to Mr. Tilton, or any other thing you did for the purpose of accomplishing that end — namely, your own vindication in the mind of Mr. Tilton.'
>
> "*Mr. Beecher:* 'I sent not one line or word, that I remember, to Mr. Tilton — I — if you will allow me to go on —'
>
> "*Judge Fullerton:* 'That is an answer to my question.' "

This is the message Henry Ward Beecher sent to Lib Tilton's husband, by Frank Moulton:

"Brooklyn, January 1, 1871.
"In trust with F. D. Moulton

"My Dear Friend Moulton:

"I ask through you Theodore Tilton's forgiveness, and I humble myself before him as I do before my God. He would have been a better man in my circumstances than I have been. I can ask nothing except that he will remember all the other hearts that would ache. I will not plead for myself. I even wish that I were dead; but others must live and suffer.

"I will die before any one but myself shall be implicated. All my thoughts are running toward my friends, toward the poor child lying there and praying with her folded hands. She is guiltless, sinned against, bearing the transgression of another. Her forgiveness I have. I humbly pray to God that he may put it into the heart of her husband to forgive me.

"I have trusted this to *Moulton* in confidence.

"H. W. BEECHER."

* Beecher's version was that he signed without reading. But on cross-examination he acknowledged the general purport of the note to be substantially what he said.

On the morrow, Henry Ward Beecher stood in Plymouth pulpit and looked out over a packed house. He wet his thick lips with his tongue.

"The text to-day—" he began. Down below him, in the costliest pew of Plymouth Church, his glance caught Henry C. Bowen's saturnine face, inscrutable behind its beard. The vast auditorium rocked before Henry Ward's eyes . . . He took a grip on himself, closed his Bible and stepped to the edge of the platform.

"The text to-day is from the fifteenth chapter of the Gospel according to St. Matthew, the twenty-fifth verse:

"'Lord, help me!'"

CHAPTER XXIII

REMSEN STREET

IT WAS a great pity that there was no telephone service in 1870. Everybody connected with what came to be known as the Beecher Scandal wrote a vast deal too freely. "In the peculiar atmosphere of this case, where people shriek in stilted English, instead of talking quietly, and where the most hideous offenses do not seem incompatible with perfect sainthood, even Mr. Beecher seems to lose his power of lucid expression," complained the New York *Times*. It would have been far better for Henry Ward if he had lost his power of any kind of expression. As Thurlow Weed's old Albany *Journal* put it, "It is Mr. Beecher's own hand which furnishes the only evidence that seriously inculpates him. He is his own accuser, and he must defend his name against himself."

A judgment natural enough when the flood of letters which distinguished the Beecher case was first released. But it fails to include a number of elements in the situation in which Henry Ward Beecher found himself in the opening days of 1871. The immediate and pressing problem was how to handle Theodore Tilton; but it was by no means the only problem. Brother Bowen of Plymouth Church was, and had been all along, Beecher's most dangerous enemy—the more dangerous as he remained in the background, outwardly friendly. And while Henry Ward was afraid of Theodore's impulsiveness, he was twice as fearful of Bowen's cold-blooded animosity.

For Henry Ward Beecher was confronted not just with the peril of his relations with Lib Tilton — that alone he might face down. Indeed, when he came at last to tell his story to a jury, he did stoutly maintain that from that fateful night in the upper room of Frank Moulton's house until Theodore Tilton appeared like an avenging angel before Plymouth Church in July 1874, not the slightest suspicion ever crossed his mind that Tilton thought him guilty of adultery with his wife. It was his story, and he stuck to it. He insisted, on oath, that what he thought Theodore Tilton and Frank Moulton and Mrs. Moulton and Mrs. Bradshaw and Tilton's mother-in-law and half of Brooklyn were talking about for three years was just that Lib Tilton had confessed to her husband that her Pastor had made "improper solicitations" of her — which, of course, was quite all right. Henry Ward admitted that Tilton had every ground for thinking this, and that he was convinced that Tilton was sincere in believing it. But adultery — no. And what he then swore he had been so contrite over that he had prayed to God to put it into the heart of the lady's husband to forgive him for was, he said, that he had advised Mrs. Tilton to leave her husband (which she had not done), that he had repeated unfounded and damaging stories about Tilton to Bowen (which he took back in a letter to Bowen on January 2, 1871), and finally that he had counseled Bowen to discharge Tilton from *The Independent* and the Brooklyn *Union* (which Bowen told Henry Ward he was going to do, anyhow).

All of this was all very well, and plainly necessary if Henry Ward were to defend Theodore Tilton's suit in which adultery was specifically set forth. But unfortunately it did not account for the fact that there was an adultery charge afloat against Henry Ward Beecher, the existence of which Beecher himself admitted in writing early in 1871. If it was not Tilton's charge, whose was it? And in heaven's name, just how many adulteries was the pastor of Plymouth Church chargeable with, anyhow? Poor Henry Ward dared not plead knowledge of Tilton's charge, because he was being sued by Tilton, and he would unquestionably lose his case if he admitted that for three years and a half he had been making stupendous efforts to keep Tilton quiet. But he was not being sued by Bowen. And so:

> "*Mr. Evarts:* 'Well, did Mr. Moulton say that Mr. Bowen charged that you had confessed adultery to him?'
> "*Mr. Beecher:* 'I — he did — yes, he said so.'"

Unhappily for Henry Ward, however, Bowen did not confine himself to simple adultery. In the letter he had written Tilton from Woodstock just after the first Mrs. Bowen's death, and in statements he had made since, he preferred far more terrible charges against the pastor of Plymouth Church. And Henry Ward's mental anguish was in no wise affected by the truth or falsity of these accusations — or Tilton's accusations, either, whatever they might be. As a minister of the Gospel and the Great Preacher he was just as surely ruined if they became public, whether any or all of them were true or not. So that if Henry Ward Beecher expressed his worry and despair during those black years in extravagant language (and he did), it must be admitted he had some reason so to do. The character of his language alone cannot fairly be cited as indicating a guilt which, after all, is of no consequence now. Its significance in this study is that it reveals a terrific and long-sustained emotional ordeal, out of which Henry Ward Beecher was to emerge a very different man. It is for this reason that documentary evidence is now here assembled.

When Frank Moulton undertook to do what a heathen could, as he expressed it, to aid Henry Ward Beecher and Theodore Tilton to settle their griefs in a Christian spirit, he had not the slightest idea what he was in for. The whole Bowen ramification to the affair came to him as a terrible shock, and he went straight to Beecher for an explanation, before he would go a step farther. According to Moulton, Henry Ward assured him that the facts were not as Bowen pictured them. He admitted, Moulton said, a little matter of what he called a "paroxysmal kiss," but insisted that Bowen could prove nothing against him. The expression "paroxysmal kiss" achieved a wide currency in the seventies. "Words are things," declared that astute old trial lawyer, William A. Beach. And from the voluminous pages of Henry Ward Beecher's writings he marshaled dozens of examples of the use of a word as rare as "paroxysmal" to annihilate Henry Ward's denial that he ever said anything of the sort.

Francis Moulton had hardly bargained for anything like this. He had conceived the affair with Lib Tilton the great weakness of a great man — deplorable, of course, but romantic at that. That there had been more than one such incident in the life of Henry Ward Beecher had never occurred to Francis Moulton. It was a day when people believed in things happening out of a clear sky.

Moulton had put his hand to the business, however; so he went on with it. His troubles were only just beginning. Promptly he squelched Theodore's inclination to publish a garrulous letter to Bowen, reviewing all the shocking details of Bowen's charges against Beecher. He set the machinery in motion to finance a literary journal, *The Golden Age*, to keep Theodore Tilton busy editing a paper of his own — what Theodore had really wanted to do for the past four years; and he arranged for arbitration of Tilton's claims against Bowen for breach of contract. He told Beecher to go on with the auctioning of the pews of Plymouth Church, and though the receipts fell below the previous year for the first time since 1862, they still came to the respectable sum of $47,309 — Henry C. Bowen paying the highest figure. In short, as Henry Ward put it, "The friend whom God has sent to me (Mr. Moulton) has proved, above all friends that ever I had, able and willing to help me in this terrible emergency of my life. His hand it was that tied up the storm that was ready to burst upon our heads."

But Brooklyn folk appear to have suffered from peculiarly ostrich-like habits. It never seemed to occur to the quartet so busily engaged in keeping dark the secret — whatever it was — of Henry Ward Beecher's relations to the Tilton family that there was danger from any other source than one of their number. Yet since the fatal hour three months before when Lib Tilton sobbed out her story on Susan Anthony's bosom, it had spread like wildfire in the radical suffrage group. After all, Henry Ward and Theodore and Lib Tilton had all belonged to that little circle. Only a year before Beecher as president of the conservative and Tilton as president of the radical wing of the suffrage movement had been exchanging public messages. Even Frank Moulton was mildly identified with suffrage activities. On the whole, the suffragists had quite as good a right as any one to gossip about Henry Ward Beecher and Lib Tilton — and without having Beecher call them "human hyenas" for it either.

What was particularly dangerous in the knowledge of the Beecher Scandal possessed by the suffrage group was that it was both first hand and complete. Henry Ward might take his solemn oath to his wife, to Plymouth Church, to a jury of twelve good men and true, or "challenge man, angels and God" — as he did on occasion — to prove him guilty of anything worse than kissing and fondling Lib Tilton during the absence of her husband. All of this was without effect on Mrs. Stanton and Miss Anthony. Both knew the whole truth. And while in general they were remarkably discreet about it, they did discuss it in their own group — and their discussion brought the horrid business right back to Henry Ward Beecher's own doorstep. For not only was his sister, Isabella Beecher Hooker, a leading member of the group, but his intimate friend and business associate, Samuel Wilkeson, Jay Cooke's publicity man, was Mrs. Stanton's brother-in-law.

"At the time of our first knowledge of the affair, Mr. Wilkeson heard of it," says Mrs. Stanton. "He besought the ladies not to make it public. To him it was a matter of money. He was stockholder in Plymouth Church, in the *Christian Union* and in 'The Life of Christ.' Now the destruction of Mr. Beecher would be the destruction of all of these. As Mr. Wilkeson expressed it, 'It would knock the "Life of Christ" higher than a kite.' Hence his concern in keeping the matter secret."

To Sam Wilkeson everything was a matter of money. He was certain he knew just how to conjure the danger to his friend Beecher, and save his own investments in the Beecher enterprises from being knocked higher than a kite, at one and the same time. He would buy Theodore Tilton with Jay Cooke's purse, as he had secured the services of Beecher's editorial pen for $15,000 worth of Northern Pacific stock. He had a free-handed way of doing one man's business with another man's money, had Sam Wilkeson — to every man his price, he figured. "Keep quiet. Don't talk. DON'T PUBLISH," he wrote Theodore — and offered him a job with Jay Cooke & Co. Tilton was hard up. But he was not for sale. He did not even reply to Sam Wilkeson.

Henry Ward, too, was climbing his Golgotha. Mrs. Morse wrote warning him of the rapidity with which knowledge of his secret was spreading. "Do you know when I hear of you cracking your jokes from Sunday to Sunday, and think of the misery you have brought upon us, I think with the Psalmist: 'There is no God.'" There was a sinister note in her letter, also: "I thought the least you could do was to put your name to a paper to help reinstate my brother (in the Custom House). Elizabeth was as disappointed as myself." As Henry Ward read it, he could see unfold before him long years filled with the increasing demands of this half-crazy woman, as he called her — now a job for her brother — later money — and more money . . .

Nor was Lib Tilton any happier. "I have had sorrow almost beyond human capacity," she wrote a friend at this time. "We have weathered the storm, and, I believe, without harm to our *Best*." Our *Best* was Beecher. And she speaks pathetically of the child she had miscarried that fateful Christmas — "a *love babe* it promised, you know," she says.

"Does God look down from Heaven on three unhappy creatures that more need a friend than these?" wrote Henry Ward of Lib, Theodore and himself.

But even in his moments of profoundest grief, Henry Ward Beecher never quite lost his shrewdness. Thanks to Frank Moulton, the danger that Theodore Tilton's accusation "was to be at once publicly pressed against me," as Beecher put it, had been dissipated. But it had all been verbal, and Henry Ward had an almost childish confidence in the efficacy of documents. He would like to have something from Theodore in writing with which he could defend himself against Mrs. Morse's future importunities, and also, perhaps, tranquilize such of his business associates as, like Wilkeson, might come into possession of the facts and be worried about their investments in him. Henry Ward went to Moulton about it, and Frank got Theodore to write, "that notwithstanding the great suffering which he [Beecher] has caused to Elizabeth and myself, I bear him no malice, shall do him no wrong, shall discountenance every project by whomsoever proposed for any exposure of his secret to the public" — which was not exactly what Henry Ward had hoped for.

Beecher's greatest worry, however, was Lib Tilton. She loved him, he knew — in fact, that was just the trouble. "Would to God, who orders all hearts, that by your kind mediation, Theodore, Elizabeth and I could be made friends again," he wrote

Moulton. "Theodore will have the hardest task in such a case; but has he not proved himself capable of the noblest things? . . . Of course, I can never speak with her again, except with his permission, and I do not know that even then it would be best. My earnest longing is to see her in the full sympathy of her nature at rest in him." And having arranged with Frank Moulton to advise Elizabeth to turn her affections back upon her husband, with Theodore's permission Henry Ward wrote Lib herself, urging her to do just as Frank Moulton should counsel her:

"I beseech of you, if my wishes have yet any influence, let my deliberate judgment in this matter weigh with you. It does my sore heart good to see in Mr. Moulton an unfeigned respect and honor for you. It would kill me if he thought otherwise . . . You and I may meet in him. The past is ended. But is there no future? — no wiser, higher, holier future? May not this friend stand as a priest in the new sanctuary of reconciliation, and mediate, and bless you, Theodore, and my most unhappy self?"

It is hard to see how Henry Ward Beecher could have done any more than this to liquidate the whole affair. If he had only stuck to it! But nowhere in his long life had Henry Ward Beecher learned the discipline of self-denial. After all, why should he give up what he called the "inspirational" quality he found in Lib Tilton now that everything was so nicely settled? For four years she had exercised "the most calming and peaceful influence over him, more so than any one he ever knew." To her he opened his heart as to no one. Once Lib had written Theodore: "Do not think it audacious in me to say I am to him a good deal, a rest, and, can you understand it, I appear even cheerful and helpful to him . . . I strive in my poor word-painting to give you the *spirit* and impression which I give him, and he to me. . . . The trinity of friendship I pray for always." Well, why not? thought Henry Ward.

It was partly Theodore's fault. Toward the end of February, and just before Frank Moulton was leaving for Florida, he sent for Beecher to come to the little house in Livingston street. Henry Ward was so eager that he got there before they had finished breakfast. Tilton swore he summoned Beecher to question him as to the paternity of little Ralph Tilton, who had been born on June 20, 1869. "I want if possible to shield him [Ralph], but I want more than that to know the truth," Theodore said. Beecher, of course, swore that what they talked about was not his, but Theodore's, sins. One can take one's choice. But both are agreed that, as they were talking, Lib Tilton came in; and thus these two met again for the first time since that night two months before, when Henry Ward had left her lying "white as marble, with closed eyes, as in a trance, and with her hands upon her bosom, palm to palm, like one in prayer."

And straightway Lib Tilton wrote her Pastor secretly — and secretly he replied. Strange, cryptic little notes, mostly without date or signature, a fragment only of what passed between these two — she thirty-seven, he fifty-eight — and both with all the world to lose by folly.

"My Dear Friend," wrote Lib. "Does your heart bound *towards all* as it used? So does mine! I am myself again. I did not dare to tell you till I was sure; but the bird has sung in my heart these *four* weeks, and he has covenanted with me never again to leave. 'Spring has come.' . . ."

And a little later there was another letter:

". . . In all the said complications of the past years, my endeavor was entirely to keep from you all suffering, to bear myself alone, leaving you forever ignorant of it. My weapons were love, a larger untiring generosity and *nest-hiding!* . . ."

So "nest-hiding" came to be a popular and somewhat ribald term in those days.

Henry Ward's answer to the first of these pathetic notes — and other secret notes of his besides — Theodore found when Lib had left his house forever — hidden away in the little closet where she kept the death-mask of her baby Paul.

"No one can ever know, none but God, through what a dreary wilderness I have wandered . . ." wrote Henry Ward in one of them. "Should God inspire you to restore and rebuild at home, and while doing it to cheer and sustain outside of it another who sorely needs your help in heart and spirit, it will prove a life so noble as few are able to live . . . If it would be a comfort to *you*, now and then, to send me a letter of true *inwardness* — the outcome of your inner life — it would be safe, for I am now at home here with my sister, and it is *permitted to you*."

"*Judge Fullerton:* 'Your wife was away, was she not?'
"*Mr. Beecher:* 'She was.' . . .
"*Judge Fullerton:* 'Do you recollect where your wife was at this time?' . . .
"*Mr. Beecher:* 'I presume she was in Florida, Sir.' "

CHAPTER XXIV

YALE

THERE was a certain quality of Greek tragedy in the fact that Nemesis overtook Henry Ward Beecher through the instrumentality of Elizabeth Cady Stanton and Susan B. Anthony. If there was one act in Henry Ward's life that was contemptible without excuse it was his attempt to prove Theodore Tilton immoral because of his association with those two women. It is perhaps, also, the most convincing measure of the frivolity of Beecher's defense. Either woman could at any moment have ruined Henry Ward Beecher. Yet even after he was dead, and Susan Anthony came to publish her diary, she deliberately suppressed the portions of it that would blast his reputation.

Victoria Woodhull and her sister, Tennessee Claflin — whose name in that day was habitually written Tennie C. — were not in any wise identified with either suffrage group, prior to January 11, 1871. On that date the National Woman's Suffrage Association held its annual convention in Washington, with Isabella Beecher Hooker in charge of the arrangements.

"Tilton should be secured by all means," Susan Anthony wrote Bella Hooker. "His wife, too. Our parlor needs her demure, motherly, angelic sweetness as much as our platform needs him. These little quiet domestic women are trump cards, nowadays. I wish I had a whole pack of them."

But on January 11, 1871, Theodore Tilton and his wife had other matters on their hands.

Elizabeth Cady Stanton was to present the customary memorial to the customary Congressional committee, which would take the customary action of dropping it in the waste basket. To their astonishment, the ladies learned that a Mrs. Victoria Woodhull of Ohio was to present a memorial of her own on suffrage to the Judiciary Committee of the House the very morning their convention was scheduled to open. None of them had ever met her. As curiosity even among suffrage workers is not unknown, the convention adjourned to hear what Victoria Woodhull had to say.

She had a great deal to say. It is of no consequence now whether her memorial was one of the unacknowledged children of the Hon. Benjamin F. Butler, or not — it was by far the ablest argument that had been produced for woman's suffrage up to that hour. Victoria herself was described as "a beautiful woman, refined in appearance and plainly dressed. She read her argument in a clear, musical voice with a modest and engaging manner, captivating not only the men but the ladies, who invited her to come to their convention and repeat it."

"Mrs. Woodhull sat sphinx-like during the convention," said the Philadelphia *Press*. "Gen. Grant himself might learn a lesson of silence from the pale, sad face of this unflinching woman. No chance to send an arrow through the opening seams of her mail . . . She reminds one of the forces in nature behind the storm, or of a small splinter of the indestructible, and if her veins were opened they would be found to contain ice." That was exactly Victoria Woodhull. She had come to New York with her sister, and opened a brokerage business, in Broad street. With the backing of Commodore Vanderbilt, they had made over half a million dollars in Harlem Railroad. In 1870 they had also started a sixteen page paper — *Woodhull & Claflin's Weekly*, with the motto "Upward and Onward," devoted to suffrage, the interests of labor, birth control, less rigidity in divorce laws, spiritualism and Victoria C. Woodhull for President. There were also the latest fashion notes from Paris, and advertisements of every reputable brokerage house in New York. On the whole, it was a much more interesting paper than the *Christian Union*.

To the type of woman whose sole emotional outlet was at the feet of Henry Ward Beecher, in Plymouth Church, "The Woodhull" and her sister were just "free lovers." Their being undeniably both young and beautiful only made it worse. They wore short skirts (that is, up to their shoetops), jackets of a mannish cut, "blue neckties and nobby Alpine hats." Their brown hair was bobbed and curly. To the average straight-haired woman that last was the final touch of infamy.

And yet, even Catherine Beecher, the very soul of the anti-suffrage movement, was agreed that "Mrs. Woodhull is a pure woman, holding a wrong social theory." And Elizabeth Cady Stanton, writing to Lucretia Mott, put the case of The Wood-hull squarely:

"I have come to the conclusion that it is a great impertinence in any of us to pry into her private affairs . . . This woman stands before us to-day as an able speaker and writer. Her face, manners, and conversation all indicate the triumph of the moral, intellectual, and spiritual . . . Women have crucified the Mary Wollstone-crafts, the Fanny Wrights and the George Sands of all ages . . . Let us end this ignoble record and henceforth stand by womanhood. If this present woman must be crucified, let men drive the spikes."

Thus Victoria Woodhull and her sister were received into the suffrage fold without reservation, with Isabella Beecher Hooker their most passionate defender. And thus, too, on May 3, 1871, it came to pass that Elizabeth Cady Stanton, quite incidentally, imparted to The Woodhull her knowledge of the relations of Henry Ward Beecher and Elizabeth Tilton.

Perhaps if Catherine Beecher and Harriet Beecher Stowe — the latter the friend of George Sand and the intimate of George Eliot — had kept their hands off, nothing would have happened. But they attacked her personal conduct with the peculiar ferocity with which women of that Victorian era dealt with their erring sisters — which was no way to treat Victoria Woodhull, of all people. On May 22, The Woodhull launched her counter-attack — an open letter ("card" as it was called in that day) to the New York *Times:*

"I do not intend," she wrote, "to be made the scapegoat of sacri-fice to be offered up as a victim to society, by those who cover the foulness of their lives and the feculence of their thoughts with a hypocritical mantle of fair profession, diverting public attention from their own iniquity in pointing the finger at me . . . My judges preach against 'free love' openly, and practise it secretly . . . For example, I know of one man, a public teacher of eminence, who lives in concubinage with the wife of another public teacher of al-most equal eminence. All three concur in denouncing offenses against morality . . . I shall make it my business to analyze some of these lives, and will take my chances in the matter of libel suits."

No names were named, but the bottom dropped out of Henry Ward's stomach, the moment he heard of it. The Woodhull did not intend that those concerned should be in any doubt — she sent for Theodore Tilton and told him whom she meant, and just what she proposed to do about it if Henry Ward Beecher and his family, his paper the *Christian Union*, and his church did not mind their own business and leave her alone. All the fabric of concealment so carefully woven through five months was suddenly ripped.

To Henry Ward Beecher it was a matter of no especial concern that shocking stories were whispered about him — indeed, it had proved no small part of his stock in trade that there had been, in Lawrenceburgh, Rebecca Whitehead; in Indianapolis, Betty Bates; in the earlier days in Brooklyn, Lucy Maria Bowen. It was of the genius of the man that he recognized the need in the hearts of the vast, emotion-starved middle class of America, hog-tied by the Calvinism of their up-bringing, haunted by their suppressions and driven by resulting fears into terror of nonconformity, to seek vicarious release in admiration of those about whom hung an aura of potential wickedness. Chorus girls might, in fact, lead the most domestic of lives. No one wanted to know it. The public that flocked to feast its eyes on the brazen beauties of the Grand Opera House in Twenty-third street demanded that its idols possess the capacity for all the scarlet sins the average man dreamed in his chaste walnut-furnished bedroom, beside the untempted mother of his children — and dared not realize. Jim Fisk in that very hour, "riding the four-in-hand of his riches, packed with courtesans," as William M. Evarts put it, was a figure of national renown, not because he was rich, but because he was lewd. It was the day when Charles Stewart Parnell was launching his tremendous career, and Roscoe Conkling stood an acknowledged leader, in an odor of private scandal.

No one felt more keenly than Henry Ward Beecher the attraction of this atmosphere of profligacy — or appreciated more fully its possibilities. From the days when he had looked up to the expelled West Pointer, Fitzgerald, at Mount Pleasant, down through his persistent intimacy with Alvord, the gambler, at Indianapolis, Beecher himself had felt the pull of a certain frailty in reputation. He knew its power over his romance-hungry middle-class public. The stories afloat about him were as much a part of his equipment as the Melton coat he wore, with its great cape that he threw over one shoulder, or his slouch hat, or his long hair, or the jewels he carried in his pocket or the flowers he was always surrounded with. They marked him out among men. They made people turn and look at him and whisper to one another. They filled his lecture halls and brought three thousand attendants to Plymouth Church. But there was a point beyond which such reputation must not go. People might whisper; they must not talk. There must be nothing in the news-papers.

For Theodore Tilton this last was quite as vital as for Henry Ward Beecher. Slowly, and with an agony that was turning his hair white, Theodore was reconquering the love of his wife. From the first, she had maintained that she had committed no sin with Henry Ward Beecher. She had, she told her husband, resisted her Pastor's importunities

"until finally she had been persuaded by him that as their love was proper and not wrong, therefore it followed that any expression of that love, whether by the shake of the hand, or the kiss of the lips, or even bodily intercourse, since it all was the expression of that which in itself was not wrong, therefore that bodily intercourse was not wrong."

But the panic into which her revelation of their relationship (whatever it was) had thrown Beecher opened her eyes a bit.

"I see clearly my sin," Lib wrote her husband, at last. "It was when I knew that I was loved, to suffer it to grow to a passion. A virtuous woman should check instantly an absorbing love. But it appeared to me in such false light. That the love I felt and received could harm no one, not even you, I have believed unfalteringly . . . Now I feel quite prepared to renew my marriage vow with you, to keep it as the Saviour requireth."

And on the anniversary of the fateful night when she had con-fessed to Theodore she wrote him:

"Oh, my dear husband, may you never need the discipline of being misled by a good woman, as I was by a good man!"

She was ready to accompany Theodore on his lecture trip the coming fall. All they needed now to mend their shattered life was silence.

And silence was just what Frank Moulton undertook to secure, come what might. He apportioned their tasks: Beecher was to keep Plymouth Church off Theodore, and Theodore was to keep Victoria Woodhull off Beecher. That the latter was highly urgent, was evident at once:

"At this very moment awful and herculean efforts are being made to suppress the most terrific scandal in a neighboring city, which has ever astounded and convulsed any community," she printed a fortnight after her first shot. "Clergy, congregation and community will be alike hurled into more than all the consternation which the great explosion in Paris carried to that unfortunate city, if this effort at suppression fail."

Tilton was promptly requisitioned to write a highly fantastic biography of the lady and publish it for her, to invite her to his house, preside at her meetings, promulgate her views on suffrage and sex relations in *The Golden Age* — ably, it must be admitted — and any other little thing that would keep her quiet. But The Woodhull was a capricious ringmaster, who seemed to crack the whip just to see them jump. Henry Ward himself met her a number of times — on how cordial terms one can only conjecture. But the fact did not deter her from writing him:

"Two of your sisters have gone out of their way to assail my character and purposes, both by means of the public press and by numerous private letters . . . You doubtless know that it is in my power to strike back, and in ways more disastrous than anything that can come to me . . . I speak guardedly, but I think you will understand me."

He did indeed understand her, and it added little to his peace of mind. For Henry Ward had his own problems. A group in Plymouth Church wanted to expel Tilton — for his association with those amazing hussies, The Woodhull and her sister! There were times when Beecher, Tilton and Moulton might have had a good laugh — if they could have laughed at all. And then there was Mrs. Morse. "My dear son," she began a letter to Henry Ward, and went promptly to the point — money. "Do you know, I think it strange you should ask me to call you 'son,'" she ended. "When I have told darling [Mrs. Tilton] I felt if you could, in safety to yourself and all concerned, you would be to me all this endearing name. Am I mistaken? 'Mother.'" It was little wonder that Henry Ward, early in February, 1872, wrote Moulton in despair:

"If I had not gone through this great *year of sorrow*, I would not have believed that any one could pass through my experience and be *alive* or *sane* . . . To *say* that I have a church on my hands is simple enough — but to have the hundreds and thousands of men pressing me, each one with his keen suspicion, or anxiety, or zeal; to see tendencies which if not stopped, would break out into ruinous defense of me; to stop them without seeming to do it; to prevent any one questioning me; to meet and allay prejudices against T. [Tilton] which had their beginning years before this; to keep serene as if I was not alarmed or disturbed; to be cheerful at home and among friends when I was suffering the torments of the damned; to pass sleepless nights often, and yet to come up fresh and full for Sunday; — all of this may be talked about, but the real thing cannot be understood from the outside, nor its wearing and grinding on the nervous system.

"God knows that I have put more thought and judgment and earnest desire into my efforts to prepare a way for T. and E. [Mrs. Tilton] than ever I did for myself a hundred-fold . . . If my destruction would place him all right, that shall not stand in the way. I am willing to step down and out. No one can offer more than that. That I do offer. Sacrifice me without hesitation, if you can clearly see your way to his safety and happiness thereby. I do not think that anything would be gained by it. I should be destroyed, but he would not be saved. E. and the children would have their future clouded. In one point of view I could desire the sacrifice on my part. Nothing can possibly be so bad as the horror of great darkness in which I spend much of my time. I look upon death as sweeter-faced than any friend I have in the world. Life would be pleasant if I could see that rebuilt which is shattered. But to live on the sharp and ragged edge * of anxiety, remorse, fear, despair, and yet to put on all the appearance of serenity and happiness, cannot be endured much longer.

"I am well-nigh discouraged. If you, too, cease to trust me — to love me — I am alone; I have not another person in the world to whom I could go."

Nor is Henry Ward altogether to be blamed that in this disheartened spirit, he wrote again, secretly, to Lib Tilton:

"Now may the God of peace that brought again from the dead our Lord Jesus, that great shepherd of the sheep, through the blood of the everlasting covenant, make you perfect in every good work to do His will, working in you that which is well-pleasing in His sight, through Jesus Christ . . . My wife takes boat for Havana and

---

* This epistle came to be known as the "ragged-edge" letter.

Florida on Thursday. I called on Monday but you were out. May the dear Lord and Saviour abide with you."

And again:

"If I don't see you to-morrow night, I will next Friday, for I shall be gone all the fore part of next week."

Of course, he was not supposed to be seeing her at all.

It must not be thought that all other activities ceased for Henry Ward Beecher during these days when he was "in the very depths of the depths," as he put it — albeit, goodness knows they might well have, considering the amount of correspondence every one concerned seemed to give way to, as to a sort of addiction. 1872 was to be Henry Ward's triumphal year. It marked twenty-five years of his service as pastor of Plymouth Church, and there was to be a tremendous celebration of the event in October. Even before that, Henry Ward Beecher was, by the terms of the endowment, the first incumbent of the Lyman Beecher Lectureship on Preaching, at Yale Divinity School, established by Henry W. Sage, deacon of Plymouth Church and one of its Trustees.

It was more than a triumph, this honor. Old Dr. Beecher had sent his unpromising son to Amherst, instead of Yale, because he was afraid the youth had neither brains nor character enough for his own Alma Mater. And here he was teaching at Yale, in a chair named for Lyman Beecher. The joke was plainly on Lyman.

It was at Yale delivering his lectures to young candidates for the ministry that Henry Ward was to "be gone all the fore part of next week," as he wrote Lib Tilton. He had been driven frantic by the menace of exposure for so many months that he had had little time to prepare anything in the way of lectures. Indeed, it was only while shaving just before the first lecture that any conception of what he was going to say formulated itself in his mind. It was fortunate, for Henry Ward was compelled to fall back upon his own personal experience for subject matter, and there was a consequent impression of verity in what he said that make his Yale Lectures stand out, sound and enduring beyond anything else in the vast mass of Henry Ward Beecher's prodigious output.

The lectures were even more autobiographical than his sermons and lecture room talks, or the little pieces he used to write for *The Independent* and Robert Bonner's *Ledger*, and now wrote for the *Christian Union*. But the incidents in Henry Ward Beecher's life were not presented as they had actually taken place. In Henry Ward's mind they no longer existed in that form. He had built him a fantasy world where what had occurred had been intensely dramatized about himself as the central figure, and things that had never happened had been created and dwelt upon until they were more real to him than the reality itself.

"When I was settled at Indianapolis, nobody was allowed to say a word on the subject of slavery," he recounted. "They were all red hot out there; and one of the Elders said: 'If an Abolitionist comes here, I will have a mob to put him down.' I was a young preacher. I had pluck; and I felt it grow on me, that that was a subject that ought to be preached upon; but I knew that they would blow me up sky high, and my usefulness in that parish would be gone. Yet I was determined they should hear it, first or last. The question was: 'How shall I do it?' I recollected one of the earliest efforts I made in that direction was a sermon on some general topic. It was necessary to illustrate a point, and I did it by picturing a father ransoming his son from captivity among the Algerines, and glorifying in the love of liberty and his fight against bondage, and all thought I was going to apply it to slavery, but I did not. I applied it to my subject, and passed on; and they all drew a long breath.

"It was not long before I had another illustration from that quarter, and so before I had been there a year, I had gone over all the sore spots of slavery—illustrating the subject of Christian experience and doctrine. It broke the ice."

There is a twofold revelation of Henry Ward Beecher in this little story. First, in all essential respects the anecdote is quite untrue. But Henry Ward believed it, none the less—precisely as he believed the legend that, alone and single-handed, against terrific opposition, he had won England to the North in 1863. And, second, upon this insecure foundation, Beecher had built him a philosophy, a creed of conduct, which he now passed on to the younger generation of ministers, going out into the world as custodians of evangelical truth. Before them he stood the epitome of success in the ministry. Talmage might preach to larger audiences, but Beecher boasted more members to his church, and folk of more substance, solid respectability and enlightened conservatism. These young men who drank in his words were to be the models of hundreds of other ministers with less education than they, the source of the thought of a whole generation of Americans to come, and their children and their children's children.

"How far should a preacher . . . give utterance to truths which are disagreeable to the hearer?" one asked.

"No rule whatever can be given in regard to that," declared Henry Ward Beecher. "Whatever provocation arises from the preacher's manner or untowardness, of course, is blameworthy in him. If he will speak truths meet for persons to hear, let him learn 'speaking the truth with love.'"

"There is no more virtue required of a man who becomes a life-long preacher of the Gospel than of a man who becomes a lawyer, a physician, a teacher, an engineer," he claims. Make Christianity comfortable.

"Whatever else you do, don't slam the door of possibility in any man's face . . . The teaching of Christ and the Apostles was that God wanted all men to be saved, and made overtures to them." Old Lyman Beecher in his little tub pulpit, laying down the law of God's moral government of the world, was as dead as Julius Cæsar, and Jonathan Edwards and John Calvin with him. In his place stood Henry Ward Beecher on the broad stage of Plymouth pulpit, surrounded on three sides by the well-dressed, prosperous, decorous holders of high-priced pews. Under his spell they sobbed, they rocked with laughter, they cheered — and the women waved their little, perfumed handkerchiefs.

"You can manage an average American audience, you can make them learn almost anything," Henry Ward told his young divinity students. "There are in any community probably six to one who will watch for the emotional and impassioned part of the sermon, saying, 'That is the preaching I want; I can understand what I feel.' They are fed by their hearts. They have as much right to be fed by their hearts as the others have to be fed by their reason."

It is not to be supposed that every evangelical minister of the land at once hailed this gospel of success as altogether superseding older teachings. Indeed, not a few dubbed Henry Ward's practical creed "Beecherism" and were frankly appalled by it. They clung to the hope that the poor in spirit might still have at least an even chance at the kingdom of heaven — yes, even that penitent servant girl who, Henry Ward told the Yale students, disgusted him because she smelt of the kitchen.

Beecher's Yale lectures extended over three years, during the greater part of which time he was under fire for his personal moral conduct. It was inevitable that many should judge his conduct by his ideas and others should judge his ideas by his conduct, and that both should feel that Henry Ward Beecher was a cross laid upon the church of Christ. Indeed, when the charge of adultery was publicly brought against Henry Ward, it was his half-brother, the Rev. Thomas K. Beecher, who voiced with least circumlocution what so many clergymen felt:

"In my judgment Henry is following his slippery doctrines of expediency and, in the cry of progress and the nobleness of human nature, has sacrificed clear, exact, ideal integrity."

Yet for all his glorification of a certain charlatanry of method, his snobbery, his opportunism, there lay at the bottom of Henry Ward Beecher's conception of the function of a minister of the Gospel the germ of an idea that was not to die:

"There is one fact that is not going to be overturned by science; and that is the necessity of human development, and the capacity there is in man of being opened up and improved. If there is one thing that can be substantiated more clearly than another, it is that the development indicated by Christianity is right along the line of nature," he declared. "And if there is one business better worth a man's thought than another, it is a profession that undertakes to educate men along this common line of nature and Christianity together, and lift them up from baselier conditions and methods to the coronal heights where understanding, moral sentiment, taste, imagination and love are intermingled.

"That is the business of the preacher."

CHAPTER XXV

FALL

IF THE unparalleled publicity which attended the various accusations of adultery brought against Henry Ward Beecher served in the final analysis no constructive purpose, then Francis Moulton played a hero's rôle — for which he received the hero's customary reward of obloquy and abuse. "I believed that the scandal would tend to undermine the very foundations of social order, to lay low a beneficent power for good in our country," Moulton said; and so believing, for three years and a half, he cajoled and bullied, sometimes led and sometimes drove his fractious team of egotists — Beecher and Tilton — in the way of peace.

So far as Beecher's side of the affair was concerned, this course met with general coöperation. Not only in Plymouth Church, but widely throughout the country, people said: "If Beecher is guilty, I don't want to know it; he is too great a man to fall; he has too many interests involved in his position and success." Indeed, it was not until the suit at law had dragged on for a couple of months that those who counted on some miraculous revelation to clear up the whole sordid business and disclose their idol an innocent and sorely persecuted man, realized that the day of miracles had passed. One by one the great newspapers dropped from him — Samuel Bowles' Springfield *Republican*, Joseph Medill's Chicago *Tribune*, Charles Dana's *Sun*, Henry Watterson's *Courier-Journal*, George Jones' New York *Times* — not in hostility, but in sorrow. "Unless Mr. Moulton and others say that Mr. Beecher did *not* confess to adultery, the *whole newspaper press* cannot save the great preacher," Edmund Clarence Stedman wrote Whitelaw Reid.

It is one of the fine things about the newspapers of the United States, however, that in 1872, before anything specific about Beecher's trouble with Tilton had come out, Victoria Woodhull peddled her story of Beecher's adultery from newspaper office to newspaper office, and found no takers. Henry Ward was approaching sixty. His life had been a singularly useful one. Even newspapers that disagreed fundamentally with his political views, his theological tenets, his social theories, and called him a "pulpit mountebank," felt that he was entitled to the benefit of the doubt.

The church-going folk of Brooklyn were not, unfortunately, actuated by quite the same lofty motives. There was something pathetic in the supreme confidence displayed by those who surrounded Henry Ward most intimately in the power of money, accompanied by a little superficial geniality, to accomplish almost anything. Early in April 1872, for example, Tilton sued Bowen for breach of contract, and some of Beecher's friends headed by H. B. Claflin promptly seized the occasion to act as arbitrators while at the same time to try to induce both Bowen and Tilton to go on record as knowing "nothing derogatory to his [Beecher's] reputation as a clergyman or a man." It was crude and not a little ridiculous, as well as quite futile. The most they obtained was a written promise by Brother Bowen no longer to indulge his amiable idiosyncrasy of accusing his Pastor of adultery, and a like pledge from Tilton to refrain from spreading Bowen's grievances. On his part, however, Henry Ward agreed that

"If I have said anything injurious to the reputation of either, or have detracted from their standing and fame as Christian gentlemen and members of my church, I revoke it all and heartily covenant to repair and reinstate them to the extent of my power."

And in the *Christian Union* he referred to Bowen as "a wise and strong man" and lauded Theodore as as "honest in his convictions as he is fearless in their utterance, and that he is manly and straightforward in the ways in which he works for what seems to him best for man and for society."

To those who wanted to believe in Henry Ward Beecher, this sort of thing was a facer. Either the stories about Beecher's relations with Mrs. Bowen and Mrs. Tilton were false — or they were true. And if they were false and deliberately circulated by the two men to Beecher's discredit, what did Henry Ward mean by publishing broadcast flattering estimates of Bowen and Tilton? So Bella Hooker, Henry Ward's half-sister, argued. She wrote Beecher to know what it did mean.

"Of some things *I neither talk, nor will I be talked with*," . . . he replied. "The only thing that can be grateful to me or useful is *silence* and a silencing influence on others . . . Living or dead, my dear sister Belle, *love me* . . ."

And Bella promptly canceled her trip to Europe and stood by to help her brother when the storm broke. For she had no doubt, after his letter, of the truth of what she had heard; nor did she ever have any doubt of it.

Henry Ward's torture had really begun. His wife was growing suspicious of the amount of time he spent at the Moultons' in Remsen street. She, also, wanted to know what it was all about — as well she might. In his own house not so much as a scrap of paper referring to the matter uppermost in Henry Ward's mind was safe from curious eyes — he had to bring them all, even Bella Hooker's letters, to Frank Moulton to keep for him. In Plymouth Church, ever since Tilton's biographical sketch of Victoria Woodhull appeared, a group had been clamorous to oust Theodore from their communion — though he had not stepped foot in the church since that tragic July night when Elizabeth told her story. At all costs Beecher must hold down this witch-burning spirit among those who had their gospel from his lips. Indeed, poor Henry Ward must be suspicious of every one. Claflin, for example, was a trustee of Plymouth Church and one of its financial mainstays. How much of the truth had Claflin learned while he was dealing with Tilton and Bowen? Henry Ward had to know where he stood; so he had recourse to Frank Moulton, as usual:

"I asked him [Claflin] if B. [Bowen] had ever made him a statement of the very *bottom facts*," he wrote Moulton. "He evaded and intimated that if he had he would hardly be right in telling me. I think he would be right in telling *you* — ought to . . . The real point to avoid is an appeal to church and then a council. It would be a conflagration . . . Don't fail to see C. [Claflin] and have a full and confidential talk."

Yes; Henry Ward was right. What he had most to fear was trial by a council of fellow ministers. There was no longer any danger of a divorce suit, with the Rev. Henry Ward Beecher of Plymouth Church as corespondent. "He [Tilton] hasn't any case to take into court," said Henry Ward. "He has condoned his wife's offense and lived with her." And that was true.

But in the constantly widening circle of those to whose ears Beecher's secret had come, there was a growing number of ministers of the gospel, simple, upright, hard-working men, nothing like so brilliant and successful as Henry Ward Beecher, but who took their work fully as seriously as ever he had taken his. To men of the stamp of Dr. Richard Salter Storrs, of the Church of the Pilgrims, Dr. William Ives Buddington, of the Clinton Avenue Congregational Church, Dr. Henry J. van Dyke, Dr. J. T. Duryea, and dozens of other Brooklyn clergymen, scandalous whisperings about the pastor of Plymouth Church were a calamity. They might like Beecher personally, understand his temptations and forgive his trespasses. But if the stories about him continued to circulate, they had as well close their churches and open theaters — or gambling houses.

Theodore Tilton had been away all winter on his lecture tour, and now he was off to Cincinnati a Greeley delegate to the Progressive Republican convention. He was no longer able, or indeed willing, to conspire to keep Victoria Woodhull silent — he had broken with her over the fury with which she attacked some of the most estimable ladies in the suffrage movement. She was running for President on a ticket with Frederick Douglass — an astounding combination in that (or any other) day — and was bitter because Theodore would not support her candidacy.

Meanwhile, Beecher did not even wait to learn who would be nominated at Cincinnati before coming out for Grant. "As Mr. Greeley stands for all Beecher believes in politically why is he not for him?" naïvely asked the *World*. Well, H. B. Claflin was a Grant elector, Bowen, naturally, was for Grant, the substantial business men of Plymouth Church were for Grant — and so was Henry Ward Beecher. Perhaps as a sop to his erstwhile political liberalism, now permanently dead, Henry Ward drew down on his gray hairs a storm of orthodox disapproval by advocating the opening of public libraries, reading rooms and picture galleries on Sunday.

"I still bear witness that a certain moral sensibility, a certain poetical element, was derived by me from a strict Puritanical observance of the Sabbath which I shall ever be thankful for,"

he said, in extenuation.

The second week in October was set for the great celebration by Plymouth Church to mark twenty-five years of Henry Ward's incumbency as pastor. The exercises lasted all week, beginning with a tremendous parade of Sunday School children past Beecher's house on Columbia Heights, with bands and banners and bouquets of flowers that covered the stoop on which Henry Ward stood to review the procession, tears streaming down his cheeks. Brother Bowen, at first superintendent of Plymouth Sunday School, was the leading speaker. Another day, devoted to the history of the founding of the church, Brother Bowen told how he had fetched Beecher from Indianapolis and persuaded him to settle in Brooklyn. If there were those who rubbed their eyes and wondered a bit, they were lost in the vast cheering throng that filled Plymouth Church and overflowed far down the street.

At the exercises of the final day of the Silver Wedding of Henry Ward Beecher with Plymouth Church, Dr. Storrs and Dr. Buddington were conspicuous. It was Storrs who had first welcomed Beecher to Brooklyn, a quarter of a century before, and it was he who now paid Henry Ward Beecher the most eloquent tribute he was ever to receive. At its close, Beecher put his arm around Storrs and kissed him before them all.

"In my preaching, a change of emphasis has been made, as compared with the emphasis aforetime given in New England theology. That theology had put the emphasis on conscience and that which represents law," said Henry Ward. "It has presented the conscience in intimate connection with fear, and conscience and fear have been largely developed as prime constituents of religion. But, partly from my own personal experience, a change of emphasis has been made in my preaching, and I have put the emphasis on Divine Love, and have made conscience and fear secondary."

In that very hour, fear stood beside Henry Ward Beecher on the broad pulpit of Plymouth Church. Four months before, Victoria Woodhull had written him again, peremptorily. He had not replied. "If it brings trouble — it must come," he wrote Frank Moulton in despair. It had come. In Boston, on September 11, at the annual convention of the American Association of Spiritualists, of which she was president, Victoria Woodhull, "with two crimson spots burning in her cheeks, her face, the saddest I ever saw, telling of wrecked hopes and a cruel battle with life," had told the whole story of Henry Ward Beecher and Elizabeth Tilton to a public audience. Reporters from every Boston paper were present, but only the Boston *Journal* said, adroitly, that "prominent New York clergymen were personally accused of the most hideous crimes."

But half Boston heard the story, just the same, and a fortnight later, when Harriet Beecher Stowe gave a reading at Tremont Temple, she also heard it; and a week after that, Henry Ward himself lectured in Boston, and he heard it. But Theodore Tilton, campaigning for Greeley in Western Pennsylvania, heard nothing. He spoke for Greeley in Brooklyn one night, and dined with Frank Moulton and Beecher before the meeting. But Henry Ward told him nothing of The Woodhull's revelations.

Theodore was surprised to find Beecher so depressed and moody after the great celebration in Plymouth Church.

"You can hope for nothing better in this world in the way of honor in your pulpit than you have achieved," Tilton said to Henry Ward, that night. "You are writing the 'Life of Christ,' the second volume is not completed, and you will have a good excuse to go to the Holy Land. It can be known to all the world that you have gone to see with your own eyes the footprints of the Master whose life you are now writing, and if you now resign it will be a fitting time to do so, and such a resignation, which heretofore would have been accompanied with suspicion and danger, would be now the surest way to provide peace for the future."

To Henry Ward Beecher the idea was a brilliant one. How he longed for that peace! He was turning the suggestion over in his mind when, a week later, *Woodhull & Claflin's Weekly* devoted almost an entire issue to an article entitled "The Beecher-Tilton Case." "We are prepared to take all the responsibilities of libel suits and imprisonment," the irrepressible sisters said. "I intend that this article shall burst like a bomb-shell into the ranks of the moralistic social camp," wrote Victoria.

It did.

Within a few hours single copies of the *Weekly* sold as high as $40. But in the crisis, the friends of the Great Preacher exhibited rather more zeal than judgment. Gen. Benjamin F. Tracy, a pillar of Plymouth Church, was United States District Attorney, and the ink was hardly dry on the offending issue of *Woodhull & Claflin's Weekly* before he had both the ladies behind the bars on a federal charge of sending obscene matter through the United States mails.

It was a fatal blunder. Many who entertained no doubt whatever of Beecher's integrity were outraged at this mobilization of the machinery of the United States government to hold two women under prohibitive bonds in an eight-by-four cell in Ludlow street jail for six months, without trial. Public sympathy shifted from Beecher to the imprisoned women. It was pointed out that Henry Ward's remedy was plainly that to which he had drawn Mr. Cunard's attention with such asperity twenty years previous.

But Henry Ward Beecher instituted no action, criminal or civil, for libel against either Victoria Woodhull or her sister, then or ever. Six months after the intrepid sisters were so cavalierly hustled into custody, the indictments against them were dismissed.

It was Bella Hooker who first flew to Henry Ward's assistance. To her he replied:

"I tread the falsehoods into the dirt from whence they spring, and go on my way rejoicing . . . Meanwhile the Lord has a pavilion in which he hides me until the storm be overpast . . . Thank you for love and truth and silence, but think of the barbarity of dragging a poor, dear child of a woman into this slough!"

The poor, dear child of a woman was Lib Tilton, who was almost forty. As Bella Hooker wrote her brother, the Rev. Thomas K. Beecher:

"So far as I can see it is he who has dragged the dear child into the slough — and left her there."

Susan Anthony was equally indignant with Henry Ward:

"The reply of your brother is not more startling, not so open a falsehood, as that to Mr. Watters [a newspaper reporter who had interviewed Beecher in regard to The Woodhull's article]: 'Of course, Mr. Beecher, this is a fraud from beginning to end?' '*Entirely.*'

"Wouldn't you think if God ever did strike any one dead for telling a lie, He would have struck then?"

Susan Anthony wrote Bella Hooker. And she added:

"For a cultivated man, at whose feet the whole world of men as well as of women sits in love and reverence, whose moral, intellectual, social resources are without limit — for such a man, so blest, so overflowing with *soul food;* — for him to ask or accept the *body* of one or a dozen of his reverent and revering devotees — I tell you *he is the sinner — if it be a sin — and who shall say it is not?*"

In many respects, Victoria Woodhull's account of the relations between Henry Ward Beecher and Elizabeth Tilton was high fantasy. She could not resist adding sensational incidents lacking even the vaguest verisimilitude. Yet despite all this embroidery, the naked fact was there: "Mrs. Tilton spoke freely of a long series of intimate and so-called criminal relations, on her part, with the Rev. Henry Ward Beecher . . . of her criminal intimacy with Mr. Beecher . . ." and so on, for pages, calling a spade a spade. She described Henry Ward's terror at the thought that the whole business might become known. "Oh! if it must come, let me know of it twenty-four hours in advance, that I may take my own life," she quoted him as crying. "I can not, can not, face this thing." Tears streamed down his cheeks, she said.

Worst of all, Victoria Woodhull defended Beecher:

"The immense physical potency of Mr. Beecher, and the indomitable urgency of his great nature for the intimacy and embraces of the noble and cultured women about him, instead of being a bad thing as the world thinks, or thinks it thinks, or professes to think it thinks, is one of the noblest and grandest endowments of this truly great and representative man," she said. "Plymouth Church has lived and fed, and the healthy vigor of public opinion for the last quarter of a century has been augmented and strengthened from the physical amativeness of Rev. Henry Ward Beecher."

Tragic as the situation suddenly became, it was not without its humor.

"She [The Woodhull] goes on to say that Beecher is just as good and pure a man as ever; that Mrs. Tilton is all right; that (in effect) adultery is all right; and only public opinion, and its resulting hypocrisy, is wrong,"

said the Hartford *Times*. Which, as a matter of fact, was precisely what Victoria Woodhull did say.

Curiously enough, Plymouth Church, by some strange reasoning, seemed to expect Theodore Tilton to issue a public denial of Victoria Woodhull's story. Henry Ward even went so far as to prepare a statement for Theodore to give out to the press exonerating him. But Tilton could see no sense in this peculiar Plymouth Church logic. "I told him [Beecher] that he was involved with Mrs. Tilton," Theodore testified, "and that if her vindication was to come, if he was a brave man, it should come by him at whatever cost." It did not come.

Instead, Henry Ward sought the legal counsel of the Hon. Benjamin F. Tracy, whose conduct of matters so far had hardly been brilliant. It became, however, even less brilliant as he went on — "an exhibition of professional treachery and personal dishonor," as one of the most distinguished members of the bar of that day characterized Tracy's performance. Indeed, if the course which Henry Ward Beecher followed when the publication of what he so aptly termed the "bottom facts" at last opened the way of candor to him was a source of surprise and grief to his friends, no little of the blame must rest upon that consummate politician who was his legal adviser.

For Henry Ward Beecher was sore beset. He saw the problem before him not as the relatively simple one of conduct in an individual free of responsibilities. Henry Ward Beecher was no such individual. Victoria Woodhull herself, in her famous article, made clear beyond any possibility of misunderstanding the revolutionary effect she expected to produce upon the moral framework of society by compelling the Great Preacher to align himself with the destructive forces clawing at the social fabric. If he gave way, thousands of young people all over the country — all over the world — would cite his example to prove illicit relationships natural, inevitable. They would say: "If Henry Ward Beecher could do thus and so, I can." And the whole cause of morality, decency and religion to which Henry Ward had devoted his life would receive a body blow at his hands. The truth itself would be made to lie — as he put it to his sister, Bella — if he were but coward enough to seek merely the relief of his own conscience by confession. It would be the triumph of those depraved women, The Woodhull and her sister, and their loose ideas, undermining the very foundations of civilization.

No; Henry Ward Beecher was not so young as he had been when he defied the Fugitive Slave Law in the interests of the larger good of humanity. But there was one last fight left in him yet. All he asked now of Tracy was to be certain that his sacrifice would not be in vain — that the law would not somehow betray him. So Tracy went to Frank Moulton and Theodore Tilton and gave his word of honor that he would not act for Beecher if the case came to court; and they showed him all the evidence they possessed. Then Tracy went back to Beecher and took his case for him. "Your story will stand up," he said. "All they have is a paper that seems to imply that you had been attempting the virtue of Mrs. Tilton without success."

Yet nobody really knew what to do about The Woodhull's story — it was so specific and detailed and unequivocal. Tracy's suggestion that Tilton go to Europe was childish; why should Theodore run away? Only Bella Hooker had an idea.

"I can endure no longer," she wrote Henry Ward. "I must see you and persuade you to write a paper which I will read, going alone to your pulpit and taking sole charge of the services."

Henry Ward came rushing around to Frank Moulton's, holding out the letter in a trembling hand.

"What do you think of the condition of a man who gets such letters as this from a member of his own family?" he cried. "What is to be done? Is there no end of trouble and complication?"

Theodore took the letter and went to Hartford, where Bella Hooker lived. He would not tell on the witness stand what he did to silence Henry Ward Beecher's sister; but Frank Moulton testified how by "charging *her* with adultery," Theodore Tilton had ended all danger to Henry Ward from that quarter. Nevertheless, from that time forward Harriet Beecher Stowe sat each Sunday in the front row of Plymouth Church, lest her sister suddenly appear.

Eunice, too, bore a cross of her own. Once Theodore Tilton rode with her on a train. "She is white-haired, and looks a dozen years older than when I last had a near view of her," he wrote Moulton. "My heart has been full of pity for her, notwithstanding the cruel way in which she has treated my good name. Her face is written over with many volumes of human suffering."

It is not to be thought that Henry Ward Beecher did not also have his moments of weakness, nor that there were not many times, before he came to his great determination, when the peace of death seemed infinitely preferable to the long martyrdom of his heroic fight in defense of the home, the family, the sacredness of domestic relations.

"The man who has been wallowing in lust, the man who has been on fire in his passions, and who by God's great goodness has been brought to an hour and a moment when, with the lurid light of revelation, his monstrous wickedness stands disclosed in him — that man ought not to wait so long as the drawing of his breath. Wherever he is, no matter how decorous his audience may be, if he does the thing that is safest and best he will rise in his place and make confession. Though it be in church, and it break the order and routine of service, he will stand up and say, 'Here I am, a sinner, and I confess my sin, and I call on God to witness my determination from this hour to turn away from it.' That is the wise course, and you would think so — if it was anybody else but yourself."

So he had preached only a few weeks after that fatal tenth of October 1868.

But the thing that was safest and best was not for Henry Ward Beecher.

Part VI: New Life

> "A minister says: 'I am very sensitive to the praise and opinion of men. When I speak, I can't get rid of the feeling of myself. I am standing before a thousand people, and I am all the time thinking about myself.' . . . What is such a man to do? Can he change his own temperament? . . . How can a man alter the laws that are laid down for him?
>
> "Well, in one sense he cannot change at all. One can make just as many prayers, write just as many resolutions, and keep just as long a journal as you please, recording the triumphs of grace over your approbativeness; and when you are screwed down in your coffin, you will have been no less a praise-loving man than when you were taken out of the cradle. That quality grows, and grows stronger in old age than at any other time. You will find that men get over some things in time . . . but if vanity is a part of their composition, old age only strengthens it, and they grow worse and worse as they grow in years."
>
> HENRY WARD BEECHER, 1872

CHAPTER XXVI
1874

Even in the matter of writing compromising letters, of exposure, public investigation and a badly tarnished name, Henry Ward Beecher was no pioneer. It was the day of spotted reputations. Dana had just published in the *Sun* the indiscreet correspondence of the Hon. Oakes Ames, in the Crédit Mobilier scandal, wrecking the fortunes of Beecher's friend, Vice-President Colfax and half a dozen members of Congress, and copiously spattering Vice-President-elect Henry Wilson and James A. Garfield. During the very period Henry Ward was passing through his hell of "anxiety, remorse, fear, despair," as he put it, James G. Blaine was penning the famous Mulligan letters that were to ruin him; Secretary of War Belknap was living on graft, and President Grant's private secretary stood revealed a member of the notorious St. Louis whiskey ring, whose shadow fell even upon the President, himself. Everywhere men in public life arraigned for their corruption were seeking to save themselves by sheer effrontery and the perjury of their friends.

It was this practical course that Gen. Tracy now urged upon Henry Ward Beecher. Months had passed since Victoria Woodhull electrified Boston with the story of Beecher's adultery with Mrs. Tilton. "Of all those whose names were given in the Woodhull publication, not one, from Beecher and Tilton down, has so much as uttered the word 'False!'," said the Cincinnati *Post*. All over the country bewildered newspaper editors were saying the same. In Troy, an enterprising journalist issued a newspaper, *The Thunderbolt*, devoted exclusively to THE BEECHER-TILTON SCANDAL. It sold like hot cakes. Dr. Joseph Treat printed and circulated an open letter to Victoria Woodhull in comparison with which anything that lady herself had previously published was mere nursery reading. Victoria and her sister reprinted the famous issue of *Woodhull & Claflin's Weekly*, with additions and comments. Distinctly, it was high time somebody did something about the wretched business, and although he did not recommend lying as a rule, said Gen. Tracy, this was one of the cases in which lying was justifiable.

But Henry Ward's New England shrewdness bade him be wary. The trouble was that, on December 16, 1872, just after the Woodhull story appeared, Lib Tilton had furnished Dr. Storrs, of the Church of the Pilgrims, a brief statement of the whole affair. "H. W. Beecher, my friend and pastor, had solicited me to be a wife to him, together with all that this implied," she wrote. Henry Ward particularly disliked this way of putting it:

"Mr. Beecher said that he would not stand in the position of a man who had solicited favors from a woman, and be put in the position of one who had been rejected by her; and I told him I sympathized with that view of the case,"

testified Frank Moulton.

Henry Ward had his own plan of disposing of the scandal. It was not without its dignity:

"*Judge Fullerton:* 'What could be worse than a keen suspicion running through your large congregation?'

"*Mr. Beecher:* 'My life could — could kill that, if I was, Sir, to go right on.'

"*Judge Fullerton:* 'Then by silence, and going right on, you meant to leave this keen suspicion afloat through the whole congregation?'

"*Mr. Beecher:* 'No, Sir; I meant to make it die.' "

But poor Henry Ward reckoned without his Victoria Woodhull. She had been impetuous and indiscreet; but Victoria Woodhull was nobody's coward. Beecher's friends had flung her into prison on a frivolous charge. Beecher himself had branded her and her sister "two prostitutes" — an accusation which he, certainly, could hardly substantiate and which no one ever did substantiate, either. In consequence of these things, however, Victoria and her sister had seen their brokerage business wrecked, their newspaper ruined. They were chevied from hotel to hotel as if they had the smallpox and denied the opportunity to earn their living by lecturing. "Very well," said Victoria, "I will make it hotter on earth for Henry Ward Beecher than hell is below!" She held a tremendous meeting in Cooper Union, at which she raked up the whole scandal again to an immense audience, and summoned Beecher to sue her for libel if it was false. Every week or so in *Woodhull & Claflin's Weekly* she ran editorials headed: "Beecher, Tilton, Bowen." Nothing could silence her. Usually so resourceful in dealing with women, Henry Ward was beside himself to know what to do with this one.

Yet in the end the very clamor deafened the ears of the public. Astutely, Beecher's friends got all of Bowen's charges into print, too. Every one knew the worst about Henry Ward Beecher. And nothing at all happened. People who had never been to church before in their lives flocked across Fulton ferry, climbed the steep hill to Columbia Heights, and waited for hours for the doors of Plymouth Church to open, just to catch a glimpse of this genial, white-haired, thick-necked man with boyish manner and disarming egoism, who at sixty stood accused of so many reputed adulteries. Never had Henry Ward Beecher been more popular.

Just the same, Henry Ward was far from happy:

"The whole earth is tranquil and the heaven is serene, as befits one who has about finished his world life," Henry Ward wrote Frank Moulton out of the gloom of these days. "I have determined to make no more resistance. Theodore's temperament is such that the future, even if temporarily earned, would be absolutely worthless, filled with abrupt charges, and rendering me liable at any hour or day to be obliged to stultify all the devices by which we have saved ourselves . . . The agreement was made after my letter through you was written. ["I ask through you Theodore Tilton's forgiveness, etc."] He had condoned his wife's fault. He had enjoined upon me with the utmost earnestness and solemnity not to betray his wife nor leave his children to a blight. I had honestly and earnestly joined in that purpose . . .

"My mind is clear. I am not in haste. I shall write for the public a statement that will bear the light of the judgment day. God will take care of me and mine . . . I have a strong feeling upon me, and it brings great peace with it, that I am spending my *last Sunday* and preaching my last sermon.

"Dear, good God, I thank thee I am beginning to see rest and triumph. The pain of life is but a moment; the glory of everlasting emancipation is wordless, inconceivable, full of beckoning glory. Oh, my beloved Frank, I shall know you there, and forever hold fellowship with you, and look back and smile at the past.

"Your loving,
"H. W. B."

And the following day, he said to Mrs. Moulton (as she swore):

"I have a powder at home on my library table which I have prepared, which I shall take, and shall sink quietly off as if going to sleep, without a struggle. I haven't any desire to live; I have nothing to live for; in fact I pray for death as a happy release from all my trials and trouble."

Of course, Henry Ward had not the remotest idea of committing suicide. Judge Fullerton quizzed him, on cross-examination, as to just what he thought was going to bring him to the glory of everlasting emancipation at that particular juncture:

"*Mr. Beecher:* 'The sovereign and releasing hand of God . . .'
"*Judge Fullerton:* 'Well, did you look for a translation?'
"*Mr. Beecher:* 'Yes.'
"*Judge Fullerton:* 'As Elijah was translated?'
"*Mr. Beecher:* 'No; but as Henry Ward Beecher would be, if God should take him.'"

Henry Ward had been right when he wrote Frank Moulton that no dependence could be placed in Theodore Tilton. In 1871 Tilton had been, according to the St. Louis *Globe*, "un-

questionably the most popular young man in America. He had
won for himself a name and influence hardly rivaled by any
other. As editor, author, lecturer, poet, he was the pet of the
literary and Christian public. His lecture tours were ovations
. . . He was dashing, fearless, truculent, clear-visioned and not
a theological slave." And now suddenly all of this was gone over
night — and through no fault of his own, that he could see.
Even his paper, *The Golden Age*, was far from prosperous. As
each new development in this conspiracy of silence seemed to
demand more and more of Theodore Tilton, that Henry Ward
Beecher might come through his peril unscathed, Tilton grew
restless and embittered. Gen. Tracy was quick to perceive the
danger; he suggested that both Tilton and Moulton go abroad
for a couple of years until the scandal could blow over.
Beecher, too, was alive to the menace in Theodore's changing
moods. It was at this period that Henry Ward sought solace
and encouragement of Emma Moulton — but found her, instead, "a section of the Day of Judgment," as he put it. Overwhelmed by hopelessness and despair, with no courage to stag-
ger a step farther up his stony Calvary, Henry Ward Beecher
wrote out his resignation as Pastor of Plymouth Church and,
but for Frank Moulton, would have presented it.

In all this wreckage that buffeted Beecher and Tilton alike,
one figure stood out admirable: Francis Moulton. Under his
quiet guidance, the first hazard had been surmounted — Victoria Woodhull. Now the second loomed — Plymouth Church.
The brethren of Plymouth Church held Tilton responsible for
Victoria Woodhull's attacks on Beecher and were bent on trying Theodore for slandering his Pastor. Martha Bradshaw was
to be the accusing witness.

Poor little Lib Tilton was distracted at the thought that there,
in the holy sanctuary of Plymouth Church where her whole
life was rooted, her pitiful story was to be dragged into the
light.

"Oh, Mattie," she cried to Mrs. Bradshaw, "how can you appear against me?"

Torn between pity and duty, Mattie Bradshaw asked her
Pastor what to do:

"I could not and would not believe that you had been otherwise
than basely calumniated," she said. "Now, Mr. and Mrs. Tilton
come and warn me not to do it if I value your welfare . . . I would

part with my right hand sooner than destroy the love and confidence which is reposed in you all over the world . . . Must I accept Theodore's awful story for truth? Do mitigate it, be it ever so little, if you can."

But Henry Ward could not, not even ever so little:

"You will do the greatest good to all parties concerned," he replied, "by . . . refusing to allow the public to meddle with domestic and private affairs."

So Martha Bradshaw refused to give her testimony before Plymouth Church — "I will not add one pang to the agony that poor Elizabeth has already endured," she said. For Beecher's letter had revealed the truth to her.

And without Mrs. Bradshaw to testify, the brethren of Plymouth Church had no case against Theodore Tilton. He appeared, of course, did Theodore, tall and grave and a little contemptuous. He said "he had come to say in Mr. Beecher's presence, and in the presence of his friends, that if he had slandered him he was there to answer to the man he had slandered; that if Beecher had aught to say against him, if he would say it, he would answer him as God was his judge."

Every one turned and looked at Beecher where he sat, imperturbable, in his great arm chair.

"Mr. Tilton asks," said Henry Ward, "if I have any charge to make against him. I have none. Whatever differences have been between us have been amicably adjusted and, so far as I am concerned, buried. I have no charges."

Which, after all, might well have contented the most insatiable of busybodies. Tilton's name was quietly dropped from the rolls of Plymouth Church, with his consent, and thus was the second of the great perils of Henry Ward Beecher conjured.

But somehow Henry Ward was profoundly depressed. One danger passed seemed merely to reveal another. And now there came to him also, over the gulf of the years, the news that Betty Bates was dead. He stood a long time at his window, looking out over the river, and the little boats that went up and down, and the gas lights that twinkled afar in the early winter dusk, and beyond all of them, the last fading color in the sky — out there, in the West, where she had died. She had not married. Between them there had been only her devotion to him, and his knowledge of it . . . Well, he was glad she was dead — now.

There were those who, in that day, blamed the church for the new peril that confronted Henry Ward Beecher so swiftly upon the heels of the last. Yet after all, Beecher was not just a private person whose sins were something between himself and his God. When the scandal which had run up and down the country for four years, in public prints and out, was so neatly hushed up by Plymouth Church, the other Congregational churches of Brooklyn were outraged. That very ecclesiastical council Henry Ward had written Moulton he so feared became at once unavoidable.

To Beecher's mind this meddling of other churches in his affairs was sheer jealousy. He had not followed the career of Lyman Beecher for half a century for nothing. He knew that if he had his church with him, he was unbeatable. When the crucial meeting at which the attitude of Plymouth Church was decided had ended, Beecher came out to find Moulton and Tilton walking up and down the street outside.

"I am all in a dripping sweat," he cried. "I have just been making the greatest speech of my life! My church will do exactly as I say! . . . We can whisk the Council down the wind! We can set them all agog!" He was quivering from head to foot with excitement, and had to hold on to the lamp post to steady himself. It was the last time that Theodore Tilton saw Henry Ward Beecher till they met in a court room.

But to the public at large, and particularly to the Congregational clergy, the whole business was a matter for grief, not triumph. "There is a feeling that we are exaggerating a case of small importance," said Dr. Storrs. "It does not seem so to us . . . We have heard much of Mr. Beecher's public services, and we feel it all. I think of him as the friend whom I have loved so long, who buried my child, and whose child I helped to bury . . . But there comes to my sight, clothed with grandeur, the form of Congregationalism which has spread across the land and made Christianity blossom over the waters. Let us maintain the purity of Congregational polity if, as I believe, it still lives."

Of this speech, Henry Ward Beecher wrote Frank Moulton: *"It ought to damn Storrs . . .* If ever a man betrayed another he has. I am in hopes that Theodore, who has borne so much, will be unwilling to be a flail in Storrs' hand to strike at a friend."

By Theodore's friend, Henry Ward meant, of course, himself. To prove it, he permitted Plymouth Church to disculpate itself to the ecclesiastical council by pleading that Theodore Tilton had been dropped from membership in Plymouth congregation as one who had brought "open dishonor upon the Christian name." As an added bit of bravado, the clerk of Plymouth Church gave out to the press a statement that "Tilton was out of his mind, off his balance, and did not act reasonably. As for Mrs. Tilton," the statement went on, "she had occasioned the whole trouble while in a half-crazed condition. She had mediumistic fits, and while under the strange power that possessed her, often spoke of the most incredible things . . . and among the rest had slandered Mr. Beecher."

Poor Henry Ward! Just when things were going so nicely, too! He hastened to denounce Shearman, the clerk of Plymouth Church, as "a mischief-maker" and wrote his heart out to Frank Moulton:

"Is there no end of trouble? Is wave to follow wave in endless succession? I felt like lying down and saying, 'I am tired — tired — tired of living or of trying to resist the devil of mischief.' . . . The shameful indelicacy of bringing the most sacred relations into such publicity fills me with horror . . . My innermost soul longs for peace; and if that cannot be, for death — that *will* bring *peace* . . ."

Just what sacred relations Henry Ward found it so shamefully indelicate to have given publicity is not altogether clear.

Henry Ward began to feel that he had had about all he could stand. And so, as a matter of fact, did Tilton. Indeed, as Theodore let one opportunity after another to denounce Beecher pass by, his own position grew weaker and Henry Ward's stronger.

For in Beecher's volatile mind, four years had worked their marvels. He now no longer fled to Remsen street at every new development, to weep bitterly again and again "until his face assumed a very peculiar redness" and Frank Moulton feared he would suffer a stroke. He held his church in the hollow of his hand. He had whisked an ecclesiastical council down the wind. The whole aspect of things had changed since that ghastly interview in the upper room at Moultons'. The basket of tricks had been turned upside down. It was no longer Henry Ward Beecher who had crept into the home of his friend and worked upon the religious mysticism of his wife to seduce her, but Theodore Tilton who had turned upon his benefactor and was trying to drag that noble man into the mire into which his association with such loose characters as Victoria Woodhull, Susan B. Anthony and Elizabeth Cady Stanton had plunged him. That was what the world wanted to believe, and what the world did believe. And no evidence produced then, or since, could alter it — or ever will. "The world will never forgive you for having condoned your wife's crime," Gen. Tracy told Tilton. It never has.

That staunch bewhiskered old Calvinist, Leonard Bacon, lifelong friend of Lyman Beecher and one of the editors of *The Independent* in the days when Theodore Tilton was a fledgling journalist, also had his say about Theodore. Bacon had been moderator of the ecclesiastical council, and when he went back to Yale, he delivered a lecture to those same divinity students whom Beecher had just been instructing in the high art of preaching. Tilton, said Dr. Bacon, was a knave and a dog, and as for Plymouth Church:

"There are many not only in Brooklyn, but elsewhere, who felt that the church had not fairly met the question, and by evading the issue had thrown away the opportunity of vindicating its pastor," he declared. "Mr. Beecher would have done better to have let vengeance come on the heads of his slanderers," said this minister of the Gospel.

Well, Theodore Tilton asked nothing better. He was sick and tired of the hole-and-corner business he had been playing for four years, protecting Beecher only to be blackguarded by Beecher's friends. If they wanted the truth, why, bless you, they should have it. Theodore Tilton had come to the end of the furrow.

If only Henry Ward Beecher had been able to sit down quietly and think back over his life a little! There had been Comegys. He had abused Comegys like a pickpocket, scolding and browbeating and disparaging the wretched distiller until Comegys turned upon Henry Ward and made him a laughingstock. There had been the South. For ten years, Beecher had fulminated, defamed, vituperated and delivered himself of bitter jeremiads against the South. It had all ended in war. He preached Love, Beecher said. Did he? These very friends of his now leading the hue and cry against Theodore Tilton were the product of his preaching. They had driven Tilton till his back was to the wall. Theodore had wanted to shield his wife. He had wanted to put behind him what he called "this sorrowful business," and begin life all over again. "I never knew a man to bear so much," said Lincoln's friend, Frank Carpenter. It was those who got their code of conduct from Plymouth pulpit who would not let Theodore Tilton abide in peace.

For Tilton had no alternative. His reputation was his earning power, and any such blow as Leonard Bacon had struck at his reputation meant that he could never succeed in rebuilding, on the wreckage Beecher had left, a new life for his wife and his children. Theodore put it to Bacon squarely, in a long letter reciting the unvarnished facts of his relations with Henry Ward Beecher since July 1870. But Leonard Bacon referred the matter to Beecher, and took water and washed his hands before the multitude, as it were.

"If Mr. Tilton publishes that letter, and Plymouth Church does not reply to it within twenty-four hours by a suit at law against Mr. Tilton, they will have no case before the Christian public," said Bacon.

So Theodore Tilton published his letter to Bacon. But Plymouth Church brought no suit at law against him, then or ever. Nor did Henry Ward Beecher.

In the last hours of the crisis, Frank Moulton was incomparable. He could not tie up the storm this time — only Beecher could do that — but he rendered it relatively harmless. He saw to it that there was no mention of adultery in Tilton's letter. Indeed, aside from a dull recital of fact, all there was to worry about was a quotation from Henry Ward Beecher himself:

"I ask Theodore Tilton's forgiveness, and humble myself before him as I do before my God. He would have been a better man in my circumstances than I have been. I ask nothing except that he will remember all the other breasts that would ache. I will not plead for myself. I even wish that I were dead . . ."

That was all.

Of course if Henry Ward Beecher had ever really lived his

contrition, instead of merely talking about it, this could have done him no harm. But in Plymouth Church and in the circle of his own intimates his life for the past four years had exhibited anything but that "anxiety, remorse, fear, despair" about which he wrote Moulton so poignantly. Henry Ward had wanted to have his cake and eat it, too, as he had done all his life; to appear humbly penitent to Theodore Tilton while at the same time he stood before Plymouth Church exultant in righteousness.

It could not be done.

Frank Moulton made one last effort to save the Great Preacher. It was Mrs. Moulton's idea. Beecher was to say, frankly, to his church and to the world that he had been unjust to Theodore Tilton, that he had been sorry for it afterwards, had expressed his contrition to Tilton as a Christian should, and been forgiven. He need not say what he had done — Tilton had not said. He could just say to his church:

"I have committed no crime, and if this society [Plymouth Church] believes that it is due it that I should reopen this already too painful subject, or resign, I will resign. I know, as God gives me power to judge of myself, that I am better fitted to-day, through trials and chastening, to do good than I have ever been."

And Theodore Tilton was ready to accept that and to authorize the destruction of the whole dossier of compromising documents in Frank Moulton's hands. It would have been the end.

Yet out of what in his character was Henry Ward Beecher to extract the humility, the simple courage, necessary to step to the front of the stage of Plymouth Church and say these contrite words? Where was there, in the atmosphere of cynical materialism, of success as God, that Henry Ward Beecher with every other man Jack in America had breathed from his cradle, any quality of probity that would enable him to say: "I have sinned. I am repentant. I am a better man for it."?

No; in the world of fantasy in which he had dwelt so long — this new world, this American world — Henry Ward Beecher conceived the duty resting upon him as something transcending any mere personal consideration of his own moral comfort. He must set an example to the world of respectability, though it cost his immortal soul. "The truth must not come out — think of the influence on society!" said the Hon. Benjamin F. Tracy.

Beecher hurried down from his luxurious country estate at Peekskill the moment he learned Tilton's letter to Bacon had been published. He was completely in Tracy's hands now, and Tracy's first instinct was intimidation. A year before, without Tilton's knowledge, Henry Ward had joined with others in contributing to the capitalization of Theodore's paper, *The Golden Age,* through Frank Moulton. So now Tracy threatened to brand both Moulton and Tilton as blackmailers unless they agreed to keep Beecher's secret — a little moral blackmail of his own. It was a ridiculous idea, and when the case finally came to trial, the court excluded all consideration of blackmail. Tracy's next inspiration was bribery. "A sum of money would or could be raised," he said, to send Tilton and his family to Europe "for a term of years." To this, Theodore wrote Beecher direct "that so long as life and self-respect continue to exist together in my breast I shall be debarred from receiving either directly or indirectly any pecuniary or other favors at your hands." Henry Ward began to lose confidence in Tracy's methods.

If there was one man in the country, however, who could, as Henry Ward expressed it, "carry me through the case no matter what the facts were," it was the Hon. Benjamin F. Butler. Beecher was a great admirer of Butler's, and ten years before had urged him for the presidency to succeed Lincoln. So now to the astute and unscrupulous Ben Butler, Henry Ward sent the equally unscrupulous if not so astute Tracy. And to Butler and Tracy were added "Tearful Tommy" Shearman, jackal of Jim Fisk and Jay Gould, to whom "no so-called 'legal' infamy was too great," W. O. Bartlett, the defender of Tweed, and John K. Porter, who was to compass the acquittal of Orville E. Babcock, the brains of the "whiskey ring."

To the guidance of these men, Henry Ward Beecher gave himself over, in the interests of society.

"I don't care who is right and who is wrong," Ben Butler put it. "This exposure will work harm. What right-minded man is there who will say there can possibly be a balance of good to the world from the publication by the parties to this trouble of all this repulsive combination of details? The thing to be advised in the case was to keep it hidden, and that advice I strongly pressed."

To this Henry Ward Beecher subscribed.

CHAPTER XXVII

CITY COURT

WHEN old Lyman Beecher was alive he was fond of telling of a minister in the days of his youth who had been tried for misconduct by his fellow clergymen:

"I used to say," chuckled Lyman, "that his friends were so committed that if he had broken the seventh commandment at noonday in the public square, they would not have given up." Of this Henry Ward now bethought himself. He appointed a Committee of six members of Plymouth Church, "to have some proper investigation made of the rumors, insinuations, or charges made respecting my conduct, as compromised by the late publication made by Mr. Tilton."

"His Committee of Investigation," said the *Liberal Christian*, "was appointed by himself, at a late hour, and from among his most devoted personal friends. This Committee from its very nature could not be impartial in its proceedings."

It was not intended to be. Stupendous efforts were made, before the Committee met, to prevent Theodore Tilton from telling all his story. But Beecher's friends managed the business wretchedly. So eager were they to get the whip hand of Tilton before he could speak that Tracy went to Lib Tilton secretly, while her husband was still ignorant that an Investigation Committee had been appointed, and begged her to save her Pastor by appearing before the Committee without Theodore's knowledge, and coached her as to just what she was to say to get on record some sort of formal denial of Beecher's adultery.

Poor Lib was frantic.

"I think I should be justified in stating falsely under the circumstances," she wailed to Mrs. Moulton. "I think for the sake of Mr. Beecher, for the sake of the influence on the world, for my position, for my children, I think it is my duty to deny it." And she did deny it.

While Tracy was thus engaged, another staunch friend of Beecher's came to Tilton:

"He is an old man," he pleaded with Theodore; "his career is nearly ended, and yours has only begun. If you will withhold your forthcoming statement, and spare this old man the blow which you are about to strike him, I will see that you and your family shall never want for anything in the world."

When this failed, Tracy was really frightened, at last.

"Make the offence anything you choose, and I will procure the passage of the report," Tracy begged Theodore Tilton. "Only of course the Committee could not bring in a report that he was guilty of adultery, or anything that compromised his character and standing as a clergyman. Make a report of that kind, and you can make it ad libitum, according to your own wish and will."

It was too late. For Lib Tilton suddenly took matters into her own hands, and left her home and her children forever, to take her stand with her Pastor.

"That this woman should lie for Mr. Beecher, that this woman should follow the fortunes of Mr. Beecher, that she should forsake husband and children, was just as natural, and as inevitable, as that she should sacrifice to him her chastity, the honor of her womanhood," said that sage old counsellor, William A. Beach. "You always find the adulteress with the adulterer."

On July 20, 1874, Theodore Tilton appeared before the Plymouth Church Committee and made a sworn statement, in detail, of Henry Ward Beecher's adultery with his wife, buttressed by a wealth of documentary evidence that seemed crushing. Two days later, Beecher issued a general denial. But it was not until twenty-five days later that he made any attempt to meet Tilton's specific accusations.

In the interim, Beecher's friends were moving heaven and earth to save him. For the original documents were still in the custody of Francis Moulton. If in some way he could be prevailed upon to deliver them up to Beecher, or even to destroy them, the reputation of the Great Preacher could be retrieved, a little damaged perhaps, but usable. Tilton's story would then stand alone, without tangible proof—and Tilton could be shouted down by the cohorts of Plymouth Church.

Everything short of murder was tried. Tilton was offered $5,000 just to release Moulton. Tracy threatened to ruin Mrs. Moulton "socially, financially and in every way" unless she prevented her husband from producing Beecher's damning letters. As for Moulton and Tilton, he would brand them publicly, from one end of the country to the other, as blackmailers, he said.

"Why, Francis D. Moulton could have been the best petted man in the City of Brooklyn if he would have been false to the truth and to his friend. [Applause.] Everybody knows it," said William A. Beach. "And yet, in the face of denunciation and disaster, never for an instant faltering in his manliness, Francis D. Moulton has pursued the even tenor of his way . . . and all the power of Beecher and his minions cannot trample him to the dust. [Loud applause.]"

There was one hour when Henry Ward Beecher, too, stood in the light:

"He placed his hand on my knee," Beecher's friend James Red-path swore, "and said: 'Oh, that is all right now; I have made up my mind . . . When I awoke this morning I saw my way clear. I shall make a clean breast of it. I shall tell the whole truth. I shall take the whole blame on myself. I shall vindicate Theodore and Elizabeth.' "

And for once he did not weep.

But it did not last. All his life Henry Ward Beecher had found that the way of success was through a swift, emotional rush, to sweep men off their feet. He knew no other way. That there were citadels of convictions in the minds of men and women that no emotional attack could reach Henry Ward had never learned. Now he must learn it, through shame, humiliation and moral soilure — now he must learn his lesson before the eyes of all the world.

Elizabeth Cady Stanton tells of this mock hearing, before his packed, self-chosen Committee, from whose report Henry Ward Beecher, with such childish naïveté hoped somehow his rehabilitation might be compassed:

"What a holocaust of womanhood we have had in this investigation! What a football the Committee, the lawyers, Mrs. Beecher and her husband have made of Elizabeth R. Tilton! What statements and counter-statements they have wrung from her unwilling lips, then, like a withered flower, 'the Great Preacher' casts her aside and tells the world 'she thrust her affections on him, unsought' — the crowning perfidy in that bill of impeachment that blackens every one who dared to hear or tell the most astounding scandal of the 19th century!

"In common with the rest of the world, members of the National Woman's Suffrage Association heard and repeated the scandal as other men and women did; and forsooth Mr. Beecher dubs them 'human hyenas' and 'free lovers,' though his own sister, Isabella Beecher Hooker, was one of the number, and who, by letters and conversations that through him and his brother were published to the world, is represented as 'insane,' 'deluded,' 'weak-minded.' Those who know Mrs. Tilton — her natural delicacy and refinement — will readily believe her true story, that, through months of persuasion and argument, her love was sought — and sealed.

"Bewildered, racked, tormented, tempest-tossed in the midst of misery and wretchedness, in her last act on leaving home, and in her statement before the Committee, a touch of grand womanhood is revealed, after all, in the face of law, gospel, conventionalism, ready to leave her home forever, she says: 'Theodore, the end has come; I will never take another step by your side.' And to her brother, in announcing her decision, she said: 'I have always been treated as a nonentity — a plaything — to be used or let alone at will; but it has always seemed to me I was *a party* not a little concerned.'

"Thus leaving her husband, children, home, she went forth to vindicate the man she loved — making his friends her friends, his God, her God! With what withering cruelty, then, his words must have fallen on her heart: 'She thrust her affections on me, unsought' — though a mutual confession of love is revealed in the course of the investigation, and recognized in the verdict. . . .

"One is surprised to see in him [Beecher] so little sense of justice towards those who, from no fault of their own, became cognizant of the whole story. To blacken such characters as Susan B. Anthony and Laura Curtis Bullard, Bessie Turner — an unreliable servant, a self-confessed tool for whomsoever might choose to use her — is the main witness against Mr. Tilton and his friends who chanced to visit his house. Her statement in regard to Miss Anthony was false, and of me was exaggerated beyond all bounds . . .

"You ask if it is possible for Mr. Beecher to maintain his position in the face of the facts. His position will be maintained *for* him, as he is the soul and center of three powerful religious rings, as he tells you himself in his statement: (1) Plymouth Church; (2) The *Christian Union*; (3) 'The Life of Christ.'

"The church property is not taxed, its bonds in the hands of the wealthy men of that organization are valuable, and the bondholders, alive to their financial interests, stand around Mr. Beecher, a faithful, protecting band, not loving truth and justice less, but their own pockets more. They are shrewd enough to know that in Mr. Beecher's downfall their bonds must be of little value.

"Next, the *Christian Union*. . . . If, then, his good name is shadowed, another circle of suffering stockholders would be brought to grief.

"As to 'The Life of Christ,' in the words of one of the fold that would, indeed, be blown 'higher than a kite' were the author proved an unworthy shepherd. I have heard that he was paid $20,-000 for that work before he put pen to paper. Then he ground out one volume which the English market refused to touch until the second was forthcoming; and thus the whole investment hangs by the eye-lids until Mr. Beecher is white-washed and sees fit to finish his work. With such wealthy circles of influence in Brooklyn and New York all depending upon the vindication of Mr. Beecher's honor and honesty, you will readily understand the number, strength and activity of his partisans, and the reason why the tone of the Metropolitan press differs so widely from that throughout the country.

"Under such circumstances, justice for Mr. Beecher is quite impossible. When the friends of Mr. Beecher thought they had silenced Mr. Moulton, our city press toasted him as a brave, generous, refined gentleman; but as soon as he opened his mouth to tell the whole truth, he became a blackmailer and conspirator.

"If the secret history of this tragedy is ever brought to light, we shall have such revelations of diplomacy and hypocrisy in high places as to open the eyes of the people to the impossibility of securing justice for any one when money can be used against him.

"When a refined gentleman and scholar like Theodore Tilton can be hurled in a day from one of the proudest positions in the country — the able editor of a great journal — and become a target for the jibes and jeers of the nation, without one authenticated accusation of vice or crime against him, his downfall is the result of no lack of moral rectitude in himself. They who try to see Theodore Tilton vindicated do but maintain the claims of common justice for those who have not the money to buy it.

"I have long known Mr. Tilton and Mr. Moulton, have visited them frequently in their pleasant homes, and seen them under trying circumstances, and know they are not the base, unreliable men represented by Mr. Beecher's statement. However, when this matter is thoroughly sifted in the civil courts, truth may be made to appear."

A very able lady, Elizabeth Cady Stanton — and never abler than in this statement. The Report made by Beecher's carefully hand-picked Committee to the brethren of Plymouth Church was precisely as Mrs. Stanton characterized it. Tracy had carried out his threat: both Tilton and Moulton were branded blackmailers, and Henry Ward Beecher so set it down in black and white and signed his name to the charges. A year later, under oath, on the witness stand, he withdrew it publicly, abjectly and miserably — as he was compelled to withdraw most of the rest of the gaudy rhetoric of his unsworn statement to Plymouth Church. But just now he rode the waves of an almost hysterical triumph, with the newspapers devoting the whole front page and a good part of the remainder of their issues to accounts of the Report of the Committee. Prof. Raymond, a professional elocutionist, read that extraordinary document to a Plymouth Church packed with Brooklyn's bravest and her best. He was frequently interrupted by hurricanes of applause. Ladies waved their handkerchiefs and cried "Bravo!" Men cheered and clapped their hands and stamped their feet.

And then, just in the middle of things, who should come down the aisle, conspicuous for his stalwart figure and shock of red hair — dapper and elegant in olive coat, white vest, white pantaloons and carrying a white slouch hat — by long odds the smartest figure that had ever graced Plymouth Church — but Francis De P. Moulton himself. At first he said nothing, but merely watched the proceedings. When, however, dissenting remarks were called for, he rose to speak. Rossiter Raymond, Henry Ward's general utility man, was on his feet in an instant, seized the floor and opened a tirade of abuse of Moulton. When he reached the point where he said that "Moulton had poisoned the public with lies," Frank Moulton raised his hand and cried, "You are a liar, Sir!"

Immediately there was a pandemonium. Brethren of Plymouth Church took pistols from their pockets and the great barnlike building was filled with cries of "Put him out!" "Give him hell!" "Rush him!"

Unarmed, Francis Moulton "stood in the midst of all the storm like a sphinx. He did not smile or move." When the vote of those opposed to the Report of the Committee was called for, he rose, "looked straight at the chairman and said, vigorously and alone, 'No!'"

The police had to use their clubs on the brethren of Plymouth Church to enable Francis Moulton — "a gentleman of honor, and of high honor," as Beecher called him — to leave the

Temple of Free Speech without being mobbed by the men —
and the women, too — of Henry Ward Beecher's Christian
flock.

Under the circumstances, it is hardly remarkable that the
whitewashing Henry Ward received from the Committee of
Plymouth Church failed to satisfy the public. Bitterly Beecher
now regretted the fervor with which he had let himself go in
his statement to Plymouth Church. He had worked infinite
damage with his silly charge of blackmail, and done himself no
good. After all, thousands of people all over the country said:
"An innocent man cannot be blackmailed!" Nor was the picture
he had drawn of himself as a sort of fat, grandfatherly, gray-
haired Joseph leaving, if not his garment, at all events a good
many indiscreet letters in the hands of a lady no longer young,
an engaging one. It had done him no good, either. For both
Tilton and Moulton were preparing replies to the Report of the
Plymouth Church Committee, and it was certain that Henry
Ward's conduct in shielding himself behind the skirts of poor
little Lib Tilton was going to come in for candid treatment.

There is something both tragic and degrading in the monstrous efforts that Beecher and his advisers made to suppress
these two statements. One has a picture of Tracy speeding to
Boston to consult Ben Butler; of Redpath, desperately trying to
save the star-lecturer of his Lecture Bureau, telegraphing
Beecher in Latin, so that even the telegraph clerks would not
know what was afoot; of Tracy bullying Mrs. Moulton, con-
triving with John Russell Young of the New York *Herald* to influence the press of the country in Beecher's favor; of Beecher's
friends destroying part of the records of his church in Lawrenceburgh; mutilating the files of Indiana newspapers kept in
the public libraries to get rid of the evidence of ancient controversies; spiriting away servants who had been employed in the
Tilton household; covering tracks, covering tracks, to save the
Great Preacher! Trying to rake up some scandal on Theodore
Tilton that would discredit him; accusing him of immorality,
forgery, insanity; pulling wires to get Frank Moulton indicted;
hounding him in his business, blackguarding him to his friends;
marshaling political and financial influences against both men.

It was a loathsome business that turned the great sacrifice of
self for society, that Henry Ward Beecher told himself he was
making, into a shabby and obscene compact with dishonor. As

the last, but by no means the least, of the services that Theodore
Tilton rendered Beecher, he put a stop to all of this humiliating
intrigue and chicanery by instituting suit against Henry Ward
Beecher for the alienation of his wife's affections. And thus the
whole matter of Beecher's fitness to be a minister of the Gospel
was swept out of the privy chambers of Plymouth Church into
a court of law.

The case of Tilton vs. Beecher was called for trial in City
Court, Brooklyn, before Chief Justice Joseph Neilson, on January 11, 1875. It ended with a disagreement of the jury on July
2, 1875, after 112 days of trial. The testimony, arguments and
exhibits ran to slightly over a million words. For six months the
newspapers of the country carried little else. The nation, still
in the grip of the panic of 1873, rendered captious and disillusioned by the discovery of a seemingly unending succession of
frauds in municipal, state and national government, gave itself
up to the Beecher Scandal as to an anodyne. Hundreds of pam-
phlets were printed and sold on every news stand, reproducing,
frequently in facsimile, Beecher's "letter of contrition," his
"ragged-edge letter" to Moulton, his "clandestine letters" to
Lib Tilton. Cartoons of Beecher, Tilton and Frank Moulton,
"the mutual friend," were sold by newsboys in the streets, and
adorned the walls of barber shops and saloons. The *Daily
Graphic* of New York issued special supplements from time to
time filled with nothing but the Beecher Scandal. The Chicago
Tribune took first rank as an American newspaper from its
enterprising handling of the case. The New York *Times* accused the New York *Tribune* of receiving five dollars a column
for printing material favorable to Beecher and, particularly,
venomous towards Tilton. Victoria Woodhull was in her element. She let her active imagination have full swing, and *Woodhull & Claflin's Weekly* came to be read everywhere as possess-
ing somehow inside information.

It was drama, gripping and tremendous, with thrills, tears, sex
interest, tragedy, and even a little comedy. Nothing approaching it had ever been witnessed before in this grandiose America
where everything was possible — even adultery on the part of
"the greatest preacher the world has seen since St. Paul preached
on Mars Hill," as John Hay called Beecher. Foreign ambassa-
dors, future Presidents of the United States, Senators, Con-
gressmen, Judges, millionaires, bishops, politicians, thronged the

dingy, narrow quarters of Brooklyn City Court. One day Victoria Woodhull came in response to a subpœna. The whole neighborhood turned out to see the hussy. But she was modestly dressed and behaved with exemplary decorum.

Yet there was little new adduced in the case in court. All the essential facts had been before the public, in the utmost detail, since July 1874. Most unwisely for his own interest, Theodore Tilton had placed his cards on the table when he came before the Plymouth Church Committee. He kept nothing back. Beecher's lawyers had six months in which to work up their defense of the Great Preacher, with all Tilton's evidence before them and unlimited funds at their disposal. Tilton declared, moreover, that even if he won his suit he would not take a penny of Henry Ward Beecher's money.

Indeed, throughout, Tilton's candor was in sharp contrast to the course followed by Beecher's friends. It appeared to be the theory of the brethren of Plymouth Church that no price would be too great for the American public to pay to retain its illusions, its idol, the full flower of that emotionalism which was the counter-swing from the strait Puritanism of early days. They were amazed and bewildered to find that, side by side with the growth of a sentimentality common to America and England in that Victorian era, another intellectual development was afoot — a restless curiosity, a skepticism, a questing of truth that was already producing discoveries in the field of science, a new outlook in the field of speculative thought, and an insatiable hunger for fact in place of fantasy in respect of life.

To this demand a new type of journalism responded. Samuel Bowles, Joseph Medill, E. L. Godkin, Charles A. Dana, were men of the new order. Their minds cut through sentimentality like a knife in cheese. They did not care a fig whether Beecher had committed adultery or not. They did not even care whether he had connived with Mrs. Morse to procure the abortion of poor little Lib Tilton's "love babe," which, said the *Sun*, "is so widely known that it is strange that the papers have kept silent about it." But these men directing the great newspapers of America were determined that the facts should not be deliberately perverted merely to save the Great Preacher — that the American public should not be forced to gulp a colossal fraud for the benefit of the scrip-holders of Plymouth Church.

From the moment the Beecher Scandal broke from the grip of the truth-hiders of Plymouth Church, it came into the hands of men with this outlook. "Nothing since the outbreak of the Civil war has excited such intense interest all over the United States as this case," quoted Charles A. Dana. "All the papers, from Brooklyn to the smallest hamlet in Oregon, are talking about it, and the whole American people are anxious to know the truth." Many of the editors of the great newspapers of the country had known all the facts for years. But so long as Beecher's delinquencies had remained his private affair, they had refrained from launching a scandal solely for the sake of sensation. But the instant the brethren of Plymouth Church asked the world to believe everything false save the unsupported and unsworn declarations of their Pastor, not even the name and fame of Henry Ward Beecher could save him.

Thus the Chicago *Tribune* published Lib Tilton's pathetic letters to her husband, written between 1866 and 1870, from whose lines peered the tragic story of her struggle, her frantic bewilderment and her despair. The same journal also printed Elizabeth Cady Stanton's cogent analysis of the whole ugly business of Plymouth Church's activities. Indeed, this Western newspaper set a pace that every daily in the country was compelled to follow and made the question of truth or falsity in the Beecher case a test of American honesty. Not to be outdone by its rival, the Chicago *Times* printed the story of Beecher and Lucy Maria Bowen — with nothing left to the imagination. The Chicago *Inter-Ocean*, in its turn, revealed the touching idyl of Betty Bates. . . .

When Tilton vs. Beecher came to trial, Theodore Tilton's case was presented simply and directly, without extraneous matter. Throughout, he handicapped his attorneys by insisting that no fault attach to Lib Tilton — "she is guiltless, sinned against, bearing the transgression of another" Beecher had written, before he changed his mind and decided that she had "thrust her affections upon him, unsought." To that first declaration Theodore Tilton rigidly held his lawyers and himself. He tried to hold Beecher to it, too. But Henry Ward Beecher was no longer interested in saving the reputation of Lib Tilton.

Beecher's case, on the other hand, was Henry Ward Beecher:

"Whenever you establish the proposition that these breaches of external morality that threaten the very fabric of society, the central point, the purity of the family, can occur without preliminary moral degradation and preparation . . . can be practised with the maintenance of all the active benevolence, and the exhibition of all the beautiful virtues of life, you have struck a blow . . . at your own wives and your own daughters," William M. Evarts, Beecher's attorney, told the jury.

And Mrs. Moulton, testifying that she urged her husband to postpone to the last moment his publication of Beecher's compromising letters, said:

"I did not want Frank to state the facts. I wanted Mr. Beecher to do it."

And when Judge Fullerton asked her what she had said to her husband, she replied:

"I said: 'Give the old man another chance.'"

The trial dragged. When it began, there were days when court could not be held because the ice in East river prevented the attorneys from reaching Brooklyn. Before it ended, one of the jurymen fainted from the heat. There was perhaps more free hand perjury than ever has been seen in a case of similar prominence. Indeed, when the trial ended there was a movement to indict Gen. Tracy for perjury. But Gen. Tracy was one of the leading Republican machine politicians of New York. There was no danger of his being indicted for anything short of murder.*

It must be admitted that, on the whole, the Beecher side of the case left a deplorable impression. While Tilton's counsel were scrupulous not to disparage Henry Ward Beecher's character a hair's breadth beyond what the evidence actually revealed, the line of defense adopted by Beecher's lawyers was unfortunate. They set out by every means to blackguard Theodore Tilton.

To the average man or woman, Henry Ward Beecher was rendered no purer by mud slung at Tilton, so many years Henry Ward's closest friend. Nor did this course in any wise clear Beecher of the charge of adultery. The spectacle of the defenders of a Christian minister vilifying men who had been that minister's acknowledged intimates was no advertisement for Beecher, Plymouth Church, or Christianity either. Nor was the savagery exhibited by Beecher's attorneys towards the op-

---

* Political lines were sharply drawn at the trial. Gen. Roger A. Pryor, of Tilton's counsel, had served in the Confederate Army.

posing witnesses any feather in the cap of the defense. At one time, Justice Neilson was compelled to rebuke Gen. Tracy for his hostility.

The worst impression was left by Beecher himself. He displayed a levity so striking that the New York *Herald* remarked that "he presents for the investigation of scientific men a psychological problem which they must despair of solving." That was before the day of behavioristic psychology. His answers on cross-examination were rarely direct; plainly he sought to put off the evil moment of an answer by discursive, irrelevant remarks. "I don't want any oration about it," Judge Fullerton warned Henry Ward, finally. Eight hundred ninety-four times, Henry Ward Beecher, always so positive and pat in his repartee from the lecture platform, answered "I can't recollect" or "I presume" or "I don't know" or similar expressions. And as Judge Fullerton took the poor man over that unhappy statement Henry Ward had made to the Plymouth Church Committee, driving him to admit that one after another of its bold assertions was without foundation in fact, it was not difficult to understand Juror Davis, who said he wanted very much to bring in a verdict for the defendant, but could not because of "Mr. Beecher's signal breakdown under the cross-examination." It was, in the end, Evarts who saved Beecher — Evarts who "stood alone amid a waste of auxiliary lawyers, fighting the case of the defense," as the *Herald* put it.

Not that there were not dramatic moments. There was one when Francis Moulton, badgered and brow-beaten by the implacable Tracy, was asked:

"*Gen. Tracy:* 'Didn't you say that Mr. Beecher was a damned perjurer and libertine?'

"*Mr. Moulton:* 'I don't know whether I said he was a damned perjurer and libertine. I may have said he was a perjurer and libertine — as he is.'"

The court room was jammed when Henry Ward Beecher took the stand in his own defense, holding a bunch of wild violets in his hand, which he sniffed from time to time, as James A. Garfield described the scene. Immediately, there was a dramatic moment, for Henry Ward Beecher refused to swear on the Bible — declared that he had conscientious scruples against it, and insisted on the New England form, with upraised hand.

There were many who saw in this merely a bit of that theatricality that Beecher loved so dearly — especially as he had sworn to all the affidavits required in the case, in the usual form; but there were others who felt that somehow, by some curious mental reservation in the use of this form of oath, Henry Ward Beecher had freed himself of the responsibility to tell the truth, the whole truth, and nothing but the truth. After all, William A. Beach pointed out, there is no commandment: "Thou shalt not lie."

Nevertheless, Henry Ward denied, specifically and weepingly, that he had been guilty of adultery with Elizabeth Tilton; or that he had ever confessed that he had been guilty to Tilton, Moulton or Mrs. Moulton — all of whom swore just as solemnly that he had so confessed to them. On the other hand, Beecher did admit on cross-examination that when James Redpath told him that Tilton had charged him with adultery, he had not denied the fact. And when Judge Fullerton questioned him about his intimacy with Mrs. Tilton, a number of surprising things were revealed:

"*Judge Fullerton:* 'Were you in the habit of kissing her?'
"*Mr. Beecher:* 'I was when I had been absent any considerable time.'
"*Judge Fullerton:* 'How frequently did that occur?'
"*Mr. Beecher:* 'Very much . . .'
"*Judge Fullerton:* 'Were you in the habit of kissing her when you went to her house in the absence of her husband?'
"*Mr. Beecher:* 'Sometimes I did and sometimes I did not.'
"*Judge Fullerton:* 'Well, what prevented you upon the occasions when you did not?'
"*Mr. Beecher:* 'It may be that the children were there then . . .'
"*Judge Fullerton:* 'Did you kiss her in the presence of the servants?'
"*Mr. Beecher:* 'Not that I ever recollect.' "

Judge Fullerton also read Beecher one of his own sermons:

"*Judge Fullerton* (reading): ' ". . . It is often better that past crimes should slumber, so far as the community is concerned . . . There be many things that are great sins, grievous and wounding, which, having been committed, the conscience of the actor leads him to feel that there is a kind of expiation, or, at any rate, a justice, which requires that he should, with open mouth, confess that which has hitherto been secret. Forsake, surely; to God confess; but it does not follow, especially

when your confession would entail misery and suffering upon
all that are connected with you, that you should make confession merely for the sake of relieving your own conscience."

'Do you recollect preaching a sermon of which that is a
part?'

"*Mr. Beecher:* 'No, Sir; I regard it as sound doctrine.'

"*Judge Fullerton:* 'And will you tell me the date when that
sermon was preached, if you please?'

"*Mr. Beecher:* 'Sunday morning, Oct. 4 . . .'

"*Judge Fullerton:* 'What year?'

"*Mr. Beecher:* '1868.'

"*Judge Fullerton* (To Judge Neilson): 'There is generally not
much done, Sir, after the sermon but the benediction.'

"*Judge Neilson:* 'Will you jury get ready to retire?'

"*Mr. Beecher:* 'There has been no collection taken up!' "

This time there was no laughter at Beecher's little joke.

Henry Ward did not always attend the trial; but Eunice
Beecher missed no day. At first, Elizabeth Tilton was also present. The three met and chatted together amiably enough, in
view of all men. Indeed, for a time, all Plymouth Church
seemed to be on hand to hang over the jury box and make noisy
demonstrations. At first, too, Beecher received large bouquets
of flowers, daily, as if he were a prima donna. After a while all
of this by-play ceased.

It was not Henry Ward Beecher, not his wife, nor little Lib
Tilton, nor even Theodore Tilton himself, tall and grave, pre-
cise of speech and punctilious of manner, nor handsome Frank
Moulton, with his easy self-possession of a man of the world,
who was the one outstanding figure of Beecher's trial. It was
Emma Moulton.

Of medium height, with brown hair and deep brown eyes
and pretty color, soft-spoken — a lady — she was the last of the
witnesses for Theodore Tilton. Of her, Beecher had written
Moulton:

"Not the least has been the great-hearted kindness and trust which
your noble wife has shown, and which have lifted me out of
despondencies often, though sometimes her clear truthfulness has
laid me pretty flat."

It did now.

"He expressed great sorrow for the misery that he had brought
upon Mrs. Tilton and himself," Mrs. Moulton swore, "upon every-

body connected with the case, but said that he felt that he had thoroughly repented, and that he was better fitted now to preach than ever before. He expressed to me his love for Elizabeth, and his great remorse and sorrow that she should ever have confessed to her husband — that it had brought nothing but — that it would bring only ruin in the end to all . . .

"He walked up and down the room in a very excited manner, with the tears streaming down his cheeks, and said that he thought it was very hard, after a life of usefulness, that he should be brought to this fearful end. And I said . . . 'No matter what comes, I will always be your friend if you will only go down to the church and confess, because that is the only way out for you . . . You can never cover such a crime as this and continue in the pulpit, except through a confession on your part . . . I don't see how you can continue in this sort of life, living a lie, going into your pulpit and preaching Sunday after Sunday.' I said: 'I have never heard you preach since I knew the truth that I haven't felt I was standing by an open grave; I cannot express to you the anguish and the sorrow that it has caused me to know what I have of your life. I believed in you since I was a girl; believed you were the only good man in this world. Now it has destroyed my faith in human nature . . . It is very hard for Mr. Tilton to be abused by your friends, and to be charged with treating his family ill — his unkindness to his wife — when he feels that you are principally the cause of all his trouble . . . Your people will stand by you; they believe in you; they will forgive this one crime that you say you have committed and which you have — which you say you have — sincerely repented for. . . .'

"His only reply was that he had repented and he believed that he had been forgiven; still he suffered greatly fearing it would come to light; that the truth would all be made known; that he suffered first for the sake of the woman who had given her love to him, for the sake of his children; he said that he would — that his children, of course, would despise him; that he could never go back to his house.

"And then I said: 'You could go up to your farm and write'; but he said: 'No, if people won't listen to me preach, they certainly won't read anything that I may write; if I cannot continue as a moral and spiritual teacher, why there is nothing left for me to do, and I had better go out of life than remain a burden to my children and my family and the Church. All my past record will be wiped out!' "

Over and over this story the cleverest lawyer of his generation took this shy little woman, so patently truthful, so obviously sincere in her sorrow over Beecher's fall. He could not shake her testimony. He only made it worse, for her story became sharper under Evarts' cross-examination, with little incidents and phrases that everybody present recognized as the very spit of Beecher.

When Emma Moulton stepped down from the witness stand, it did not matter a particle what the jury might decide. The judgment of history was recorded.

CHAPTER XXVIII

HELL

IF A jury of his neighbors could not agree that Henry Ward Beecher was not an adulterer, the rest of the country may be forgiven for not being quite certain about it, either. "The amount of Beecher's innocence must be uncommonly great if one may judge by the time and trouble it takes to prove it," wrote John Bigelow. And he added: "Though all the parties, witnesses and medley in the case were educated in his church, and were or had been members of it, I have yet to hear of one who seemed to have more hesitation in lying than in picking his teeth . . . I think that the tree that brings forth such fruit might as well be hewn down and cast into the fire, whatever may be the verdict on the fornication question. If Plymouth Church ever had any usefulness, it seems to have outlived it." As far away as England, George Meredith wrote: "Guilty or not, there is a sickly snuffiness about the religious fry that makes the tale of their fornications and adulteries absolutely repulsive to read of, and but for the feeling of the reptile sarcasm in our bosoms, it would disgust one more than a chronicle of the amours of costermongers." Marse Henry Watterson called Beecher "a dunghill covered with flowers," and let it go at that. "The close of the Beecher dispensation," said the Baptist Chicago *Standard*.

Plymouth Church did its best to convince the world that the failure of the jury to reach a verdict was just the same as acquittal. The Friday night prayer meeting after the case ended was crowded to the sidewalk, and hysterical with triumph, when Beecher gave out the hymn:

"Christ leads me through no darker rooms
Than He went through before;
He that into God's kingdom comes
Must enter through this door."

Plymouth Church voted $100,000 to help pay the expenses of the trial and ten thousand copies of the speeches of Gen. Tracy and William M. Evarts in defense of Beecher were printed and sent to every library, college and important church in the country — where they remain to this day, the only accessible information on the Beecher case.

Yet the New York *Times* put the secular judgment of Beecher plainly enough:

"Sensible men throughout the country will in their hearts be compelled to acknowledge that Mr. Beecher's management of his private friendships and affairs has been entirely unworthy of his name, position, and sacred calling."

The *Advance*, Edward Beecher's old paper, expressed the view of the religious press at large:

"On his own showing he . . . has exhibited a degree of moral weakness and cowardice almost incredible were it not proved sadly true . . . There is good ground to believe not only that he thought there was, but there actually was, reason for shame and remorse."

And Tom Appleton, the "Sidney Smith of America," summed up the popular verdict: "Mankind fell in Adam, and has been falling ever since, but never touched bottom till it got to Henry Ward Beecher."

If Henry Ward retained any illusions that he had been exonerated, they were speedily dispelled. He went first to Twin Mountain House, New Hampshire, where it had been his habit to conduct what he called a summer parish, in a big corner room of the hotel, with the Golden Rule hanging on the wall. Here came many from Plymouth Church. They amused themselves hugely by holding a mock Beecher-Tilton trial for the edification of such of the natives as had been unable to attend the original performance in Brooklyn. Into the midst of this uproarious merry-making, that Henry Ward enjoyed so wholeheartedly, the shadow of the Great Scandal suddenly thrust its finger. Indeed, poor Henry Ward was to learn that that shadow was never to be very far from him, for the remainder of his days.

Just now it was particularly disconcerting. At the height of the excitement in 1874, when Frank Moulton had finally made all the documents in the case public, popular clamor had driven Beecher to swear out a complaint against Moulton for criminal libel. Now the case was to come to trial.

Henry Ward was appalled. He had managed to worry through one cross-examination, but he had no desire ever to try another. Besides, in the case with Tilton he had been the defendant, able to guide the conduct of his case as he chose. In the pending action, however, he would merely be a prosecuting witness, which was a very different business. In the previous case, though Theodore had punctiliously waived all his rights in the matter of his wife appearing as one of Beecher's witnesses, Henry Ward's attorneys had not dared subject her to Judge Fullerton's questioning. Now, Beecher would have no way of preventing Lib Tilton being called to testify. It was a prospect he envisaged with consternation. His lawyers had fought hard and successfully to keep out of the Tilton case every collateral question touching Beecher's moral character. But now Henry Ward could just see Ben Butler, as Moulton's attorney, ripping into everything he had ever done since he was born.

In great haste, Henry Ward wrote the District Attorney to drop the charge against Frank Moulton.

One of the greatest trials of Henry Ward Beecher's life was that when he made enemies, he made such two-fisted ones. There had been Comegys, the Lawrenceburgh distiller, and Henry C. Bowen, and Theodore Tilton, and now Francis Moulton.

"I am indicted of criminal libel in charging Rev. Henry Ward Beecher with criminal intercourse with a female member of his congregation," Moulton wrote the District Attorney. "The charge is true; he knows it to be true; and whatever the imperfections of man's tribunals, the Supreme Ruler will some day reveal the truth." And he published his letter, broadcast in the press, daring Beecher to sue him for libel. Indeed, Frank Moulton had no intention of waiting for the Supreme Ruler to act. He clamored to be tried. And when a nolle prosequi freed him from the charge, he sued Beecher for malicious prosecution and carried the case to the Supreme Court. Theodore Tilton was financially ruined, and could not renew his action against

Beecher if he wanted to. But Francis Moulton now took his place, and gave Henry Ward Beecher no peace. "Pulpit or Prison!" he declared should be Beecher's alternative. He offered to leave it to any jury, in any court Henry Ward Beecher might pick.

It was small wonder that Beecher returned to Plymouth Church in the fall with his face hardened and a new truculence in his manner. His first act was to clean house in Plymouth Church. Every man or woman who had not stood by him would have to go. Mattie Bradshaw left of her own accord, and a number of others with her. But Emma Moulton made no move. So the brethren of Plymouth Church dropped her from the rolls, as they had done with Tilton. And straightway Emma Moulton moved for a new ecclesiastical council to consider whether Plymouth Church was a Congregational body or not.

But Henry Ward Beecher had lost his fear of ecclesiastical councils. He knew just how to handle them. The delegates to this one, according to the New York *Sun*, were carefully "selected for having said or done or written something to vindicate or favor Mr. Beecher"—and Dana published a list of the leading delegates with their connections with Beecher. "The whole thing is a farce," said the *Sun*.

It seemed to be. Mrs. Moulton was not permitted to be represented or to testify before the Council. Francis Moulton's letter stating that he was "prepared to prove Henry Ward Beecher guilty of adultery and perjury, by evidence both oral and documentary," was ignored. Presumably the church was not interested in adultery in its ministers. Deacon West's demand that Beecher be tried was buried in Committee. But Henry Ward Beecher challenged man, angels and God to state aught against him. "As long as God knows and my mother knows, I don't care for anybody else," he cried. "I am tired of this world." He wept.

"The speaker changed the throng into a weeping multitude," said the *Sun*. "The sobs of one lady were accompanied by a scream."

The hour of the final struggle between Henry C. Bowen and Henry Ward Beecher had struck. Bowen had played his cards carefully. He was still a member of Plymouth Church, and as such he had a right to be heard, and he demanded that right. In the end, he got it.

It was snowing — just such another night as that fatal one six years before when Beecher had followed Frank Moulton to his meeting with Theodore Tilton in the upper room at Moulton's house. But this time the streets of Brooklyn Heights were black with people. A platoon of police had been called out to keep them in order. Admission to Plymouth Church was by ticket only. The building was packed.

When Henry C. Bowen rose to speak, there was a storm of hisses. A woman screamed "Yah! Yah! Yah!" He could hardly make himself heard, and before he had finished the brethren of Plymouth Church were shouting, "We've had enough of you! Sit down!" Henry Ward looked at the ceiling.

There was a sort of passion in the way in which Brother Bowen told of how he had conceived the church, raised the funds for it, and launched it on its amazing career. Of Beecher he said:

"I gave $1,000 to the purchase of a country seat for him at Lenox. I contributed money to send him to Europe . . . I paid his expenses when he was ill . . . At last there came to my knowledge evidence of his guilt which astounded and overwhelmed me, and which I was compelled to carry a weary and secret burden . . . I received from a lady whom, under the circumstances, I was compelled to believe . . . full and explicit confession of adultery with Mr. Beecher . . . Mr. Beecher declared to her . . . that he had always been unhappy in his marriage relations; that he did not really love his wife and never had . . ."

Eunice Beecher never took her eyes from Bowen's face. Bowen went on with his tragic story. The lady of whom he spoke had a key to Beecher's study in Plymouth Church. They used to meet there. Then one day she saw another woman coming from Beecher's study, who also had a key . . . It killed her. In a few months she was dead . . .

"My knowledge is so certain that it can never be shaken by any denials or protestations or oaths, past or future," Bowen ended. He did not give the lady's name, then or ever. He did not have to. There was not a man or woman in Plymouth Church who did not know of whom he spoke.

So the brethren of Plymouth Church expelled Henry C. Bowen from their communion, and Henry Ward Beecher at last reigned supreme on Brooklyn Heights. For one by one the other Congregational ministers of Brooklyn left the Congregational Association of which Beecher was a member and formed a less hectic one of their own. Henry Ward Beecher stood alone — but he stood triumphant.

All his life, two terrific, compelling, dynamic forces had strained and throbbed and seethed and flamed in Henry Ward Beecher; two turbulent, overmastering desires: his hunger for love — what Victoria Woodhull had so quaintly called his "physical amativeness" — and his hunger for power.

The first of these terrible hungers was assuaged. It had made him impetuous, unconquerable; it had lent him a quickening of perception and passion in expression; it had brought him exaltation and an inexhaustible swelling of the heart that bound men and women to him the more closely as they were emotionally starved — as he had been. It had been a consuming fire in his veins, too, that clouded his vision and enthralled him, swept him into infatuation and left him suddenly "on the sharp and ragged edge of anxiety, remorse, fear, despair." Over and over again, he had been its intoxicated victim. But he had somehow known how to sublimate, from the very stimulation of the fever that burned within him, an energy, an enthusiasm, a penetrating sympathy that reached into the secret hearts of men. These were his genius. Victoria Woodhull understood Henry Ward Beecher perfectly. She was perhaps the only human being who ever did.

It was gone, this particular hunger. Burned out. All he had left of it was the momentum, and a sort of mechanical formula for dealing with men — a habit of expression, convincing still because it was formed when its springs ran blood.

With these as equipment, and his hunger for power as a motive force, Henry Ward Beecher at sixty-four set out to build him a new world.

His first task was to get back his audience. The Tilton trial had cost the *Christian Union* (no longer his in fact, but his in sympathy) 30,000 subscribers — and Harriet Beecher Stowe the bulk of her savings. Beecher's publishing house had become bankrupt. Henry Ward was even uncertain of his lecture field.

Goodness knows why Henry Ward Beecher ever had any doubts on the score of his drawing power as a lecturer. He could have recited logarithmic tables for all his audiences cared. They paid as high as ten dollars premium for tickets. They flocked to look at him, to learn what manner of man this was

who had faced down accusations of adultery in the very teeth
of proof they had all read every line of. They looked in the
mirror of his face to see if guilt ever really did reveal itself —
and went away well pleased. His lecture trip was a sensation
from one end of the country to the other. It restored to Henry
Ward every vestige of his shaken self-confidence, and brought
him back to Brooklyn arrogant and redeemed in his own eyes
beyond any power ever again to touch him. It did more. For
the wages of sin (or the reputation of it) was $600 a lecture,
and Henry Ward Beecher largely rehabilitated his finances as
well as his self-esteem by the trip.*

Also, it taught him something. He had lost none of his New
England shrewdness, and he saw at once that his old lecture
themes were outworn. Crowds might come to gape at him once,
but if he wanted them to come again, he would have to find
something more concrete to talk about than the Uses of the
Beautiful. This new post-war America was interested in the
uses of the practical. What Henry Ward Beecher had to find
was some striking, specific message, some rising cause certain of
success, into the vanguard of which he could step, not as one
tardy in arriving (as he had been in the anti-slavery movement),
but as the leader awaited.

There was at that moment just such a cause ripe for Beecher's
espousal — Civil Service Reform. President Hayes was in the
throes of his struggle with Roscoe Conkling to break the grip of
the corrupt Republican machine that had looted New York
ever since Grant entered the White House. Men of the caliber
of Carl Schurz, George William Curtis and William M. Evarts
stood with Hayes against any more corruption.

But the victory was not yet clear enough for Henry Ward
Beecher to champion the cause of political honesty that Theodore Tilton had preached so long. Beecher was a Grant man,
"first, middle and last," he said. He hoped to see his hero nominated again in 1880. Meanwhile, he stood staunchly by Conkling, Chester A. Arthur and the spoilsmen. "I read with disapproval of the movement . . . to 'scratch the ticket,'" he declared at a Conkling meeting. "For myself, I intend to do no
scratching."

He tried the support of Russia in her holy war against the in-

* According to James Redpath, Mr. Beecher received a guarantee of as
much as $1,000 a lecture.

fidel Turk. But the theme that served Gladstone so well was a matter of total indifference to the American public. Henry Ward was forced to look elsewhere.

Under his very nose was all Henry Ward Beecher required. That sympathy with the down-trodden and oppressed he never wearied of celebrating, as he had exhibited it towards the slave twenty years before, had its most poignant and immediate appeal at his own door in 1877. Never in the history of the country had the lot of those who toiled for meager wage been so shocking. In the past four years, the burden of the financial panic of 1873 had been adroitly shifted from the promoters and speculators who had made colossal fortunes out of the development of railroads and industry to the broad, patient back of labor. Three million workers were unemployed out of a total population of only some forty-five million. Whole families literally died of starvation in great cities, oppressed by wealth. All over the industrial East, strikes broke out, not as any organized effort, but as a last gesture of despair.

The situation cried aloud for a man of great heart, careless of his own interest, to preach from the second chapter of the Epistle of St. James. After all, Henry Ward was somewhat in the position of James the Just himself.

It was when the last unbearable reduction in the wages of the railway workers had been ordered and the country was aflame with conflict that Henry Ward Beecher seized the banner that awaited him. Thirty policemen and a corps of secret service men protected him:

"Is the great working class oppressed?" he asked. "Yes, undoubtedly it is . . . God has intended the great to be great and the little to be little . . . The trade union, originated under the European system, destroys liberty . . . I do not say that a dollar a day is enough to support a working man," thundered Henry Ward Beecher. "But it is enough to support a man! . . . Not enough to support a man and five children if a man would insist on smoking and drinking beer . . . But the man who cannot live on bread and water is not fit to live."

As the slogan of a great crusade in the leadership of which Henry Ward Beecher could reconquer the esteem of the American public, this bread-and-water doctrine somehow lacked pulling power. Plymouth Church applauded it roundly; but in less refined circles Henry Ward was mercilessly car-

tooned, with his $20,000 a year salary and at least an equal
amount drawn from lectures, as hardly in a position to ask his
fellow man to bring up five children on a dollar a day. He must
seek some other cause to champion.

Until 1877, Hell, for the great mass of church-going folk in
England, and even more in the United States with its persisting
Calvinistic tradition, was not a state of mind but a place quite
as real as any to which one could buy a ticket at a railway sta-
tion. Indeed, it was a good deal more real than some of the
suburban developments around New York — such as Harlem,
for example. And until that same year, Canon Farrar of Westminster Abbey, only forty-six, was not particularly distinguished among clergymen. But by the evening of November 11,
1877, Frederick Farrar was well on the way to be one of the
most distinguished men of his day. For that morning, in the
sacred and historic precincts of Westminster Abbey, he had
abolished Hell for good and all. "I had to repudiate a doctrine
which had been more or less universally preached by the majority of Christians for fifteen hundred years," as he put it. He
did repudiate it, and in no equivocal fashion, either. And instead
of being struck dead by an enraged deity, he was congratulated
by Dean Stanley, and by Cardinal Manning, and summoned by
the Bishop of London to preach at St. Paul's. Within a fortnight, Canon Farrar began to receive letters from every part of
the globe telling him what a stupendous thing he had done. As a
leading London clergyman said to him: "You have spoken out
what nearly every one of us secretly thought."

It certainly was what Henry Ward Beecher had been secretly
thinking for a long time — probably even at the very moment
when he sat in the witness chair in City Court, excoriating
Theodore Tilton as an immoral man for believing precisely
that. Henry Ward Beecher was like that. All his life what he
had attacked most violently had been what was already gaining
the upper hand in his consciousness. His bitterest censures were
of views which he was on the point of adopting. Those to
whose friendship he clung most closely were the very ones of
whose way of life he was most severely critical. His one infal-
lible method of dealing with temptation was to denounce it
roundly first — then yield.

Of course there were bound to be many who hastened to
point out that Henry Ward Beecher had as strong a personal

reason as any man for at least hoping there might be no Hell. Yet that phase of the matter really played no part in Beecher's prompt espousal of Canon Farrar's view of eternal punishment. Long since, Henry Ward had convinced himself completely that he had been the victim of a deep plot in the Tilton affair, that the high fantasy of his own story of his relations with Lib Tilton was the solemn truth. What did play a major part in Henry Ward's decision was the imperious necessity that he find something, immediately, to bury the past in the public mind — and Hell would serve as well as anything. Better, in fact. For the almost universal acclaim with which Farrar's views had been hailed was an excellent augury for Henry Ward Beecher — it was precisely the type of sensational but successful cause to champion that Beecher most needed.

So five weeks after Canon Farrar had abolished Hell in Westminster Abbey, Henry Ward Beecher gave the brethren of Plymouth Church the thrill of their lives:

"If now, you tell me that this great mass of men, because they had not the knowledge of God, went to heaven, I say that the inroad of such a vast amount of mud swept into heaven would be destructive of its purity; and I cannot accept that view. If, on the other hand, you say that they went to hell, then you make an infidel of me; for I do swear, by the Lord Jesus Christ, by his groans, by his tears, by the wounds in his hands and in his side, that I will never let go of the truth that the nature of God is to suffer for others rather than to make others suffer . . . To tell me that back of Christ is a God who for unnumbered centuries has gone on creating men and sweeping them like dead flies — nay, like living ones — into hell, is to ask me to worship a being as much worse than the conception of any medieval devil as can be imagined. But I will not worship the devil though he should come dressed in royal robes and sit on the throne of Jehovah. I will *not* worship cruelty. I *will* worship Love — that sacrifices itself for the good of those who err, and that is as patient with them as a mother is with a sick child."

It was a good thing for old Lyman Beecher that he was safely dead.

CHAPTER XXIX

DELMONICO'S

HELL served Henry Ward Beecher admirably. The inconstant public, with mind directed upon eternity, speedily forgot his unhappy dollar-a-day speech. They even forgot the charges of adultery in arguing whether there was a Hell for adulterers to go to. Of course Beecher did not stick to his guns on eternal damnation. He had never stuck to his guns in his life and he hardly knew how to. Within a week, he was recanting in Plymouth pulpit:

"Is there a Hell to go to?" he asked, and answered himself: "Yes; one here and one hereafter."

About the one hereafter he spoke with no authority; but on the one here, he should have been an expert. For hardly had his transgression been sealed in a bag, as it were, scarcely had he reconquered his lecture field, reëstablished himself in popular estimation, if not as either a very bold or a very far-sighted leader, at least as a leader, when the horrid business burst out anew, and once more the Beecher Scandal filled whole pages of the newspapers.

Poor little Lib Tilton had been rather an expert on hells herself since that fateful July night eight years before, when she sobbed out her tragic story at Theodore's feet. In the course of Beecher's trial, she had risen in the court room one day and demanded her right to clear her name. But Beecher's lawyers were having all they could do just then to clear the Great Preacher's name; they could not be bothered with Lib Tilton. Since the trial, she had lived on the interest of a trust fund of $10,000 established by some of Beecher's friends. But now even that had been stopped. She opened a little private school, on the promise of the brethren of Plymouth Church to send their children there. But shortly the brethren of Plymouth Church bethought themselves that Elizabeth Tilton was not a proper person to teach children. So the school failed. Her hair was white, now — just like Eunice Beecher's. Theodore supported the children "sumptuously," Mrs. Morse said, by lecturing. His two daughters he sent to Europe to school. He lived alone in a tiny room on Second avenue. Theodore Tilton needed no money for himself.

What Lib Tilton did at this highly inappropriate moment for Henry Ward Beecher, and why she did it, she herself stated in a letter to her friend and legal adviser which every newspaper in the country published:

"A few weeks since, after long months of mental anguish, I told, as you know, a few friends whom I bitterly deceived, that the charge brought by my husband, of adultery between myself and the Rev. Henry Ward Beecher, was true, and that the lie I had lived so well the last four years had become intolerable to me.

"That statement I now solemnly reaffirm, and leave the truth to God, to whom also I commit myself, my children, and all who must suffer.

"I know full well the explanations that will be sought for this acknowledgment: desire to return to my husband, insanity, malice — everything save the true one — my quickened conscience, and the sense of what is due the cause of truth and justice. . . .

"ELIZABETH R. TILTON.

"Brooklyn, April 13, 1878."

Lib Tilton knew her Plymouth Church. All of those reasons were assigned to her action, and more besides. Henry Ward, lecturing in northern New York, gave out a statement that sounded uncannily like that one of Shearman's,* whose "shameful indelicacy of bringing the most sacred relations into such publicity fills me with horror," Henry Ward had said then. But now Beecher went Shearman one better. Not only, said he, was Lib Tilton a clairvoyant, doing things as if in a trance and saying things in an abnormal state, but "at such times she would grovel in the dust and roll in the gutter, even kissing the feet of those to whom she most felt herself under obligation," he told the reporters.

Theodore was lecturing, too, out in Iowa. He would say nothing.

To thousands of honest and sincere men and women in 1874, it had seemed of vital importance to save the Great Preacher. Feeling ran so high that, so long as Beecher himself did not admit adultery, vast numbers neither knew nor cared what evidence was brought out in court. But now all of this passion and prejudice that had so confused the judgment four years before

* Page 261.

had died down. Lib Tilton's brief pathetic statement was read in cold blood, and with a new insight into the whole affair.

"The long and bitter struggle to set at naught the consequences of guilt, and the keen torture which every new phase of this wretched business must bring to an organization like that of Mr. Beecher, form one of the most pitiful episodes of human experience," said the New York *Times*. "Mrs. Tilton's latest confession will probably abate not one jot of the attachment with which Mr. Beecher's friends have clung to him, and their implicit faith in his innocence is likely to stand a much ruder test than this. But, it can hardly fail to deepen the indignation with which those convinced of Mr. Beecher's guilt regard the spectacle of the gospel of truth and purity being expounded by one who has so flagrantly defied its precepts."

So, many thought, even among the most generous minded.

Shortly, Theodore Tilton gave up the struggle to make headway against the deadly undertow the propaganda of Plymouth Church had set running against him — the speeches of Beecher's attorneys at the trial that the brethern of Plymouth Church had given such universal circulation, the efforts of Beecher's partisans among the clergy everywhere to prevent Tilton from earning his living by lecturing. "The world will never forgive you for your agency in destroying Henry Ward Beecher," William C. Kingsley had said to Theodore. Beecher was a long way from being destroyed; but the world had not forgiven Tilton.

So one day, Theodore Tilton left the United States for good and all, and took him a little attic room in an old, old house on the Isle St. Louis, in Paris. There he lived and wrote poetry, and every afternoon played chess in the Café de la Régence, opposite the Comédie Française — with Judah P. Benjamin, who had been Secretary of State of the Confederacy. When Judah Benjamin died an exile in 1884, Theodore played his chess games with Jules Grévy, twice President of the French Republic. And when Theodore Tilton himself came to die, in 1907, he was buried beside Jean François Millet, in Barbizon.

But for Henry Ward Beecher there was no such escape. Theodore Tilton had lost in the struggle, and nobody cared what became of him. But Henry Ward Beecher had won. He must play the rôle of victor to the last curtain.

Hell was, of course, much too fruitful and appropriate a subject of discussion for Henry Ward Beecher to let go of, even had he desired to return to the faith of his fathers — which he did not. He had always recanted, after the repercussion of the first shock of any new departure of his — but almost always resumed the attack, chastened but persistent. He did now, in respect of Hell:

"If I thought that God stood at the door where men go out of life ready to send them down to eternal punishment, my soul would cry out: 'Let there be no God!' " he preached. "My instincts would say: 'Annihilate him!' "

But negation of eternal damnation was hardly a philosophy by which one may live, even at sixty-five. Henry Ward Beecher must find such a philosophy, not simply for his sermons and his lectures; he had to have that, it was true. But also he had occasionally to look into his own soul. And one day perhaps, he might have to face his Maker.

It was not easy going for Henry Ward Beecher. All his life emotion had taken the place of thought, and emotion now was all he had to work with. There had been a time when Beecher believed he had ideas of his own. He was beginning to understand that he never had had, and never would have — that the tortuous processes of thought were not for him. But the swift lightning-stroke of intense emotional reaction — that was his, supremely, sublimely. And he had learned to impart it to others, to infuse great audiences with what he felt — not didactically and priggishly, as he had tried to do with those unhappy Young Men at whom he lectured in Indianapolis, but with candor, disconcerting and unashamed, out of his own suffering, his own agony.

Where a few hundred learned of Canon Farrar's great sermon in Westminster Abbey, tens of thousands had the glad tidings that Hell had been abolished from Henry Ward Beecher.

"Men learn, and *must* learn, of God, of the divine government and of the future, through their own experience," he said. "I see that organized life begins at absolute simplicity, develops new organs, increases in complexity. Thus a unity is reached made up of many organs; later a unity of groups of organs, and when you rise to human beings there is not simply one faculty, and there are not merely single faculties, but there are groups of faculties superinduced one over another; there are animal passions, and social affections, and moral sentiments, and over them all imagination and reason."

Herbert Spencer might not have recognized his concepts via Beecher. But it was a vast deal nearer to Spencer, to rationalism, than ninety-nine in an hundred of Beecher's hearers were apt to get by their own efforts. And when Henry Ward Beecher carried such ideas as this into the Middle West and the South, on his lecture tours, he entered upon a service beside which his vacillations on slavery and his mythical conquest of England in 1863 were mere exercises in preparation.

Unfortunately for Beecher there was, as he admitted, "nothing in this world that is such a stimulus to me as an audience. It wakes up the power of thinking and wakes up the power of imagination in me." This stimulus became, in short, not only all it had always been in the life of the Great Preacher, but the impetus he now drew from crowds had also to supplant that personal adulation, worship and passionate devotion that had formerly come to him from Lib Tilton and Lucy Maria Bowen and Betty Bates and so many others. He must have more crowds and more applause, as a furnace must constantly be stoked with fuel.

It was this imperious need, rather than mere personal ambition, that beguiled Henry Ward Beecher into politics, where he had no contribution of idealism to make, and a vast deal of ethical authority to lose. The politics of the late seventies and early eighties required a coarse moral texture that developed nothing of value to the world in Henry Ward Beecher.

His hunger for publicity, for the limelight, for the outward trappings of power, led Henry Ward Beecher into countless minor absurdities in these closing years of his life. He never seemed to grow up. At sixty-five he accepted the post of chaplain of the thirteenth regiment of the National Guard of New York, and paraded the streets of Boston on horseback, in uniform — a lamentable, unsoldierly figure, with his white hair flying. The unregenerate poked fun at him and when a public subscription was taken up to send the regiment to Canada for Queen Victoria's birthday, there was the comment that "the snobs it is who have foisted the man Beecher upon the regiment, and who have placed it in the ridiculous position of acting as his bodyguard while he goes and mouths his adulation to the Queen of Great Britain."

Also, Henry Ward revealed a considerable practical worldliness acquired since the days, not ten years before, when a little band of Communists held Paris, and Beecher declared that the middle and upper classes had had their chance, and now the workers were to have theirs. Then, he had prophesied that class divisions in America would become sharper and sharper. But now he assured the Army of the Potomac that any such radical social theory as this was "an absurdity only this side of insanity. . . . It will tend to organize labor as distinguished from capital in an antagonistic spirit. . . . Labor-unions," he said, "are the worst forms of despotism that ever were bred by the human mind. [Applause.] The Army and the great generals," he declared, "have proved themselves to be safer guides than have been our civil leaders [Great applause.]."

Gen. Hooker, whom Henry Ward had accused of drunkenness to his English audience in 1863, spoke next on the program.

It was in the campaign of 1880 that Beecher's political activities assumed proportions to reawaken the old ambitions he had cherished after his triumphal return from England in 1863. Henry Ward was for Grant. While Conkling was conducting the fight against Blaine for Grant's nomination in Chicago, Beecher was offering up prayers in Plymouth Church for Grant's success. But the country had had all it could stand of the shameless political debauchery of Grant and Conkling. Garfield, with "his record as a harmonizer and a legislative compromiser" and the shadow of the Crédit Mobilier still upon him, was hardly better; Chester A. Arthur, Conkling's satellite, was as lacking in moral fiber as "Elegant Oakey" Hall, who used to preside at Henry Ward's political meetings in the flourishing Tweed days. But to Garfield and Arthur, Beecher rallied with enthusiasm. "For God and Garfield!" was his slogan. And at the Academy of Music in Brooklyn he shocked even Plymouth Church by introducing Col. Robert Ingersoll, with a thumping eulogy of that distinguished agnostic.*

It was during this same campaign that James G. Blaine summoned Henry Ward to the Fifth Avenue Hotel and read him the riot act for circulating gossip about him. It was a stormy interview, and when Beecher emerged it was with a bitter hatred of Blaine that was in nowise lessened when Garfield's cabinet was announced. The faithful were well taken care of, but Henry Ward Beecher was not even mentioned for an ambassadorship. Blaine was widely believed to have had quite as much

* Printed in the New York *Herald*, Oct. 29, 1880.

to do with Garfield's appointments as the President himself. Henry Ward never forgave Blaine.

It was during this campaign, also, that Herbert Spencer and the Rev. William Arthur between them, in a series of letters to the *Tribune*, demolished the legend of that British hostility to the North in 1863 which Henry Ward Beecher was popularly credited with having altered over night by his famous English speeches. But a legend is a legend, and not to be lightly brushed aside. Mere facts failed to convince even Henry Ward of the fabulous character of the tale of his exploit he had come to believe and to enjoy reciting at every opportunity.

It was plain that Henry Ward Beecher as a politician was ready to sleep in anybody's bed. He did little harm by it. He wrote almost nothing, now, on any subject, and by his political speeches he was not even able to carry Plymouth Church. On the other hand, the importance he was given on the program of political meetings, and the applause which his strongly partisan appeals evoked from audiences already sympathetic to just such appeals, were precisely the stimulus he needed to launch him with full steam in those theological waters where what he said might be of real and lasting value. Where years before he had purged the dross of himself in his relationships with women, and so risen to the heights of those earlier chapters of "The Life of Christ" that had been conceived in the little house in Livingston street, so now he seemed to get rid of what was coarse in his make-up in the give-and-take of political debate. By sating, in gross political affiliations, his tendency to opportunism, equivocation and compromise he appeared to be enabled to liberate himself, to soar clear and free in his interpretation of man's relation to the universe.

It was not only appropriate, therefore, but inevitable that in the heat of a political campaign in which Beecher's rôle was a tawdry one, he should have preached a sermon that constituted the second stanza of the message Henry Ward Beecher was to leave with his generation:

"It is a gigantic lie," he said, "told with much circumstantiality, that man was created perfect, and then fell . . . The world is as God meant it to be. There was no trick. God did not make a bad job and then paint it pretty and plaster it up. Such an idea is not worthy of Him. In the childhood of thought such ideas might prevail; that they continue in the manhood of the world is pitiable and confounding . . . In a sense God made laws to be broken — that is, He knew that nascent and imperfect beings would break them. The idea is to be disclaimed and trampled under foot that men must do thus and thus, or be destroyed . . . I don't hold the theory of Atonement . . . I hold that the Divine Nature broods over the human family everywhere, and tenderly stirs men to rise from a lower to a higher state of action."

"The truths of the Bible are not to be swallowed whole," he maintained, "but to be sifted." And when the old familiar pressure that always converged upon Henry Ward whenever he gave voice to any startling idea and hustled him into prompt repudiation gathered about him, this time he would not. He stood in Plymouth pulpit, the tears streaming down his cheeks. There was something in his smooth-shaven face, something in its curious lack of tension, that made those who watched him closely think of that brilliant young Irish poet, Oscar Wilde, just coming into prominence. But in Henry Ward's face there were heavy lines now from his nose to the corners of his mouth. His thinning white hair hung stringy about his face. Under his chin the great cords and hollows of old age were plainly visible. He was fat and a little pathetic. But he had won his freedom at last. He would not surrender:

"I have never expressed any theology but my own," he said. "If I am not permitted to hold fellowship with other churches, let it be so. I will not engage in controversy. I have not many years here — I cannot afford to spend them foolishly."

And he wept. But he did not recant.

Indeed, Henry Ward found himself suddenly very like Aladdin, when he had got over his first fright of the genii. Having won at last, in agony and tears, his final emancipation from the influence of Lyman Beecher that had so tortured him through almost seventy years, he found few disposed to dispute his right to make and preach his own theology. He withdrew from the Brooklyn Association of Congregational Ministers with a great flourish, so that, he said, his associates might not be held responsible for his radical views. But as he stated those views in detail, they proved to "lead the Westminster Catechism in orthodoxy, and shame Andover Theological Seminary on account of her departure from the truth." No one could understand what Beecher had in mind — "was it for the purpose of making a Beecher sensation, and to fill the house with a gaping multitude who crowd the doors to learn the difference between Tweedledee and Tweedledum?" they asked.

How could they understand that Henry Ward Beecher must in some public and irrevocable way burn his bridges behind him, if he were not once more to yield to his old fears and come fleeing back to the safe bosom of conservatism? He had few years remaining to him, as he said. There was no time left for tergiversations. The opportunity to make his new stand clear to others besides himself came to Henry Ward, providentially, a month later.

Herbert Spencer was returning to England after a visit to the United States that had set all the intellectuals of the country agog. "Probably there never was anywhere before or since as widespread an interest in philosophy as the American interest at that time in Spencer's," said Henry Holt. "The ablest thinker of them all, and the ablest man that has appeared for centuries," Beecher called Spencer. Even the newspapers printed columns of Herbert Spencer — to the consternation of the copy readers.

Spencer's visit had been in a sense the first world recognition of the American, not just as an inventor, a shrewd merchant, an organizer and to some extent a romancer, but as a potential thinker in lines unrelated to practicality. It was eminently fitting that at the farewell dinner given to the philosopher at Delmonico's, Henry Ward Beecher should stand forth as the type of what America had to offer in the intellectual field.

"Henry Ward Beecher . . . delivered the greatest speech I ever heard," Henry Holt records. "Beecher's face got so flushed as to make one think of apoplexy."

"I began to read Spencer's works more than twenty years ago. They have helped me through a great many difficulties," said Henry Ward. "Whoever gives me a thought that dispels the darkness that hangs over the most precious secrets of life, whoever gives me confidence in the destiny of my fellow-men, whoever gives me a clearer standpoint from which I can look to the great silent One, and hear Him even in half, and believe in Him, not by the tests of physical science, but by moral intuition — whoever gives that power is more to me than even my father and my mother; they gave me an outward and physical life, but these others emancipated that life from superstition, from fears, and from thralls, and made me a citizen of the universe."

It was at once confession and trumpet call. Man cannot advance impelled by fear. The philosophy of Love alone — of all-enfolding benevolence and philanthropy as the sufficient remedy for the world's ills — to which throughout his life Henry Ward Beecher had pinned his faith, had failed him. Emotionalism may intoxicate for a time, but it cannot clothe the naked soul. Safety is in truth — and truth is in knowledge, not sentimentality.

But the distinguished guest of the evening was not profoundly impressed.

"The proceedings," he notes in his autobiography, "were somewhat trying to sit through."

He makes no mention of Henry Ward Beecher.

CHAPTER XXX

REDEMPTION

It is not to be supposed that any divine inspiration visited Henry Ward Beecher that night at Delmonico's. He said he gave voice to "truths that lay on the horizon of my mind for thirty years." Thirty years would have made Beecher antedate Darwin, and may be taken as rhetorical. Nevertheless, the truths that Henry Ward brought forth under the warming influence of an appropriate occasion and a sympathetic audience had in fact been germinating in his mind a long time.

Indeed, one must go back to those terrible days of 1858, of the last great religious revival that had so torn and tortured poor Henry Ward, sucked into the vortex of the ancient conflict between flesh and spirit. Then, he had stood between the intense emotionalism in which Lucy Maria Bowen constituted at once his partner and his peril, and the eager, questioning intellectuality of his young friend Theodore Tilton. He was caught and drawn down into the whirlpool then. But when he clambered out at last, it was to Tilton he wrote in 1867 of a fresh intent:

"It seems to me that I discern, arising in studies in Natural Science, a surer foothold for these [evangelical] views than they have ever had. In so far as theology is concerned, if I have one purpose or aim, it is to secure for the truths now developing in the sphere of Natural Science a religious spirit & harmonization with all the cardinal truths of religion which have thus far characterized the Christian system."

In 1867, however, Henry Ward Beecher was hardly ready for any such drastic alteration of the foundations of his faith. In the first place, he knew very little about "the truths now developing in the sphere of Natural Science." Knowledge of the work of Darwin and Huxley was not yet sufficiently widespread to have reached so casual a student as Henry Ward Beecher. In the second place, a whole undergrowth of inhibitions and suppressions, still cluttering his own mind, would have to be cleared away before he could build anew.

Foremost among these was that hunger for love and faith in the omnipotence of its emotional expression that had held him thrall all his life. In the very hour he was writing Theodore of the new sphere he seemed to see opening before him, Henry Ward Beecher stood on the brink of the last and the most devastating of his plunges into passionate adventure. And when that adventure led him to the sharp and ragged edge of anxiety, remorse, fear, despair, it was to no new vision Henry Ward turned for strength. He clutched desperately at the only salvation he knew, crying from Plymouth pulpit:

"When I come before the Eternal Judge and say, all aglow: 'My Lord and God!' will He turn to me and say . . . 'You did not come up the right road . . . Go down!' I to the face of Jehovah will stand and say: 'God! I won't go to hell! I will go to heaven! I love Thee. Now damn me if Thou canst. I love Thee!' And God shall say, and the heavens flame with double and triple rainbows, and echo with joy: 'Dost thou love? Enter in and be forever blessed!' "

But God said no such thing to Henry Ward Beecher.

Instead, the years passed and one discomfiting experience after another compelled Henry Ward to seek solider spiritual foothold or sink. One by one he threw overboard the baggage of Lyman Beecher's theology — election, total depravity, eternal punishment, the divine inspiration of the Bible — until he stood as naked as David before Goliath, and as unafraid:

"I am a cordial Christian evolutionist. I would not agree by any means with all of Spencer, nor all of Huxley, Tyndall and their school. They are agnostic. I am not — emphatically. But I am an evolutionist and that strikes at the root of all medieval and orthodox modern theology," he wrote Dr. Kennard in 1883. "Men have not fallen as a race. Men have come up. No great disaster met the race at the start," he went on. "Any theory of atonement must be one which shall meet the fact that man was created at the lowest point, and, as I believe, is, as to his physical being, evolved from the animal race below him, but as to his moral and spiritual nature is a son of God . . .

"My life is drawing to an end. A few more working years only have I left. No one can express the earnestness which I feel that, in the advance of science, which will inevitably sweep away much rubbish from the beliefs of men, a place may be found for a higher spirituality — for a belief that shall have its roots in science and its top in the sunlight of faith and love. For that I am working and shall work as long as I work at all . . .

"The discussion has begun. God is in it. It must go on. It is one of those great movements which come when God would lift men to a higher level . . ."

To his astonishment, Henry Ward found himself in this in a goodly company of distinguished personalities, from President McCosh of Princeton to the Duke of Argyle. He found, too, that this new theme only increased the number of those who flocked to hear his lectures, to the profit alike of his prestige and his pocket. It was during this memorable summer of 1883 that he and Mrs. Beecher and his manager, Maj. Pond, made a tour all the way to the Pacific Coast.

"I am not afraid of seeing Christianity swept away," he repeated over and over again on this trip. "Anything that can be swept away ought to be swept away. But I hold that the foundations of God stand sure, and in the near future this very doctrine of evolution that so alarms many of the churches and many ministers will prove to be a soil down into which the roots of Christian doctrine will go, and they will be no longer controvertible."

A spiritual calm descended at last upon Henry Ward Beecher. He had found something to believe that he could preach without cant.

That summer, too, Plymouth Church gave Henry Ward a momentous celebration of his seventieth birthday, and Judge Neilson, who had presided at the trial of Tilton vs. Beecher, attended. What with his newly achieved harmonization of his inner conflicts in the field of belief, and with the cordiality with which he had been received from one end of the country to the other on his lecture tours, and now with this significant public testimonial on his birthday, Beecher began to feel that the past was dead. The time had come, he thought, for a general popular acknowledgment of that fact.

Four years before, when Garfield was nominated, Henry Ward told Maj. Pond that he had abandoned all idea of ever being President of the United States. But Garfield, the logical candidate to succeed himself, was dead, and as the time for presidential nominations once more approached, bitter dissension in the Republican ranks presented a tempting prospect to one who had been as faithful and as distinguished a party man as Beecher.

So in the preliminary campaign Henry Ward backed Chester A. Arthur for the nomination, despite the highly damaging report of the Jay Commission on Arthur's administration of the New York custom house, just as he had taken the stump for Garfield, despite the latter's Crédit Mobilier record. For Arthur was far from a strong contender, and it was by no means beyond the bounds of possibility that some nationally known figure, not too deeply embroiled in factional political squabbles, such as — well, such as Henry Ward Beecher — might finally be fixed upon as a compromise candidate.

It was a bitter blow to Henry Ward when Blaine was chosen. He hated Blaine as only an apostle of love knew how to hate. Yet having stood for Grant and Garfield and Arthur and Conkling and every Republican spoilsman and grafter in nation and State for thirty years, Beecher could hardly display a sudden queasiness over Blaine's reputation for personal honesty. Besides, he had pledged himself in advance to support the Republican nominee when Blaine was a leading candidate. As for the Democratic party, he had just declared that "it had not shown that it had learned a single lesson from the great struggle of the last twenty-five years."

Eleven days after the Democrats nominated Governor Cleveland of New York to oppose Blaine, George William Curtis, Carl Schurz, Thomas Wentworth Higginson, President Eliot of Harvard and President Seelye of Smith College, together with what was left of the old Radical Republican group of the previous decade, called an independent convention in New York. In this distinguished gathering Blaine's reputation was torn to rags and Grover Cleveland's candidacy endorsed. But

of the "Mugwumps" sponsoring this action Henry Ward
Beecher was not one.

For Henry Ward was in a quandary. More than any one else
he had been instrumental in making and keeping Plymouth
Church a Republican stronghold. Many of Blaine's staunchest
supporters were among those who had stood by Beecher with
unquestioning loyalty in the dark days of Henry Ward's sorest
need. To these men he must offer a better reason for deserting
the Republican standard than a prophetic sensing that the hour
had struck for a popular rebuke of Republican corruption. Unfortunately, the only reason Henry Ward could think of to
give for his defection convinced no one. He claimed that, on
September 29, 1877, "at the hospitable board of a private
house," * James F. Joy, President of the Wabash railroad, had
told him that some unnamed third person had solicited a bribe
from him [Joy] on behalf of Blaine, then Speaker of the House
of Representatives. At best the story was third-hand gossip
that gathered no added authority from having been locked in
Beecher's breast for seven years. But as Henry Ward at first
did no more than "mention it privately among my intimate
friends," as he put it, Blaine's partisans in Plymouth Church
were hardly disturbed. There was plenty of real evidence
against the Plumed Knight to keep them busy.

It was not until the campaign had got well under way that
Henry Ward Beecher was struck by a shaft that penetrated all
the protective walls he had built up about his innermost consciousness during ten years of struggle and agony. It was almost as if fate had determined to clamp the Great Preacher in
an inexorable grip and compel him to search his own soul to
the last dark corner. For while Henry Ward had so far taken
no active part in the campaign, he had been candid enough in
declaring his opinion — "put me down against Blaine one hundred times in letters two feet long!" he cried. Blaine, he said,
had gone "a-whoring after votes."

And then, in mid-campaign, a story ran like wildfire from
mouth to mouth: Cleveland was an immoral man; he was an
adulterer; he had an illegitimate child, born in Buffalo on September 14, 1874 — just at the very moment moral turpitude
was a subject occupying Beecher's own undivided attention.
Eunice Beecher promptly wrote the Governor about it — "like

* It was Joy's own house.

a mother," he said. And Cleveland manfully admitted the charge. It was true.

For Henry Ward Beecher it was a terrific crisis. He was like a man naked in the presence of a great multitude. He could feel the eyes of all of those to whom he had been so outspoken in his contempt of Blaine's loose moral code upon him. He could not get away from the eyes of Eunice Beecher under their beetling brows. Worst of all, he could not escape his own eyes, turned inward. An adulterer! Cleveland was an adulterer! Good God, why couldn't he have been a forger or a burglar!

There was only one way out for Henry Ward Beecher. Somewhere in the recesses of his mind he saw Cleveland and himself as one. Cleveland's fight was his fight, and Cleveland's victory would constitute a vicarious exorcism of the shadow that had lain over his own life all these years. He must see it through. And he must win it.

"When in the gloomy night of my own suffering I sounded every depth of sorrow, I vowed that if God would bring the day-star of hope I would never suffer brother, friend or neighbor to go unfriended should a like serpent seek to crush him. That oath I will regard now," he cried to a vast audience in Brooklyn. "I will imitate the noble example set me by Plymouth Church in the day of my calamity. They were not ashamed of my bonds. They stood by me with God-sent loyalty. It was a heroic deed. They have set my duty before me, and I will imitate their example."

He could hardly have confessed his own transgression, his common cause with Cleveland in that one capital respect, in plainer words. "As for the sin of Cleveland in the Halpin case, when divested of exaggerations, so far from being an encouragement to sin, it will be a vivid example and warning to ambitious young men to avoid evil and maintain social purity," said Henry Ward. "Cleveland has already suffered loss, mortification and damage for the commission of a grievous sin." After all, who should know better than Henry Ward Beecher? He had come a long way in the forty years since he had so solemnly expelled Owen Tuller from his church. Was there never to come a day when a man might say: "See; I have paid for my sin. Let me go in peace!"?

Everything he had Henry Ward threw into the fight for Cleveland's triumph—and his own salvation. He was seventy-one. But he campaigned as if he were twenty-one, haranguing an open air meeting in Wall street, shouting down turbulent hecklers in Jersey City, holding four thousand people spell-bound in the Academy of Music in New York, packing the immense barn of Brooklyn Rink to the doors. He cited all his past public services to prove the disinterestedness of his course:

"I became an Abolitionist the moment I was born," he thundered. "It grew with my strength. My earliest work, outside of my professional work, was in the anti-slavery cause." (*Loud cheers.*)

Men who had known Beecher for years were amazed and appalled at the Beecher they suddenly saw revealed. Thomas Wentworth Higginson campaigned with him. "Beecher . . . is the only man I have spoken with in public of whom I felt ashamed," he wrote. "There was a coarse jauntiness in his way of treating the attacks on Cleveland that disgusted me." The *Tribune*, for thirty-five years Beecher's unfaltering partisan, was equally frank: "For the first time in a Presidential canvass he voiced the bitterness of his own heart. Such humor as he displayed was envenomed with spite, and sometimes degenerated into coarse buffoonery." "I had tasted blood," Henry Ward himself said, sadly, afterwards. "I had to go on tasting it."

But poor Henry Ward had to swallow bitterer draughts than blood before that hideous campaign was ended.

For this was a very different business to the relatively private matter of the accusations of adultery brought against Beecher ten years before. The dominance of a great political party was at stake. The continuance in power of a financial and industrial hierarchy that had ruled the country for twenty-four years was threatened. Tremendous property interests and stupendous organizations of privilege, whose faithful servant James G. Blaine had been, were in peril. Millions of eyes in every corner of the land searched Henry Ward Beecher's past to stop his mouth with it.

They did not stop his mouth. But they brought to light a number of things that had slipped even Henry Ward's mind. They found that he had made unsubstantiated charges against Comegys, the Lawrenceburgh distiller, and had had to retract them; that he had engaged in a bitter controversy with the Rev. Joel Parker, over "Uncle Tom's Cabin," in the course of which Henry Ward had been sharply accused of signing that gentleman's name without his authorization; that Beecher and Mr. Cunard had called one another liars in the public prints with great relish and no decision; that Henry Ward had made statements about Leonard Bacon's son for which he had been forced to apologize as untrue; that he had accused Fighting Joe Hooker of being drunk at the battle of Chancellorsville and when summoned to produce his evidence before a Congressional Committee, had been compelled to admit that he had none; that when Henry J. Raymond, of the New York *Times*, lay dead, it was Henry Ward Beecher who circulated scandalous (and unfounded) gossip about the manner of his death. And finally, to cap it all, James Joy cabled from London a sweeping and categorical denial of Henry Ward's pet story about Blaine. He had never said anything of the sort to Beecher, Joy declared, and no such incident as Beecher had been recounting ever took place.

But Henry Ward was beyond caring what any one said about him. Only one thing meant anything to him: Cleveland must be elected and so exonerated that Henry Ward Beecher might thus achieve vindication in his own eyes. Ten days before election Beecher issued what his old friends of the *Tribune* termed a call to all the adulterers of the State to support Cleveland:

"If every man in New York State to-night, who has broken the seventh commandment, voted for Cleveland, he would be elected by 200,000 majority," Henry Ward Beecher shouted to the young voters of the Brooklyn Y. M. C. A. "There are men in Brooklyn who will say: 'I have been bumming with Cleveland at night.' I say to any such man: 'You were bumming on your own hook, and were so drunk that you couldn't see who was bumming with you!' "

"As an expert in such matters Mr. Beecher must know better than I," dryly remarked the Hon. Benjamin F. Butler, who was running for President himself on the People's Party ticket.

"A vote for Butler is a vote in the mud!" retorted Henry Ward.

It was a wild campaign. Yet with a curious irony it was the Hon. Benjamin F. Butler, not Henry Ward Beecher, who finally did bring about the election of Grover Cleveland. Perhaps Henry Ward in his zeal overestimated the number of adulterers in the Empire State; or it may be some of them basely betrayed his candidate. For Cleveland's margin in New York was only 1,149 votes, and Ben Butler took, largely from Blaine, 17,004 votes that would have elected the Plumed Knight.

Friday night before election the greatest political parade the country ever saw passed down Fifth avenue. Miles upon miles of men carrying torches marched five hours and a half shouting "Blaine! . . . Blaine! . . . Blaine! . . ." "It was as if the ground was aflame in solid avenues of fire."

Henry Ward Beecher watched from the shadows, his face ashen, his hands trembling. And in his heart he prayed.

The elevation to the Presidency of the United States of the acknowledged father of Maria Halpin's illegitimate son was an epochal event any way one may care to take it. To Henry Ward Beecher it was deliverance. The fear that had stood at his elbow all his life was gone forever. What William James calls the moral and intellectual discordancy that had kept Henry Ward in turmoil for years was dissolved. In its place inner harmony and outward sureness took possession of him. Peace had come at last to the troubled spirit of the Great Preacher.

It was Beecher's last excursion into politics, and high time. "I have never witnessed a clergyman active in the collision of party politics," old Lyman Beecher used to say, "without feeling and perceiving that others felt that the man was out of his place and religion disgraced." It had proved so abundantly with Henry Ward, at all events. First to last political polemics had led him astray. From the days when Harry of the West was his idol down to this last rough-and-tumble fight, with adultery lay and clerical overshadowing the real issues of the campaign, politics betrayed Henry Ward Beecher. As a political idealist his epitaph might suitably be written: He generally managed to be on the winning side.

In Plymouth Church, the brethren were content to let bygones be bygones. "Mr. Beecher is not the man who fails to see the drift in current events in such a case," said Brother S. V. White. "He acted on the impulse of popularity, feeling proud to stand somewhat alone." There was a great deal of truth in that, too. They had begun to know their Henry Ward Beecher in Plymouth Church.

But in the real work that remained before him in the few years he could still hope to labor, Beecher by no means stood alone. Emerson and Agassiz were household names. John Stuart Mill's "Three Essays on Religion" had had the church world in a state of ferment for a quarter of a century. Renouvier was almost as venerable as Henry Ward himself, and Renan an Academician in good and regular standing. A minister of the gospel no longer had to creep into a scientist's precincts under cover of darkness — he could purchase John Fiske's books and read his evolution at his leisure. For one abreast of current thought the difficulty was not to acquire knowledge of the Darwinian hypothesis, but to escape it. Spencer and Huxley enjoyed a vogue that John Wesley might have envied.

The fact was that poor Henry Ward was out over his depth again. For seventy years he had steeped himself in that mysticism which Prof. Joly has described as "wrapped up in and filled with the love of God." He had not reasoned his faith. He had felt it, as the appropriate and sufficient channel for his desire of self-realization. And now he could not go back and begin all over again. Try as he would, he could not. In the gathering dusk of his life, Henry Ward Beecher sounded bottom in tragedy: he saw the truth, but it could not make him free.

Even so, Henry Ward was not beaten yet. He got Prof. James Dwight Dana of Yale to furnish him with a succinct definition of evolution, and used that. Occasionally, he jumbled his authorities a bit. Once he cited Dr. Rowland Williams, dead some fifteen years, as the Brompton lecturer on "The Relations Between Religion and Science," actually the performance of Frederick Temple.* But Beecher's audiences had never heard of Dr. Williams, or the Archbishop of Canterbury, either. It was not his authorities for what he said that thrilled them, but his message:

"The old theory of sin, then — which will be exterminated, I think, by the new light thrown upon the origin of man and the conditions by which the race has developed — is repulsive, unreasonable, immoral, and demoralizing. I hate it. I hate it because I love the truth, because I love God, and because I love my fellowmen. The idea that God created the race, and that two of them

* Bishop of Exeter in 1869; Brompton Lecturer in 1884; Bishop of London in 1885; Archbishop of Canterbury in 1896.

without experience were put under the temptation of the arch-fiend (or whatever the 'creature' was), and that they fell into disobedience of what they did not understand anything about, and that God not only thrust them out of the Garden of Eden, as no parent would ever treat a child in his own household, but that he then transmitted the corruption that was the result of disobedience through the countless ages, and spread it out and out and out, and kept it on through the system of nature, mingling damnation on the right and on the left, before and behind — I hate it, because I love God! I abhor it, because I love justice and truth. People say to me: 'It is generally understood that you are not a Calvinist.' John Calvin can take care of himself. But I am a teacher of righteousness. I am a lover of mankind. It is my business to make the truth, the path in which men's thoughts travel, just as plain as I can, and take out all the obstructions that tend to unbelief. Among the mischievous things of this kind is this whole theory of sin and its origin that lie at the base of the great evangelical systems of Christianity. I say it is hideous, it is horrible, it is turning creation into a shambles and God into a slaughterer, and the human race into a condition worse a thousandfold than that of beasts. . . . Man is made to start and not to stop; to go on, and on, and up, and onward, steadily emerging from the controlling power of the physical and animal conditions in which he was born and which enthrall him during his struggle upward, but ever touching higher elements of possibility, and ending in the glorious liberty of the sons of God."

Women in huge bustles and tight-fitting basques, wearing nobby little bonnets above their bangs, to whom the works of E. P. Roe and Bertha M. Clay were literature, and men with long, sweeping mustaches, wearing puffy Ascot ties, sat on the edge of their seats and listened to this gospel of freedom, spellbound. Dwellers still in that Puritan prison from which Henry Ward Beecher had made his escape at such price, they too hated the old idea of sin and damnation and hell and a respectable but joyless existence. In all their narrow, emotion-starved middle-class lives they would never have read Darwin or Spencer or Huxley, or understood a word of it if they had. But they came to hear Henry Ward Beecher and went away uplifted and rejoiced, with a new hope in life.

"We are God-builders," said he. "As our character is, so our God is. If we are base and cruel, then our ideas of God are base and cruel. If we are fine and spiritual, then our ideas of God are fine and spiritual; so that if we want a pure and noble religion we must first become pure and noble ourselves. The way to religion is through moral experience. . . . The qualities which men have found admirable, pure, just, holy, true and good in any generation they have gathered together and have ascribed to them universality and infinity and called the result God. . . . The moral qualities are not only divine in themselves but are constituent letters in forming our idea of divinity."

"The Kingdom of God is not a place," Beecher declared. "All those who have their inward and nobler nature developed until they feel in themselves the inspiration of God's presence and love are inhabitants of that kingdom; and none others are." The Bible, too, he disposed of: "The doctrine of inspiration that teaches us that God wrote it, men do not believe," he proclaimed. "Ministers may assert it officially in the pulpit, but they do not personally believe it." And in Plymouth Church, at least, his audience cheered.

Up and down the land for two years went Henry Ward Beecher, no longer young, but indomitable, carrying this message of release, the more eagerly welcomed as he was in no sense contumacious about it. "I am not an extremist," he insisted. "I am not in favor of any revolutionary haste in changing the economy that now rules." Nor was he. All his life he had preached against the liquor traffic. But he served wine in his own house and made presents of bottles of port to his friends. All his life, too, Beecher supported the missionary work of the evangelical churches. Yet he declared that "I am entirely opposed to collecting $100,000, $200,000, $300,000 every year and sending missionaries to China, and then refusing to allow the Chinamen to come here and breathe our air."

It was in 1886 that Henry Ward Beecher revisited England, after twenty-three years. This time he took Mrs. Beecher and the faithful Pond along. It was a personal triumph—a round of public receptions and of lectures that netted him $11,600, while Pond made a fat volume of the account of the trip. But in that larger world, where Darwin had so recently died and Spencer and Huxley still dwelt; where hundreds of clergymen in high place were evolutionists without clamor, and the doctrine that had proved so daring when expounded from the lecture platform in Minnesota or Alabama was just a commonplace, Henry Ward Beecher suddenly perceived that he really had no message at all. Of the significance of the forward strides of science in the nineteenth century he had no better than a child's conception. He merely felt that the old order was wrong — felt it passionately, urgently, compellingly. But of the new order Henry Ward Beecher had no vision. His work was done.

On Beecher's return from England, William Cleaver Wilkinson, an old colleague of *The Independent* days, went to hear him preach:

"To me the sight was inexpressibly pathetic," he writes. "The large, smooth-shaven, rubicund face of the preacher set off most strikingly the silver of his hair, streaming in long locks behind the ears. Fullness of blood which is the life seemed to be imported by the warm color of the skin; but the hoary head betokened the inevitably stealing frost of age. If I had seen before me an old age crowning a fruitful life without reproach, the sight would still have been one to move tears! Not tears of disappointment, of regret, of remorse, of passionate shame! As the case stood, indignation, reprobation, were half laid to sleep in the arms of over-persuading pure sorrow and sympathy. The sight became simply, and, as I have said, unspeakably affecting."

In his last sermons, Henry Ward seemed to forget evolution. He could talk only of Love, as the very old hark back to the memories of childhood . . .

The world was half asleep in the Spring of 1887. Yet stirring in its sleep. Millions whose chains were economic, not spiritual, looked to Henry George as a Messiah . . . Woman's suffrage at last became effective in Kansas . . . In Washington, the Divine Sarah played "Camille." She had a tiger cat that she had fetched from Ecuador as a pet . . . Barnum and Forepaugh's circus was coming to town . . .

In England, James McNeill Whistler exhibited "a portion of the most memorable etched work executed in our time" at the Hogarth Club. Charles Stewart Parnell and the Irish members created a riot in Parliament — "shouts, defiant gestures and insults were freely exchanged." Sir Michael Hicks-Beach had enough of it as Chief Secretary for Ireland. It was Arthur James Balfour who succeeded him. . . . The Prince and Princess of Wales invited Mrs. James Brown Potter to dinner . . .

At Friedrichsruhe, Otto von Bismarck and Francesco Crispi, their courses almost run, bound future generations to war by the Triple Alliance. . . . In Abyssinia, the Italian army was neatly reduced to mincemeat at Massowah . . . The French Minister of War ordered all private soldiers to wear beards — *poilus*. . . . Having won a war against Serbia, Prince Alexander was ousted as sovereign of Bulgaria — by Russia gold, it was charged . . . Hwangti succeeded to the Celestial Throne, a pathetic child brow-beaten by his mother . . . Queen Victoria planned her jubilee . . .

"The Zola school continues its disgusting work, and seems to find abundance of readers," complained Appleton's Cyclopædia. But all was not dark. "Björnstjerne Björnson . . . has lately been lecturing on the subject of Chastity, and takes the very highest ground," the same authority records . . . One John Rowlands, later known to fame as Sir Henry M. Stanley, set out from Zanzibar to rescue Emin Pasha. But Emin Pasha's name was not Emin Pasha, either. It was Schnitzer. He was an Austrian . . .

Immigrants arriving from Europe in vast droves craned their necks to stare at the Statue of Liberty Enlightening the World, newly erected in New York harbor . . . The forty-ninth Congress, having prohibited polygamy in the United States, adjourned after an all-night session on March fifth. . . .

A few hours later, Henry Ward Beecher suffered a stroke of apoplexy. . . .

His son's house, where he lay unconscious, was besieged by callers. But curiously enough few were distinguished. . . . President Cleveland sent a long message to Mrs. Beecher . . . Maj. Pond denied for the press that Queen Victoria had cabled her sympathy. . . . Bulletins were issued by the Great Preacher's physicians every few hours . . . On Sunday, the congregation of Plymouth Church sang "Love Divine" to the tune of "Beecher." . . .

Henry Ward never recovered consciousness. He died on March eighth.

The body of Henry Ward Beecher lay in state in Plymouth Church, whose barren walls were banked with the flowers he loved. Company "G" of the thirteenth regiment of the National Guard furnished a military guard of honor for their departed chaplain. It might have been a general lying there . . .

Forty thousand people filed by to view the remains, ninetenths of them women. On the sidewalks, peddlers hawked chromos of Henry Ward Beecher at ten cents each. Neither the President nor Governor Hill sent representatives to the funeral. After a sharp debate, the Chicago association of Congregational ministers voted against sending a message of condolence to the widow . . .

"There was an American stamp and seal upon the man," said the *Tribune*. "A great sentimentalist," said Dana in the *Sun*.

Only a few carriages followed the body of Henry Ward Beecher to Greenwood. The show was over . . .

In Paris, Theodore Tilton was playing chess in the Café de la Régence. A newspaper man came in and quietly slipped him a cablegram: "BEECHER DEAD. INTERVIEW TILTON."

For a long time Theodore Tilton sat staring out of the window . . . Crowds were marching down the rue St. Honoré cheering Boulanger — Le Général Révanche. They sang a marching song:

> "Et chacun le suivra!
> Pour cortège il aura
> La France entière!"

Theodore Tilton turned back at last and bowed to his adversary with that formal, old-world courtesy that had always been his.

"I beg your pardon, Sir," he said. "Is it my move?"

Brooklyn Heights settled down to normal somnolence once more. Plymouth Church was deserted, save for workmen removing the dead flowers. In the streets, stirred by Spring, children were playing, shouting up and down. Something in the day had reminded them of a little ditty. They sang it now at their play:

> "Beecher, Beecher is my name —
> Beecher till I die!
> I never kissed Mis' Tilton —
> I never told a lie!"

APPENDIX I

Acknowledgment

THE author desires to acknowledge his indebtedness to Dr. Gregory Stragnell for his invaluable aid in the analysis of the psychology of Henry Ward Beecher; to the Rev. Jean S. Milner, Pastor of the Second Presbyterian Church of Indianapolis; to Robert S. Fletcher, Librarian of the Converse Memorial Library of Amherst College, Miss Violet Gert Williams, Assistant Librarian of the Young Men's Mercantile Library Association of Cincinnati, and Miss Esther McNitt, of the Indiana State Library; and to Mrs. Emma Bonner Forbes, Miss Annie Beecher Scoville, Mrs. Annie Merrill Foster, Mrs. Alice Tilton Gardin, Mrs. Harriet Stanton Blatch and Mrs. Franklin Woodruff Moulton, for access to original material.

APPENDIX II

A List of the Sources

EVERY reference of fact made in this book may be found verified in this bibliography of the books consulted by the author. Because some readers may wish to consult the sources of the direct quotations made by the author, such a list is given in Appendix III.

Jacob Abbot: "New England and Her Institutions." Boston. 1835.

Lyman Abbott: "Henry Ward Beecher." New York. 1903.

Charles Francis Adams: "An Autobiography. 1835–1915." Boston. 1916.

E. D. Adams: "Great Britain and the American Civil War." London. 1925.

Henry Adams: "The Education of Henry Adams." Boston. 1918.
"History of the United States of America During the Second Administration of James Madison." New York. 1891.

Felix Adler: "Henry Ward Beecher." New York. 1887.

The Advance, Chicago, Ill.

Seth Ames: "Works of Fisher Ames, edited by Seth Ames." Boston. 1854.

Amherst College: Converse Memorial Library. *Memorabilia.*

Annals of Congress. 1810–1811.

Athenian Society, Amherst College: *Records.*

Atlantic Monthly, Boston, Mass. Vols. XIII and LXXXII.

George L. Austin: "Life and Times of Wendell Phillips." Boston. 1888.

Adam Badeau: "The Vagabond." New York. 1859.

Ballou's Pictorial Drawing-Room Companion, Boston, Mass. Vol. X.

John Henry Barrows: "Henry Ward Beecher, the Shakespeare of the Pulpit." New York. 1893.

David Bartlett: "Modern Agitators; or Pen-portraits of living American reformers." New York. 1855.

H. Bateman: "Biographies of 250 Distinguished Men." New York. 1871.

Charles and Mary Beard: "History of the United States." New York. 1921.
"The Rise of American Civilisation." New York. 1927.

Catherine Beecher: "Educational Reminiscences and Suggestions." New York. 1874.

Charles Beecher: "The Duty of Disobedience to Wicked Laws." 1851.

"Review of the 'Spiritual Manifestations.'" New York. 1853.

Edward Beecher: "Narrative of Riots in Alton in Connection with the Death of Rev. Elijah P. Lovejoy." Alton, Ill. 1838.

Henry Ward Beecher: "Address of Henry Ward Beecher at the Brooklyn Rink, October 22, 1884." New York. 1884.

"The Conflict of Northern and Southern Theories of Man and Society." Rochester, N. Y. 1855.

"A Dissuasive from Moral Intolerance. Address by H. W. Beecher at Bloomington, Ind." Indianapolis, Ind. 1845.

"Driving Fast Horses Fast," in "Catalogue of Trotting Stock the Property of Robert Bonner, at his Farm near Tarrytown, N. Y., and His Stable in This City." New York. 1898.

"Evolution and Religion." New York. 1886.

"Freedom and War." Boston. 1863.

"Henry Ward Beecher and Theodore Parker." Boston. 1859.

"The Hidden Manna and the White Stone. A Sermon by Mr. Beecher, July 6, 1866, with Appendix by Mrs. Beecher." Brooklyn. 1892.

"Lecture: Chicago, Feb. 7, 1883." Chicago. 1883.

"The Means of Securing Good Rulers. A Sermon Delivered on the Occasion of the Death of Noah Noble, late Governor of Indiana." Indianapolis, Ind. 1844.

"Norwood; or Village Life in New England." New York. 1868.

"Patriotic Addresses." New York. 1887.

"Seven Lectures to Young Men on Various Important Subjects; Delivered Before the Young Men of Indianapolis, Ind., During the Winter of 1843–44." Indianapolis, Ind. 1844.

"Star Papers." New York. 1855.

"Thirteen Years in the Gospel Ministry." Brooklyn. 1860.

"The Two Letters on Reconstruction of the Southern States. Written by Henry Ward Beecher in 1866." New York. 1884.

"Why I Am a Free-Trader. Address at the Chicago Conference, Nov. 12, 1885." New York. 1886.

"Why the Republican Party Should Be Trusted." Brooklyn. 1880.

"Woman's Duty to Vote. Address at the 11th National Woman's Rights Convention, New York, May 10, 1866." New York. 1867.

"Woman's Influence in Politics. An Address Delivered by Henry Ward Beecher, at the Cooper Institute, New York, Feb. 2, 1860." Boston, 1860.

"Yale Lectures on Preaching." New York. 1872.

"Yale Lectures on Preaching. Second Series." New York. 1873.

Sermons in *The Independent, The Methodist, The Christian Union,* "Plymouth Pulpit," etc.; articles in *The Ledger, The Independent, The Christian Union,* etc.; editorials in *The Western Farmer and Gardener, The Independent, The Christian Union,* etc.; unpublished letters to Robert Bonner, Mrs. Catherine Dickinson Sweetser, etc.; Journal and other papers in possession of Miss Annie Beecher Scoville.

Mrs. Henry Ward Beecher: "Dawn to Daylight; The Simple Story of a Western Home. By a Minister's Wife." New York. 1859.

"The Law of a Household." Boston. 1910.

"Mr. Beecher as I Knew Him." Ten articles published in *The Ladies' Home Journal,* October, 1891–August, 1892.

Appendix to "The Hidden Manna and the White Stone."

Articles in the New York *World, The Mother at Home and the Household Magazine, The Christian Union,* etc.

Lyman Beecher: "Autobiography." New York. 1864.

"The Means of National Prosperity. A Sermon Delivered at Litchfield, Conn., on the Day of the Anniversary of Thanksgiving, Dec. 2, 1819." New York. 1820.

"A Plea for the West." Cincinnati. 1835.

"Resources of the Adversary, and the Means of Their Destruction. Sermon." Boston. 1827.

William C. Beecher and Rev. Samuel Scoville, assisted by Mrs. Henry Ward Beecher: "A Biography of Rev. Henry Ward Beecher." [Family Biography.] New York. 1888.

"Beecher's Career; The Great Public Orator Sketched. From $40 to $35,000 a Year. His Life and Experiences in America and England." Supplement to the *Family Herald.* New York.

"The Beecher-Tilton Controversy. A Graphic Record of the Most Remarkable Social Sensation in the World's History, a Gigantic Conspiracy or Unparalleled Hypocrisy. Truth Stranger than Fiction." Chicago, Ill. 1874.

"The Beecher-Tilton Investigation. The Scandal of the Age." Philadelphia. 1874.

"The Beecher-Tilton Scandal. A Complete History of the Case, with Mrs. Woodhull's Original Statement." Brooklyn. 1874.

"The Beecher-Tilton War." New York. 1874.

"The Beecher Trial. A Review of the Evidence. Reprinted from the New York *Times* of July 3, 1875." New York. 1875.

E. Porter Belden: "New York: Past, Present and Future." New York. 1850.

Eugene Benson: "New York Journalists: Theodore Tilton." In *The Galaxy,* September, 1869.

J. Richard Beste: "The Wabash." London. 1855.

John Bigelow: "Retrospections of an Active Life." New York. 1913.

William Birney: "James G. Birney and His Times." New York. 1890.

Joseph Bucklin Bishop: "Notes and Anecdotes of Many Years." New York. 1895.

James G. Blaine: "Twenty Years in Congress." Norwich, Conn. 1884–1886.

Bonner Correspondence: Unpublished letters from Henry Ward Beecher and Mrs. Beecher to Robert Bonner. In possession of Mr. Bonner's daughter, Mrs. Francis Forbes.

Boston *Daily Advertiser, Globe, Morning Journal.*

Henry C. Bowen's Scrapbook compiled in the office of *The Independent.* Presented to the New York Library by his grandson, Dr. Hamilton Holt.

Eliza Southgate Bowne: "A Girl's Life Eighty Years Ago." New York. 1887.

Bradshaw Manuscript: Unpublished recollections of Mrs. John Bradshaw, in possession of the Second Presbyterian Church of Indianapolis.

Mary Brainerd: "Life of the Rev. Thomas Brainerd." Philadelphia. 1870.

L. W. Brastow: "Representative Modern Preachers." London. 1904.

L. P. Brockett: "Men of Our Day." Philadelphia. 1868.

Brooklyn *Argus, Daily Eagle, Sunday Press.*

Brookville *American,* Brookville, Ind.

Junius Henri Browne: "The Great Metropolis: A Mirror of New York." Hartford. 1869.

Oscar Browning: "The Fall of Napoleon." London. 1907.

James, Lord Bryce: "The Essential Unity of Britain and America." In *The Atlantic Monthly,* Vol. LXXXII.

James Silk Buckingham: "The Eastern and Western States of America." London. 1842.

George W. Bungay: "Off-hand Takings; or Crayon Sketches of the Noticeable Men of Our Age." New York. 1854.

Benjamin F. Butler: "Butler's Book." Boston. 1892.

"The Battle of the Giants: A Debate on the Roman Catholic Religion, held in Cincinnati, between the late Alexander Campbell, founder of the 'Christian' church, and the Right Rev. John B. Purcell," etc. Cincinnati. 1875.

The Catholic World. New York. Vol. XII.

Edward Channing: "History of the United States." New York. 1925.

Chicago *Inter-Ocean, Post and Mail, Times, Tribune.*

Frank S. Child: "The Boyhood of Henry Ward Beecher. The

Record of a Litchfield Beecher Day." New Preston, Conn. 1887.

"The Christian Diadem, A Family Keepsake." New York. 1853.

Christian Observer and St. Louis Presbyterian. Louisville, Ky.

The Christian Union. New York.

Cincinnati *Daily Gazette, Herald, Post.*

Charles Cist: "Cincinnati in 1841: Its Early Annals and Future Prospects." Cincinnati. 1841.

Joseph I. C. Clarke: "My Life and Memories." New York. 1925.

Philip S. Cleland: "A Sermon Delivered July 4, 1841, in the Presbyterian Church, Greenwood, Ind., by Rev. P. S. Cleland. Published by Request of the Executive Committee of the Greenwood and Vicinity Anti-Slavery Society." 1841.

Francis J. Clerc: "Mount Pleasant Classical Institution: Reunion of 1865." Brooklyn. 1865.

The Congregationalist. Boston.

Congressional Globe, 31st and 33rd Congresses.

Congressional Record. Vol. LVI.

Connecticut Post and New Haven Visitor. New Haven, Conn.

Converse Memorial Library, Amherst College: *Memorabilia;* manuscript sermon of Henry Ward Beecher; unpublished letters, etc.

George S. Cottman: Article in Indianapolis *Press,* April 17, 1900.

Olatia Crane: "The Gutierres-Magee Expedition." Manuscript thesis. University of Texas. 1903.

The Crescent. Payson, Ill.

William Augustus Croffut: Article in *Indianapolis Sentinel,* May 28, 1882.

George R. Cutting: "Student Life at Amherst College." Amherst. 1871.

Theodore L. Cuyler: "Recollections of a Long Life." New York. 1912.

G. S. Darewin: "Synopsis of the Lives of Victoria C. Woodhull (now Mrs. John Biddulph Martin) and Tennessee C. Claflin (now Lady Cook) the two First Lady Brokers and Reformers of America." London. 1891.

W. E. Davenport: "A Bibliography of Henry Ward Beecher."

James C. Derby: "Fifty Years Among Authors, Books and Publishers." New York. 1884.

J. B. Dillon: "A History of Indiana." Indianapolis, Ind. 1859.

John Ross Dix: "Pulpit Portraits; or Pen-pictures of Distinguished American Divines." Boston. 1854.

William Dorling: "Great Modern Preachers." London. 1875.

Frederick Douglass: "Life and Times of Frederick Douglass." Boston. 1892.

John E. P. Doyle: "Plymouth Church and Its Pastor, or Henry Ward Beecher and His Accusers." Hartford. 1874.

Jesse Duncan: "A Treatise on Slavery." Vevay, Ind. 1824.

William H. Emory: "Notes of a Military Reconnaissance from Fort Leavenworth, in Missouri, to San Diego, in California, including parts of the Arkansas, Del Norte, and Gila rivers." Washington. 1848.

The Era. London.

Edmund B. Fairfield: "Wickedness in High Places." Mansfield, O. 1874.

Frederick William Farrar: "Eternal Hope. Sermons — November and December 1877." New York. 1878. Article in "That Unknown Country." Springfield, Mass. 1888.

Henry Bradshaw Fearon: "Sketches of America." London. 1818.

Annie Fields: "Life and Letters of Harriet Beecher Stowe." Boston. 1897.

Charles Grandison Finney: "Autobiography." London. 1882.

Calvin Fletcher: Original unpublished diary in custody of the Indiana State Historical Commission.

Timothy Flint: "Recollections of the Past Ten Years, passed in the valley of the Mississippi, from Pittsburgh and the Missouri to the Gulf of Mexico, etc." Boston. 1826.

Thomas Floyd-Jones: "Backward Glances." New York. 1914.

Henry Fowler: "The American Pulpit: Sketches Biographical and Descriptive of Living American Preachers, etc." New York. 1856.

O. B. Frothingham: "Theodore Parker." Boston. 1874.

P. R. Frothingham: "Edward Everett." Boston. 1925.

The Galaxy. New York. Vol. VIII.

W. P. and F. J. Garrison: "William Lloyd Garrison: 1805–1879. The Story of His Life, Told by His Children." New York. 1885–1889.

Genius of Universal Emancipation. Mt. Pleasant, O.

James Gould: "An Oration Pronounced at Litchfield on the Anniversary of the Independence of the United States of America, in the Year M,DCC,XCVIII." Litchfield, Conn. 1798.

"The Great Brooklyn Romance. All the Documents in the Famous Beecher-Tilton Case, Unabridged. Portraits and Facsimiles." New York. 1874.

"The Great Scandal. History of the Famous Beecher-Tilton Case. All the Documents and Letters." New York. 1874.

Horace Greeley: Editorial in the New York *Tribune*, Sept. 3, 1866.

Greencastle *Visitor*. Greencastle, Ind.

W. C. Griswold: "Life of Henry Ward Beecher." Centerbrook, Conn. 1887.

Ida Husted Harper: "Life and Work of Susan B. Anthony." Indianapolis, Ind. 1898.

Hartford *Daily Times*, Hartford, Conn.

Charles H. Haswell: "Reminiscences of an Octogenarian of the City of New York." New York. 1896.

Julian Hawthorne: "Nathaniel Hawthorne and His Wife." Boston. 1892.

I. T. Hecker: "Beecherism and Its Tendencies." In *Catholic World*, January, 1871.

Mary Thacher Higginson: "Thomas Wentworth Higginson: The Story of His Life." Boston. 1914.

Newell Dwight Hillis: "Lectures and Orations by Henry Ward Beecher, edited by N. D. Hillis." New York. 1913.

Morris Hillquit: "Socialism in the United States." New York. 1910.

B. A. Hinsdale: "The Old Northwest." Boston. 1899.

"History of Woman Suffrage." Edited by E. C. Stanton, S. B. Anthony, M. J. Gage and I. H. Harper. New York. 1881.

Charles Fenno Hoffman: "A Winter in the West." New York. 1835.

William R. Holloway: "Indianapolis: an Historical and Statistical Sketch of the Railroad City." Indianapolis, Ind. 1870.

Oliver Wendell Holmes: "Our Minister Plenipotentiary." In the *Atlantic Monthly*, January, 1864.

Henry Holt: "Garrulities of an Octogenarian Editor." New York. 1923.

Philip Hone: "Diary of Philip Hone." New York. 1889.

Charles F. Horner: "The Life of James Redpath." New York. 1926.

John R. Howard: "Remembrance of Things Past, a Familiar Chronicle of Kinsfolk and Friends Worth While." New York. 1925.

Joseph Howard, Jr.: "Life of Henry Ward Beecher." Philadelphia. 1887.

A. S. Hoyt: "The Pulpit and American Life." New York. 1921.

Frederic Hudson: "Journalism in the United States from 1690 to 1872." New York. 1873.

The Independent. New York.

Indiana Farmer and Gardener (Vol. I. of *Western Farmer and Gardener.*)

Indiana State Journal. Indianapolis, Ind.

Indianapolis *Free Democrat, Journal, Semi-Weekly Journal, Sentinel.*

Robert Green Ingersoll: "The Works of Robert G. Ingersoll. Dresden Edition." New York. 1903.

William James: "The Varieties of Religious Experience." London. 1902.

Oliver Johnson: "Garrison and His Times." Boston. 1881.

Jules Charles Henri Joly: "The Psychology of the Saints." New York. 1913.

Mrs. Jane Merrill Ketcham: Unpublished reminiscences in possession of her daughter, Miss Susan M. Ketcham.

Manuscript History of the Second Presbyterian Church of Indianapolis, in possession of Miss Julia Graydon Sharpe.

P. K. Kilbourne: "Sketches and Chronicles of the Town of Litchfield, Connecticut, historical, biographical, and statistical, together with a complete official Register of the Town." Hartford. 1859.

Horatio C. King: "An Account of the Services of the Silver-Wedding Week in Plymouth Church, Brooklyn, N. Y." Edited by Horatio C. King. New York. 1873.

Thomas W. Knox: "Life and Work of Henry Ward Beecher." Hartford. 1887.

"Catalogue and History of Foundation and Endowment of Lane Theological Seminary." Cincinnati. 1848.

Elsie Lathrop: "Early American Inns and Taverns." New York. 1926.

Lawrenceburgh *Political Beacon*. Lawrenceburgh, Ind.

Frank Leslie's Illustrated Weekly. New York.

The Liberal Christian. New York.

The Liberator. Boston, Mass.

Abraham Lincoln: "Complete Works." New York. 1920.

Harriet Raymond Lloyd: "Life and Letters of John Howard Raymond." New York. 1881.

J. T. Lloyd: "Memorable Men of the Nineteenth Century: III. Life of Henry Ward Beecher." London. 1881.

Henry Cabot Lodge: "Life and Letters of George Cabot." Boston. 1877.

London and Westminster Review. London. 1838.

"A Looking-glass for Henry Ward Beecher; or Satan In, Satan Out — in the Pulpit, in the Press. The Devil's Last and Great Victory. By a Classmate of Henry Ward Beecher." New York. 1875.

John E. Lovell: "United States Speaker." New Haven, Conn. 1833.

Hugh McCulloch: "Men and Measures of Half a Century." New York. 1899.

John Bach McMaster: "A History of the People of the United States from the Revolution to the Civil War." New York. 1895.

"A History of the People of the United States During Lincoln's Administration." New York. 1927.

David Macrae: "The Americans at Home." Edinburgh. 1870.

Emma M. Maffitt: "Life and Services of John Newland Maffitt." New York. 1906.

Edward Deering Mansfield: "Personal Memories, Social, Political and Literary, with Sketches of Many Noted People. 1803–1843." Cincinnati. 1879.

Frederick Marryatt: "Second Series of A Diary in America." Philadelphia. 1840.

Charles F. Marshall: "The True History of the Brooklyn Scandal." Philadelphia. 1874.

Harriet Martineau: "The Martyr Age in the United States of America." In *London and Westminster Review*, December, 1838.

"Retrospect of Western Travel." London. 1838.

Carlos Martyn: "Wendell Phillips." New York. 1890.

Bradhurst Field Maunsell: "Memories of Many Men and Some Women." New York. 1875.

Samuel Joseph May: "Memoir of Samuel Joseph May." Boston. 1873.

William C. Meigs: "Life of John C. Calhoun." New York. 1917.

Memphis *Appeal*. Memphis, Tenn.

George Meredith: "Letters of George Meredith." New York. 1912.

George Spring Merriam: "The Life and Times of Samuel Bowles." New York. 1885.

Samuel Merrill: Manuscript reminiscences in possession of his daughter, Mrs. Annie Merrill Foster.

Middlesex Gazette. Middletown, Conn.

"More Uncensored Recollections." London. 1926.

Forrest Morgan: "Connecticut as Colony and State." Hartford. 1904.

B. G. Morris: "Life of Senator Morris." Cincinnati. 1856.

Abner Morse: "A Genealogical Register of the Inhabitants and History of the Towns of Sherborn and Hilliston." Boston. 1856.

The Mother at Home and the Household Magazine. New York. Vol. I.

"Mount Pleasant Classical Institution. Catalogue & C." Amherst. 1828.

"Catalogue of the Mt. Pleasant Classical Institution." Amherst. 1829.

Hugo Münsterberg: "On the Witness Stand." New York. 1925.

The Nation. New York.

National Intelligencer. Washington, D. C.

National Police Gazette. New York.

A. Nettleton and Lyman Beecher: "Letters of the Rev. Dr. Beecher and Rev. Mr. Nettleton on the 'New Measures' in Conducting Revivals of Religion." New York. 1828.

A. Nevins: "American Social History." New York. 1923.

New England Society of New York: Anniversary, 1873.

New York *Courier and Enquirer, Daily Graphic, Daily News, Evening Post, Express, Herald, Journal of Commerce, Press, Sun, Times, Tribune.*

Thomas Nichols: "Forty Years of American Life." London. 1864.

E. P. Oberholtzer: "Jay Cooke: Financier of the Civil War." Philadelphia. 1907.

Frank M. O'Brien: "The Story of 'The Sun.'" New York. 1918.

Rollo Ogden: "Life and Letters of E. L. Godkin." New York. 1907.

Leon Oliver: "The Great Sensation. History of the Beecher-Tilton-Woodhull Scandal." Chicago. 1873.

Albert Bigelow Paine: "Th. Nast." New York. 1904.

John Parsons: "A Tour Through Indiana in 1840. The Diary of John Parsons of Petersburg, Virginia." New York. 1920.

James Parton: "Famous Americans of Recent Times." Boston. 1867.

W. W. Patton: Letter to Plymouth Church Investigating Committee, Aug. 27, 1874. In "The Great Brooklyn Romance," Section 48.

"The Phase of Religion Developed by the Tilton-Beecher Scandal. By a Layman." New York. 1875.

The Philistine. East Aurora, N. Y. October, 1900.

"Pictorial History of the Beecher-Tilton Scandal. Its Origin, Progress and Trial. Illustrated with 50 Engravings, Portraits, etc." New York. 1874.

Pittsburgh *Commercial.* Pittsburgh, Pa.

Plymouth Chimes. Brooklyn.

"Plymouth Collection of Hymns and Tunes; for the Use of Christian Congregations." (Introduction by Henry Ward Beecher.) New York. 1858.

"Manual of Plymouth Church." 1854.

"Memorial of Revival in Plymouth Church, 1858." New York. 1859.

"Plymouth Pulpit." New York. 1868. Vol. I.

James B. Pond: "Eccentricities of Genius." New York. 1900.

"A Summer in England with Henry Ward Beecher." New York. 1887.

Roger A. Pryor: "Brief. Supreme Court, Second Department. F. D. Moulton, Plaintiff and Appellant, vs. Henry Ward Beecher, Defendant and Respondent."

Puck. New York.

Richard J. Purcell: "Connecticut in Transition." Washington. 1918.

Andrew Reed and James Matheson: "A Narrative of the Visit to the American Churches by the Deputation of the Congregational Union of England and Wales." New York. 1835.

The American Home Missionary Society: Annual Reports for 1838, 1839, 1840 and 1847.

James Ford Rhodes: "History of the United States from the Compromise of 1850 to the Final Restoration of Home Rule at the South in 1877." New York. 1910.

Charles Edward Russell: "The Story of Wendell Phillips." Chicago. 1914.

The Saturday Review. London.

Carl Schurz: "The Reminiscences of Carl Schurz." New York. 1907.

Second Presbyterian Church of Indianapolis, Indiana: *Records.*

W. B. Selbie: "The Psychology of Religion." Oxford. 1924.

Frederick W. Seward: "Seward at Washington as Senator and Secretary of State." New York. 1891.

The Shrine. Amherst, Mass. 1831–1833.

N. Sizer: "Biographical Sketch of Henry Ward Beecher" in *The Christian Diadem.* New York. 1853.

Matthew Hale Smith: "Sunshine and Shadow in New York." Hartford. 1869.

"Successful Folks." Hartford. 1878.

Oliver H. Smith: "Early Indiana Trials and Sketches. Reminiscences." Cincinnati. 1858.

Theodore Clarke Smith: "Life and Letters of James A. Garfield." New Haven, Conn. 1895.

Herbert Spencer: "An Autobiography." London. 1904.

Homer B. Sprague: "Recollections of Henry Ward Beecher." Newton, Mass. 1905.

The Standard. Chicago, Ill.

Henry B. Stanton: "Random Recollections." New York. 1886.

T. Stanton and Harriet Stanton Blatch: "Elizabeth Cady Stanton." New York. 1922.

Laura Stedman and George M. Gould: "Life and Letters of Edmund Clarence Stedman." New York. 1910.

Charles Edward Stowe: "Life of Harriet Beecher Stowe. Compiled from Her Letters and Journals by Her Son." London. 1889.

C. E. and Lyman Beecher Stowe: "Harriet Beecher Stowe: The Story of Her Life." Boston. 1911.

Harriet Beecher Stowe: "The Mayflower; or Sketches of Scenes and Characters Among the Descendants of the Pilgrims." (Introduction by Catherine Esther Beecher.) New York. 1843.

"Men of Our Times." Hartford, Conn. 1868.

"Uncle Sam's Emancipation; Earthly Care, a Heavenly Discipline; and Other Sketches. By Mrs. Harriet Beecher Stowe. With a Sketch of Mrs. Stowe's Family." Philadelphia. 1853.

"Uncle Tom's Cabin; or Life Among the Lowly." Boston. 1852.

Catherine Dickinson Sweetser: Unpublished letter from Henry Ward Beecher, Nov. 14, 1835.

David Swing: "The Message of David Swing to His Generation."
New York. 1913.

Synod of the Presbyterian Church of Indiana (New School):
Records.

Lewis Tappan: "The Life of Arthur Tappan." New York. 1870.

Ebenezer Smith Thomas: "Reminiscences of the Last Sixty-five
Years, Commencing with the Battle of Lexington. Also
Sketches of His Own Life and Times." Hartford. 1840.

J. H. Thomas: "An Historical Sketch of the Presbyterian Church
of Lawrenceburgh, Indiana." Lawrenceburgh. 1887.

Joseph Parrish Thompson: "A Memoir of David Hale." New York.
1850.

Noyes L. Thompson: "History of Plymouth Church." New York.
1872.

The Thunderbolt. Troy, N. Y.

Theodore Tilton: "The American Board and American Slavery.
Speech of T. Tilton in Plymouth Church, Brooklyn, January 28, 1860." Brooklyn. 1860.

"The Golden Age Tracts No. 3. Victoria C. Woodhull. A Biographical Sketch by Theodore Tilton." New York. 1871.

"Letters to His Wife: 1865–1870." Section 44 in "The Great
Brooklyn Romance."

Articles and editorials in *The Independent,* the Brooklyn *Union,*
etc.; Addresses to the New England Society of New York, the
American Equal Rights Association, etc.

Mrs. Theodore Tilton: "Letters to Her Husband: 1866–1870." Section 43 in "The Great Brooklyn Romance."

Theodore Tilton vs. Henry Ward Beecher. Action for crim. con.
Tried in the City Court of Brooklyn. Verbatim Report in
Three Volumes. New York. 1875.

(*Note: The "Official Report of Trial of Henry Ward Beecher.
Notes and References, edited by Austin Abbott." Two volumes. New York. 1875, is neither official nor complete.*)

George Francis Train: "My Life in Many States and Foreign
Lands." New York. 1902.

Joseph Treat, M.D.: "Beecher, Tilton, Woodhull, the Creation of
Society. All four of them are exposed, and if possible reformed,
and forgiven, in Dr. Treat's celebrated letter to Victoria C.
Woodhull." New York. 1874.

Frances Milton Trollope: "The Domestic Manners of the Americans." New York. 1901.

William Seymour Tyler: "A History of Amherst College During
the Administration of Its First Five Presidents from 1821 to
1891." New York. 1895.

United States Circuit Court, Eastern District of New York. *Complaint:* Edna Dean Proctor vs. Francis D. Moulton, Sept. 17, 1874.

United States War Department. Military Academy. Orders No. 20, 1827. Engineer Department, May 9, 1827.

Emily Noyes Vanderpoel: "Chronicles of a Pioneer School. From 1792 to 1833. Being the History of Miss Sarah Pierce and Her Litchfield School." Cambridge, Mass. 1903.

Vanity Fair. New York.

Daniel Van Pelt: "Leslie's History of Greater New York." New York. 1898.

Robert Bruce Warden: "Private Life and Public Services of Salmon Portland Chase." Cincinnati. 1874.

Charles Dudley Warner: "Book of Eloquence." New York. 1853.

Henry Watterson: Editorial in the Louisville *Courier-Journal.*

Noah Webster: "A Plea for a Miserable World, etc." Boston. 1820.

Thurlow Weed: "Autobiography." Boston. 1883.

Western Farmer and Gardener. Indianapolis, Ind.

Alain C. White: "The History of the Town of Litchfield, Connecticut: 1720–1920." Litchfield. 1920.

William Cleaver Wilkinson: "Modern Masters of Pulpit Discourse." New York. 1905.

Rowland Williams: "Bunsen's Biblical Researches" in "Essays and Reviews." London. 1861.

F. P. Williamson: "Beecher and His Accusers." Philadelphia. 1874.

Woodhull & Claflin's Weekly. New York.

Victoria C. Woodhull (Mrs. John Biddulph Martin) and Tennessee C. Claflin (Lady Cook): "The Human Body the Temple of God." London. 1890.

William Wesley Woollen: "Biographical and Historical Sketches of Early Indiana." Indianapolis, Ind. 1883.

APPENDIX III

Sources for the Direct Quotations

SOME readers of this book may wish to consult the sources of the direct quotations made by the author, in order to derive additional pleasure and information from a further reading of the material out of which the author has quoted only snatches. Therefore, a list of these sources is appended. Whenever the reader finds material within quotation marks in the text, he need only refer to the page and line number given below, to discover which of the books, listed in Appendix II, has been quoted from, and which page of the book.

CHAPTER I

Page 3, line 10, this sentence from Browning, p. 32. *Page 4, line 2*, these phrases from Fearon, pp. 121, 139. *Page 4, line 18*, this phrase from Adams: *History*, II, p. 126. *Page 5, line 4*, this phrase from Vanderpoel, p. 15. *Page 5, line 6*, this phrase from L. Beecher: *Autobiography*, I, p. 284. *Page 6, line 17*, these phrases from L. Beecher: *Auto*. I, p. 285. *Page 6, line 20*, this phrase from Lodge, p. 442. *Page 6, line 33*, these phrases from Gould. *Page 7, line 11*, these phrases from Fearon, p. 114. *Page 8, line 32*, this phrase from Griswold, p. 6. *Page 8, line 38*, these sentences from L. Beecher: *Auto*. I, p. 339. *Page 9, line 10*, these phrases from L. Beecher: *Auto*. II, pp. 23–24. *Page 9, line 15*, this sentence from L. Beecher: *Auto*. I, p. 344. *Page 9, line 18*, this sentence from L. Beecher: *Auto*. I, p. 337. *Page 10, line 40*, this sentence from Vanderpoel, p. 149.

CHAPTER II

Page 11, line 8, this phrase from L. Beecher: *Auto*. I, p. 323. *Page 11, line 32*, this phrase from Vanderpoel, p. 170. *Page 12, line 8*, this phrase from Ames, II, p. 294. *Page 12, line 12*, this phrase from *Middlesex Gazette*, March 19, 1806. *Page 12, line 23*, this phrase from L. Beecher: *Auto*. II, p. 53. *Page 12, line 29*, this phrase from L. Beecher: *Auto*. I, p. 351. *Page 13, line 28*, this sentence from Bowne, p. 102. *Page 13, line 37*, these sentences from L. Beecher: *Auto*. I, pp. 356–357. *Page 14, line 3*, this sentence from Stowe:

Men of Our Times, pp. 506–507. *Page 14, line 8*, these sentences from L. Beecher: *Auto.* I, p. 355. *Page 14, line 24*, this paragraph from *Christian Union*, Jan. 3, 1872. *Page 14, line 41*, these sentences from L. Beecher: *National Prosperity*. *Page 15, line 22*, this sentence from Hoyt, p. 28. *Page 15, line 29*, this paragraph from L. Beecher: *Auto.* I, p. 149. *Page 16, line 27*, these phrases from *Christian Union*, May 21, 1870. *Page 16, line 39*, this phrase from *Christian Union*, May 21, 1870. *Page 17, line 3*, this phrase from Stowe, p. 512; L. Beecher: *Auto.* I, p. 407. *Page 17, line 11*, this phrase from White, p. 34. *Page 17, line 18*, these sentences from L. Beecher: *Auto.* I, p. 460. *Page 17, line 20*, this phrase from Child, p. 11. *Page 17, line 35*, these sentences from L. Beecher: *Auto.* I, p. 390. *Page 18, line 23*, this paragraph from Child, pp. 12–13. *Page 18, line 38*, this paragraph from Child, pp. 11–13. *Page 19, line 25*, this phrase from Child, p. 12. *Page 19, line 30*, this paragraph from Fields, p. 27; Joseph Howard, p. 37.

CHAPTER III

Page 20, line 16, this phrase from L. Beecher: *Auto.* II, p. 70. *Page 20, line 20*, this phrase from L. Beecher: *Auto.* II, p. 29. *Page 21, line 12*, this paragraph from Mansfield, p. 87. *Page 21, line 38*, these phrases from Flint, pp. 175–176. *Page 22, line 36*, this sentence from L. Beecher: *Auto.* I, p. 530. *Page 23, line 16*, this sentence from L. Beecher: *Auto.* II, p. 62. *Page 23, line 29*, this phrase from L. Beecher: *Auto.* II, p. 90. *Page 24, line 2*, these sentences from Finney, p. 72. *Page 24, line 15*, this paragraph from L. Beecher: *Auto.* II, p. 101. *Page 24, line 25*, this paragraph from Nettleton, pp. 83, 91. *Page 25, line 7*, this paragraph from Finney, pp. 265–266. *Page 25, line 18*, this phrase from Catherine Beecher, p. 24. *Page 25, line 20*, this phrase from Harriet Beecher Stowe in *Family Biography*, p. 82. *Page 25, line 28*, this paragraph from Stowe, p. 517. *Page 26, line 2*, this paragraph from *Norwood*, p. 159. *Page 26, line 17*, this paragraph from Henry Ward Beecher in *Family Biog.*, p. 84. *Page 27, line 27*, this sentence from Stowe, p. 519. *Page 27, line 31*, this sentence from Thomas K. Beecher in *Family Biog.*, p. 91.

CHAPTER IV

Page 27, line 34, these phrases from Webster, p. 61. *Page 28, line 15*, this phrase from Mt. Pleasant Catalogue, 1828, p. 2. *Page 28, line 23*, this phrase from Mt. Pleasant Catalogue, 1828. *Page 28, line 26*, MS. letter in Amherst Library. *Page 29, line 4*, these phrases from L. Beecher: Sermon, 1827. *Page 29, line 28,* these phrases from Mt. Pleasant Catalogue, 1828. *Page 29, line 31,* this phrase from Clerc, pp. 9, 12. *Page 29, line 37,* this phrase from *Christian Union,* July 14, 1880. *Page 30, line 38,* these sentences from Stowe, p. 522. *Page 31, line 22,* this paragraph from Henry Ward Beecher in *Family Biog.,* pp. 105–106. *Page 32, line 14,* this paragraph from Original document; *Family Biog.,* p. 105. *Page 32, line 25,* this phrase from Henry Ward Beecher in *Family Biog.,* p. 107. *Page 34, line 30,* this sentence from Lovell: *Preface. Page 35, line 23,* this sentence from Mt. Pleasant Catalogue, 1829.

CHAPTER V

Page 36, line 2, this paragraph from MS. letter in Amherst Library. *Page 36, line 22,* this paragraph from MS. letter in Amherst Library. *Page 37, line 2,* this phrase from L. Beecher: *Plea for the West,* p. 56. *Page 37, line 12,* these phrases from L. Beecher: *Auto.* II, pp. 221, 224. *Page 37, line 32,* this sentence from L. Beecher: *Auto.* II, p. 228. *Page 38, line 6,* this paragraph from L. Beecher: *Auto.* II, p. 224. *Page 39, line 12,* these phrases from Holmes, *Atlantic Monthly,* XIII, p. 107. *Page 39, line 28,* this phrase from Morse, pp. 31–32. *Page 40, line 21,* these sentences from Henry Ward Beecher: *Journal* in *Family Biog.,* pp. 110–111. *Page 41, line 13,* these phrases from Tyler, p. 47, footnote. *Page 41, line 30,* this phrase from Cutting, p. 94. *Page 42, line 21,* this paragraph from C. E. and L. B. Stowe, p. 75. *Page 43, line 7,* this sentence from Sprague, pp. 5–6. *Page 43, line 10,* this sentence from *Ladies' Home Journal,* Oct. 1891. *Page 43, line 24,* this sentence from Henry Ward Beecher in *Family Biog.,* p. 129. *Page 43, line 41,* this sentence from MS. *Commencement Address:* Alonzo Gray, 1834, Amherst Library. *Page 44, line 22,* this phrase from Athenian Society Records, June 5, 1833. *Page 44, line 29,* this phrase from Cutting, p. 59.

CHAPTER VI

Page 46, line 11, this paragraph from H. W. Beecher: *Wendell Phillips. Page 47, line 28,* this paragraph from Johnson, pp. 44–45. *Page 48, line 8,* this phrase from Johnson, pp. 89–90. *Page 48, line 21,* this phrase from Tappan, p. 129. *Page 48, line 31,* this paragraph from L. Beecher: *Auto.* II, p. 323. *Page 48, line 34,* this phrase from Johnson, p. 45. *Page 49, line 19,* this paragraph from *London and Westminster Review,* Dec. 1838. *Page 50, line 3,* this sentence from Tilton vs. Beecher, I, p. 478. *Page 50, line 14,* these sentences from

N. Y. *Times*, Aug. 12, 1871. *Page 50, line 33*, this paragraph from *Christian Union*, Oct. 8, 1870. *Page 51, line 10*, these sentences from L. Beecher: *Plea for the West*, p. 29. *Page 51, line 16*, these sentences from Reed and Matheson, I, p. 113. *Page 51, line 39*, this paragraph from Martineau, II, page 55. *Page 52, line 3*, this phrase from L. Beecher: *Plea for the West*, p. 56. *Page 52, line 22*, this phrase from Stanton, p. 29. *Page 52, line 36*, this phrase from Lane Seminary Catalogue, 1848; Cist, p. 124. *Page 53, line 5*, this phrase from L. Beecher: *Auto*. II, p. 321. *Page 53, line 9*, this phrase from MS. letter to Mrs. Sweetser, Nov. 14, 1835. *Page 54, line 16*, this paragraph from L. Beecher: *Auto*. II, p. 357. *Page 54, line 27*, these sentences from L. Beecher: *Auto*. II, p. 383. *Page 54, line 36*, this paragraph from Tappan, p. 233. *Page 54, line 40*, this sentence from *Lectures to Young Men*: Dedication.

CHAPTER VII

Page 55, line 5, this phrase from *Genius of Universal Emancipation*, April, 1834, p. 61. *Page 55, line 14*, this sentence from *London and Westminster Review*, Dec., 1838. *Page 55, line 29*, this paragraph from L. Beecher: *Auto*. II, p. 345. *Page 56, line 13*, this paragraph from E. S. Thomas, II, pp. 200–201. *Page 56, line 18*, this sentence from Trollope, p. 127. *Page 56, line 36*, this sentence from *A Looking-glass for Henry Ward Beecher*, p. 19. *Page 56, line 38*, this phrase from Trollope, p. 94. *Page 57, line 1*, these phrases from *Lectures to Young Men*, pp. 138–139. *Page 57, line 4*, these sentences from Henry Ward Beecher: *Journal* in *Family Biog.*, p. 146. *Page 57, line 10*, this sentence from Henry Ward Beecher: *Journal* in *Family Biog.*, pp. 145–146. *Page 57, line 15*, this paragraph from Henry Ward Beecher: *Journal* in *Family Biog.*, p. 144. *Page 57, line 25*, this phrase from Marryatt, p. 100. *Page 57, line 30*, this paragraph from Hoffman, II, p. 131. *Page 58, line 24*, this phrase from *Ladies' Home Journal*, Oct., 1891. *Page 59, line 2*, this phrase from Stowe, p. 536. *Page 59, line 14*, this phrase from Brainerd, p. 81. *Page 59, line 31*, this phrase from Birney, p. 244. *Page 60, line 12*, this paragraph from C. E. Stowe, p. 82. *Page 61, line 28*, these sentences from C. E. Stowe, pp. 84–86. *Page 61, line 37*, this phrase from Maunsell, p. 185. *Page 62, line 9*, this phrase from Warden, p. 244. *Page 62, line 14*, these sentences from Trollope, p. 84.

CHAPTER VIII

Page 63, line 8, these phrases from Hillis, p. 320. *Page 63, line 26*, this paragraph from Henry Ward Beecher in *Family Biog.*, p. 155.

Page 64, line 21, these phrases from Campbell-Purcell Debate, p. 356. *Page 64, line 34,* this paragraph from Henry Ward Beecher in *Family Biog.,* p. 167. *Page 65, line 14,* this paragraph from *Ladies' Home Journal,* Nov., 1891. *Page 65, line 31,* this phrase from Ketcham, p. 66. *Page 66, line 26,* this phrase from *A Looking-glass for Henry Ward Beecher,* p. 19. *Page 67, line 1,* this phrase from *Christian Union,* Dec. 6, 1871. *Page 67, line 23,* this sentence from Mrs. Beecher: *Dawn to Daylight,* p. 80. *Page 68, line 27,* this phrase from *Western Farmer & Gardener,* I, p. 31. *Page 68, line 33,* this phrase from Buckingham, II, p. 414. *Page 69, line 12,* this phrase from Edward Beecher, p. 22. *Page 69, line 24,* these phrases from Morris, p. 70. *Page 69, line 32,* these phrases from Edward Beecher, p. 151. *Page 70, line 13,* this sentence from N. Y. *World,* May 22, 1882. *Page 70, line 26,* these sentences from *Yale Lectures,* I, p. 146.

CHAPTER IX

Page 71, line 12, these sentences from Henry Ward Beecher: *Journal* in *Family Biog.,* p. 158. *Page 71, line 16,* this phrase from J. H. Thomas, p. 8. *Page 71, line 25,* this phrase from *American Home Miss. Soc. Proceedings,* XII, p. 14. *Page 72, line 16,* this paragraph from L. Beecher: *Auto.* II, pp. 430–431. *Page 72, line 31,* this paragraph from *Christian Union,* May, 1887. *Page 73, line 9,* this paragraph from Henry Ward Beecher in *Family Biog.,* pp. 165–166. *Page 74, line 12,* this paragraph from Lawrenceburgh *Political Beacon,* July 7, 1838. *Page 74, line 32,* this paragraph from Lawrenceburgh *Political Beacon,* July 7, 1838. *Page 76, line 6,* these sentences from Buckingham, II, pp. 395–396. *Page 77, line 18,* this phrase from Birney, p. 155. *Page 77, line 29,* this phrase from Second Church Records, p. 11. *Page 77, line 39,* these sentences from Lawrenceburgh *Political Beacon,* July 13, 1839.

CHAPTER X

Page 78, line 9, this phrase from Ketcham, p. 66. *Page 78, line 21,* this phrase from Nevins, p. 4. *Page 79, line 3,* this phrase from Cottman. *Page 79, line 20,* this sentence from Mrs. Beecher: *Dawn to Daylight,* p. 139. *Page 79, line 24,* these sentences from Ketcham, pp. 69, 71. *Page 79, line 27,* this sentence from Ketcham, p. 70. *Page 79, line 41,* this paragraph from Parsons, pp. 156–157. *Page 80, line 4,* these phrases from Mrs. Beecher: *Law of a Household,* p. 1. *Page 80, line 10,* this sentence from Ketcham, pp. 69–70. *Page 80, line 20,* these phrases from Synod Records, Vol. I, pp. 459–462. *Page 80, line*

28, this paragraph from Synod Records, I, pp. 31–51. *Page 80, line 34,* this sentence from Synod Records, I, pp. 31–51. *Page 81, line 2,* these sentences from Hillis, p. 190. *Page 81, line 7,* this phrase from Duncan, p. 110. *Page 82, line 12,* this paragraph from Fletcher Diary. *Page 82, line 36,* this sentence from Merriam, II, p. 49. *Page 83, line 7,* these sentences from Ketcham, p. 71. *Page 83, line 14,* these sentences from *Ladies' Home Journal,* Dec., 1891; Croffut. *Page 83, line 17,* these paragraphs from *Yale Lectures,* II, p. 299. *Page 84, line 20,* this sentence from Stowe, p. 510. *Page 84, line 35,* this phrase from Synod Records, I, pp. 492–496. *Page 85, line 1,* this phrase from Cleland, p. 11. *Page 85, line 16,* these phrases from Ketcham MS., p. 9. *Page 86, line 21,* this paragraph from *Yale Lectures,* I, p. 11. *Page 86, line 30,* these sentences from J. T. Lloyd, p. 32. *Page 86, line 36,* this phrase from Second Church Records, p. 21.

CHAPTER XI

Page 87, line 4, this phrase from Ketcham MS., p. 9. *Page 87, line 5,* this phrase from Chicago *Times,* July 27, 1874. *Page 88, line 6,* this paragraph from Sermon on Governor Noble. *Page 88, line 11,* this phrase from Bradshaw MS. *Page 88, line 27,* this sentence from Derby, p. 467; Fletcher Diary, June 15, 1842. *Page 88, line 38,* this paragraph from Henry Ward Beecher in *Family Biog.,* p. 191; *Yale Lectures,* I, p. 47; J. T. Lloyd, p. 35. *Page 89, line 30,* this paragraph from *Lectures to Young Men,* pp. 50–51. *Page 90, line 3,* this paragraph from L. Beecher: *Auto.* II, pp. 476–477. *Page 90, line 30,* this phrase from Second Church Records, pp. 33–34. *Page 90, line 35,* this phrase from Second Church Records, pp. 55–56. *Page 91, line 5,* this phrase from Second Church Records, p. 81. *Page 91, line 15,* these phrases from *Lectures to Young Men,* Preface. *Page 91, line 19,* these sentences from *Lectures to Young Men,* p. 90. *Page 91, line 21,* this sentence from *Lectures to Young Men,* p. 127. *Page 91, line 24,* this sentence from *Lectures to Young Men,* p. 43. *Page 91, line 27,* this phrase from *Lectures to Young Men,* p. 46. *Page 91, line 29,* this phrase from *Lectures to Young Men,* p. 131. *Page 91, line 32,* this phrase from *Lectures to Young Men,* pp. 131–132. *Page 92, line 1,* this phrase from *Lectures to Young Men,* pp. 138–139. *Page 92, line 3,* these phrases from *Lectures to Young Men,* pp. 140, 163. *Page 92, line 5,* this phrase from *Lectures to Young Men,* p. 133. *Page 92, line 10,* these sentences from *Lectures to Young Men,* p. 147. *Page 92, line 29,* this paragraph from *Lectures to Young Men,* pp. 181, 184, 191. *Page 92, line 41,* this phrase from *Indiana State Journal,* Sept. 4, 1844. *Page 93, line 4,* this phrase from Synod Records, I, p. 597. *Page 93, line 34,* this phrase from Catherine Beecher: *Introduction to The*

Mayflower by Harriet Beecher Stowe, p. VIII. *Page 94, line 24,* this paragraph from Woollen, p. 354. *Page 95, line 37,* this phrase from *Lectures to Young Men,* p. 50. *Page 96, line 6,* this phrase from Synod Records, II, pp. 632–633. *Page 96, line 8,* this phrase from Synod Records, II, p. 628. *Page 96, line 24,* these sentences from *Indiana State Journal,* Jan. 29, 1845. *Page 97, line 18,* these paragraphs from *Indiana State Journal,* Mar. 4, 1846.

CHAPTER XII

Page 98, line 7, this paragraph from O. H. Smith, pp. 94–95. *Page 98, line 28,* these phrases from Bradshaw MS. *Page 99, line 18,* this phrase from Mrs. Beecher, pp. 161–162. *Page 99, line 27,* this phrase from Ketcham, p. 79. *Page 100, line 14,* this paragraph from N. L. Thompson, pp. 36–39. *Page 100, line 23,* these phrases from Cottman. *Page 101, line 12,* these phrases from Second Church Records, p. 81. *Page 101, line 24,* this sentence from *Lectures to Young Men,* p. 165. *Page 101, line 37,* this paragraph from Henry Ward Beecher to William T. Cutter, December 15, 1846, *Family Biog.,* pp. 210–213. *Page 102, line 6,* this phrase from N. Y. *Journal of Commerce,* June 17, 1846. *Page 103, line 21,* this sentence from Sermon: January 8, 1860. *Page 103, line 32,* this phrase from Am. Home Miss. Soc., XXI, pp. 3–4. *Page 104, line 12,* this paragraph from *Indiana State Journal,* May 24, 1847. *Page 104, line 29,* this paragraph from Brookville, Ind., *American,* September 3, 1847. *Page 104, line 33,* this phrase from Second Church Records. *Page 105, line 5,* this sentence from Indianapolis *Journal* cited in New York *Times,* June 5, 1882. *Page 105, line 11,* this phrase from Fletcher Diary, September 2, 1845. *Page 105, line 35,* this paragraph from Ketcham MS., p. 16. *Page 106, line 18,* these phrases from Belden, p. 55. *Page 107, line 38,* this paragraph from N. L. Thompson, p. 209. *Page 108, line 11,* these paragraphs from N. Y. *Tribune,* May 18, 1847; N. L. Thompson, pp. 51–56.

CHAPTER XIII

Page 109, line 33, this paragraph from King, p. 60. *Page 110, line 12,* this paragraph from *Journal of Commerce,* Dec. 6, 1847. *Page 110, line 22,* this paragraph from Haswell, p. 189. *Page 111, line 29,* this paragraph from N. Y. *Tribune,* October 24, 1848. *Page 112, line 28,* this phrase from *Independent,* May 23, 1850. *Page 113, line 19,* this sentence from N. Y. *Sun,* Mar. 3, 1876. *Page 115, line 34,* this phrase from Maffitt, p. 26. *Page 115, line 38,* this phrase from *In-*

dependent, Nov. 18, 1852. *Page 116, line 16*, this paragraph from *Independent*, Jan. 24, 1850. *Page 116, line 34*, this phrase from *Congressional Globe*, 31st Cong., 1st Sess., Appendix, pp. 115–127. *Page 117, line 12*, this paragraph from *Independent*, Feb. 21, 1850. *Page 118, line 1*, this phrase from Channing, VI, p. 98. *Page 118, line 15*, this paragraph from *Independent*, May 9, 1850. *Page 118, line 25*, this sentence from *Independent*, May 9, 1850.

CHAPTER XIV

Page 119, line 2, this phrase from *Independent*, Nov. 14, 1850. *Page 119, line 12*, this phrase from Austin, p. 134. *Page 120, line 3*, this paragraph from Martyn, p. 231. *Page 120, line 7*, this sentence from *Independent*, May 9, 1850. *Page 120, line 16*, this sentence from C. E. Stowe, p. 130. *Page 120, line 37*, this sentence from *Ladies' Home Journal*, Dec., 1891. *Page 121, line 2*, these sentences from *Ladies' Home Journal*, Dec., 1891. *Page 121, line 16*, this paragraph from Barrows, p. 109; Joseph Howard, p. 127. *Page 122, line 4*, this phrase from C. E. Stowe, p. 145. *Page 123, line 13*, these sentences from *Star Papers*, pp. 85–88. *Page 123, line 34*, this paragraph from Channing, VI, pp. 104–105. *Page 125, line 10*, this paragraph from C. E. Stowe, p. 476. *Page 125, line 29*, this phrase from *Independent*, May 8, 1851. *Page 125, line 39*, these phrases from *Independent*, Nov. 14, 1850. *Page 126, line 6*, this sentence from *Independent*, Apr. 24, 1851. *Page 126, line 10*, this phrase from *Independent*, Feb. 5, 1852. *Page 126, line 18*, this paragraph from *Independent*, Feb. 5, 1852. *Page 126, line 29*, this paragraph from *Independent*, June 2, 1853. *Page 126, line 36*, these sentences from Greeley in N. Y. *Tribune*, cited in *Independent*, June 2, 1853. *Page 127, line 13*, this paragraph from *Independent*, June 2, 1853. *Page 127, line 26*, this paragraph from *Independent*, Nov. 14, 1850. *Page 127, line 30*, this sentence from Treat, p. 16.

CHAPTER XV

Page 128, line 20, these sentences from *Independent*, Feb. 17, 1859. *Page 129, line 15*, these sentences from *Lectures to Young Men*, pp. 182–183. *Page 129, line 22*, these phrases from *Independent*, May 14, 1857. *Page 129, line 33*, this phrase from Charles Beecher: *Spiritual Manifestations*, p. 75. *Page 130, line 2*, these phrases from *Independent*, May 23, 1850. *Page 130, line 33*, this paragraph from *Independent*, Feb. 16, 1854. *Page 131, line 16*, this sentence from

Derby, p. 475. *Page 132, line 15*, this phrase from *Independent*, Jan. 24, 1856. *Page 133, line 8*, this paragraph from *Congressional Globe*, 33rd Cong., 1st Sess., pp. 278–279. *Page 133, line 17*, this phrase from *Independent*, Apr. 24, 1851. *Page 133, line 22*, this sentence from *Independent*, Oct. 12, 1854. *Page 133, line 31*, this sentence from Seward, II, p. 226. *Page 134, line 1*, these sentences from *Independent*, Feb. 23, 1854. *Page 134, line 13*, this paragraph from *Independent*, Mar. 23, 1854. *Page 134, line 34*, this phrase from Ogden, pp. 117–118; N. Y. *Daily News*, Nov. 8, 1856. *Page 135, line 3*, these sentences from Henry Ward Beecher: *Conflict of Northern and Southern Theories*. *Page 135, line 8*, these sentences from N. Y. *Tribune*, Nov. 30, 1860. *Page 135, line 19*, this paragraph from *Independent*, June 26, 1856. *Page 135, line 26*, this paragraph from *Independent*, Sept. 22, 1859. *Page 136, line 29*, this paragraph from Van Pelt, II, p. 220. *Page 137, line 25*, these sentences from *Independent*, Sept. 15, 1853. *Page 137, line 39*, this phrase from Hone, II, p. 393. *Page 138, line 27*, this phrase from *Independent*, Sept. 8, 1853. *Page 139, line 16*, this phrase from *Independent*, Apr. 5, 1855.

CHAPTER XVI

Page 140, line 10, this sentence from Pittsburgh *Commercial*, cited in Chicago *Tribune*, Aug. 3, 1874. *Page 141, line 4*, these paragraphs from Brockett, pp. 612–613. *Page 141, line 9*, this phrase from *Independent*, Jan. 5, 1854. *Page 141, line 25*, this paragraph from *Independent*, Mar. 29, 1855. *Page 141, line 34*, this paragraph from *Independent*, Dec. 3, 1857. *Page 141, line 37*, these phrases from *Indiana State Journal*, Dec. 8, 1846. *Page 142, line 12*, this paragraph from *Independent*, Mar. 3, 1859. *Page 143, line 3*, this paragraph from Tilton vs. Beecher, II, p. 11. *Page 144, line 34*, this paragraph from *Independent*, Oct. 27, 1859. *Page 145, line 2*, this paragraph from *Independent*, Sept. 29, 1859. *Page 145, line 12*, this paragraph from *Independent*, Jan. 22, 1857. *Page 145, line 19*, this phrase from *Independent*, Mar. 11, 1858. *Page 145, line 21*, this phrase from *Liberator*, Apr. 30, 1858. *Page 145, line 26*, this sentence from *Memorial of Revival*, p. 59. *Page 146, line 4*, this paragraph from *Independent*, Jan. 12, 1860. *Page 146, line 12*, this paragraph from *Independent*, Dec. 8, 1859. *Page 146, line 16*, this phrase from *Independent*, Apr. 21, 1859. *Page 146, line 32*, this paragraph from Theodore Tilton to Henry Ward Beecher, Nov. 30, 1865, T. vs. B., II, p. 11. *Page 147, line 1*, this sentence from Senator Carpenter to Theodore Tilton, Sept. 18, 1871, *Woodhull and Claflin's Weekly*, Oct. 7, 1871. *Page 148, line 10*, this paragraph from *Beecher and Parker*, p. 18. *Page 148, line 37*, this paragraph from *Freedom and War*, pp. 13–22. *Page*

149, line 17, this paragraph from Tilton: *American Board and American Slavery. Page 149, line 25,* these phrases from Mrs. Beecher: N. Y. *World,* Apr. 19, 1896. *Page 149, line 29,* these sentences from Mrs. Beecher: N. Y. *World,* Apr. 12 and 19, 1896. *Page 149, line 37,* these sentences from *Woman's Influence in Politics. Page 150, line 18,* this paragraph from N. Y. *Evening Post,* Aug. 16, 1867. *Page 151, line 5,* this phrase from *Independent,* Aug. 14, 1856. *Page 151, line 6,* this phrase from *Independent,* Aug. 7, 1862. *Page 151, line 15,* this paragraph from N. Y. *Tribune,* Nov. 30, 1860.

CHAPTER XVII

Page 152, line 7, these sentences from Badeau, p. 280. *Page 152, line 10,* this phrase from Nichols, I, p. 337. *Page 152, line 11,* this phrase from O. B. Frothingham, p. 441. *Page 152, line 23,* this phrase from *Ballou's Pictorial,* Vol. X, p. 60. *Page 152, line 25,* this phrase from Bungay, pp. 104–115. *Page 153, line 3,* this sentence from Brooklyn *Sunday Press,* Apr. 20, 1873. *Page 153, line 23,* this phrase from N. L. Thompson, p. 109. *Page 154, line 3,* this paragraph from *Freedom and War,* pp. 36, 43, 51. *Page 154, line 8,* this sentence from *Independent,* May 9, 1850. *Page 154, line 36,* these sentences from *Freedom and War,* pp. 50, 64, 71. *Page 155, line 12,* these sentences from *Freedom and War,* pp. 93, 102, 103. *Page 155, line 19,* this phrase from *Independent,* July 31, 1862. *Page 155, line 21,* this sentence from *Independent,* Jan. 16, 1862. *Page 156, line 27,* this phrase from *Independent,* Mar. 6, 1862. *Page 156, line 28,* this phrase from *Independent,* Mar. 20, 1862. *Page 156, line 35,* this paragraph from *Independent,* Nov. 3, 1864. *Page 157, line 5,* this phrase from Rhodes, III, p. 428. *Page 157, line 24,* this phrase from *Independent,* Dec. 19, 1861. *Page 157, line 31,* this phrase from C. F. Adams, p. 161. *Page 158, line 29,* this paragraph from *Independent,* July 10, 1862. *Page 158, line 30,* this phrase from *Independent,* July 17, 1862. *Page 158, line 33,* these sentences from *Independent,* July 17, 1862. *Page 158, line 38,* these sentences from *Independent,* July 24, 1862. *Page 159, line 8,* these sentences from *Independent,* Mar. 20, 1862. *Page 159, line 30,* this paragraph from *Independent,* Aug. 7, 1862. *Page 159, line 40,* these sentences from *Independent,* Sept. 11, 1862. *Page 160, line 20,* this paragraph from *Independent,* Dec. 14, 1862. *Page 161, line 16,* this sentence from Bryce: *Atlantic Monthly,* Vol. LXXXII, p. 25. *Page 161, line 25,* this paragraph from Weed, I, p. 645. *Page 161, line 33,* this paragraph from Rhodes, III, p. 599. *Page 162, line 3,* this sentence from *Independent,* Jan. 8, 1863. *Page 162, line 14,* these phrases from H. R. Lloyd, p. 411. *Page 162, line 34,* this paragraph from E. D. Adams, II, p. 184, footnote. *Page 162, line 39,* these sentences from Beard: *American Civilization,* II, p. 82. *Page 163, line 12,* this paragraph from Hawthorne, II, p. 281. *Page 163, line 18,* these sentences from London *Era,* Oct. 25, 1863.

CHAPTER XVIII

Page 163, line 26, this sentence from Stowe, p. 557. *Page 163, line 33,* this phrase from N. Y. *Times,* June 9, 1865. *Page 164, line 2,* this phrase from *Independent,* July 30, 1863. *Page 164, line 11,* this phrase from N. Y. *Tribune,* Oct. 13, 1863. *Page 164, line 38,* this paragraph from London *Era,* Aug. 16, 1863. *Page 165, line 2,* this phrase from London *Saturday Review,* Oct. 3, 1863. *Page 165, line 23,* this phrase from *Independent,* Dec. 26, 1861. *Page 165, line 24,* this phrase from London *Saturday Review,* Oct. 31, 1863. *Page 166, line 3,* this paragraph from Hamilton Wright Mabie in Abbott, p. 253. *Page 166, line 16,* this phrase from N. Y. *Tribune,* Nov. 7, 1863. *Page 166, line 23,* these sentences from N. Y. *Times,* Nov. 18, 1863. *Page 166, line 33,* these sentences from Stowe, p. 564. *Page 168, line 2,* this phrase from *Independent,* Aug. 7, 1862. *Page 168, line 5,* this phrase from N. Y. *Times,* Nov. 18, 1863. *Page 168, line 22,* this sentence from Lincoln: II, p. 567. *Page 168, line 25,* this phrase from N. Y. *Times,* Nov. 4, 1863. *Page 168, line 28,* this phrase from Hudson, p. 673. *Page 169, line 7,* this phrase from Bonner Correspondence: Feb. 3, 1865. *Page 169, line 34,* these sentences from Bonner Correspondence: May 20, 1865. *Page 170, line 11,* these sentences from *Independent,* May 11, 1865. *Page 170, line 15,* this phrase from *Independent,* Apr. 13, 1865. *Page 170, line 35,* this paragraph from *Patriotic Addresses,* p. 696. *Page 170, line 18,* this paragraph from *Independent,* May 11, 1865. *Page 172, line 4,* this phrase from N. Y. *Times,* Oct. 23, 1865. *Page 172, line 10,* these sentences from *Daily News,* cited in *Independent,* Oct. 26, 1865. *Page 172, line 20,* this phrase in *Independent,* Nov. 9, 1865. *Page 172, line 23,* this phrase from *Cleveland Letters,* p. 13. *Page 172, line 27,* this phrase from Sermon: Oct. 22, 1865. *Page 173, line 6,* these phrases from Greeley in N. Y. *Tribune,* Sept. 3, 1866. *Page 173, line 11,* this sentence from *Independent,* Sept. 6, 1866. *Page 173, line 13,* this sentence from *Independent,* Sept. 13, 1866. *Page 173, line 39,* this phrase from Henry Ward Beecher to Dr. Tyng, Sept. 6, 1866 in *Family Biog.,* pp. 470–471. *Page 174, line 2,* these sentences from *Independent,* Sept. 13, 1866. *Page 174, line 17,* these sentences from *Independent,* Oct. 25, 1866. *Page 174, line 34,* this paragraph from *Independent,* Oct. 25, 1866. *Page 175, line 2,* this paragraph from T. vs. B., I, p. 503.

CHAPTER XIX

Page 175, line 5, these phrases from Garrison, IV, p. 91. *Page 176, line 12,* this sentence from Harper, I, p. 234. *Page 176, line 35,* these sentences from Mrs. Beecher in N. Y. *World,* Apr. 12, 1896. *Page 176, line 38,* this phrase from Mrs. Beecher in N. Y. *World,* Apr. 19, 1896. *Page 176, line 41,* these phrases from Mrs. Beecher in N. Y. *World,* May 10, 1896. *Page 177, line 4,* this phrase from Mrs. Beecher in N. Y. *World,* May 17, 1896. *Page 178, line 5,* this phrase from Chicago *Tribune,* Aug. 2, 1874. *Page 178, line 9,* these phrases from Chicago *Tribune,* Aug. 1, 1874. *Page 178, line 12,* this phrase from Chicago *Post and Mail,* July 24, 1874. *Page 179, line 28,* this phrase from *Independent,* June 28, 1860. *Page 179, line 29,* this sentence from Brooklyn *Argus,* Sept. 18, 1874. *Page 181, line 23,* these phrases from *Vanity Fair,* Mar. 22, 1862. *Page 181, line 31,* these sentences from Derby, pp. 470–471. *Page 182, line 5,* this sentence from Bonner Correspondence, Feb. 3, 1865. *Page 182, line 11,* these sentences from Bonner Correspondence, Feb. 8, 1865. *Page 182, line 19,* these sentences from Bonner Correspondence, undated letter. *Page 182, line 30,* this phrase from Bonner Correspondence, May 20, 1865. *Page 182, line 40,* these sentences from T. vs. B., II, p. 742. *Page 183, line 7,* this phrase from Harper, I, p. 463–465. *Page 183, line 21,* these sentences from *Independent,* Sept. 21, 1865. *Page 183, line 28,* these phrases from *Independent,* Dec. 27, 1866. *Page 183, line 40,* this phrase from N. Y. *Sun,* July 23, 1874. *Page 184, line 4,* this phrase from Harper, I, p. 465. *Page 184, line 16,* these sentences from T. vs. B., I, p. 488. *Page 184, line 28,* this paragraph from Mrs. Tilton: *Letters to Her Husband. Page 184, line 41,* this sentence from *Independent,* Jan. 18, 1866. *Page 185, line 31,* this paragraph from T. vs. B., I, p. 485. *Page 185, line 35,* these phrases from Tilton: *Letters to His Wife. Page 185, line 40,* this phrase from T. vs. B., I, p. 499. *Page 185, line 41,* this phrase from T. vs. B., I, p. 489. *Page 186, line 11,* this paragraph from T. vs. B., I, p. 499. *Page 186, line 22,* this phrase from T. vs. B., III, p. 20. *Page 186, line 22,* this phrase from Mrs. Tilton: *Letters to Her Husband. Page 186, line 33,* this paragraph from *Norwood,* pp. 277–278. *Page 186, line 40,* these sentences from T. vs. B., Exhibit D–60; I, p. 491; III, p. 890.

CHAPTER XX

Page 187, line 9, this sentence from T. vs. B., III, p. 74. *Page 187, line 13,* this phrase from *Norwood,* p. 21. *Page 187, line 17,* this sen-

tence from Harper, I, p. 464. *Page 187, line 27*, this paragraph from
T. vs. B., Exhibit D–68. *Page 188, line 1*, these phrases from *Independent*, Nov. 21, 1867. *Page 188, line 3*, this phrase from *Independent*, May 9, 1867. *Page 188, line 22*, this phrase from Plymouth
Church Manual, 1854. *Page 189, line 41*, these sentences from *Independent*, Sept. 14, 1865. *Page 190, line 15*, this phrase from *Lectures
to Young Men*, p. 184. *Page 190, line 21*, these sentences from *Independent*, Dec. 5, 1867. *Page 190, line 25*, this sentence from Derby,
pp. 456–457. *Page 191, line 10*, this paragraph from N. Y. *Times*,
July 11, 1868. *Page 191, line 16*, this phrase from Tilton: *Letters to
His Wife*. *Page 191, line 30*, these sentences from N. Y. *Times*, Oct.
10, 1868. *Page 192, line 7*, this sentence from Derby, p. 465. *Page
193, line 20*, this sentence from T. vs. B., II, Exhibit D–96. *Page 193,
line 37*, this phrase from N. Y. *Times*, Jan. 8, 1869. *Page 194, line 15*,
this paragraph from Harper, I, p. 276. *Page 194, line 34*, this phrase
from H. Adams: *Education of Henry Adams*, pp. 271–272. *Page 195,
line 10*, this sentence from N. Y. *Times, Review of Beecher Case*,
p. 11. *Page 195, line 15*, this phrase from T. vs. B., III, p. 59. *Page
195, line 19*, these phrases from Mrs. Tilton: *Letters to Her Husband*. *Page 195, line 22*, this phrase from Mrs. Tilton: *Letters to Her
Husband*. *Page 195, line 26*, these sentences from Harper, I, p. 464.
Page 196, line 10, this phrase from J. R. Howard, p. 255. *Page 196,
line 17*, this sentence from Chicago *Tribune*, Oct. 2, 1874. *Page 196,
line 39*, this paragraph from J. R. Howard, p. 271. *Page 197, line 23*,
this phrase from N. Y. *Times*, Dec. 5, 1869. *Page 197, line 33*, these
sentences from Hudson, p. 653. *Page 198, line 22*, these sentences
from N. Y. *Times*, Aug. 5, 1875. *Page 198, line 26*, this phrase from
Brooklyn *Eagle*, Dec. 27, 1875. *Page 198, line 36*, these phrases from
Oberholtzer, II, p. 165. *Page 199, line 6*, this phrase from Oberholtzer, II, pp. 190–191. *Page 199, line 8*, this phrase from Brooklyn
Eagle, Dec. 27, 1875. *Page 199, line 17*, these sentences from *The
Nation*, Oct. 8, 1874. *Page 199, line 22*, these sentences from T. vs.
B., Exhibit D–89. *Page 199, line 30*, these sentences from N. Y. *Sun*,
Mar. 3, 1876. *Page 200, line 18*, this paragraph from Theodore Tilton's sworn statement: N. Y. *Sun*, July 22, 1874. *Page 201, line 3*,
these paragraphs from *Independent*, July 14, 1870.

CHAPTER XXI

Page 203, line 17, this sentence from Harper, I, p. 352. *Page 203,
line 29*, this sentence from Harper, I, p. 274. *Page 203, line 32*, this
phrase from *Patriotic Addresses*, p. 956. *Page 203, line 35*, this phrase
from N. Y. *Tribune*, Apr. 11, 1873. *Page 203, line 37*, this phrase
from N. Y. *Times*, Oct. 25, 1871; J. T. Lloyd, p. 227. *Page 204, line*

1, this sentence from *Hist. Woman Suff.*, II, pp. 808–809. *Page 204, line 8*, this sentence from *Christian Union*, Sept. 10, 1870. *Page 204, line 30*, this paragraph from Tilton: *Letters to His Wife. Page 204, line 33*, this phrase from Benson. *Page 205, line 24*, this sentence from N. Y. *Sun*, July 22, 1874. *Page 206, line 14*, these sentences from N. Y. *Herald*, July 28, 1874: T. vs. B., II, p. 309. *Page 206, line 34*, this paragraph from Brooklyn *Argus*, Sept. 18, 1874. *Page 206, line 36*, this phrase from T. vs. B., I, p. 534. *Page 208, line 40*, this phrase from T. vs. B., II, p. 750. *Page 209, line 8*, these sentences from T. vs. B., III, p. 15. *Page 209, line 32*, this sentence from N. Y. *Sun*, Feb. 7, 1876. *Page 210, line 2*, these phrases from T. vs. B., I, p. 68. *Page 210, line 9*, this phrase from T. vs. B., I, p. 68. *Page 210, line 16*, this paragraph from the N. Y. *Sun*, Feb. 7, 1876. *Page 210, line 22*, this phrase from T. vs. B., I, p. 68. *Page 210, line 25*, this phrase from T. vs. B., I, p. 75, Exhibit 4. *Page 211, line 10*, this sentence from N. Y. *Sun*, Mar. 3, 1876. *Page 211, line 24*, this phrase from T. vs. B., III, p. 412. *Page 211, line 37*, this sentence from T. vs. B., II, p. 759. *Page 212, line 19*, this sentence from Plymouth Church Manual, 1854.

CHAPTER XXII

Page 212, line 32, this phrase from T. vs. B., I, p. 771. *Page 212, line 34*, this phrase from T. vs. B., I, p. 721. *Page 214, line 30*, this sentence from *Independent*, Dec. 22, 1870. *Page 215, line 14*, these sentences from T. vs. B., I, p. 68. *Page 215, line 39*, these phrases from *Independent*, Nov. 7, 1867. *Page 216, line 11*, these sentences from T. vs. B., I, p. 61. *Page 216, line 14*, this sentence from T. vs. B., III, p. 25. *Page 216, line 24*, these sentences from T. vs. B., I, p. 62. *Page 217, line 4*, this sentence from N. Y. *Sun*, Apr. 16, 1878. *Page 218, line 5*, these phrases from T. vs. B., I, p. 761. *Page 218, line 8*, these sentences from T. vs. B., III, p. 28. *Page 218, line 17*, these sentences from T. vs. B., III, p. 35. *Page 218, line 23*, this phrase from T. vs. B., I, p. 396. *Page 218, line 36*, this sentence from T. vs. B., I, pp. 62, 398. *Page 219, line 4*, this phrase from N. Y. *Sun*, Aug. 14, 1874. *Page 219, line 32*, this letter from T. vs. B., I, p. 75. *Page 220, line 29*, these sentences from T. vs. B., I, p. 64. *Page 220, line 39*, these sentences from T. vs. B., I, p. 188. *Page 221, line 18*, these sentences from T. vs. B., I, p. 215. *Page 222, line 4*, this phrase from N. Y. *Sun*, Mar. 3, 1876. *Page 222, line 30*, this sentence from Benson. *Page 223, line 2*, this phrase from T. vs. B., I, p. 64. *Page 223, line 19*, these sentences from T. vs. B., III, p. 50. *Page 223, line 38*, this letter from T. vs. B., I, p. 65. *Page 224, line 12*, this sentence from N. Y. *Times*, Jan. 2, 1871.

CHAPTER XXIII

Page 224, line 19, this sentence from N. Y. *Times*, cited in *Beecher-Tilton Scandal*, p. 138. *Page 224, line 25*, this sentence from Albany *Journal*, cited in *Beecher-Tilton Scandal*, p. 142. *Page 225, line 17*, this phrase from T. vs. B., III, p. 50. *Page 226, line 5*, these sentences from T. vs. B., II, p. 785. *Page 226, line 34*, this phrase from T. vs. B., I, pp. 66, 402–403; Complaint: Proctor vs. Moulton, Circuit Court of the U. S., East. Dist. of N. Y., Sept. 17, 1874. *Page 226, line 36*, this phrase from T. vs. B., III, p. 833. *Page 227, line 26*, this sentence from T. vs. B., I, p. 82, Exhibit 11. *Page 228, line 2*, this phrase from N. Y. *Sun*, Aug. 14, 1874. *Page 228, line 8*, this phrase from N. Y. *Sun*, Feb. 19, 1876. *Page 228, line 27*, these sentences from Brooklyn *Argus*, July 18, 1874. *Page 228, line 37*, these phrases from T. vs. B., II, p. 308. *Page 229, line 7*, these sentences from T. vs. B., I, p. 80. *Page 229, line 16*, these sentences from N. Y. *Sun*, Aug. 22, 1874. *Page 229, line 18*, this sentence from T. vs. B., I, p. 82. *Page 229, line 23*, this phrase from T. vs. B., III, p. 90. *Page 229, line 36*, this phrase from T. vs. B., I, p. 82. *Page 230, line 6*, these sentences from T. vs. B., I, p. 82. *Page 230, line 18*, this paragraph from T. vs. B., I, p. 82. *Page 230, line 23*, this word from T. vs. B., III, p. 860. *Page 230, line 26*, this phrase from T. vs. B., I, p. 488. *Page 230, line 32*, these sentences from T. vs. B., I, p. 460. *Page 231, line 2*, this sentence from T. vs. B., I, p. 617. *Page 231, line 9*, this phrase from N. Y. *Sun*, Aug. 14, 1874. *Page 231, line 19*, these sentences from T. vs. B., I, p. 83, Exhibit 12. *Page 231, line 24*, these sentences from T. vs. B., I, p. 84, Exhibit 15. *Page 232, line 2*, these sentences from T. vs. B., I, p. 84, Exhibit 13. *Page 232, line 7*, these sentences from T. vs. B., III, p. 80.

CHAPTER XXIV

Page 232, line 29, these sentences from Harper, I, p. 357. *Page 233, line 16*, these sentences from Harper, I, p. 376. *Page 234, line 5*, this sentence from Harper, I, p. 378. *Page 234, line 15*, this paragraph from Stanton and Blatch, II, pp. 136–137. *Page 234, line 41*, this paragraph from T. vs. B., I, pp. 87–88. *Page 236, line 22*, this phrase from T. vs. B., III, p. 819. *Page 236, line 31*, this paragraph from T. vs. B., I, p. 541. *Page 236, line 35*, this sentence from T. vs. B., I, p. 682, Exhibit 106. *Page 237, line 11*, these sentences from *Woodhull & Claflin's Weekly*, June 3, 1871. *Page 237, line 26*, these sentences from T. vs. B., II, p. 829. *Page 237, line 39*, these sentences from

T. vs. B., I, p. 118. *Page 238, line 35,* these sentences from T. vs. B., I, pp. 86–87: "Ragged-edge letter." *Page 239, line 2,* these sentences from T. vs. B., I, pp. 85–86. *Page 239, line 5,* this sentence from T. vs. B., I, p. 87. *Page 240, line 28,* these paragraphs from *Yale Lectures,* I, p. 166. *Page 241, line 11,* these sentences from *Yale Lectures,* I, p. 101. *Page 241, line 14,* this sentence from T. vs. B., III, p. 997. *Page 241, line 19,* these sentences from *Yale Lectures,* I, p. 23. *Page 241, line 30,* this sentence from *Yale Lectures,* I, p. 110. *Page 241, line 35,* these sentences from *Yale Lectures,* I, p. 54. *Page 242, line 14,* this sentence from N. Y. *Sun,* Aug. 22, 1874. *Page 242, line 30,* these paragraphs from *Yale Lectures,* I, pp. 20–21.

CHAPTER XXV

Page 243, line 3, this sentence from N. Y. *Graphic,* Aug. 21, 1874. *Page 243, line 13,* this sentence from T. vs. B., III, p. 947. *Page 243, line 23,* this sentence from Stedman and Gould, I, pp. 514–515. *Page 244, line 4,* this phrase from T. vs. B., I, p. 237; II, p. 299. *Page 244, line 14,* this sentence from T. vs. B., I, p. 237. *Page 244, line 19,* these phrases from *Christian Union,* Apr. 17, 1872. *Page 244, line 31,* these sentences from N. Y. *Sun,* Aug. 22, 1874. *Page 245, line 22,* these sentences from T. vs. B., I, p. 87. *Page 245, line 28,* these sentences from T. vs. B., I, p. 743. *Page 246, line 15,* this sentence from N. Y. *World,* Aug. 17, 1872. *Page 246, line 25,* this sentence from N. Y. *Tribune,* Apr. 23, 1872. *Page 247, line 18,* this paragraph from N. L. Thompson, p. 212. *Page 247, line 22,* this sentence from T. vs. B., I, p. 119. *Page 247, line 28,* this phrase from Memphis *Appeal,* Nov. 17, 1872. *Page 247, line 32,* this sentence from Boston *Journal,* Sept. 12, 1872. *Page 248, line 12,* this paragraph from T. vs. B., I, p. 421. *Page 248, line 20,* these sentences from *Woodhull & Claflin's Weekly,* Nov. 2, 1872. *Page 249, line 10,* these sentences from N. Y. *Sun,* Aug. 22, 1874. *Page 249, line 15,* this sentence from N. Y. *Sun,* Aug. 22, 1874. *Page 249, line 30,* these paragraphs from Brooklyn *Argus,* Sept. 18, 1874. *Page 250, line 16,* this paragraph from *Woodhull & Claflin's Weekly,* Nov. 2, 1872. *Page 250, line 22,* this sentence from Hartford *Times,* May 14, 1873. *Page 250, line 33,* this sentence from T. vs. B., I, pp. 422–423. *Page 250, line 38,* this phrase from T. vs. B., III, p. 1,013. *Page 251, line 2,* this phrase from T. vs. B., I, p. 87. *Page 251, line 37,* these sentences from T. vs. B., III, p. 516. *Page 252, line 4,* these sentences from N. Y. *Sun,* Aug. 22, 1874. *Page 252, line 10,* these sentences from T. vs. B., I, p. 424. *Page 252, line 14,* this phrase from T. vs. B., I, pp. 301, 424. *Page 252, line 25,* these sentences from N. Y. *Sun,* Aug. 22, 1874. *Page 253, line 2,* this paragraph from T. vs. B., III, p. 960.

Page 255, line 10, this sentence from Cincinnati *Post*, cited in *Woodhull & Claflin's Weekly*, Feb. 15, 1873. *Page 255, line 29*, this sentence from T. vs. B., I, p. 137. *Page 255, line 34*, this sentence from T. vs. B., I, p. 91. *Page 256, line 6*, these sentences from T. vs. B., III, p. 92. *Page 256, line 11*, this phrase from T. vs. B., I, p. 330; III, p. 894. *Page 256, line 19*, this sentence from T. vs. B., II, p. 615. *Page 257, line 22*, this letter from T. vs. B., I, p. 100. *Page 257, line 28*, this paragraph from T. vs. B., I, p. 721. *Page 257, line 38*, these sentences from T. vs. B., III, p. 128. *Page 258, line 6*, these sentences from St. Louis *Globe*, cited in N. Y. *Herald*, Aug. 3, 1874. *Page 258, line 18*, this phrase from T. vs. B., III, p. 960. *Page 258, line 36*, this phrase from T. vs. B., II, p. 460. *Page 259, line 4*, these sentences from T. vs. B., I, pp. 327–328. *Page 259, line 8*, these phrases from T. vs. B., I, pp. 327–328. *Page 259, line 11*, this sentence from T. vs. B., II, pp. 460. *Page 259, line 20*, this phrase from T. vs. B., I, p. 336. *Page 259, line 26*, these sentences from Marshall, p. 34. *Page 260, line 23*, these sentences from T. vs. B., I, p. 438. *Page 260, line 37*, these sentences from N. Y. *Sun*, March 26, 1874. *Page 261, line 2*, these sentences from T. vs. B., I, p. 104. *Page 261, line 8*, this phrase from T. vs. B., I, p. 111. *Page 261, line 15*, these sentences from T. vs. B., I, p. 105. *Page 261, line 25*, this paragraph from T. vs. B., I, pp. 104–105. *Page 261, line 36*, this phrase from T. vs. B., I, p. 402. *Page 262, line 12*, this sentence from T. vs. B., I, p. 423. *Page 262, line 28*, these sentences from T. vs. B., I, pp. 111–112. *Page 263, line 9*, these phrases from N. Y. *Times*, July 30, 1874. *Page 263, line 24*, this sentence from N. Y. *Times*, July 30, 1874. *Page 263, line 38*, these sentences from T. vs. B., I, p. 65. *Page 264, line 22*, this paragraph from T. vs. B., I, p. 115. *Page 264, line 40*, this sentence from T. vs. B., III, p. 310. *Page 265, line 14*, these phrases from T. vs. B., I, p. 439; III, p. 517. *Page 265, line 18*, this phrase from T. vs. B., I, p. 439. *Page 265, line 22*, this phrase from T. vs. B., II, p. 895; III, pp. 102–103, 296, 304. *Page 265, line 29*, this phrase from N. Y. *Times*, Aug. 5, 1874. *Page 265, line 39*, this paragraph from N. Y. *Graphic*, July 25, 1874.

CHAPTER XXVII

Page 266, line 6, this sentence from L. Beecher: *Auto.* I, p. 157. *Page 266, line 11*, this phrase from *Great Brooklyn Romances:* Section 18. *Page 266, line 15*, these sentences from *Liberal Christian*,

Oct., 1875. *Page 266, line 30*, these sentences from T. vs. B., I, p. 722. *Page 267, line 5*, these sentences from Brooklyn *Argus*, Sept. 18, 1874. *Page 267, line 12*, this paragraph from T. vs. B., I, p. 446; N. Y. *Sun*, Sept. 12, 1874. *Page 267, line 21*, this paragraph from T. vs. B., III, p. 891. *Page 268, line 11*, these sentences from T. vs. B., III, p. 952. *Page 268, line 11*, these sentences from T. vs. B., II, p. 727. *Page 270, line 39*, these paragraphs from Chicago *Tribune*, Oct. 1, 1874. *Page 271, line 40*, this phrase from T. vs. B., III, p. 38. *Page 273, line 39*, this phrase from Bishop, p. 43. *Page 274, line 35*, this phrase from N. Y. *Sun*, Aug. 22, 1874. *Page 274, line 37*, this phrase from N. Y. *Sun*, Feb. 7, 1876. *Page 275, line 8*, these sentences from N. Y. *Sun*, Aug. 6, 1874. *Page 275, line 35*, this phrase from N. Y. *Sun*, Aug. 31, 1874. *Page 276, line 6*, these phrases from T. vs. B., III, p. 663. *Page 276, line 14*, this sentence from T. vs. B., I, p. 753. *Page 277, line 7*, this phrase from N. Y. *Herald*, Mar. 21, 1875. *Page 277, line 11*, this sentence from T. vs. B., III, p. 87. *Page 277, line 15*, these phrases from T. vs. B., III, p. 851. *Page 277, line 22*, this phrase from N. Y. *Times*, July 3, 1875. *Page 277, line 25*, this phrase from N. Y. *Herald*, Feb. 12, 1875. *Page 277, line 33*, these sentences from T. vs. B., I, p. 281. *Page 278, line 33*, these sentences from T. vs. B., III, p. 20. *Page 279, line 3*, these sentences from *Plymouth Pulpit*, I, No. 3. *Page 279, line 15*, these sentences from T. vs. B., II, p. 118. *Page 279, line 38*, this sentence from T. vs. B., I, p. 118. *Page 280, line 41*, these paragraphs from T. vs. B., III, pp. 959–962.

CHAPTER XXVIII

Page 281, line 20, these sentences from Bigelow, V, pp. 151–152. *Page 281, line 26*, this sentence from Meredith, I, pp. 245–246. *Page 281, line 27*, this phrase from Louisville *Courier-Journal*, cited in *Beecher-Tilton Scandal*, p. 143. *Page 281, line 28*, this phrase from Chicago *Standard*, cited in N. Y. *Sun*, Aug. 1, 1874. *Page 282, line 4*, these lines from N. Y. *Times*, July 3, 1875. *Page 282, line 16*, this sentence from N. Y. *Times*, July 3, 1875. *Page 282, line 22*, these sentences from *Advance* in H. C. Bowen's Scrapbook, VII, p. 65. *Page 282, line 26*, this sentence from *More Uncensored Recollections*, p. 137. *Page 283, line 35*, these sentences from N. Y. *Times*, Sept. 15, 1875. *Page 284, line 22*, these phrases from N. Y. *Sun*, Feb. 21, 1876. *Page 284, line 36*, these sentences from N. Y. *Sun*, Feb. 19, 1876. *Page 285, line 12*, these sentences from N. Y. *Sun*, Mar. 2, 1876. *Page 285, line 33*, this sentence from N. Y. *Sun*, Mar. 3, 1876. *Page 287, line 32*, this phrase from Joseph Howard, p. 502. *Page 287, line 37*, these sentences from N. Y. *Times*, Oct. 9, 1879. *Page 288, line 35*, these sentences from N. Y. *Times*, July 30, 1877. *Page 289, line 26*, this sentence from Farrar in *That Unknown Country*, pp. 269–272. *Page 290, line 33*, this paragraph from *Evolution and Religion*, p. 166.

CHAPTER XXIX

Page 291, line 10, these sentences from N. Y. *Herald*, Dec. 14, 1877. *Page 292, line 20*, this letter from N. Y. *Times*, Apr. 16, 1878. *Page 292, line 26*, this phrase from T. vs. B., I, pp. 104–105. *Page 292, line 31*, this phrase from N. Y. *Sun*, Apr. 17, 1878. *Page 293, line 13*, this paragraph from N. Y. *Times*, Apr. 16, 1878. *Page 293, line 22*, this sentence from Brooklyn *Argus*, Sept. 18, 1874. *Page 294, line 9*, these sentences from N. Y. *Times*, Nov. 10, 1879. *Page 294, line 40*, this paragraph from *Evolution and Religion*, pp. 152, 158–159. *Page 295, line 12*, these sentences from Henry Ward Beecher in *Family Biog.*, p. 685. *Page 295, line 39*, this phrase from *Puck*, May 21, 1879. *Page 296, line 12*, these phrases from *Patriotic Addresses*, pp. 820–822. *Page 296, line 24*, this phrase from T. C. Smith, p. 1,102. *Page 296, line 29*, this phrase from *Puck*, Jan. 12, 1881. *Page 298, line 7*, these sentences from N. Y. *Tribune*, July 5, 1880; J. T. Lloyd, pp. 121–122. *Page 298, line 9*, this sentence from N. Y. *Times*, July 7, 1880. *Page 298, line 26*, these sentences from N. Y. *Times*, July 12, 1880. *Page 299, line 2*, these phrases from N. Y. *Tribune*, Oct. 16, 1882. *Page 299, line 15*, this sentence from Holt, pp. 51–52. *Page 299, line 16*, this sentence from *Evolution and Religion*, p. 127. *Page 299, line 40*, this paragraph from Holt, pp. 51–52. *Page 300, line 12*, this sentence from Spencer, II, p. 407.

CHAPTER XXX

Page 300, line 17, this phrase from *Evolution and Religion*, p. 417. *Page 301, line 3*, this sentence from T. vs. B., I, p. 485; Exhibit D–64. *Page 301, line 29*, these sentences from Wilkinson, p. 21. *Page 302, line 17*, these paragraphs from *Congregationalist*, July 27, 1901. *Page 302, line 32*, this paragraph from Lecture: Chicago, Feb. 7, 1883. *Page 303, line 33*, this phrase from Chicago *Tribune* cited in N. Y. *Tribune*, Oct. 13, 1884. *Page 304, line 14*, this phrase from N. Y. *Herald*, Sept. 27, 1884. *Page 304, line 21*, this phrase from N. Y. *Tribune*, Oct. 12, 1884. *Page 304, line 33*, this phrase from Paine, p. 497. *Page 304, line 34*, this phrase from J. T. Lloyd, p. 325. *Page 305, line 25*, this paragraph from *Brooklyn Rink Speech*. *Page 305, line 33*, these sentences from Brooklyn *Eagle*, Oct. 23, 1884. *Page 306, line 9*, these sentences from N. Y. *Times*, Oct. 16, 1884. *Page 306, line 15*, these sentences from Higginson, p. 310. *Page 306, line 20*, these sentences from N. Y. *Tribune*, Oct. 24, 1884. *Page 306, line 21*, these sentences from N. Y. *Times*, Nov. 8, 1884. *Page 307, line 30*, this paragraph from N. Y. *Sun*, Oct. 29, 1884. *Page 307, line 32*, this sentence from N. Y. *Sun*, Nov. 1, 1884. *Page 308, line 9*, this sentence from James, p. 167. *Page 308, line 26*, this phrase from N. Y. *Tribune*, Oct. 29, 1884. *Page 308, line 38*, these sentences from Joly, p. 40. *Page 309, line 17*, this phrase from Selbie, p. 53. *Page 310, line 25*, this paragraph from Adler, p. 12. *Page 311, line 7*, this paragraph from *Evolution and Religion*, p. 96. *Page 311, line 11*, these sentences from *Evolution and Religion*, p. 139. *Page 311, line 15*, these sentences from Knox, pp. 54–55. *Page 311, line 29*, this sentence from Pond, p. 72. *Page 312, line 20*, this paragraph from N. Y. *Tribune*, Mar. 6, 1887. *Page 312, line 32*, this phrase from N. Y. *Tribune*, Mar. 6, 1887. *Page 312, line 35*, this phrase from N. Y. *Tribune*, Mar. 8, 1887. *Page 314, line 7*, this phrase from N. Y. *Sun*, Mar. 10, 1887.

APPENDIX IV

Index